Political Repression

PENNSYLVANIA STUDIES
IN HUMAN RIGHTS

Bert B. Lockwood, Jr., Series Editor

A complete list of books in the series
is available from the publisher.

Political Repression

Courts and the Law

Linda Camp Keith

PENN

UNIVERSITY OF PENNSYLVANIA PRESS

PHILADELPHIA

Published by
University of Pennsylvania Press
Philadelphia, Pennsylvania 19104-4112
www.upenn.edu/pennpress

Printed in the United States of America
on acid-free paper

10 9 8 7 6 5 4 3 2 1

Library of Congress Cataloging-in-Publication Data

Keith, Linda Camp
Political repression : courts and the law / Linda Camp Keith.—1st ed.
p. cm.—(Pennsylvania studies in human rights)
Includes bibliographical references and index.
ISBN 978-0-8122-4381-9 (hardcover : alk. paper)
1. Political persecution. 2. Human rights. 3. Civil rights. 4. Constitutional law. 5. Judicial independence. I. Title. II. Series: Pennsylvania studies in human rights.
JC585.K37 2011
323'.044—dc23

2011030589

In memory of Neal and Steve
for their enduring guidance

Contents

Chapter 1

Introduction

The constitution [of Jordan] provides for freedom of speech and press; however, the government imposed significant restrictions on these rights in practice. Citizens generally were able to criticize the government openly, although journalists exercised caution in regard to the king, the royal family, the GID [General Intelligence Directorate], and sensitive topics such as religion. Government intimidation and the threat of fines and detention led to self-censorship of journalists during the year. (U.S. Department of State 2007)

The constitution [of Egypt] prohibits arbitrary arrest and detention; however, during [2007], police and security forces conducted large-scale arrests and detained hundreds of individuals without charge under the Emergency Law. Continuing a trend begun in 2005, the government arrested and detained hundreds of activists affiliated with the banned-but-tolerated Muslim Brotherhood (MB), generally for periods lasting several weeks. (Ibid.)

The constitution [of Zimbabwe] provides for an independent judiciary; however the judiciary was under intense pressure to conform to government policies and the government repeatedly refused to abide by judicial decisions. (Ibid.)

On a documentary level the world seems to have converged upon a set of ideals regarding states' human rights behavior and the appropriate institutions to promote and protect those ideals. At the turn of the new century the global script for state legitimacy calls for a written constitution or the equivalent, with an embedded bill of rights, democratic processes and institutions, and, increasingly, a judicial check on state power to protect an internationally recognized set of human rights. Evidence of formal acceptance of these norms is overwhelming. The formal commitment to international human rights norms approaches near universality as each of the core conventions composing the international human rights regime claims state parties representing from 75 to 99 percent of the global set of states: 173 states are parties to the International Convention on the Elimination of All Forms of Racial Discrimination (89 percent),[1] 164 have ratified or acceded to the International Covenant on Civil and Political Rights (84 percent),[2] 160 are parties to the International Covenant on Economic, Social and Cultural Rights (83 percent),[3] 186 have ratified or acceded to the Convention on the Elimination of All Forms of Discrimination Against Women (96 percent),[4] 146 are parties to the Convention Against Torture and Other Cruel, Inhuman or Degrading Treatment or Punishment (75 percent),[5] and 193 are parties to the Convention on the Rights of the Child (99 percent), making it the most universally accepted of these core human rights instruments[6] (UN Treaty Collection, accessed December 2009). Currently, around 90 percent of nation-states have a written constitution or set of basic laws that constitute paramount domestic law (Elkins, Ginsburg, and Melton 2009, 49), 65 percent of which contain "an explicit declaration regarding the independence of the central judicial organs" (Constitutional Design Group 2008, 1). Much of the constitution writing in the last half of the twentieth century has resulted from the postcolonial emergence to independence of almost 100 countries, and, as Go (2003) notes, most of these states have rewritten their original post independence constitutions at least once. Beer (1992) calls the latter decades of the twentieth century "an era of unprecedented experimentation in forms of government and law under written constitutions, as colonialism ended and each newly independent state sought its constitutional identity while other countries responded to challenge by revising or amending basic laws" (1). Postcolonial constitutions accounted for roughly two-thirds of all the world's constitutions by the 1970s, and by the 1990s, postcolonial constitutions, combined with those of the ex-Soviet countries and other secessionist countries, made up more than four-fifths of the constitutions of the world (Beer 1992). All but

10 percent of current postcolonial constitutions have a section devoted to rights provisions under a separate title (Go 2003, 81). Go posits that the post-colonial documentary constitutions are remarkable in that there is "no immediately necessary condition between having an independent state and writing a single-document constitution," nor is there any imperative that they be similarly constituted and yet "all existing constitutions share some basic features" (72). For Go, these patterns "affirm that documentary constitutionalism has become a globally shared mode of organizing sociopolitical formations" (72). Beer would concur. As early as 1992, he saw that "these historic decades of frenetic constitution making activity" reflected "a convergence in the world towards relatively few living traditions of modern law, and the beginnings of mutual comprehension among legal scholars and practitioners of these different traditions" (1). Furthermore, he argues that this period saw "the achievement of at least formal global political consensus on the centrality—once national independence and stability are achieved—of human rights to sound and moral government and law" (1).

While the progress toward universal formal adherence to this global model is remarkable, the substantive meaning of this progress is much less clear. On one hand, numerous scholars and human rights proponents express at least some optimism that this proliferation of formal rights protections will translate into actual state protection of human rights in those countries adopting the legal provisions (for example, Ackermann 1989; Elster 1993; Finer, Bogdanor, and Rudden 1995). Scholars presume that regimes will be less willing to abuse rights that are clearly and publicly promised in a legally binding document (for example, Rosenthal 1990, 401) and expect that such formal promises may pressure a regime to give in to public demands for these fundamental protections (see Elster 1993; Finer, Bogdanor, and Rudden 1995). Some scholars within international relations expect that international human rights discourse and interaction will have a transformative effect even beyond that which leads states to make such formal commitments, and others expect that transnational networks of nongovernmental organizations will help to hold regimes accountable for their promises in law (Koh 1996; Keck and Sikkink 1998; Risse, Ropp, and Sikkink 1999). Other scholars point to states' general propensity to comply with their legal obligations (Henkin 1979; Chayes and Chayes 1993). On the other hand, numerous scholars question the effectiveness of formal mechanisms, speculating that constitutions may provide more window dressing than substantive protection for human rights (Howard 1991, 3) and expressing concern that many constitutions may simultaneously limit the very rights they delineate in terms of the state's interests or the public good (Ludwikowski 1996, 227). Realists within international relations question states' motivation to commit to international human rights treaties and emphasize the weakness of treaty mechanisms and the anarchic nature of the international system (Hoffmann 1956; Waltz 1979; Mearsheimer 1994). Others would temper our expectations, urging us to take a very long-term view of the transition to constitutionalism; they argue that the process is often a repeated trial-and-error process through which countries may over time adapt general constitutional principles to the more particularized circumstances of the individual state (An-Na'im 2003, 2006).

Others are pragmatic and note that, yes, constitutional provisions "may accurately reflect the *serious intent* of a government and a people on a problem of governance or rights, but history, economy, and/or sociopolitics may make the achievement of the goal in the short run improbable or impossible" (Beer 1992, 11). Some pragmatists argue that "not all constitutions are dishonoured all the time and that certain parts of certain constitutions are obeyed most of the time" and that "very few are entire fictions, bearing no relationship whatsoever to what goes on" (Finer, Bogdanor, and Rudden 1995, 2–3). Empirically we will see in subsequent chapters that while repression of civil liberties has lessened over time, repression of personal integrity rights has not improved, despite the level of documentary provision of human rights. A growing body of empirical studies has largely supported the pessimists' expectation in regard to both human rights treaties and constitutional provisions of fundamental rights. In addition, the judiciary has not appeared to be the guarantor of rights that is often assumed. As we will see in the sections below, at best these studies suggest only a strongly qualified optimism that the universality of these norms and their widespread formalization will lead to improved human rights: the associated improvement is limited, it occurs only in regard to some rights, and it occurs only under a limited set of circumstances. I agree with Beer that the "relationships are often complex between printed provisions, government policies, and social practices" (1992, 11); and here I seek to examine the effect of a subset of these provisions within the broad set of domestic and international circumstances that shape a state's repression of its citizens' fundamental human rights. I believe that in order to understand fully the impact of constitutional provisions for rights and freedoms (and provision for an independent judiciary) on state repression, we should first understand better why states adopt or maintain these provisions in their constitutions. In this book I engage in what I believe is the first systematic large-*N* cross-national examination of why states make these formal commitments. I then use this theoretical and empirical understanding to inform our study of judicial independence and my ultimate interest, state repression of personal integrity rights and civil liberties.

State Repression of Internationally Recognized Human Rights

The breadth of universally recognized human rights has grown substantially, encompassing an exhaustive list of both first-generation and second-generation rights.[7] Within the human rights subfield, however, the empirical literature has largely focused on the first generation of human rights, and often even more narrowly upon a subset of these rights, personal or physical integrity rights, namely the right to be free from arbitrary physical harm and coercion. Critics could argue that the narrow focus of this field reflects a Western bias that tends to emphasize individual rights over communal rights and duties, and political rights and civil liberties over economic and social rights. There might be some validity to such a criticism, but I believe that this work also reflects a theoretical interest in the nature of political conflict and in the tools that regimes use in order to control or modify the behavior of its citizens, particularly challengers of the regime. To some degree the focus also reflects a prioritization of limited resources and attention, in which scholars may have felt compelled to focus on the most egregious abuses of human rights—a set of rights that also happen to be more universally accepted and less controversial than other categories of human rights. Indeed, as Davenport (2007c) notes in a recent review of the subfield, it is surprising actually that so little attention has been paid to the study of repression and "the evils done by presidents, the police, military, secret service, national guard, and death squads against those within their territorial jurisdiction," especially "given the duration of this practice, the vast numbers of its victims, the range of legal, political, and religious restrictions condemning such activity, the many social movements and human rights organizations dedicated to the elimination of this behavior, and the centrality of relevant action to some of the most prominent ideas and political figures in human history" (1). This focus, to some extent, reflects the relative ease of conceptualizing and measuring these rights, compared to economic, social, and cultural rights. But more importantly the repression of this set of rights represents the sort of repression that usually can be avoided; these types of violations are "usually perpetrated directly by government officials and thus are more easily dealt with by a change in government policy, in direct contrast to violations of economic and social rights, which are often less amenable to change" (Poe and Tate 1994, 854). Thus while my study is clearly set within the broader human rights field, my focus here is limited to political repression rather than to human rights violations more generally. I believe that this work will inform not only studies of political repression but also newly emerging studies of violence against women and the growing body of research that examines the impact of the law on a broader set of rights, including second-generation rights.

Davenport (2007c) carefully distinguishes political repression from human rights violations, arguing that political repression does not necessarily require that a law or norm be violated, in contrast to human rights violations. I believe that most acts of repression do in fact repress or violate internationally recognized human rights norms, such as the right to personal or physical integrity and a broad range of civil liberties promoted in the Universal Declaration of Human Rights, which is "now accepted as declaratory of customary international law" (Reisman 1990, 867) and protected in the International Covenant on Civil and Political Rights and the Convention Against Torture, conventions for which there is near-universal formal acceptance.[8] Throughout the book I use the terms "political repression" and "human rights abuse" and variations of these terms to identify the same behavior. I believe the usage is appropriate for the context of my study, and it allows some rhetorical freedom and variety. Ultimately, I agree with both Davenport's definition of political repression, which he draws somewhat from Goldstein (1978), and with his assessment of the goals that state actors seek to achieve through the use of repression: "By most accounts, repression involves the actual or threatened use of physical sanctions against an individual or organization, within the territorial jurisdiction of the state, for the purpose of imposing a cost on the target as well as deterring specific activities and/or beliefs perceived to be challenging to government personnel, practices or institutions" (2). As Davenport notes in his review of the quantitative literature dedicated to the study of state repression, this work has been unified in its focus on the problem of order and has been "fundamentally concerned with why and how political authorities use coercive power domestically amid potential and existing challenges and challengers" (2007c, 1–2). Most cross-national studies of political repression have tended to focus on one of two dimensions of state repression, rarely on both—either addressing the more severe form of repressions, violations of personal integrity (imprisonment, torture, killing, and disappearances) (for example, Poe and Tate 1994; Poe, Tate, and Keith 1999; Cingranelli and Richards 1999a, 1999b; Keith 2002a), or addressing the broader category of civil liberties restrictions or "negative sanctions" as they are sometimes referred to in the literature (for example, Davenport 1995a, 1995b, 2007a, 2007b; Keith 2002b; Howard and Carey 2004; Walker and Poe 2002). Davenport (2007b) argues that while the two forms of repression share the goal of attempting to influence behavior and attitudes, they achieve the goal differently; civil rights restrictions modify behavior through constraining and channeling opportunities, and personal integrity abuses such as killing and disappearances modify behavior through eliminating actors. Thus it may be shortsighted to perceive repression as one-dimensional. However, as Davenport notes, thus far most explanatory variables have similarly influenced both categories of repression, and therefore it is highly likely that "comparable processes underlie the coercive strategies" (487). While my previous work has largely fit within the first category of repression, in this book I examine both categories. And while, like Davenport, I do find both categories of repression similarly influenced by the same agentic and structural factors, significant differences emerge in regard to the influence of domestic and external threats, constitutional provisions, and, in some limited instances, the role of the judiciary.

Why Do States Repress Their Own Citizens?

While most of the current empirical work on political repression has approached states' behavior from the perspective of international relations theory (primarily a "soft" rational-choice perspective), I seek to expand the theoretical underpinnings that encompass a broader set of subfields in political science, including public law and comparative politics. I do not expect to be able to offer an overarching grand theory that synthesizes the theoretical concerns of these subfields; however, I do believe that the dominant theories share features that may be incorporated under the "organizing concepts" of opportunity and willingness that Most and Starr set forth (1989), and which they argue appropriately encompass both macro and micro approaches (23). I believe the concepts are useful here for structuring the somewhat disparate approaches through which these diverse fields attempt to understand political repression or human rights abuse.

Most and Starr conceptualize *opportunity* as "a shorthand term for the possibilities that are available within any environment," and which thus "represents the total set of environmental constraints and possibilities" (1989, 23). They conceptualize *willingness* as "a shorthand term for the choice (and the process of choice) that is related to the selection of some behavioral option from a range of alternatives" and the subsequent employment of "available capabilities to further some policy over others" (23). They derive their notion of these two overarching concepts from the work of the Sprouts (1956, 1965, 1968, and 1969), in particular from these authors' conceptualization of the "ecological triad," which is composed of an entity (with its policy/choice processes), its context or environment, and the relationship or interaction between the entity and the environment (27). According to Most and Starr, "The ultimate entities—single decisionmakers or small groups of decisionmakers—are surrounded by factors that structure the nature of the decision, the options available, the consequences, costs and benefits of those options. Individuals, then, make choices within a complex set of *incentive structures*. This can be captured only looking at all three parts of the ecological triad. Opportunity and willingness . . . encompasses all three aspects of the triad" (29). As Friedman and Starr (1997) note, the value of the framework is that "it highlights the notion that all independent variables explaining social phenomena can be characterized as either agentic or structural variables" (6). Most and Starr (1989) conceptualize interaction between agent/entity and structure/environment with the metaphor of a menu that provides "a number of behavioral choice/possibilities" that do not determine the diner/actor's choice but that limit it (28). As Friedman and Starr note, "factors based in both the agent (values, preferences, resources, etc.) and the structure (prices, size of portion, reputation for certain dishes, etc.) will make certain choices more or less likely" (6).

The framework fits the soft rationalism of the political repression literature (for example, Gurr 1986; Poe, Tate, and Keith 1999; Poe 2004; Keith and Poe 2004; Davenport 2007a, 2007c). These scholars assume that political leaders are rational actors and that they choose from a menu of repressive tools that they see as the most effective means to achieve their chief end, which is to stay in power. And I assume that the most pervasive factor that increases leaders' willingness to repress is a threat to the leaders' rule, whether real or perceived, and that the more serious the threat, the more willing state leaders are to employ repression (Keith and Poe 2004). Or, as Davenport (2007a) argues more broadly, state actors utilize actual or threatened physical sanctions in order to impose "a cost on the target as well as deterring specific activities and/or beliefs perceived to be challenging to government personnel, practices or institutions" (2); however, state actors carefully weigh the costs and benefits of engaging in repressive action, and also consider a menu of alternative mechanisms of control, as well assessing the odds of achieving their goals with these tools (4 and citations therein).

This framework is broad enough to encompass one of the long-standing debates within international relations (for example, Katzenstein 1996a, 1996b; Finnemore and Sikkink 1998) that has informed a substantial empirical literature examining a variety of human rights–related behavior—the debate over "norms versus interests," as it has been termed (Rosenblum and Saleyhan 2004). Generally, realists and rational functionalists perceive states as rational actors whose behavior is based primarily based upon narrow self-interest and is largely a function of the state's calculation of the benefits and costs (Waltz 1979; Keohane 1984). State commitments to international human rights norms are perceived as "cheap talk" (Mearsheimer 1994) that gives way to more substantive interests of the state when in conflict. Conversely, constructivists emphasize the emergence and diffusion of international human norms through networks of domestic and transnational actors, who not only shape the discourse of international human rights but also rally publics to convince states to formally accept and to adhere to these norms (for example, Keck and Sikkink 1998; Risse, Ropp, and Sikkink 1999). In addition, states are expected to comply with these norms because states have a propensity to comply with their legal obligations (Henkin 1979) or because they generally aspire to comply with the norm of *pacta sunt servanda* (agreements must be kept) (Chayes and Chayes 1993). These approaches fall within Most and Starr's framework in that they perceive that a regime's *opportunities* to use the tools of repression are either facilitated or constrained by its environment at both the domestic and international levels. In addition, the approaches assume that the *willingness* of a regime to employ these tools may be "intimately related to a decision maker's calculations of advantage and disadvantage, of cost and benefit, that decision makers consider on both conscious and unconscious levels," and they assume that these decision makers "see their own behavior constrained within a range of opportunities presented by the environment (governmental, domestic, and international)" (Most and

Starr 1989, 34). Constructivist perspectives emphasize the transformative power of international normative discourse on human rights and on activism by transnational actors (international organizations and nongovernmental actors) who support local efforts to press for human rights commitment and who also, through repeated interactions with state actors, socialize states to accept new norms. Thus, constructivists would argue that international socialization changes both the menu of appropriate choices and the values through which the regime will evaluate the choices.

The opportunity and willingness framework is also appropriate for the public law perspective, which posits that a potentially repressive regime would be constrained by a written constitution with a bill of fundamental rights and freedoms that are protected by an independent judiciary empowered with judicial review (for example, Rosenthal 1990; Ramseyer 1994; Prillaman 2000; Mutua 2001). Written bills of rights greatly extend the reach of the rule of law and provide individual protection from the overextension of governmental power, providing new duties and standards of justice and fairness that both politicians and bureaucrats are now required to meet; and, more importantly, they represent "catalogues of very important interests and activities over which the individual rather than the state has been given final control" (Beatty 1994, 16). In addition, the law itself may serve as a socializing agent, and, coupled with a strong civil society and a judiciary that is at least somewhat independent, may cultivate a budding rights consciousness within the state (MacGuigan 1965; Martin 1991; Murphy 1993; Tate and Vallinder 1995; Epp 1998). Or, as James Madison (1788) stated, "political truths declared in that solemn manner . . . become incorporated with the national sentiment, and counteract the impulses of interest and passion" (297–300). Thus, bills of rights and a judiciary empowered with judicial review could potentially change the menu of appropriate choices, change the costs of inappropriate choices, and influence the values through which the regime will evaluate the choices.

The framework is also appropriate for the "domestic democratic peace" perspective in comparative politics. Opportunity is constrained because the structure and limited nature of democratic governments make extensive use of repression more difficult and costly to arrange. Willingness is dampened because democracy "provides citizens (at least those with political resources) the tools to oust potentially abusive leaders from office before they are able to become a serious threat" (Poe and Tate 1994, 855); thus the cost of repression is increased (Davenport 1999). Willingness is also lessened because strong democracies provide a variety of alternative mechanisms through which conflict can be channeled for possible resolution (Poe, Tate, and Keith 1999; Davenport 2007c), and it is also dampened by "the socialization processes that guide citizens of democratic polities toward the belief that nonviolent means of resolving conflicts are preferred over violence" (Poe, Tate, and Keith 1999, 293). As Davenport (1999) notes, it is not just the institutions of democracy but also "the norms (of compromise, toleration, and facilitation) accompanying these institutions" that influence the decisions of the rulers by "increasing the cost of human rights violations as well as decreasing the value to quiescence" (96). He also argues that these alternative mechanisms "weaken the justification for coercive activity by reducing the likelihood for human conflict and facilitating the conveyance of grievances" (Davenport 2007c, 11).

Here I have identified briefly some the core assumptions of the dominant theories that I believe share features that may be incorporated under Most and Starr's "organizing concepts" of opportunity and willingness. Ultimately, I argue that state actors' choices to employ the tools of repression are shaped by factors based in the agent (for example, democratic values, ideological preferences, and resources), structure (for example, competitive party system or independent judiciary), and environment (for example, domestic and external threats). These factors influence which options (tools of repression) are available or deemed appropriate as well as shape the consequences and the costs and benefits of employing the tools of repression. In Chapter 2 I address in more detail the theories of repression, and in the subsequent chapters I explore more fully specific hypotheses for the various forms of state commitment and repression.

Plan of the Book

In Chapter 2 I examine the dominant theories of political repression that span three subfields in political science, and place them within the opportunity and willingness framework. I then examine extant large-*N* cross-national empirical studies, place my results here within that literature, and identify their contribution to the development of that field. In Chapter 3 I address the "standard model" that has developed over time, expanding it to cover a much longer period and to reflect developments within the literature in regard to the influence of democracy and the availability of new measures of specific individual rights. Through these analyses I address more thoroughly the conflicting expectations regarding the effect of military regimes and Marxist/Marxist-Leninist regimes. I find that the standard model as a whole continues to perform in explaining a broad range of acts of political repression, and I use these base models as the foundation for analyses in the following chapters that examine that effect of the judiciary and the law on state repression. Throughout these models I control for fixed effects. In Chapter 4 I expand the standard model to account for state embeddedness in global society, examining the role of global and regional norms, the influence of international nongovernmental organizations (INGOs), and memberships in international governmental organizations and human rights treaties. I also broaden my focus to liberal economic theory and examine the influence of World Trade Organization membership, trade, and foreign direct investment. This chapter presents a substantive examination of the role of judicial independence: why states commit formally to the norm of judicial independence, whether these formal commitments make a difference, and the circumstances that shape the actual achievement of judicial independence within the state. I believe these analyses are the first systematic cross-national empirical examinations of these questions. I also present a new measure of *de facto* judicial independence and examine its relationship with both categories of repression. Throughout these analyses, I control for fixed effects and selection effects. I also examine interactions between judicial independence and the transnational network and domestic circumstances. In Chapter 5 I examine state bills of rights, specifically, constitutional commitments to individual freedoms and due process rights, first examining factors that influence commitment, especially prior commitment to the International Covenant on Civil and Political Rights (ICCPR). I believe these analyses are the first large-*N* cross-national empirical examination of the question of why states adopt particular constitutional provisions. I then examine the influence of that commitment on repression of the specific rights promised in the provisions, controlling for selection effects, fixed effects, and examining interactions between these rights and judicial independence and the presence of INGOs. In Chapter 6 I examine thoroughly the influence of a variety of types and levels of threats to regimes on the repression of personal integrity rights and restriction of civil liberties. Ultimately, I examine the effectiveness of state of emergency provisions in models that are conditioned on the level and type of threat. Throughout these analyses I control for fixed effects as well as selection effects. Finally, in Chapter 7 I examine the implications of the research in terms of our theoretical and empirical understanding of state repression as well as the potential policy implications of protecting human rights. I discuss candidly the limitations of these analyses and point the way forward for future research.

Chapter 2

Empirical Theories and Studies of Political Repression

On April 26, just after the announcement that Faure won the election, several cities erupted in violence. The government [of Togo] deployed security forces to quell demonstrations. Security forces fired tear gas indiscriminately into crowds. After dispersing large crowds, they began a house-by-house campaign of violence against supposed opposition supporters in reprisal for protesting alleged electoral fraud. Security forces targeted neighborhoods thought to be opposition strongholds, killing persons in their houses and shooting at those who tried to flee. (U.S. Department of State 2005)

Several hundred Falun Gong adherents reportedly have died in detention [in China] due to torture, abuse, and neglect since the crackdown on Falun Gong began in 1999. For example, Falun Gong groups alleged that more than 50 persons died in custody in June through August, many from torture in detention camps. (U.S. Department of State 2003)

On February 24, Sucre state police in Cumana [Venezuela] used tear gas canisters and pellet guns

> against students at the University Institute of Technology who were protesting peacefully noncompletion of the cafeteria. One student, Angel Castillo Munoz, died as a result of being hit in the head by rubber bullets and falling unconscious into an area flooded by tear gas. Police reportedly continued to fire, despite students' attempts to surrender, resulting in a delay of medical care to the injured. (U.S. Department of State 1999)

Why Do States Repress Their Own Citizens?

While most of the current empirical work on political repression has approached states' behavior from the perspective of international relations theory (primarily a "soft" rational-choice perspective), I seek to expand the theoretical underpinnings of a broader set of subfields in political science, including public law and comparative politics. As I noted in Chapter 1, I do not aim to offer an overarching grand theory that synthesizes the theoretical concerns of these subfields; however, I argue that these theories express commonalities that I incorporate under Most and Starr's (1989) organizing concepts of opportunity and willingness. I believe these concepts are useful here for structuring the somewhat disparate approaches through which these diverse fields attempt to understand political repression or human rights abuse. Most and Starr conceptualize opportunity as "a shorthand term for the possibilities that are available within any environment" that as such "represents the total set of environmental constraints and possibilities," and they conceptualize *willingness* as "a shorthand term for the choice (and the process of choice) that is related to the selection of some behavioral option from a range of alternatives" and the subsequent employment of "available capabilities to further some policy over others" (23). These two overarching concepts are derived from the Sprouts' "ecological triad," which is composed of an entity (with its policy/choice processes), its context or environment, and the relationship or interaction between the entity/agent and the environment (1956, 1965, 1968, and 1969). Most and Starr argue that state decisionmakers are surrounded by factors that structure the nature of their decisions that form a complex set of incentive structures. They conceptualize the interaction between agent/entity and structure/environment with the metaphor of a menu that provides "a number of behavioral choice/possibilities" (28), and they argue that "factors based in both the agent (values, preferences, resources, etc.) and the structure (prices, size of portion, reputation for certain dishes, etc.) will make certain choices more or less likely" (Friedman and Starr 2007, 6). This framework fits the underlying soft rationalism of the political repression literature. Most human rights scholars assume that political leaders are rational actors in that they choose from a menu of policy options and employ the tools of repression because they see those tools to be the most effective means to stay in power. I assume throughout this book that the most pervasive factor that increases leaders' willingness to repress is a threat to the leaders' rule, whether real or perceived, and that the more serious the threat, the more willing state leaders are to employ repression to deter or impose a cost on actions or views that challenge the regime or its policies. I argue, however, that state actors carefully weigh the costs and benefits of engaging in repressive action, and also consider a menu of alternative mechanisms of control, as well as assessing the odds of achieving their goals with these tools. In the sections that follow I address the general theoretical expectations in more detail, and in the subsequent chapters I will explore these theories more fully and derive testable hypotheses. In the second half of this chapter I examine the body of empirical work on political repression and place this work within that literature.

Key Theoretical Perspectives on Repression of Human Rights

Rational Actor Theories

As noted above, much of the human rights literature takes a soft, rational actor approach. Even though the earliest empirical studies largely focused on the domestic environment, over time human rights studies have drawn increasingly upon the dominant theory in international relations, especially as the compliance literature has grown. As the rational approach has been applied to states' human rights behavior, the literature has gradually broadened beyond the approach's assumption of a unitary state actor, and has expanded its focus to domestic institutions and actors, as we will see below. The rational actor approaches fall easily within Most and Starr's framework in that these approaches would generally perceive a regime's opportunity and willingness to use the tools of repression to be either facilitated or constrained by both the domestic and international environment.

(NEO)REALISM AND RATIONAL FUNCTIONALISM

Both realists and rational functionalists perceive states as unitary rational actors that primarily behave on the basis of self-interest; thus they would argue that decisions by the state on whether to adhere to international human rights norms or to engage in repression would largely be a function of the state's calculation of the benefits and costs of engaging the various choices. As these are international relations approaches, their perspective on state repression and human rights behavior more generally focuses on the role of the international human rights regime and international organizations, and more specifically on state decisions to join human rights treaties, and the subsequent decision of whether or to what extent to comply with the legal obligation. Realists in international relations (Morgenthau 1948; Hoffmann 1956; Waltz 1979; Gilpin 1987) emphasize the dominance of power and the norm of sovereignty in a weak and decentralized international legal system, which they argue diminishes the likelihood that legal authority will constrain the behavior of states. They posit that any observed compliance with international norms or treaties simply reflects a convergence of interests that will dissipate once the state's material interests conflict with its normative commitments (Hoffmann 1956; Waltz 1979; Mearsheimer 1994). Thus, realists ultimately remain skeptical about the development of international law beyond serving the interests of the most powerful states, which they argue typically do not have sufficient self-interest to impose sanctions for violations of international human rights law (Krasner 1993; Donnelly 1998). Both realists and rational functionalists note that the formal mechanisms for monitoring and enforcing human rights commitments are deliberately weak, thus allowing states to engage in cheap talk with little or no direct costs. In addition, these treaties lack the potential effects of market forces, reciprocal benefits, or potential retaliation from other state parties that typically motivate compliance with international financial agreements (Neumayer 2005). At the same time regimes may face domestic circumstances that make compliance with international norms too costly, even for well-intentioned states, particularly in the face of perceived or real internal threats to the regime.

Rational functionalists also perceive state behavior as being interest-driven and recognize the dominant value of state sovereignty; however, they argue that international agreements provide a means through which states can cooperate to solve problems that they cannot achieve unilaterally, and therefore states are willing to sacrifice some measure of sovereignty for this benefit (Bilder 1989). While the mutual benefits of interstate cooperation through trade and monetary agreements readily come to mind, it is much more difficult to identify the mutual benefit of agreements that regulate activities such as human rights that are purely *internal* to the state rather than interactions among states (Moravcsik 2000). However, it is possible that states may acquire indirect benefits, such as bilateral or multilateral aid, through participation in the international human rights regime. In addition, they may avoid reputational costs, particularly identification as a "pariah state," for failure to participate in the regime. While rational functionalism has tended to focus on the question of formal commitment to human rights treaties, the theory is increasingly applied to the question of compliance with international norms or treaties, with the expectation that, given the weak enforcement mechanisms of the agreements and the low probability of sanctions, compliance will most likely be driven by calculations related to reputation (Simmons 2000; Hathaway 2005).

In the context of the human rights literature, these approaches typically focus on the commitment to and compliance with international norms, specifically human rights treaties; however, international human rights norms broadly speaking, and human rights treaty commitments more specifically, are both strongly associated with expectations that these norms and/or commitments will be translated into domestic law and policy and protected by domestic institutions, particularly the judiciary. To the extent that the adoption or maintenance of constitutional provisions for core rights represents compliance with international treaty commitments, realists would expect that commitment to these norms in constitutional documents would simply reflect a convergence of interests that, once again, would dissipate once the state's material interests conflicted with the formal commitments, and thus the state would be likely to ignore or change its constitutional commitments when it was no longer beneficial to its goals. In other words, the commitments would not be likely to alter the menu of policy choices, especially if the regime's primary interest, staying in power, was threatened from within or without. It is, however, more likely that formal commitments to international human rights norms through domestic constitutions will be associated with stronger legal remedies for violations and enforcement mechanisms than those of human rights treaties. Specifically, constitutions that provide for an independent judiciary increase the potential costs of the regime's choice to engage in political repression. The third stream of the rational actor approach addresses the influence of the judiciary and domestic institutions more broadly.

DOMESTIC INSTITUTIONS/DEMOCRATIC PEACE

A third stream within the rational actor perspective dismisses the assumption of a unitary state actor and instead recognizes the role of numerous domestic actors and institutions within the state (particularly in democratic regimes) that may affect the regime's menu of acceptable policy options or its calculation of costs and benefits related to commitment to international national human rights norms and with subsequent (non)compliance to formal commitment to the norms. Poe, Tate, and Keith (1999) argued that state leaders have less opportunity and less willingness to employ the tools of repression when faced with domestic or international conflict (293 and citations therein). As I noted above, opportunity is constrained because the structure and limited nature of democratic governments, which may include separation of powers and/or checks and balances, make it difficult for state actors to coordinate extensive use of repression. The necessity to utilize repression as a tool to solve conflict can be mitigated in democracies because they provide a variety of alternative mechanisms through which conflict can be channeled for possible resolution (Poe, Tate, and Keith 1999; Davenport 2007c), in turn, weakening the state's justification for coercive state action. The need to employ the tools of repression is also dampened by "the socialization processes that guide citizens of democratic polities toward the belief that nonviolent means of resolving conflicts are preferred over violence" (Poe, Tate, and Keith 1999, 293). The democratic norms of compromise, toleration, and facilitation may influence the decisions of the rulers by "increasing the cost of human rights violations as well as decreasing the value to quiescence" (Davenport 1999, 96). The cost of repression is increased in democracy as the electoral process "provides citizens (at least those with political resources) the tools to oust potentially abusive leaders from office before they are able to become a serious threat" (Poe and Tate 1994, 855).

It is not just democratic electoral processes but also the legal institutions associated with democratic systems that can provide the public and other political actors with the tools and venues through which they can hold the regime accountable should it fail to keep its formal commitments, both domestic (Keith 2002b) and international (for example, Keith 1999; Neumayer 2005; Hathaway 2007; Powell and Staton 2009). A truly independent judiciary, in particular, "should be able to withstand incursions upon rights because (1) the courts' power and fiscal well-being are protected, (2) the courts have some ability to review the actions of other agencies of government, and (3) the judges' jobs are constitutionally protected" (Keith, Tate, and Poe 2009, 649). Powell and Staton (2009) posit that in states where the courts are influential (effective), the use of repression may lead to rights claims in which the regime will incur a loss of resources as punishment for violating its obligations (154). In addition, nongovernmental organizations (NGOs) may initiate human rights litigation and form with courts what Moustafa refers to as "judicial support networks," which consist of domestic and transnational institutions and associations that support the judiciary's independence and power, which in turn are necessary for activists to pursue their claims (Moustafa 2008, 2007, 44).

These general explanations tend to assume a rather monolithic set of democracies, although it should be noted that most empirical human rights studies ultimately test the level of democratization rather than assuming a simple dichotomy. Most studies also tend to assume a linear association, at least in their empirical models. Recent theoretical and empirical work suggests that these often-unstated assumptions do not accurately reflect the true relationship between democracy and repression. Some scholars argue that there is "more repression in the middle," with full autocracies and democracies applying relatively low amounts of repression (with the latter being the least coercive) and mixed and transitional regimes, which combine elements of autocracy and democracy, being the most coercive (Regan and Henderson 2002, 120, modifying Fein 1995). Reagan and Henderson argue that autocratic regimes are suspicious of attempts to subvert their rule, and "in the face of an overarching state police machinery, the public is cowed and quiescent and made more accepting of domination, such that violent repression by the autocratic state is less likely" (123). However, they argue that the insufficiently developed infrastructure of semi-democratic regimes does not allow for the efficient channeling of opposition or dissent into the political arena, and the fragility of the institutions of government and the more limited range of options available encourage these leaders to respond harshly to opposition threats out of fear of political usurpation (124). In more recent work, both Davenport and Armstrong (2004) and Bueno de Mesquita et al. (2005) argue that the relationship between democracy and repression has been misspecified and that a threshold effect is a more accurate characterization. Specifically, Davenport and Armstrong argue that

> until there is a particular combination of institutions and behavioral factors in place, authorities will not be compelled to respect human rights. Below this critical point, the constraints are not comprehensive or severe enough to deter repressive action nor are the social control mechanisms well enough situated to provide viable alternatives for state repression. As these institutions and behavioral patterns gain strength beyond some threshold and the country's over-all level of democracy increases, however, the repressive behavior used by authorities should decrease. Above the critical point, constraints become too significant to ignore, and democracy functions as an acceptable substitute for influencing citizens. (542)

Other scholars have perceived democracy as multi-dimensional, following Lasswell (1950) and Dahl (1971), and have sought to understand which dimensions of democracy are more likely to lessen the use of political repression (Gleditsch and Ward 1997; Keith 2002a; Bueno de Mesquita et al. 2005).

Scholars also have attempted to distinguish between types of autocracy. For example, scholars have examined the role of military regimes (McKinlay and Cohen 1975; Poe and Tate 1994; Poe, Tate, and Keith 1999, Davenport 2007b) and Marxist-Leninist regimes (Mitchell and McCormick 1988; Poe and Tate 1994; Poe, Tate, and Keith 1999). The expectation that military regimes are more willing and able to use the tools of repression than other regimes has been well established, extending back to the work of McKinlay and Cohen (1975), who found that military regimes were more likely than civilian ones to suspend constitutions and to ban assemblies and political parties. As Poe and Tate (1994) noted, this increased willingness of a military regime to employ coercive means against its civilian population is not surprising, as "military juntas are based on force, and force is the key to coercion" (858). And as Poe, Tate, and Keith (1999, 293) argued, because the leaders in a military regime have direct control of the instruments of coercion, they will also be likely to face fewer constraints and barriers than other leaders if they choose to act repressively. As Poe and Tate (1994) noted, "since military rule is by definition antithetical to democracy, it might be that any apparent relationship between military rule and state terrorism is spurious, a result of a failure to control for the democratic/nondemocratic nature of the regime" (858). Davenport (2007b) argues that in "political systems where the agents of repression (i.e., the military) directly wield power, there is a higher likelihood that repressive behavior—especially violent activity—would be applied out of habit, familiarity, an impulse to meet specific organizational norms, and a desire to expand prestige in/control over the political system" (486). However, Davenport points out that there is a significant scholarship that disagrees with some of these assumptions: "Others have noted that the armed forces tend to shy away from their area of expertise and implementing repressive behavior. Indeed, the hesitancy of the 'professional soldier' to interfere in domestic politics because of organizational norms is a constant theme in older research . . . persisting up to the present" (491 and citations therein). Additionally, he argues that a military regime will have less need to resort to "overt manifestations of coercive power" because "such power is signaled by the presence of the military itself" (491). As we will see below, empirical studies have been rather mixed in determining the influence of military regimes.

Most recently, Davenport (2007b) has argued that different types of autocratic regimes vary in their use of repression. He challenges the general assumption that all autocratic regimes uniformly lack alternative mechanisms of sociopolitical control and thus resort to coercive power. He argues that research on autocratic regimes has demonstrated that in fact they vary significantly in the strategies they use (490 and citations therein). In particular, he distinguishes two extreme types: *personalist systems* and *single-party systems*, with some regime types such as military regimes and hybrid systems in between. He argues that in personalist systems, which are the most isolated of all, "repressive behavior emerges when autocratic leaders are isolated and have involved a smaller number of actors in the political process," and "the likelihood of repressive behavior is increased as those inside the ruling clique attempt to protect themselves from those that do not have any institutional means to influence government policy/practice" (486). And he argues that single-party systems, which are the least insulated, are the least repressive of autocratic regimes because "authorities have involved more individuals/organizations," and the likelihood of repression is thus lower because "those in power are able to use alternative mechanisms of control to influence the population by 'channeling' them through established political institutions" (486). Davenport admits that the extent to which a single-party system provides alternative mechanisms of solving grievances or promoting alternative mechanisms of control may be weak, but nonetheless, "they do provide some venue within which discussion/aspirations/activism can take place—in a sense, it may be the only 'show in town,' but at least there is a show" (490). As we will see below, his empirical analyses support these expectations. Vreeland (2008) also argues that the domestic political institutions of authoritarian regimes are not monolithic; he posits that an authoritarian regime that faces multiple legal political parties may have an incentive to concede to the parties' pressure to make a small concession and commit to international human rights norms. Ginsburg (2003) makes a similar argument in regard to authoritarian regimes' adopting constitutional constraints such as judicial review.

The repression literature has approached with some caution the expectation that leftist regimes will be more likely to repress than non-Marxist regimes, and, as we will see below, that hesitancy has been justified empirically. Nonetheless, policymakers such as former U.S. ambassador to the United Nations Jeane Kirkpatrick have argued that Marxist or Marxist-Leninist regimes are the world's most repressive regimes, and political scientists have treated the assertion to be at least a testable hypothesis (Mitchell and McCormick 1988; Poe and Tate 1994; Poe, Tate, and Keith 1999). For example, Mitchell and McCormick (1988) find that such regimes are in fact more repressive on at least one of their dimensions of repression than are non-Marxist "authoritarian" regimes (480–81, 493–95). Poe and Tate (1994) noted that "such a finding is not surprising if one takes seriously the tenets of Marxist-Leninist theory about the need for a dictatorship of the proletariat" (858); however, the results of their analyses tended to support critics of U.S. foreign policy that had taken Kirkpatrick and the Department of State to task for unfairly linking all socialist regimes with repression. As we will see below, the relationship appeared only in analyses using human rights measures as reported by the Department of State, suggesting that the leftist regime measure may have been simply controlling for a Department of State bias. Subsequent analyses that have expanded the time frame beyond the 1980s have failed to support the hypothesis that leftist regimes are more repressive; in fact the analyses have suggested just the opposite (Poe, Tate, and Keith 1999; Keith 2002). As Keith (2002) notes, there are two likely explanations. First, in Marxist or Marxist-Leninist regimes control of society and personal freedoms has often been so complete that the regime might be less likely than its non-leftist counterparts to need to engage in these more severe abuses of personal integrity rights to maintain order. Second, as Duvall and Stohl (1983) and Lopez and Stohl (1992) have argued, human rights repression may have an "'afterlife,' which affects the behavior of people long after the observable use of coercion by state agents has ended" (Lopez and Stohl 218). Thus, past repression in leftist regimes may actually reduce the need for future repression or the need for more severe forms of repression, such as those measured by personal integrity rights abuse.

The domestic institutions perspective fits firmly within the opportunity and willingness framework. Domestic institutions can either reduce or increase the cost of the choice to employ repression. The limited nature of democratic governments makes extensive use of repression more difficult and costly to arrange, and the electoral processes associated with democracies give citizens the potential to periodically change governments and thus increase the cost of repression. Democratic norms of compromise, toleration, and facilitation along with alternative processes for conflict resolution remove repression from the menu of appropriate policy tools, except in extraordinary circumstances. On the other hand, the nature and norms of military regimes may increase the perception that state coercion of citizens belongs in the menu of appropriate government responses, and the regime may face little cost or few barriers in choosing to employ the tools of repression. However, the past and current environment may lessen the need of military and leftist regimes to engage in overt coercive state action. The mere power of the military's presence may obviate that need, and the leftist regimes' overwhelming control of every dimension of society may lessen its need to engage in more severe forms of repression.

Theories Related to International Norms and Socialization

Another set of theoretical approaches generally focuses on transnational or international interaction and socialization, which are believed to drive the creation of and commitment to international human rights norms, rather than rationalist calculations. These perspectives emphasize the transformative power of international normative discourse on human rights and the role of activism by transnational actors (international organizations and nongovernmental actors), who through repeated interactions with state actors socialize states to accept new norms and who also support local efforts to press for a commitment to human rights. Thus, this perspective's emphasis is on the processes through which state actors adopt formal constraints on the state's opportunity to repress and through which state actors eventually internalize international human rights norms or values, which over time remove many of the tools of repression from the state's menu of appropriate policy options. Two of these approaches are particularly relevant to the study of political repression: the transnational advocacy networks perspective and the world society approach.

TRANSNATIONAL ADVOCACY NETWORKS

The transnational advocacy networks perspective (Keck and Sikkink 1998; Risse, Ropp, and Sikkink 1999) posits that international human rights norms are diffused through networks of transnational and domestic actors who "bring pressure 'from above' and 'from below' to accomplish human rights change" (Risse and Sikkink 1999, 18). Risse and Sikkink identify a process of socialization through which international norms are internalized and implemented domestically, and they identify three types of causal mechanisms that they deem to be necessary for enduring internalization of human rights norms: (1) the process of instrumental adaptation and strategic bargaining; (2) the process of moral consciousness-raising, argumentation, dialogue, and persuasion; and (3) the processes of institutionalization and habitualization (5).

Risse and Sikkink note that the first process, which typically occurs early in the socialization process, is essentially compatible with rational-choice assumptions: state actors make tactical concessions in pursuit of instrumental or material interests, such as releasing political prisoners to retain bilateral aid. In other words, state actors "adjust their behavior to the international human rights discourse without necessarily believing in the validity of the norms" (12). Risse and Sikkink note that sometimes repressive governments will return to repression once the pressure decreases, as Kenya did in the early 1990s. Sometimes, however, the regimes change their discursive practices and start institutionalizing international norms into domestic law for instrumental reasons, and "this in turn opens space for the domestic opposition to catch the government in its own rhetoric"; at this point "instrumental and communicative rationality intertwine," and thereafter it is very difficult for the regime to deny the validity of human rights norms (15).

Risse and Sikkink argue that the argumentative/persuasion process is still "not sufficient to socialize states into norms-abiding practices" and caution that we cannot consider norms to be internalized in domestic practice until actors comply with the norms irrespective of individual beliefs about their validity (16). Thus, they propose a final type of socialization process, in which norms are gradually institutionalized to such an extent that human rights norms are incorporated as part of the "'standard operating procedure' of domestic institutions" (17). Once this stage of institutionalization is reached, changes in government and individual state actors matter less because norms are simply taken for granted and are implemented independently of the moral consciousness of the individual actors (17).

Ultimately, Risse, Ropp, and Sikkink (1999) present a five-phase spiral model that assumes that political repression triggers activation of a transnational network of NGOs that invokes human rights norms and applies pressure on the repressive state to make concessions; the repressive state denies the validity of the human rights norms as a subject for international jurisdiction and instead asserts the norm of nonintervention; the regime eventually makes some tactical concessions to the transnational network; the regime then becomes trapped in its own rhetoric and concessions, which can lead to either the opposition bringing about a regime change or a process of gradual liberalization; the regime accepts international norms (ratifies treaties and institutionalizes domestically), and ultimately we see rule-consistent behavior due to the regime's acceptance of the validity of human rights and to increased scrutiny under the monitoring and reporting mechanisms of the treaties.

WORLD SOCIETY APPROACH

A second perspective, the world society approach (for example, Boli-Bennett 1976; Meyer et al. 1997) perceives states to be embedded in an integrated cultural system that "promulgates cognitive frames and normative prescriptions that constitute the legitimate identities, structures, and purposes of modern nation-states" (Cole 2005, 477). Thus, with the proliferation of treaties codifying human rights norms, states' legitimacy or "good nation" identity is increasingly linked to the formal acknowledgment of these norms (Cole 2005; Wotipka and Ramirez 2007). As Go (2003) notes, the approach posits that newly emerging or independent states will be likely to adopt standardized forms of government, and over time will appear to be similar to other nation-states around the world. As noted in Chapter 1, he finds strong evidence that "documentary constitutionalism has become a globally shared mode of organizing sociopolitical formations" (72). Further, he argues that the approach suggests not only that all states have constitutions, but also that all constitutions come in a very similar package because the larger world system dictates that they should. This perspective posits three mechanisms through which states are influenced by the world polity: the degree of participation in global civil society, particularly membership in international governmental organizations (IGOs) and international nongovernmental organizations (INGOs) (Boli and Thomas 1997); participation in international human rights conferences (Goodman and Jinks 2004); and normative bandwagoning (Finnemore and Sikkink 1998). However, as Cole notes, many states join the traditionally weak human rights regime "not out of deep commitment, but because it signals their probity to the international community," and thus "a decoupling is endemic to the human rights regime" (2005, 477). As Hafner-Burton and Tsutsui (2005) note, this convergence in organization forms and policies does not necessarily lead to changes in state repression, as formal changes are often nominal (1383 and citations therein).

I believe these approaches fall within Most and Starr's framework in that they perceive that a regime's opportunities to use the tools of repression are either facilitated or constrained by both the domestic and global environment and influenced by both domestic and transnational actors. The constructivist emphasis on the transformative power of international normative discourse and repeated interactions with state actors assumes that states are socialized to accept new norms. Thus, constructivists would argue that international socialization changes both the menu of appropriate choices and the values through which the regime will evaluate the choices.

Liberal Economic Theory

There are two schools of thoughts concerning the somewhat indirect relationship between human rights and global economic interdependence. As Gilpin (1987) notes, liberals believe that an interdependent economy, and trade in particular, facilitates economic development:

> Liberalism maintains that an interdependent world economy based on free trade, specialization, and international division of labor facilitates domestic development. Flows of goods, capital, and technology increase optimum efficiency in resource allocation and therefore transmit growth from the developed nations to the less developed countries. Trade can serve as an "engine of growth" as the less-developed economy gains capital, technology, and access to world markets. This is a mutually beneficial relationship since the developed economies can obtain cheaper raw materials and outlets for their capital and manufactured goods. (266)

Ultimately, liberal trade policies are expected not only to facilitate economic development but also to contribute to an improvement in social and political conditions in less economically developed states, and over time to lead to the emergence of a middle class that increasingly make rights demands upon their government (Lipset 1959)—which will ultimately foster democracy and civil liberties (Meyer 1998; Moran 1998). As Apodaca (2001) notes, according to the positive model of globalization theory, the new globalization/economic liberalization "is privileging individuals and weakening abusive governments" (590). On the other hand, the dependency theory critique of liberal economic theory argues generally that more economically developed states exploit less economically developed states, which leads to uneven development and hinders the socioeconomic growth of the states whose economies are vulnerable to the demands of multinational corporations (MNCs) and multilateral lending institutions. This malign view of developing countries' integration into the global economy holds that "economic globalization exploits the developing world by means of cheap labor, minimal skill transmissions, restrictions on technology transfers and on long-term commitments to stay and invest," and thus "foreign capital reinforces and strengthens repression in developing countries" (Apodaca 2001, 591). Ultimately, the less economically developed state's options are constrained by its economic relationships with the developed world, and its decisions are made to benefit MNCs and domestic elites rather than to look out for its own citizens. Thus, the two positions disagree on how globalization would affect the cost/benefit structure of using coercive force. And they also disagree about what controls the menu of appropriate policy tools and priorities—the values and interests of the general public or those of MNCs and economic elites that. As we will see in the next section, empirical evidence has been rather mixed.

Public Law Perspective

The opportunity and willingness framework is also appropriate for the public law perspective, which would posit that a potentially repressive regime would be constrained by a written constitution with a bill of fundamental rights and freedoms that are protected by an independent judiciary empowered with judicial review (for example, Rosenthal 1990; Ramseyer 1994; Prillaman 2000; and Mutua 2001). Written bills of rights greatly extend the reach of the rule of law and provide individual protection from the overextension of governmental power, providing new duties and standards of justice and fairness that both politicians and bureaucrats are now required to meet, and, more importantly, they represent "catalogues of very important interests and activities over which the individual rather than the state has been given final control" (Beatty 1994, 16). In addition, the law itself may serve as a socializing agent and, when coupled with a strong civil society and a judiciary that is at least somewhat independent, may cultivate a budding rights consciousness within the state (MacGuigan 1965; Martin 1991; Murphy 1993; Tate and Vallinder 1995; Epp 1998). Thus, bills of rights and a judiciary empowered with judicial review could potentially change the menu of appropriate choices, change the costs of inappropriate choices, and influence the values through which the regime will evaluate the choices. Empirical evidence has been somewhat mixed, however. I next turn to the body of empirical literature on political repression.

The Empirical Literature on Political Repression

Over the last two decades we have seen tremendous growth in the body of empirical research that has sought to explain states' human rights behavior, which in part has been driven by the creation and dissemination of large-*N* cross-national data sets. This research has primarily focused on two categories of human rights behavior that fall within the broader concept of political repression; however, increasingly, global cross-national studies have sought to explain other human rights, such as economic or basic needs rights, workers' rights, women's rights, and asylum or refugee rights. While this book's focus continues within the larger set of studies, those examining political repression, I expect that the research here will also substantially inform studies of the broader set of human rights. And because this study is also informed in part by those studies, I try to incorporate their findings where appropriate.

Measuring Political Repression

As Davenport (2007) notes, most cross-national studies of human rights tend to focus on two dimensions of state repression separately—primarily addressing the more severe category of repressions, violations of personal integrity (imprisonment, torture, killing, and disappearances) (for example, Poe and

Tate 1994; Poe, Tate, and Keith 1999; Cingranelli and Richards 1999a, 1999b; Keith 2002a), or, to a somewhat lesser extent, addressing the broader category of civil liberties restrictions, or negative sanctions as they are sometimes referred to in the literature (for example, Davenport 1995a, 1995b, 2007a, 2007b; Keith 2002; Walker and Poe 2002; Howard and Carey 2004). Studies of abuses of personal integrity have tended to dominate the field, in part because of the egregious nature of the repression, but also in part because, as Risse et al. (1999) note, "these basic 'rights of the person' have been most accepted as universal rights, and not simply rights associated with a particular political ideology or system" (3). Studies of personal integrity abuse have tended to employ the dominant indicators in the field: the Political Terror Scale (PTS) or Cingranelli and Richard's (CIRI) physical integrity measures. The Political Terror Scale (PTS) was originally developed by Stohl and others (Gibney and Stohl 1988; Poe 1992; Gibney and Dalton 1996) and is maintained by Gibney (2011). The CIRI measures are similar to the Political Terror Scale, but the dimensions are disaggregated to measure imprisonment, torture, disappearances, and killings separately (Cingranelli and Richards 1999a, 1999b); however, they are frequently used as an additive index. Studies of the second category of repression, civil liberties restrictions, have also tended to use two dominant measurements: Taylor and Jodice's (1983) negative sanctions (Davenport 1995a, 1995b, 1996) and Freedom House's (McColm 1990) Civil Liberties Index (Keith 2002b; Walker and Poe 2002; Davenport 2007b). While most literature to date has focused on political repression as *either* restrictions of civil liberties *or* violations of personal integrity, Davenport's (2007a) most recent work conceptualizes state repression in terms of the degree of lethality that encompasses both the violence dimension captured within the PTS measure and the restrictions captured within the Freedom House measure. These measures will be discussed and examined more fully in Chapter 3.

Major Findings in the Empirical Literature

Political scientists have created a significant body of research examining both domestic and international influences on political repression. In the past couple of decades we have seen the creation and dissemination of large cross-national data sets that encompass all countries and increasingly longer periods. Over time, both our measurements and statistical methodologies have improved substantially. The majority of large-*N* cross-national studies of state repression have typically focused on explanatory factors that are primarily domestic. These factors largely reflect rational actor assumptions, and they capture both agent (regime) and environment dimensions (domestic threat and opposition and socioeconomic conditions). As Davenport and Armstrong (2004) note, over time a "standard" model has emerged in the repression literature (Poe and Tate 1994; Poe, Tate, and Keith 1999 and citations therein). The standard model has typically included measures of domestic threats or opposition, regime type (democracy, autocracy, military, and leftist), and socioeconomic conditions (economic development, population, and colonial legacy). These influences represent the most consistently studied expectations in the cross-national literature. Some of these factors have proven to be more significant than others in empirical analyses. I discuss these findings in the section that follows. Each of the eight conditions in this standard model represents the domestic context or environment of the state, with one exception (international war, which is a part of the broader state concern with threats to the regime). This context either creates or constrains the regime's opportunities to repress or affects the regime's decision-making calculation of the advantage or disadvantage to exercising repressive tools as a means to achieve its policy goals. The body of empirical work has gradually expanded beyond domestic influences to examine a variety of international or transnational influences, including bilateral aid, multilateral lending programs, international treaty regimes, trade relations, and foreign investment. In this section I seek to identify the most important factors that have been shown to constrain or facilitate a state's choice to employ the tool of repression, while at the same time identifying some of the weaknesses that still limit our understanding of such behavior. I discuss domestic influences first, then the international or transnational influences, noting, of course, that increasingly these contexts are difficult to separate from each other.

Domestic Influences

DOMESTIC THREATS AND OPPOSITION

Theoretically, the most significant environmental factor in state repression may be the presence of significant domestic opposition or a perceived challenge to the regime's hold on power, especially if there is a threat (actual or perceived) that the regime's challengers may resort to violent tactics. The regime may choose to employ coercive force to prevent, contain, or punish such threats. The most potentially disruptive form of domestic threat, civil war, has received the most empirical attention, and its effect has been demonstrated to be the strongest of many factors, in terms of impact, statistical robustness, and consistency across a variety of measures of repression and other human rights behavior (for example, Poe and Tate 1994; Davenport 1995c; Cingranelli and Richards 1999a; Keith 1999, 2002a, 2004; Richards 1999; Poe, Tate, and Keith 1999; Apodaca 2001; Regan and Henderson 2002; Davenport and Armstrong 2004; Keith and Poe 2004; Bueno de Mesquita et al. 2005; Abouhard and Cingranelli 2006). To illustrate its magnitude, Poe, Tate, and Keith (1999) demonstrate that an ongoing civil war would increase the level of repression over time by around 1.5 on a 5-point scale of repression, with other factors in the model held equal (308).

Political scientists have also sought to understand the impact of less severe forms of threat, as well as other dimensions of threat, such as variety of strategies and frequency of conflict. Davenport (1995c) found that deviance from past norms of conflict, the frequency of conflict, and the variety of strategies engaged each increases the likelihood that a state will resort to civil liberties restrictions; however, once these factors are controlled, the presence of domestic violence becomes statistically insignificant. As Davenport notes, "the insignificance of this variable is probably attributed to the fact that its presence generally leads to the implementation of *other* tools of behavioral control including state-sponsored terrorism, armed attacks and political executions" (701). Davenport (1999) confirmed these findings generally, but also found that the presence of domestic violence decreased the odds of negative sanctions. I further test Davenport's supposition that this negative effect is likely because the regime engages in different forms of repression when violence is present, especially since the empirical literature on personal integrity rights has consistently demonstrated this expectation.

Poe et al. (2000) found that the repressive response to domestic threats was dependent not only upon the level of the threat but also upon the prior level of repression. Generally the greater the level of the threat, the more likely a regime was to engage in coercive force, although some regimes did in fact engage in repression even when they were not seriously threatened. However, where repression levels were already high, nonviolent protest and nonviolent rebellion had little or no effect, but these threats did have some effect on repression in states that had exercised only low to moderate levels of repression in the past. On the other hand, violent opposition or rebellion increased the level of repression regardless of the prior level of repression, unless repression was already quite high. The analyses also showed that regimes responded in most cases by lessening the repression once the threat ceased; this result suggests that regimes do weigh the potential cost of engaging in political repression, perhaps in fear of their supporters' defecting if repression continues once the threat diminishes or perhaps in response to the economic costs in terms of resources or the loss of support of international actors (Poe et al. 2000, 58). Regan and Henderson (2002) also found that the level of threat was positively associated with repression, and that the impact of threat was greater than that of regime type. They also found that when controlling for threat, less-developed states with intermediate levels of democracy had the greatest odds of using coercive force. Political scientists now have multiple measures capturing a fuller range of repressive tools that regimes have at their disposal, as well as multiple measures capturing the most significant dimensions of threat. In Chapter 6 I examine more fully the theoretical expectations in regard to both internal and external threats, as well as formal regulations of regime behavior during times of threat.

REGIME CHARACTERISTICS

Democracy: As I noted above, political democracy has proven to be one of the more potent and consistent explanators in political repression models; almost four decades of research support the expectation that higher levels of democracy are associated with lower levels of repression, across both categories of repression (for example, Hibbs 1973; Ziegenhagen 1986; Mitchell and McCormick 1988; Henderson 1991; Poe and Tate 1994; Davenport 1995c, 1999, 2007a; Poe, Tate, and Keith 1999; Richards 1999; Zanger 2000; Apodaca 2001; Keith 2002a; Bueno de Mesquita et al. 2005). As discussed above, more recent studies of democracy's influence on repression have urged us to look beyond a simple linear relationship and have indeed demonstrated that the relationship is not as simple as we have generally theorized. Gartner and Regan (1996) and Regan and Henderson (2002) demonstrated that the impact of democracy on human rights abuse is curvilinear when controlling for the level of threat, with semi-democracies more likely to repress than full democracies and autocracies. Their work was, however, limited to only less-developed countries.

Davenport and Armstrong (2004) demonstrate that we have probably misspecified democracy's role in our models, specifically showing that democratization tends to have no impact until it reaches a critical threshold. Using the Polity measure of democracy, they find that at the lower levels of the scale (below 8) there is no impact, but as states progress into the intermediate level there is some negative effect on repression, and as states reach the highest level of democracy there is a strong negative effect (548). Other scholars have perceived democracy as a multidimensional concept and have sought to understand which dimensions of democracy are more likely to lessen the use of political repression (Gleditsch and Ward 1997; Keith 2002a; Bueno de Mesquita et al. 2005). Gleditsch and Ward (1997) examined empirically the components of the Polity measure and demonstrated that the measure is primarily driven by its executive constraint dimension and that the other dimensions, which measure patterns of executive recruitment and the extent and competitiveness of participation, were "not especially powerful in determining the degree of democracy" (380). They conclude that to use the data "summarily to classify modern polities as democracies directs attention away from the actual data that have been collected on authority patterns" (380). Thus, they urged scholars to move beyond discrete classification of "democracy" or "autocracy" and to focus more on the sub-dimensions of this measure. Studies of political repression do not use the Polity data as a dependent variable, nor do we typically use the data to divide countries into two discrete categories; rather, we use the index to control for the level of institutional democracy attained in the country.

Nonetheless, Keith (2002a) followed Gleditsch and Ward's suggestion and tested the four components of the Polity democracy measure separately; two of the components produced statistically significant relationships: constraint on the chief executive and the competitiveness of political participation. While Ward and Gleditsch's analysis revealed that the Polity democracy measure was largely driven by executive constraint, Keith found the competitiveness of political participation to be a more powerful explanator. Not surprisingly, the combined maximum impact of the two individual components was approximately equal to that achieved by the composite measure. Regardless of the construction of the democracy measure, its impact was one of the largest in the analysis. Bueno de Mesquita et al. (2005) confirmed this result, and also demonstrated that improvement of the state's level of democracy did not make a difference in human rights until the state achieved full democracy, supporting Davenport and Armstrong's analysis. Additionally, they demonstrated that the significant components of democracy had a sharp threshold effect, and they concluded that "real improvements in human rights do not occur smoothly but reflect a discontinuous step function achieved only when a society becomes fully democratic" (453). Ultimately, they concluded that accountability through a competitive party system is a critical feature of democracy, but for it to be effective in reducing human rights abuses, institutional foundations must first be put into place. In Chapter 3 I engage in a thorough examination of democracy, its various components, and effects.

Types of Autocracy: Currently, Davenport's work (2007b) represents the most comprehensive examination of autocratic regimes' use of political repression, in particular demonstrating that there is variation among types of autocratic regimes in their use of repression. He uses Geddes' (1999) categorization of autocratic regimes, which distinguishes two extreme types on this dimension: personalist systems and single-party systems, with some regime types such as military regimes and military hybrid systems fitting in between. His work demonstrates that only military regimes influence the level of restrictions, and they do so in a negative direction. When he adds interactions for the end of the Cold War, the military regime's effect remains, but then he finds that both personalist and single-party regimes are less repressive. In regard to personal integrity rights, the military regime's effect disappears, and only the single-party autocracy measure influences the level of repression, and it does so in a negative direction. Controlling for the various types of autocracy removes the effect of the leftist regime variable, which as discussed above has performed somewhat inconsistently in previous work.

Marxist-Leninist Regimes: The expectation that leftist regimes will be more likely to repress than non-Marxist regimes has not been consistently supported, even though it has been considered a part of the standard model. While Mitchell and McCormick (1988) did find that leftist regimes were more repressive than non-Marxist authoritarian regimes, Poe and Tate (1994) found such a link only when employing measures of human rights based on Department of State reports, which suggested quite plausibly a bias in the Department of State reports of the 1980s. Subsequent analyses that expanded the time frame beyond the 1980s have failed to support the hypothesis that leftist regimes are more repressive; in fact, the analyses have suggested the opposite (Poe, Tate, and Keith 1999; Keith 2002a, Keith, Tate, and Poe 2009). Thus, past repression in leftist regimes may actually reduce the need for future repression or the need for more severe forms of repression, such as those measured by abuse of personal integrity rights. Interestingly, Davenport (2007b) found that that a leftist regime is more likely to increase civil liberties restrictions, but, as with the studies above, that regime type decreases the odds of personal integrity abuses. The latter finding is not unexpected, since he uses the same data set (Poe, Tate, and Keith 1999; Keith 2002a); however, it is interesting that when he adds the autocracy types to his model, the effect of a leftist regime disappears altogether. I explore the Marxist/Marxist-Leninist influence further in the next chapter, examining the influence on both the broader category of civil liberties restrictions and the more severe personal integrity abuse. I continue to compare the measures based on Amnesty International reports with those based on Department of State reports to control for possible ideological biases.

Military Control: Despite the strong theoretical arguments that would lead us to expect that military regimes will be more repressive than nonmilitary regimes, empirical evidence has been rather mixed. Poe and Tate (1994) found no such effect; however, subsequent studies of longer periods yielded the expected effect, although its impact remained somewhat minor (Poe, Tate, and Keith 1999; Keith, Tate, and Poe 2009). These studies have employed Madani's (1992) classification, which follows McKinlay and Cohen (1975), where military regimes are defined as those that have come to power "as a consequence of a successful coup d'état, led by the army, navy or air force, that remained in power with a military person as the chief executive, for at least six months in a given year" (Madani 1992, 61; see McKinlay and Cohen 1975, 1). This operationalization also includes a small number of mixed regimes "with either a civilian as the chief executive and several military persons in the cabinet or a military head of government who nominated a civilian as the head of government and himself worked behind the scenes" (Madani 1992, 61).

Davenport (2007b), who utilizes a different categorization of military regimes, also fails to find an effect for military or hybrid military regimes on personal integrity abuse but does find evidence that military regimes are *less* likely to restrict the broader civil liberties category of repression (as defined and measured by Freedom House). Davenport uses Geddes' (1999) somewhat broader definition, which delineates military regimes as those in which "a group of officers decides who rules and influences policy" (Davenport 2007b, 493; Geddes 1999, 4). He also includes in his analysis a military-personalist hybrid measure that fails to demonstrate any effect on either type of repression. Thus, as a whole the empirical analysis suggests that military regimes are not more likely to engage in personal integrity abuses such as torture, killing, and disappearances, and, even more interesting, that military regimes may be less likely to engage in restrictions on civil liberties. In explaining these different results Davenport notes: "It seems reasonable to suggest that these political systems reduce civil liberties restrictions because they tend to avoid involving themselves with the political processes which are normally responsible for these repressive activities (i.e., legislatures and courts) . . . and more inclined to use repressive techniques which are more directly within the realm of their expertise—physical violence" (500).

While I find Davenport's explanation plausible, there is evidence of military regimes' curbing freedom of the press, detaining protestors, and engaging in lower forms of repression. The nature of the Freedom House civil liberties measure also makes it somewhat problematic to assume that it does not capture physical violence, as its survey on civil liberties does include questions about political terror, physical harm, and violence. Also, as I read Davenport's table, the military-regime measure did not have a statistical effect on any of the personal integrity models, a result that parallels previous findings (Poe, Tate, and Keith 1999). I continue to explore this perplexing relationship in each of the following chapters.

THE DOMESTIC SOCIOECONOMIC ENVIRONMENT

Economic Development and Growth: As I noted above, one of the earliest-identified and most consistent influences on political repression is the effect of the level of economic development or wealth (McKinlay and Cohen 1975, 1976; Mitchell and McCormick 1988; Henderson 1991; Poe and Tate 1994; Keith 1999, 2002a; Poe, Tate, and Keith 1999; Richards 1999). Most recent studies have consistently used per-capita gross national product or gross domestic product (GDP) to measure economic development and growth, and most have supported the hypothesis that higher levels of economic development do lead to less state repression, regardless of the category of repression. However, these studies have demonstrated that the size of the impact is typically not substantively significant; coefficients on average approach zero, especially when the models incorporate factors beyond the limited standard model, many of which represent a more viable policy alternative to improve human rights conditions than the level of increase in economic development that would be required to produce even a modest improvement (for example, Keith 2002a; Keith, Tate, and Poe 2009). Over time economic growth has been dropped from many models because of its repeated failure to achieve statistical significance; nonetheless, I continue to test it here, as the time frame of my current dataset represents the largest period under study thus far. In the section on international factors that follows I discuss the impact of other important economic factors that have a transnational character and are more controversial in regard to their influence.

Population Size and Growth: As with the domestic economic environment, population size and level of growth are seen as conditions associated with popular unrest stemming from scarcity within the state. Population size, typically logged, has consistently been shown to positively increase levels of repression, but, as with economic development, population growth has proven to be insignificant as studies of repression have extended over time and controlled for additional influences. I continue to examine these dimensions of population in subsequent chapters.

Colonial Experience: Over time the inclusion of a control for British colonial experience has become standard in explanatory models of state repression (for example, Davenport and Armstrong 2004; Keith 1999, 2002a; Poe and Tate 1994; Poe, Tate, and Keith 1999; Howard and Carey 2004). Interestingly, though, the results have been somewhat inconsistent. For example, the variable was not statistically significant in Poe and Tate's early work, which examined repression in the 1980s, but the variable was statistically significant in all four of their models in their 1999 study (Poe, Tate, and Keith), which expanded the data back to 1976 and forward to 1993. However, Keith (2002a) and Keith, Tate, and Poe (2009), which extended the analyses forward to 1996 and added measures of constitutional protections and institutional provisions, found the measure to be statistically insignificant. Keith (2004) found some evidence of colonial influences, in that rights-related constitutional provisions performed better in countries with Iberian colonial experience; and Keith and Ogundele (2007) found that in Sub-Saharan Africa former francophone colonies had better human rights protection than anglophone ones and that constitutional protections and institutional provisions of former francophone colonies outperformed those of anglophone ones. In my work here, I examine these findings fully, along with other colonial legacies such as the type of legal system.

Domestic Law and the Judiciary

A growing body of empirical studies has examined the question of whether constitutional provisions for rights and an independent judiciary constrain the likelihood that states will repress their own citizens. Most of these studies have examined the role of specific rights typically embedded in bills of rights, and to a lesser extent institutional constraints such as provisions for an independent judiciary, state of emergency clauses, or provisions for federalism. The earliest analyses (Boli-Bennett 1976; Pritchard 1986) found evidence that not only were the constitutional provisions not associated with improved rights behavior, but also the associations were in the opposite direction, suggesting a harmful effect. However, Blasi and Cingranelli (1996) found some evidence of a weak direct effect. These early studies tended to utilize simple bivariate analysis of the association between constitutions and various rights measures, and additionally they tended to be limited to a single year; thus the generalizability of the results is significantly limited. Over time the analyses have become more statistically sophisticated, and the depth of analysis has extended to longer periods and a broader set of countries, beginning with Davenport (1996), which presents a rigorous and comprehensive analysis of the impact of constitutional provisions on state use of negative sanctions on its citizens. He, too, finds limited effects: only three constitutional indicators (out of fourteen) demonstrate a statistically significant effect on state repression, and several other provisions appeared to increase sanctions, although their coefficients did not achieve statistical significance. As Davenport notes, his sample is limited and not representative of the world and his time frame ends in 1982, well before the development of constitutions in the Third Wave of democratization and the post-Communist era. Nonetheless, the initial skepticism generated by his analysis continues across subsequent studies. Cross (1999) finds no statistically significant association between constitutional provisions for reasonable searches and human rights protection, but he does find that judicial independence increases the probability of political rights and protection against unreasonable searches and seizures. Cross's effort to analyze the impact of judicial independence on human rights is commendable; however, his measure of judicial independence is the subjective rating devised by the late Charles Humana (1992) which provides no replicable operationalization of the concept of judicial independence. Additionally, the study is limited to a small, not fully representative sample of countries.

My previous work has built upon these early studies, expanding the analysis to the global set of countries across a twenty-year period and also expanding the set of constitutional provisions. Keith (2002a) examined ten constitutional provisions associated with internationally recognized human rights and found some evidence to support the optimistic perspective, and while the traditional freedoms associated with bills of rights (freedom of speech, religion, assembly, association, and press) were not found to improve state protection against personal integrity abuse, provisions for public and fair trials did significantly improve states' behavior, even when controlling for the broad range of factors known to influence this type of behavior. In addition to the failure of the basic constitutional freedoms to influence human rights, neither the provision for the right to writ of habeas corpus nor a provision banning state torture influenced states' human rights behavior. Keith's (2002b) examination of the impact of seven provisions increased the likelihood that states would protect fundamental freedoms and rights; these included provision for separation of powers, guaranteed terms of office for judges, fiscal autonomy for the judiciary, and a ban against exceptional courts. However, again, the remaining provisions failed to produce the expected effect; these included the provision for exclusive judicial authority and finality in its decision-making process, along with the provision for enumerated qualifications for judges. Keith cautioned that her analysis is limited to formal provisions for judicial independence, which do not guarantee that the judiciary actually achieves the level of independence that would be necessary to stand against the regime in protecting fundamental rights. In this book I seek to address that need.

Prior to Howard and Carey (2004) there was not a systematic replicable measure of actual judicial independence available for all countries that went beyond formal provisions. A few studies have created subjective ratings for a significant albeit nonrandom set of countries; however, these evaluations are not replicable (for example, Johnson 1976; Cross 1999; La Porta et al. 2004). Howard and Carey created an indicator of *de facto* judicial independence based on assessments within the Department of State's human rights country reports that measure the degree to which judiciaries function in practice independently of the executive and legislature, are free from corruption and bribery, and afford basic criminal due process protections to criminal defendants. Howard and Carey do find that across a ten-year period and the global set of countries the level of judicial independence does influence states' provision of civil and political rights. While I applaud Howard and Carey's standards-based measure of judicial independence, I have concerns about the use of their measure in regard to our human rights analysis, because one of the measure's three components considers whether the state "afford[s] basic criminal due process to criminal defendants" (287). This component seems at best indirectly related to consensus definitions of judicial independence, as we will see in Chapter 4. More importantly, my strong interest in exploring the potential influence of judicial independence on human rights leads us to be very sensitive to possible overlaps between operationalizations of independent variables linked to human rights and our primary human rights measures, the Political Terror Scale (Gibney and Dalton 1996), frequently referred to as a measure of the abuse of personal integrity, and Cingranelli and Richards' measures of physical integrity (Cingranelli and Richards 1999). Both measures assess the degree of abusive or politically motivated state behavior, including imprisonment, torture, disappearance, and extrajudicial killings, which seem by their very nature to deny basic due process rights. Even if, arguably, the targets of the abuse are not in fact criminals, we are still measuring in our dependent variable the same forms of abuse, which encompass an abuse of procedural due process as well. Thus, we are left with the need for a more appropriate measure of *de facto* judicial independence, and in Chapter 4 I will present an alternative measurement that builds upon Howard and Carey's work.

The mixed results described above have continued to appear in more recent work. Keith and Poe (2004) found that, as expected, certain provisions for states of emergencies, which have been promoted by international organizations such as the International Lawyers Association and the International Commission of Jurists, have unintended consequences and are associated with increased levels of human rights abuse during most types of internal threat, while under some circumstances other provisions have the intended effect. Our combined model (Keith, Tate, and Poe 2009) again found rather mixed effects for constitutional provisions for bills of rights, judicial independence, and states of emergency, with several provisions producing a beneficial effect, and many producing either no effect or a harmful effect.

Overall, then, recent empirical analyses suggest that there is some justification for the optimistic expectation that legal provisions for rights and judicial independence (both *de jure* and *de facto*) may increase the level of state human rights protections. However, confidence in the generalizability of these results is somewhat constrained by some of the limitations associated with these previous studies. First, none of these studies extend beyond 1996, which limits our understanding in regard to the most of the post-Cold War period. Second, the studies examine a wide range of human rights behavior, but typically each study examines only one type or measure of behavior, and thus the empirical tests are not as robust as they could be. Third, only Keith (2002b) and Howard and Carey (2004) examine the global set of countries. Fourth, most of the studies examine one set of constitutional provisions in isolation from the others. Fifth, the studies do not examine the full set of causal links or the paths of influence; for example, they do not explore the path from formal judicial independence to actual judicial independence to human rights protection, nor do they deal with issues of endogeneity. Finally, the studies lack an appropriate measure of judicial independence, at least in regard to core human rights, such as personal integrity abuse. In Chapters 4 through 6 I take steps to deal with these issues in a rigorous manner.

International or Transnational Influences

EXTERNAL THREATS/INTERNATIONAL WAR

As noted above, the expected nexus between international war and civil conflict was demonstrated by Stohl's early work (1975, 1976) to the extent that international war increased the level of domestic violence. And at least one early study examined the effect of international wars on repression; Rasler's (1986) study of the twentieth-century United States found evidence that administrations did indeed increase levels of repression during wars. Subsequently, large-*N* studies have confirmed the effect of participation in international wars on domestic political repression (Poe and Tate 1994; Poe, Tate, and Keith 1999; Cingranelli and Richards 1999a, 1999b), and over time international war has become a key component of the standard model of human rights behavior (Keith 1999, 2002; Richards 1999; Apodaca 2001; Davenport and Armstrong 2004; Abouharb and Cingranelli 2006, 2008; Landman 2005). It is interesting to note that the impact of international war is substantially lower than that of civil wars. For example, Poe, Tate, and Keith (1999) find the impact of participation in a civil war to be at least three times the impact of being a participant in an international war. This result is somewhat intuitive even though external threats such as interstate war are potentially more serious than civil wars; often civil wars are a greater threat to a regime because of the proximity and ability of the opposition to inflict damage, especially compared to some interstate wars, which may be fought far away from at least some of the belligerents' states, such as in the Persian Gulf War or the war in Iraq. In Chapter 6 I continue our examination of a variety of threats, both external and internal, and their interactive effects, especially in regard to the independence of the judiciary.

BILATERAL, MULTILATERAL, AND GLOBAL ECONOMIC INFLUENCES

Bilateral Aid. U.S. foreign assistance is a significant component of U.S. foreign policy and has received considerable attention by scholars, commentators, and critics of the United States, especially during the Cold War. Most scholarly attention has sought to determine what factors actually affect U.S. aid allocation and has been especially concerned with whether a state's human rights practices affect these decisions as mandated by Congress or whether geopolitical and economic interests truly drive these decisions (for example, Carleton and Stohl 1987; Cingranelli and Pasquarello 1985; Poe 1992; Poe et al. 1994; Poe and Sirirangsi 1994; Meernik, Krueger, and Poe 1998; Apodaca and Stohl 1999; Neumayer 2003a, 2003b, 2003c). Considerably less attention has been given to the question of whether U.S. aid influences human rights practices of recipient states. Regan's (1995) study is the only empirical study I am aware of that examines this question specifically, beyond two studies supported by the U.S. Agency for International Development (USAID) itself (Finkel et al. 2006, 2008) and a study by Knack (2004), a senior research economist for the World Bank who examined the impact of western foreign assistance on democratization in recipient states. While there are strong theoretical links between aid and improved human rights practices, both direct and indirect, there is also some justification to expect that aid will not influence human rights or that it might have a harmful effect. While Knack agrees that foreign aid can potentially contribute to democratization by providing support for electoral processes, strengthening legislatures and independent judiciaries, promoting of civil society organizations, and improving education and per-capita income levels, he argues that it may also undermine some components of democratization such as accountability and stability. Not only are we left with mixed theoretical expectations, but also the small number of empirical studies examining this question have been somewhat mixed in their findings, though generally pessimistic that aid will reduce levels of political repression. Beginning with Shoultz's (1981) early analysis of U.S. economic aid to Latin America, we see that aid was sometimes used to support dictatorial regimes and sometimes used to overthrow nonrepressive regimes for more repressive ones that supported key U.S. policy goals during the Cold War. Regan's (1994) cross-national analysis of U.S. economic aid in 1979–1988 found that it accounted for little change in recipient states' human rights behavior. In fact, he found that it would take a $250 million increase in economic aid to a state to produce a 1-point change in his 15-point repression scale. It is tempting to attribute these findings to the limited period or geographic region (in the case of Shoultz) under analysis, especially since it is the height of the Cold War and, in the case of Regan, to attribute the result to the possibility that his aggregate index may not appropriately capture all the potential variations in state repression.

However, two comprehensive analyses of the USAID democracy and governance aid commissioned by USAID itself have consistently demonstrated that while spending in the other subsectors of aid (elections, civil society, and governance) all produce the desired effects, spending on the human rights component of the rule-of-law program has a strong negative effect on states' human rights protection, regardless of numerous controls, including controls for endogeneity, and regardless of which measure of human rights is employed (Finkel et al. 2006, 2008). As the investigators note in the final report of their second study, their "effort to untangle the web of relationships that may underlie this distressing and presumptively anomalous relationships and to model them statistically has been largely unsuccessful in its basic purpose" (Finkel et al. 2008, 57). Apodaca (2001) has examined the influence of bilateral aid from OECD Development Assistance Committee countries during 1990–1996, and while she does find that the bilateral aid reduced the likelihood of repression, the size of its impact is rather small, and it achieves only marginal statistical significance. Apodaca is more optimistic about her findings than subsequent work supports. Knack (2004) also examined the influence of foreign aid from the OECD countries, but over a twenty-five-year period (1975–2000) that overlaps somewhat with the fifteen-year period of Finkel et al.'s 2008 study (1990–2004) and is inclusive of Apodaca's entire period. In his more extensive analysis Knack found no effect from either of his measures of development assistance on either of his two measures of democracy. As Knack admits, his data do not allow for the disaggregation of aid intended to promote democracy from aid intended for other purposes, and thus urges some caution in interpreting his results. Thus, while scholars seem somewhat reluctant to accept these null or negative findings, we are left with the dilemma that aid may actually promote political repression, at least under some circumstances, as indeed Knack posited as a counterhypothesis. Recent empirical studies of the influence of multilateral aid programs have been just as pessimistic.

Multilateral Aid/Structural Adjustment Programs. While some scholars might argue that there are direct links between structural adjustment programs and improved human rights through the program requirements of a reduced or limited state, most neoliberal arguments link structural adjustment programs indirectly to human rights practices through increased levels of economic growth or wealth, which have been weakly linked to increased human rights protection. Critics, however, argue that the programs have harmful effects on the economic well-being of citizens, especially women and the poor (for example, Buchmann 1996; Sadasivam 1997; Zack-Williams 2000; Fields 2003), and on workers' rights (Abouharb and Cingranelli 2008); and other scholars have argued that regimes' reduction in subsidies, social welfare programs, and public employment have led to mass protests to which recipient states have responded with repressive action (for example, Pion-Berlin 1984; Keith and Poe 2000; Abouharb and Cingranelli 2008). In addition, increasingly rigorous analyses have consistently demonstrated that the programs do not even lead to economic growth (for example, Pion-Berlin 1984; Harrigan and Mosley 1991; Rapley 1996; Prezworski and Vreeland 2000; van de Walle 2001; Vreeland 2003); thus even the hypothesized indirect benefits seem unlikely.

These results bring into serious question the expectation that the loans will lead to improved human rights, since this influence is expected to come indirectly through economic growth and political stability. Interestingly, empirical studies have also demonstrated that the programs do not lead to increased political stability but rather increase the probability of civil conflict (for example, Sidell 1988; Di John 2005; Keen 2005; Abouharb and Cingranelli 2008). A growing number of empirical studies have addressed specifically the impact of these programs on human rights. The earliest empirical study to my knowledge is Pion-Berlin's (1984) analysis of the impact of International Monetary Fund (IMF) loans on repression in Argentina during 1958–1980, which demonstrated that the stabilization programs increased repression against labor groups. Subsequent studies of personal integrity abuse have also demonstrated a link between these programs and increased state imprisonment, torture, killing, and disappearances (Franklin 1997; Keith and Poe 2000). The most comprehensive and rigorous study to date (Abouharb and Cingranelli 2008) demonstrates that not only do the structural adjustment programs (both IMF and World Bank) fail to deliver economic development, but also the agreements fail even to promote increased political stability. They demonstrate that instead, the deleterious economic and social effects of the agreements have destabilized the countries with increased levels of civil conflict—antigovernment demonstrations, riots, and rebellion in particular. The increased civil conflict in turn increases the state's level of physical integrity abuse (torture, murder, disappearance, and political imprisonment). Indeed, the likelihood of physical integrity abuse increases the longer the state participates in a structural adjustment agreement, even when controlling for selection effects and most of the known factors that affect such abuse. And similarly, the longer the state participates in a structural adjustment agreement, the weaker the state's protection is of worker rights. Thus, we are left with overwhelming evidence that multilateral aid is generally harmful to a broad range of rights, and that some components of bilateral aid have either no effect or a deleterious effect. The evidence in regard to trade openness and foreign economic penetration is mixed but somewhat more optimistic than that of the aid relationship.

Trade Openness and Foreign Economic Penetration. Empirical studies that have tested the liberal perspective on the linkage between trade and human rights protection, though small in number, have consistently confirmed these expectations (Apodaca 2001, 2007; Harrelson-Stephens and Calloway 2003). Apodaca (2001, 2007) found that exports had the third-strongest impact in predicting personal integrity abuses in 1990–1996, with only democracy and conflict producing larger effects. Her model controls for several important domestic conditions (conflict, population, democracy, and education expenditures) and international factors (conflict, bilateral and multilateral aid, foreign direct investment, and portfolio investment). Harrelson-Stephens and Calloway (2003) examine three measures of trade openness over a significantly longer period than Apodaca (1976–1996): trade openness (the sum of exports and imports divided by GDP, which captures the level of trade but not the symmetrical nature of trade between states), level of exports relative to GDP, and a 4-point trade liberalization index. They find that, when controlling for the standard human rights model, each of their trade openness measures does demonstrate a decrease in the likelihood of state repression in three separate models, supporting liberal expectations. However, they do caution that the coefficients are rather small. But given the effect over time through the lagged dependent variable, they calculate .5 decrease in the 5-point personal integrity abuse scale in ten years' time. This is roughly comparable to the impact that Poe, Tate, and Keith (1999) found for the presence of international war and about half the effect they found for economic development, which, interestingly, fails to achieve statistical significance in Harrelson-Stephens and Calloway's model. Apodaca's (2007) study, which covers a longer period (1989–2002) than her first study, confirms her earlier finding even though she employs a different measure of trade openness (exports plus imports as a percentage of GDP). Thus much of the initial empirical evidence does support the liberal perspective that open trade has a positive effect on at least one dimension of human rights, the right to personal integrity.

The evidence examining the effect of foreign investment has been much more inconsistent and in one study has varied depending upon the category of repression. Apodaca (2001) found that foreign direct investment (FDI) did lead to moderate decreases in repression of personal integrity rights for the period 1990–1996; however, she also found that the portfolio investment did not have a statistically significant effect. She had in fact hypothesized that this type of investment, which tends to be "short-ventures, highly mobile, and subject to capital flight," places more restrictions on the regime's taxing and spending policy options, and in particular restricts spending on social welfare programs while doing little to enhance economic growth (595). In her 2007 study of the years 1989–2002 the effect of FDI disappears, although here her model is more focused on the media and thus controls for an additional set of measures than in her 2001 study. She does not include the portfolio measure here either, so the results are somewhat difficult to compare. Richards, Gelleny, and Sacko's (2001) analysis of both categories of political repression in 1981–1995 provides some additional insight into these mixed findings. They also find that FDI reduces the likelihood of political repression, but only in regard to the civil liberties restriction category, not the personal integrity category. This finding contradicts Apodaca's earlier study of the seven-year period but fits with her longer study. However, contrary to Apodaca, they find that portfolio investment decreases the odds of repression of personal integrity rights but has no effect on civil liberties restrictions. They also find that foreign debt increases the repression of civil liberties restrictions but has no effect on personal integrity rights. Ultimately, these mixed results suggest that it is still premature to draw firm conclusions about the effect of foreign investment.

International Treaties

Most empirical studies of state compliance with international human rights treaty obligations focus on the state's provision or protection of the guaranteed rights embedded in the document. The bulk of the empirical compliance literature, while grounded in rich theoretical debate concerning the influence of human rights treaties, has largely been limited to tests of whether being a state party produces a positive or negative effect, when controlling for a variety of factors. It does not enable us to determine which of the mechanisms that are hypothesized to be at work are actually operative. Realist theory views treaty commitments as cheap talk and therefore predicts no effect or perhaps even a negative effect. Rationalist theory does not provide as clear an expectation, but because of the lack of direct benefits from compliance and the weak enforcement mechanisms that make noncompliance relatively costless (except, possibly, in terms of reputation), treaties would be expected to have a weak effect at best. The decoupling effect posited by the world society approach would predict that we would observe no direct effect and a negative effect over time. Thus, three theories predict little or no effect or even a negative effect. The expectations of the domestic institutions approach would be conditional, expecting better human rights, but only in democratic regimes or regimes with effective legal institutions. The normative perspectives, however, would predict compliance due to norm diffusion and the effect of transnational human rights networks, but perhaps would make the expectations contingent upon the strength of the networks (Neumayer 2005).

Empirical evidence of the influence of participation in an international human rights treaty has been mixed. For example, Keith (1999) finds no effect from the International Covenant on Civil and Political Rights (ICCPR) on personal integrity rights or civil rights and liberties, unless controlling for state derogations. Hathaway (2002) finds that most treaties within the human rights regime do not significantly affect human rights behavior, and that participation in some of the treaties, such as the Genocide Convention and the Convention Against Torture (CAT), produces negative effects, a result that is confirmed by Hafner-Burton and Tsutsui (2005) in regard to a wide range of treaties. On the other hand, the two most exhaustive compliance studies (Landman 2005 and Simmons 2009) found consistent evidence of an association between rights behavior and state commitment to a variety of treaties within the international human rights regime. Landman finds that commitment to the ICCPR and the CAT, even while controlling for the level of reservations, decreased state repression of personal integrity rights, torture, and civil and political rights. Simmons extends Landman's work and finds that participation in the ICCPR, the Convention on the Elimination of All Forms of Discrimination Against Women (CEDAW), and the Children's Convention are associated with the provision of several related rights. In the case of the CAT and the ICCPR in regard to fair trials she finds that the influence is limited to a narrow set of circumstances. For example, the impact of the CAT is conditioned on the strong rule of law. In most empirical studies of compliance, the theoretical mechanisms (for example, cost/benefit calculations and power relationships) are merely assumed rather than directly tested in the models. Kelley's (2007) work on bilateral nonsurrender agreements represents a significant exception and takes advantage of a unique opportunity to test particular costs that a state could not have anticipated when it became a party to the Rome Statute. Contrary to realist expectations, she finds that approximately half of the countries pressured by the United States went against their own self-interest and resisted the pressure, incurring diplomatic and sometimes economic costs. She does find some evidence to support realist assumptions in that states that have Generalized System of Preferences (GSP) status with the United States, poor states, and members of the "Iraq coalition of the willing" were more likely to sign nonsurrender agreements.

We find another notable exception within the asylum literature. A growing body of research has examined the United States' obligations under the Geneva Convention Relating to the Status of Refugees and under the CAT to respect the norm of *nonrefoulement*.[1] Most of these empirical studies have demonstrated that U.S. foreign policy interests (security and trade relationships) and domestic policy interests (economic and national security concerns) influence decisions on who receives a grant of asylum in the United States (Rosenblum and Salehyan 2004; Salehyan and Rosenblum 2008; Rottman, Fariss, and Poe 2009; Keith and Holmes 2009). Overall, the weak association of human rights with treaty commitment supports realist expectations. However, most of these studies do not specifically operationalize and test the underlying assumptions that would predict no effect; thus our confidence in this conclusion is rather weak. Moreover, Kelley's findings and those in the asylum literature, which account more directly for realist and rationalist assumptions, suggest that interests may not matter as much as the realists think; and, indeed, their analyses demonstrate that norms and domestic political contexts also matter.

Assumptions of the domestic institutions approach have received much more specific empirical attention than those of realist and rationalist theory; presumably because scholars can more readily observe and more directly measure domestic institutional contexts than cost/benefit calculations or the diffusion of norms. Several studies have examined the conditional or interactive effect of democratic regimes on treaty compliance. When Hathaway (2002) limited her analysis to democratic regimes she continued to find no effect of the ICCPR and negative effects of the CAT on human rights behavior;

but she did find that participation in the Genocide Convention, CEDAW, and the ICCPR's Optional Protocol produces a significant positive effect on related human rights. Neumayer (2005) examines whether the impact of ratification is conditional upon regime type, and finds that in pure autocracies, ratification of the CAT and the ICCPR is associated with worse human rights practices, but that ratification has a "more and more beneficial effect" as democracy strengthens.[2] Landman (2005) conceptualizes and models ratification as a function of the underlying processes of democratization, economic development, and global interdependence, which he finds influence human rights moderately but consistently across the various treaties that constitute the international human rights regime. It is difficult to separate out the influence of democratic institutions in his human rights analysis, although we do know that the relative weight of democratization is likely to be rather small because its effect on ratification is minor relative to that of other factors. As reported above, Powell and Staton's (2009) study of the CAT makes a significant contribution by moving our attention to the domestic legal system. They find that as the effectiveness of the judiciary increases, the joint probability of ratifying the CAT in full and then violating the treaty decreases; however, they find only mixed evidence that the joint probability of not ratifying and torturing increases with an effective judiciary in place. Kelley (2007) also demonstrates that states with a stronger domestic commitment to the rule of law are less likely to violate their treaty commitment by signing a nonsurrender agreement.

Finally, if we broaden the scope of compliance to include the asylum literature, Salehyan and Rosenblum (2008) make a significant contribution, demonstrating that public and media attention to immigration and asylum issues increases the impact of humanitarian concerns in U.S. asylum outcomes. However, their findings in regard to congressional influence on human rights concerns in asylum outcomes are less encouraging, as the effect is contingent upon partisan politics and whether congressional hearings are framed in terms of immigration enforcement, which reduces the humanitarian dimension of the outcomes, or in terms of refugee and asylum issues, which increases the importance of the humanitarian dimension. Overall, the literature clearly demonstrates that domestic institutions and politics influence a state's compliance with its treaty obligations, and that the influence of democratic institutions extends beyond the traditional electoral components to the judiciary and the rule of law.

Measuring norms is probably the most difficult task that empiricists face in testing normative approaches, and thus most empirical studies of compliance have examined surrogate indicators. Powell and Staton (2008) test regional and global norms, as indicated by past rates of torture, in their CAT models; however, they find little evidence that norms influence state torture practices. Kelley's (2007) study of bilateral nonsurrender agreements provides the best opportunity to examine the influence of norms on state values. She finds that even while controlling for a significant number of realist assumptions, states that have demonstrated a prior normative affinity for the International Criminal Court (ICC) are less likely to sign nonsurrender agreements; however, she does not find that human rights norms influence signing of the nonsurrender agreements. Even though the asylum literature has consistently demonstrated that security and material interests strongly influence U.S. asylum decisions, these studies have also consistently demonstrated that humanitarian norms (especially human rights conditions) do influence U.S. compliance with its commitments under international law (Rosenblum and Salehyan 2004; Salehyan and Rosenblum 2008; Rottman, Fariss, and Poe 2009; Keith and Holmes 2009). The presence of transnational networks or civil society pressure (typically measured as the number of INGOs in which citizens have membership) is much easier to measure than the presence of norms; however, the direct link between treaty ratification and civil society pressure is not typically tested in human rights models. Both Hafner-Burton and Tsutsui (2005) and Powell and Staton (2008) find that as the number of INGOs to which citizens belong increases, so does the level of protection of human rights. Neumayer (2005) provides the most rigorous analysis, examining specifically the effect of treaty commitment on human rights behavior, conditioned upon the strength of civil society organizations. His results are mixed: he does find that the stronger the state's participation in INGOs, the greater the beneficial effect of ratification of the CAT on human rights behavior; however, the results do not hold for ICCPR ratification. He also finds mixed results in regard to regional treaties.

For example, ratification of the Inter-American torture convention with INGO participation is beneficial, but the effect does not hold for the European torture convention. Overall, the observable effect of norm diffusion is weak and inconsistent at best. The evidence of a strong positive influence by NGOs on states' human rights practices is more convincing; however, we must keep in mind that the civil society link through treaty ratification is not directly demonstrated except in Neumayer's work. In the following chapters I continue to explore the role of norms diffusion and treaty ratification in regard to state commitment to constitutional freedoms and subsequent state rights behavior.

Moving the Literature Forward

In this book I seek to build upon this substantial body of human rights literature, examining the core assumptions of multiple subfields in political science through the organizing concepts of opportunity and willingness, arguing that state actors' choice to employ various tools of repression is shaped factors based in both the agent (for example, democratic values, ideological preferences, resources, etc.), the structure (for example, competitive party system or independent judiciary) and environment (for example, domestic and external threats). I argue that these factors influence which options (tools of repression) are available or deemed appropriated and that they shape the consequences and costs and benefits of employing the tools of repression. I also seek to move the literature forward in several ways. I expand what has become known as the "standard model" of repression forward in time to cover almost three decades and the global set of states. I expand the standard model to reflect developments in the literature concerning the conceptualization and measurement of democracy, and I explore measurement issues in regard to civil liberties. I also explore more thoroughly the conflicting expectations in the literature regarding the effect of military regimes and Marxist/Marxist-Leninist regimes. Subsequently, I expand the standard model to account for state embeddedness in global society and liberal economic theory. This book's primary contribution lies in the substantive examination of the role of judicial independence. I first address why states commit formally to the norm judicial independence, and then examine the circumstances that shape the actual achievement of judicial independence within the state. I also present a new measure of *de facto* judicial independence and examine its relationship with both categories of repression. Throughout these analyses I model and control for selection effects. I also examine interaction between judicial independence and the transnational network and domestic circumstances. I also examine state constitutional commitment to individual freedoms and due process rights, first examining factors that influence commitment, especially prior commitment to the ICCPR and then examining the influence of that commitment on repression of the specific rights promised in the provisions, controlling for selection effects. Finally, I examine the influence of threats on repression of personal integrity rights and restrictions of civil liberties. Ultimately, I examine the effectiveness of states of emergency provisions in models that condition the level and type of threat. I believe these analyses offer one of the rigorous assessments of the role of the judiciary and the role of law on state decisions to repress their own citizens.

Chapter 3

The Standard Model of Human Rights

December 2001, Gbarnga, Liberia: Students rioted to protest the killing of a fourth grade boy by the police commander; the police killed two more students during the demonstration in front of the police station. (U.S. Department of State 2001)

October and December 2008, Central Yerevan, Armenia: Newspaper editors Nikol Pashinian and Shogher Matevosian were arrested after participating in a march with supporters of the former President Levon Ter-Petrosian, a vocal critic of the government, and two months later the Gyumri-based television channel Gala TV was harassed by government officials following its broadcasting of Levon Ter-Petrosian's campaigning activities. (Amnesty International 2009)

October 2005, Gambia: The government arrested and detained opposition leaders who had publicly criticized or who had expressed political views in disagreement with the government. (U.S. Department of State 2005)

May 2001, Liberia: Security forces detained 24 persons from a truckload of internally displaced persons fleeing fighting: it is believed that detainees were transported to the Gbatala military base; however, they have not been seen since. (U.S. Department of State 2001)

February 2007, Abidjan, Côte d'Ivoire: Moustapha Tounkara and Arthur Vincent, two young mobile phone salesmen, were arrested by members of the national security forces; their bullet-riddled bodies were found the next day. (Amnesty International 2007)

October 2005, Azerbaijan: The Court of Grave Crimes sentenced seven opposition leaders to between two and a half and five years in prison on alleged charges for their role in post-election violence; their convictions were based on confessions allegedly extracted under torture. (Human Rights Watch 2005)

August and September 2005, Ecuador: The state police arrested Washington Enrique Vilela Barra and Luis Antonio Cevallos Barre; their bodies were found the following day. Military officers patrolling the northern province of Sucumbios opened fire with no warning on a vehicle, killing Servio Pena Jimenez and seriously injuring Ramon Zamora Zamora. (U.S. Department of State 2005)

2004, Indonesia: Security forces continued to commit unlawful killings of rebels, suspected rebels, and civilians in areas of separatist activity, and the government largely failed to hold soldiers and police accountable for such killings and other serious human rights abuses. (U.S. Department of State 2004)

January 2004, Democratic Republic of Congo: Authorities at a military prison placed two civilians in front of freshly dug graves and then proceeded to bludgeon them to death with hammers. (Ibid.)

February 2004, Nepal: State soldiers killed 17-year-old Subhadra Chaulagain and 18-year-old Reena Rasaili, who were reportedly attempting to flee custody; it is alleged that the girls, who were accused by the Royal

Nepalese Army of being Maoists, were captured, beaten, and raped before being killed. (Ibid.)

March 2004, Haiti: Five Haitian National Police officers arrested five youths from the pro-Aristide neighborhood of La Saline in Port-au-Prince; the next day their bodies, bearing signs of torture, were found near the airport. (Ibid.)

February 2000, Russia (Chechnya): The military used indiscriminate force in areas of significant civilian populations, resulting in numerous deaths, and also engaged in extrajudicial killings. For example, Russian riot police and contract soldiers executed at least 60 civilians in Aldi and Chernorechiye, suburbs of Grozny. (U.S. Department of State 2000)

January through October 1999, Burundi: Soldiers killed more than 55 civilians in Mubone, Kabezi commune, in May soldiers killed 11 Hutu civilians, including women and children, in July soldiers killed 30 civilians in Kanyosha commune, in August soldiers shot and killed an estimated 50 civilians in Kanyosha commune and used grenades and machine guns to kill an unknown number of civilians in Ruziba, Bujumbura Rural province, and in October a soldier shot and killed six persons, including three children and two women, at the Ruyaga regroupment site in Bujumbura Rural province—the army claims the civilians were collaborating with rebels. (U.S. Department of State 1999)

The long list above presents a very few examples of countless acts of political repression occurring throughout the world every year despite a near-universal commitment among nation-states not to engage in these behaviors. Social scientists committed to the study of human rights or contentious state politics have produced a substantive and growing body of empirical research that seeks to identify the factors that motivate these actors to engage in repression, and what circumstances enhance or constrain their opportunity and their willingness to utilize coercive tools against their own citizens. In this chapter I address the "standard model" that has developed over time, expanding it to cover a much longer period and broadening the model to reflect the subsequent developments in the literature regarding our conceptualization and measurement of democracy and to make use of newly available measures of specific individual rights. Because I find that the standard model as a whole continues to perform well in explaining a broad range of acts of political repression, I use these base models as the foundation for the analyses in the following chapters that examine that effect of the judiciary and the law on state repression.

Conceptualizing and Measuring Repression

I agree with Davenport's (2007c) broad definition of political repression, which, while drawing generally on Goldstein (1978), still accurately reflects the consensus of the current literature: "By most accounts, repression involves the actual or threatened use of physical sanctions against an individual or organization, within the territorial jurisdiction of the state, for the purpose of imposing a cost on the target as well as deterring specific activities and/or beliefs perceived to be challenging to government personnel, practices or institutions" (2). Consensus among scholars dissipates somewhat when the focus narrows to the more specific nature of repression—in particular, whether repression should be conceptualized as being composed of a single dimension, or whether it is composed of multiple, distinct dimensions related to the form of coercion (for example, violence or coercion; see Stohl and Lopez 1984; Davenport 2007a), the breadth of the target (for example, actual dissenters or potential dissenters; see Wilkinson 1976), and the required resources, capabilities, and potential costs (see Mitchell and McCormick 1988; McCormick and Mitchell 1997). Most large-*N* cross-national studies of political repression have tended to focus on two forms of state repression separately—either addressing the more severe forms of repression, violations of personal integrity (imprisonment, torture, killing, and disappearances) (for example, Poe and Tate 1994; Poe, Tate, and Keith 1999; Cingranelli and Richards 1999a, 1999b; Keith 2002a; Keith, Tate, and Poe 2009), or addressing the broader category of civil liberties restrictions, or "negative sanctions," as they are sometimes referred to in the literature (censoring the press, restricting freedom to assemble peacefully, or curbing religious freedoms) (for example, Davenport 1995a, 1995b, 2007a, 2007b; Keith 2002; Howard and Carey 2004; Walker and Poe 2002). The theoretical perspectives of the models employed in these studies are largely indistinguishable. Davenport (2007b) argues that while the two forms of repression share the same goal—to influence behavior and attitudes—they attempt to achieve the goal differently: civil liberties restrictions modify behavior through constraining and channeling opportunities; whereas personal integrity repression, such as killing and disappearances, modifies behavior through eliminating actors. Thus, it may be shortsighted to perceive repression as one-dimensional. However, as Davenport notes, to date most explanatory variables have similarly influenced both categories of repression, and therefore it is highly likely "that comparable processes underlie the coercive strategies" (487).

Davenport's (2007a) work makes a substantial contribution to the field in that he specifically explores the question of whether state-sponsored restrictions and state-sponsored violence are equivalent behaviors. While the literature clearly agrees that states' primary objective in employing coercive methods is to maintain or achieve political order, Davenport distinguishes how states pursue this goal. He argues that when states choose to restrict their citizens' freedoms, "their goal is less to remove individuals/groups from society than it is to mold them within it," and thus restrictions "establish parameters within which individuals (victims as well as bystanders) modify their behavior in an attempt to avoid sanctions in the present and future" (47). He then posits that states have a different goal in employing violent tools of repression, specifically arguing that "killing citizens eliminates a part of society deemed unacceptable while compelling acquiescence or guided change in others" (47). Davenport posits that it is useful to consider combinations of strategies that regimes may employ to take advantage of different cost/benefit structures or to communicate different messages. He suggests four basic combinations that are theoretically illustrative, although he ultimately creates and tests nine categories. The four combinations include the two extremes on a continuum: on one end the government does not engage in restrictions or violence, and at the other end the government engages in significant levels of both restrictions and violence. In between, the government either engages in significant amounts of restrictions but not violence, or the government engages in significant amounts of violence but not restrictions. Davenport argues that each combination allows government authorities distinct sets of costs and benefits. For example, "restrictions without violence allow government officials to regulate behavior without provoking the negative ramifications associated with state-sponsored violence," and "violence without restrictions allows authorities to eliminate challengers but avoids the administration, monitoring, and pretense of legality commonly affiliated with civil liberties restrictions" (49). Davenport's empirical analysis reveals that some factors known to influence repression generally affect certain categories of repression in opposing directions. For example, conflict and development/modernization decrease the probability of a state's resort to less lethal forms of repressive action, yet these same factors increase the probability of a resort to more lethal repression. He also demonstrates that democracy generally increases the probability that a regime will employ less lethal forms of repressive activity while decreasing the probability that it will employ more lethal methods. As I demonstrate in the measurement section below, I am not confident that the current measures of repression allow us to capture firmly the distinction between lethal and nonlethal dimensions.

Davenport's debate reflects an earlier debate among scholars who have examined personal integrity abuse and disputed whether this singular category of repression is itself multidimensional or unidimensional. Mitchell and McCormick (1988) have argued that the tools of repression within this subset are substantively distinct, and thus while "arbitrary political imprisonment was certainly reprehensible, resort to torture and killing was a distinct, and qualitatively worse, activity" (484). Poe and Tate (1994) disagreed, claiming that it could "be persuasively argued that the two dimensions postulated by Mitchell and McCormick stem, in reality, from the one dimension that Stohl and his colleagues tap [in their Political Terror Scale]—that both torture/killing and imprisonment are rooted in a regime's willingness to repress its citizens when they are considered a threat" (855). McCormick and Mitchell (1997) disagree with Poe and Tate, contending instead that "human rights violations differ in type not just amount, such that they cannot be clearly represented on a single scale," and in particular they argue that the use of imprisonment and the use of torture and killing are "quite different types of government activity, with differing consequences for the victims, differing use of governmental resources and capabilities, and differing costs for the government, both domestically and internationally" (514). They argue that governments or their agents engage in a calculation of costs and benefits when choosing among the tools of repression. However, their empirical analyses demonstrate only thin differences in predictor variables across two types of personal integrity abuse (imprisonment and torture). With one exception, the differences were tied to the level of achieved statistical significance, and most of these measures were ones that have performed thinly or inconsistently in other analyses that cover a longer period; McCormick and Mitchell's analysis covers only the years 1984 and 1987. The one exception they find, civil war, has been one of the two predictors that have consistently achieved the highest level of statistical and substantive significance in personal integrity models, and civil war fails to achieve statistical significance in only one of the years the authors studied. Poe, Tate, and Keith (1999) note that the similarities Mitchell and McCormick find are "impressive given the differences in design: their use of two dimensions of repression as dependent variables, their not using a lagged dependent variable (as we had), and the necessity of their using smaller (cross-sectional) samples of countries [which] led to much larger standard errors in their reanalysis, making statistical significance more difficult to achieve, a factor that accounts for several of their divergent findings" (299). Poe, Tate, and Keith also raised theoretical concerns about analyzing the components of repression separately, because doing so does not take into account that the behaviors are substitutable policy options, and the fact that the choice to use one tool may either prevent or render unnecessary the use of the other (see Most and Starr 1989, 97–132). For example, killing one's political opponents eliminates the need to imprison them. Disappearance may also be substitutable for imprisonment and may in many cases actually hide murder. I continue to conceptualize repression of personal integrity rights as a unidimensional phenomenon. As we will see below, Cingranelli and Richards' (1999b) Mokken scaling of their nine-point physical integrity rights index strongly suggests that this subset of rights is indeed unidimensional.

Measuring Repression

Social scientists seeking to measure state repression or coercive action empirically face significant measurement issues similar to those that challenge all large-*N* cross-national studies. Mitchell et al. (1986) provide an accurate summary of the challenge: data sets must "(1) have broad coverage across countries and time, (2) be based on multiple sources, (3) be reliable and valid, (4) have intensiveness (depth of coverage), (5) have extensiveness of coverage (multiple indicators), and (6) be sensitive to differences across countries and time" (22). Measurements must capture the scope (the degree of potential harm inflicted), the intensity (frequency and concentration of occurrence), and the range (size and type of target population) of the repression (14–16). The two earliest popular measurements of political repression, Taylor and Jodice's (1983) State Coercive Behavior (part of *The World Handbook of Political and Social Science Indicators*) and Freedom House's Civil Liberties Index, represent significant data-collection efforts, but each fails to some degree to meet these criteria, as I will demonstrate below. Most empirical studies to date, however, have primarily addressed the more severe form of repression, violations of personal integrity (imprisonment, torture, killing, and disappearances) (for example, Poe and Tate 1994; Poe, Tate, and Keith 1999; Cingranelli and Richards 1999a, 1999b; Keith 2002a), and have tended to employ the dominant indicators in the field: the Political Terror Scale (PTS) or the (CIRI) physical integrity rights measures, both of which I believe come much closer to meeting the criteria set forth by Mitchell et al. (1986) than do the two early measures of civil liberties restrictions. The Political Terror Scale was originally developed by Stohl and others (Stohl and Carleton 1985; Gibney and Stohl 1988; Poe 1992; Gibney and Dalton 1996) and is maintained by Mark Gibney (Gibney 2011).

The two standards-based PTS measures are based on assessments contained in the yearly human rights country reports published by Amnesty International and the U.S. Department of State in regard to the occurrence of political imprisonment, execution, disappearances, and torture. The ordered indices range from 1 to 5. The coding categories and their criteria are:

(1) Countries [are] under a secure rule of law, people are not imprisoned for their views, and torture is rare or exceptional. . . . Political murders are extremely rare.
(2) There is a limited amount of imprisonment for nonviolent activity. However, few persons are affected, torture and beating are exceptional. . . . Political murder is rare.
(3) There is extensive political imprisonment, or a recent history of such imprisonment. Execution or other political murders and brutality

may be common. Unlimited detention, with or without trial, for political views is accepted.

(4) The practices of level 31 are expanded to larger numbers. Murders, disappearances are a common part of life. . . . In spite of its generality, on this level terror affects primarily those who interest themselves in politics or ideas.

(5) The terrors of level 41 have been expanded to the whole population. . . . The leaders of these societies place no limits on the means or thoroughness with which they pursue personal or ideological goals. (Gastil 1980, 37, as quoted in Carleton and Stohl 1985, 212–13)[1]

While the two measures are highly correlated (.81 in the data set here), the country coverage varies. The country coverage in the Department of State–based measure reflects the universal set of independent states, except in a couple of the early years under study here.[2] The measure based on Amnesty International reports is less complete because, as a human rights NGO, its mission has been to respond to human rights abuse, and thus it has tended to focus on states with problematic human rights records (Poe and Tate 1994, 869; Poe, Carey, and Vazquez 2001, 655–56). Specifically, the Department of State–based measure tends to cover 20 to 40 more states than the one based on the Amnesty International reports. In previous work we wanted to take advantage of having two measures based on different reports of human rights, so we dealt with this issue of uneven country coverage by substituting Department of State scores for the missing scores in the Amnesty International–based data, and vice versa for the less frequently missing State Department–based data (Poe and Tate 1994; Poe, Tate, and Keith 1999; Keith, Tate, and Poe 2009). I continue this practice here, and I conduct parallel analyses with each of the political terror scales.

Cingranelli and Richards (1999b) have created another measure that is useful in capturing the level of state repression. Their physical integrity rights measures are somewhat similar to Gibney and Stohl's Political Terror Scale, but four components of repression (imprisonment, torture, disappearances, and killings) are measured separately on a three-point scale that captures the frequency of violations: frequent (fifty or more) violations (0), some (one to fifty) violations (1), and no violations (2). The authors note that their categories rest on events-based criteria whenever possible: countries with 50 of more confirmed violations are scored zero; countries with less than 50 violations but than zero confirmed violations are scored one; and countries with no violations are scored two. A brief description of the variables follows (for the fuller description see http://ciri.binghamton.edu/documentation.asp).

Disappearance: Disappearances are cases in which people have disappeared, political motivation appears likely, and the victims have not been found. Knowledge of the whereabouts of the disappeared is, by definition, not public knowledge. However, while there is typically no way of knowing where victims are, it is typically known by whom they were taken and under what circumstances. A score of 0 indicates that disappearances have occurred frequently in a given year; a score of 1 indicates that disappearances occasionally occurred; and a score of 2 indicates that disappearances did not occur in a given year.

Extrajudicial Killing: Extrajudicial killings are killings by government officials without due process of law. They include murders by private groups if instigated by government. These killings may result from the deliberate, illegal, and excessive use of lethal force by the police, security forces, or other agents of the state whether against criminal suspects, detainees, prisoners, or others. A score of 0 indicates that extrajudicial killings were practiced frequently in a given year; a score of 1 indicates that extrajudicial killings were practiced occasionally; and a score of 2 indicates that such killings did not occur in a given year.

Political Imprisonment: Political imprisonment refers to the incarceration of people by government officials because of: their speech; their nonviolent opposition to government policies or leaders; their religious beliefs; their nonviolent religious practices, including proselytizing; or their membership in a group, including an ethnic or racial group. A score of 0 indicates that there were many people imprisoned because of their religious, political, or other beliefs in a given year; a score of 1 indicates that a few people were imprisoned; and a score of 2 indicates that no persons were imprisoned for any of the above reasons in a given year.

Torture: Torture refers to the purposeful inflicting of extreme pain, whether mental or physical, by government officials or by private individuals at the instigation of government officials. Torture includes the use of physical and other force by police and prison guards that is cruel, inhuman, or degrading. This also includes

> deaths in custody due to negligence by government officials. A score of 0 indicates that torture was practiced frequently in a given year; a score of 1 indicates that torture was practiced occasionally; and a score of 2 indicates that torture did not occur in a given year. (http://ciri.binghamton.edu/documentation/ciri_variables_short_descriptions.pdf)

Cingranelli and Richards' (1999) scores are based on the combined reports of human rights practices in the Department of State and Amnesty International country reports, with the Amnesty reports controlling in the case of any conflicts. The measures are frequently used as an additive index. The index behaves as a unidimensional scale. The CIRI scores have the advantage of being disaggregated when theoretical or empirical inquiry justifies it—for example, when examining specifically the effect of the Convention Against Torture on state torture practices. The events-based nature of scales can be potentially problematic, since fifty instances of torture or killing in China would not be of the same magnitude as fifty instances in Jamaica, given the great disparity in population size. Events-based measures, while less subjective than standards-based measures, assume a higher degree of accuracy in reporting than is likely to be achieved in these reports. The categorical nature of the scores also requires somewhat arbitrary numerical cutoffs in which a state that kills forty-nine people receives a lower score than one that kills fifty. The additive index then compounds these problems, and also suffers from an inherent limitation of additive indices in that countries receiving the same score may engage in very different human rights practices. For example, a country with no political imprisonment and no torture but high levels of killing and disappearances will receive a cumulative score of 4, as will a country with no killings or disappearances but high levels of imprisonment and torture. Similarly, a country that has one incident each of imprisonment, torture, killing, and disappearance will also receive a score of 4. Clearly, the nature of repression in these states differs in magnitude and lethality. Despite the differences in the operationalization of the measures and the different use of the sources on which they are based, the PTS and CIRI measures are highly correlated. Cingranelli and Richards (1999) report an overall correlation of .79 between their index and the PTS scales (408). In the data set here, the CIRI Index is highly correlated with the Department of State–based PTS measures, at .83, and with the Amnesty-based PTS measures, at .76. The CIRI data are not available for two of the years under study here, since those data begin with 1981. As is increasingly the norm, I take advantage of both the CIRI and PTS measures, keeping in mind the inherent limitations and advantages of each. I also invert the CIRI Index to represent repression of rights rather than the realization of rights. As noted above, the two earliest popular measurements of political repression, Taylor and Jodice's (1983) State Coercive Behavior measures and Freedom House's Civil Liberties Index, represent significant data-collection efforts, but I believe these measures do not meet fully the Mitchell et al. (1986) criteria at least for the purpose of capturing state repression of civil liberties. Taylor and Jodice's negative sanctions measurements are events-count measures, which are limited in country and time coverage. They have been criticized as potentially incomplete measures because they are based on newspaper reports, which typically suffer from problems such as threshold effects, fatigue effects, and newshole effects, although some scholars suggest these problems are overstated (Davenport 2007c). Mitchell et al. note that the collection of the Taylor and Jodice data is shaped by a focus on legal actions of the state, which tends to ignore illegal actions, such as political murders that the state does not officially recognize or claim (19). Freedom House's standards-based civil liberties measure has been criticized for its cultural and ideological (Western, conservative) biases, for the inconsistencies of its scales' content over time, for being impressionistic, and for lacking replicability and reliability (Mitchell et al. 1986). However, Freedom House has improved the specification and standardization of the measurement over time, and thus the measure has become less impressionistic (Poe and Tate 1994). Freedom House currently reports that "The civil liberties questions are grouped into four subcategories: Freedom of Expression and Belief (4 questions), Associational and Organizational Rights (3), Rule of Law (4), and Personal Autonomy and Individual Rights (4). Raw points are awarded to each of these questions on a scale of 0 to 4, where 0 points represents the smallest degree and 4 the greatest degree of rights or liberties present" (Freedom in the World 2010). The four subcategories and point structures are reported as follows:

Freedom of Expression and Belief:

1. Are there free and independent media and other forms of cultural expression? (*Note*: In cases where the media are state-controlled but offer pluralistic points of view, the survey gives the system credit.)

2. Are religious institutions and communities free to practice their faith and express themselves in public and private?
3. Is there academic freedom, and is the educational system free of extensive political indoctrination?
4. Is there open and free private discussion?

Associational and Organizational Rights:

1. Is there freedom of assembly, demonstration, and open public discussion?
2. Is there freedom for nongovernmental organizations? (*Note*: This includes civic organizations, interest groups, foundations, etc.)
3. Are there free trade unions and peasant organizations or equivalents, and is there effective collective bargaining? Are there free professional and other private organizations?

Rule of Law:

1. Is there an independent judiciary?
2. Does the rule of law prevail in civil and criminal matters? Are police under direct civilian control?
3. Is there protection from political terror, unjustified imprisonment, exile, or torture, whether by groups that support or oppose the system? Is there freedom from war and insurgencies?
4. Do laws, policies, and practices guarantee equal treatment of various segments of the population?

Personal Autonomy and Individual Rights:

1. Do citizens enjoy freedom of travel or choice of residence, employment, or institution of higher education?
2. Do citizens have the right to own property and establish private businesses? Is private business activity unduly influenced by government officials, the security forces, political parties/organizations, or organized crime?
3. Are there personal social freedoms, including gender equality, choice of marriage partners, and size of family?
4. Is there equality of opportunity and the absence of economic exploitation?

Freedom House then appears to create an additive index, which can range from 0 to 60 points, and the points in turn are converted from an additive index to an inverted seven-point scale. Unfortunately, this process brings with it the potential problems discussed above in regard to the CIRI Index, and the conversion to the seven-point scale makes it difficult to assess the substantive significance of placement on the scale. Since 2006 Freedom House has begun reporting the subcategory scores—a significant improvement. Unfortunately, this change does not cover any of the years under study here.

A small but significant body of studies of state repression of civil liberties has utilized either the Freedom House Civil Liberties Index (for example, Keith 2002b, Walker and Poe 2002; Davenport 2007b) or the Taylor and Jodice's *negative sanctions* measurements (for example, Davenport 1995a, 1995b, 1996). I have previously used the Freedom House Civil Liberties measure[3] but continue to have concerns about the appropriateness of its content for some of my analyses. In particular, two of the four categories do not specifically examine civil liberties protection per se, but rather in the case of category 3 (rule of law) measure circumstances and institutions that may facilitate or hinder the protection of civil liberties: freedom from war and insurgencies and judicial independence. This category also measures equal protection under the law, which is primarily a civil rights issue not a civil liberties issue and thus would entail different theoretical expectations. For example, civil liberties issues typically involve a trade-off or balance between order and freedom, whereas civil rights issues typically involve a trade-off or balance between freedom and equality. The third category also measures political terror (personal integrity rights). The fourth category (personal autonomy and individual rights) captures a broad range of economic, social, and civil rights, with only one component that would represent a potential civil liberty (freedom of movement). This category as a whole is largely based on equality issues; thus the abuse of these rights may appropriately be classified as oppression of social and economic privileges regardless of whether the individual challenges or opposes the government (see Bissell et al. 1978, as cited by Stohl and Lopez 1984, 7) and thus would fall outside our definition of repression above.

Fortunately, scholars now have access to new measures within the CIRI data set that allow them to examine separately some core individual liberties. Of particular interest to me, they include individual measures of separate civil liberties such as freedom of speech and press, as well as freedom of assembly and association. They also include a measure of freedom of religion. While the range of civil liberties covered is clearly more limited, the measures do not suffer from many of the shortcomings of the Freedom House measure. I continue to utilize the Freedom House measure in the standard model analysis for the sake of replication and to build upon previous work; but I also examine the model with the three separate core civil liberties from the CIRI data set. Cingranelli and Richards (2010) operationalize these three variables as follows:

> *Freedom of Speech and Press:*
> This variable indicates the extent to which freedoms of speech and press are affected by government censorship, including ownership of media outlets. Censorship is any form of restriction that is placed on freedom of the press, speech, or expression. Expression may also be in the form of art or music. There are different degrees of censorship. Censorship denies citizens freedom of speech and limits or prevents the media (print, online, or broadcast) to express views challenging the policies of the existing government. In many instances, the government owns and operates all forms of press and media. Government censorship and/or ownership of the media (including radio, TV, Internet, and/or domestic news agencies) are coded: (0) Complete, (1) Some, (2) None.[4]
>
> *Freedom of Assembly and Association:*
> It is an internationally recognized right of citizens to assemble freely and to associate with other persons in political parties, trade unions, cultural organizations, or other groups. This variable evaluates the extent to which the freedoms of assembly and association are subject to actual governmental limitations or restrictions (as opposed to strictly legal protections). Despite the international recognition of the right to assembly and association, in some states, citizens are prohibited by government from joining, forming, and participating in political parties of their choice. Citizens in many states are prohibited from protesting or publicly criticizing government decisions and actions. In more than a few states, organizations critical of a government or those that are perceived to have political agendas are not allowed to hold

demonstrations, and their activities are severely curtailed and closely monitored by the state. Citizens' rights to freedom of assembly and association are coded: (0) Severely restricted or denied completely to all citizens, (1) Limited for all citizens or severely restricted or denied for select groups, and (2) Virtually unrestricted and freely enjoyed by practically all citizens.

Freedom of Religion:
This variable indicates the extent to which the freedom of citizens to exercise and practice their religious beliefs is subject to actual government restrictions. Citizens of whatever religious belief should be able to worship free from government interference. Additionally, citizens should be able to hold no religion at all. Citizens should be able to freely practice their religion and proselytize (attempt to convert) other citizens to their religion as long as such attempts are done in a noncoercive, peaceful manner. Members of the clergy should be able to freely advocate partisan political views, oppose government laws, support political candidates, and otherwise freely participate in politics. Some important questions to consider include: Does the government respect rights including the freedom to publish religious documents in foreign languages? Does religious belief affect membership in a ruling party or a career in government? Does the government prohibit promotion of one religion over another and discrimination on the grounds of religion or belief? Does the government restrict the teaching or practice of any faith? Does the government discriminate against minority religious groups? Government restrictions on religious practices are coded: (0) Severe and Widespread, (1) Moderate, and (2) Practically Absent. (Cingranelli and Richards 2010)

The operationalization and coding instructions of these three rights measures indicate that the measures are standards-based and do not contain the events-count component that the CIRI physical integrity measures include. One potentially significant drawback is that two of the three measures combine pairs of civil liberties (freedom of speech with freedom of press and freedom of association with freedom of assembly). It is likely that states would perceive the press's exercise of its freedom as more threatening than citizens' exercising freedom of speech, and thus states may perceive a higher benefit to repressing the press than citizens' speech. Similarly, citizens engaging in freedom to assemble may represent a more visible and immediate threat to the regime than those exercising the right of association, and thus the state may respond differently to the exercise of the two freedoms. These distinctions could be theoretically important, but we remain unable to explore them empirically at this point.

While most of the literature to date has focused on political repression as *either* restrictions on civil liberties *or* violations of personal integrity, Davenport's (2007a) most recent work conceptualizes state repression in terms of the degree of lethality in personal integrity rights abuse captured within the PTS measure and the civil liberties restrictions captured within the Freedom House measure. As discussed above, Davenport argues that the use of violent tools of repression differs from employing nonviolent coercive methods in terms of goals and cost/benefit calculations. Davenport creates nine categories of repressive behavior by dividing each scale into low, medium, and high levels/scores, and then overlaying the level of violence with the level of restrictions.[5] His analysis does demonstrate some significant differences among predictors of the levels of repression. While I recognize the insightful contribution of this conceptualization, I have concerns arising from the necessity of relying on the problematic Freedom House Civil Liberties Index. Specifically, the measure is constructed from fifteen questions, of which only one relates directly to *violent* state behavior. Each answer, as noted above, is rated on a five-point scale in regard to the degree of freedom/repression. Answers to the questions are added up for a total score and then converted to an inverted seven-point scale. It seems impossible to know where, within this scale, violence may be present and to what degree it is employed, especially since seemingly only 4 of 60 points are specifically related to violence in the first place.[6] As I noted above, Freedom House has only lately begun to report the component (subcategory) scores that may be useful to continue Davenport's exploration in later studies. These concerns ultimately lead me to restrict the analysis in this book to parallel examinations of personal integrity abuse and civil liberties restrictions using both the CIRI individual measures and the Freedom House civil liberties measure to enrich our understanding more broadly and to test the robustness of the Freedom House measure. Next, I present a view over time of the repression of personal integrity rights worldwide as measured by the two Political Terror Scales and the CIRI index, and civil liberties restrictions as measured by the Freedom House civil liberties index, as well as the three separate CIRI measures.

Political Repression Across the Globe

Figure 3.1 presents the percentage of countries over time that fall into each category of repression in the Political Terror Scale based on Amnesty reports. Several interesting trends emerge. First, the rank ordering of the five levels remains rather stable over time. Mid-levels of repression (levels 2 and 3) are consistently the most dominant condition over the entire twenty-seven-year period. The severest level of repression affects the smallest proportion of states, typically between 5 and 10 percent. At the other extreme, the lowest level of repression is experienced by a relatively small percentage of states, usually between 5 and 15 percent, with the exception of the early 1990s, when it reaches almost 25 percent. The proportion of states experiencing the second-highest level of repression ranges between 10 and 20 percent. Second, over time we see significant fluctuation in the percentage of countries in each level, especially with the end of the Cold War era, which led to the creation of

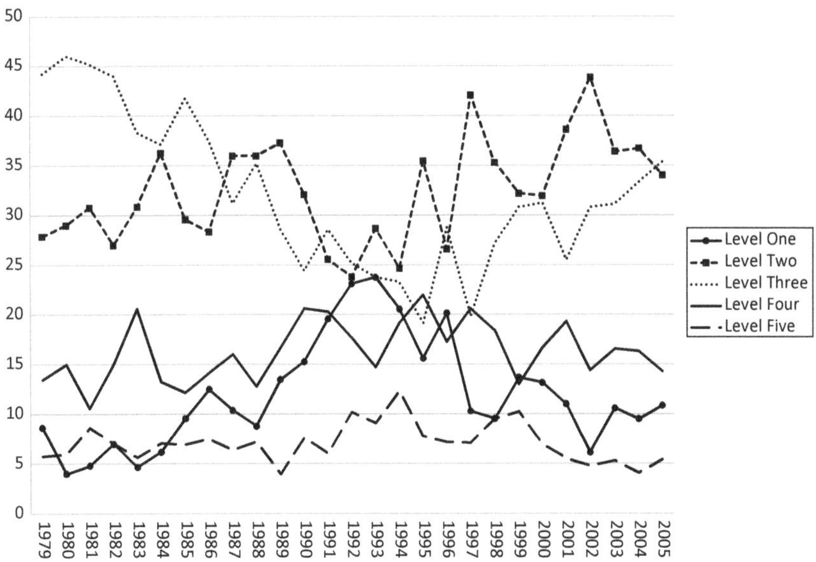

Figure 3.1. Political Terror Scale Based on Amnesty International Reports, 1979–2005

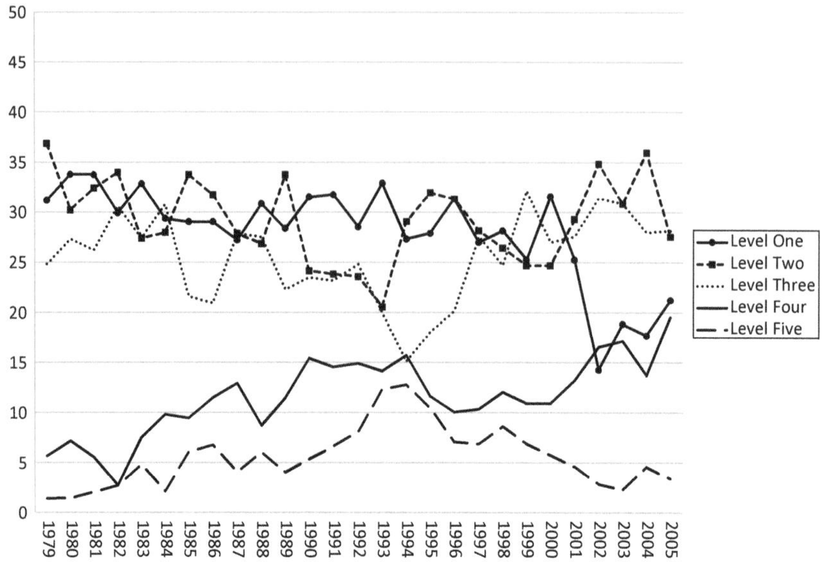

Figure 3.2. Political Terror Scale Based on State Department Reports, 1979–2005

many newly independent states; this result may be due in part to the incomplete and varying state coverage by Amnesty International discussed above. Third, despite significant fluctuation over time, the percentage of states at the uppermost and lowest levels of repression end up approximately the same in 2005 as they were in 1979, and the percentage of states at the two mid-levels of repression end up converging at around 35 percent each.

Figure 3.2 presents the Political Terror Scale based on repression as reported by the U.S. Department of State country reports. As I noted above, the State Department–based scales have much broader country coverage than the Amnesty-based scales. The data in this figure represent a near universal set of countries and thus represent a more accurate picture. As expected, once we are able to examine the fuller set of countries, we see a significant difference in the percentage of countries achieving the lowest level of repression or no repression, which now range from 25 to almost 35 percent, with the exception of the last four years in the analysis. We continue to see that countries experiencing the highest level of repression represent the smallest segment of countries (ranging from 2 to 12.5 percent), which is somewhat lower than with the Amnesty International–based scale. Level 4 repression represents the

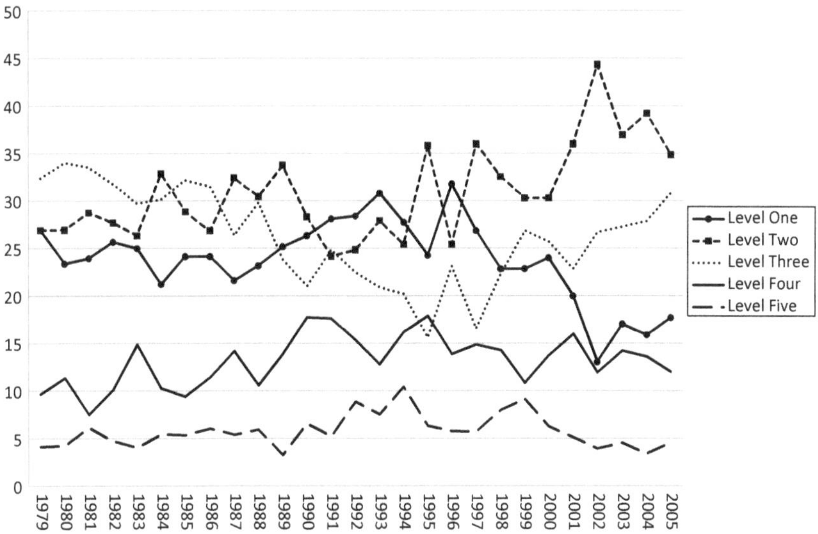

Figure 3.3. Political Terror Scale Based on Amnesty International Reports with State Department Data Filling in Country Gaps, 1979–2005

second-smallest segment here. And we see that mid-levels of repression affect approximately the same percentage of states over time as the lowest level of repression, with some variation over time, and with levels 2 and 3 converging in 2005.

As noted above, in previous work, we have dealt with the inconsistent coverage in the Amnesty-based scores by substituting Department of State scores for the missing data. Figure 3.3 presents the trends for the Amnesty-based scales that have been adjusted according to this practice. The adjustment clearly makes a difference in the share of countries experiencing the lowest level of repression (level 1), which now amounts to 18 to 33 percent of states instead of 5 to 15 percent. The percentage of countries experiencing only level 1 and level 2 repression is significantly higher; however, the percentage of states experiencing the higher end of repression remains the same. Missing data are not as significant a problem with the Department of State reports, but I do adjust the missing data to reflect the Amnesty score if available, and, as expected, there is little change in the trends (see Figure 3.4).

Human rights scholars have also noted that in addition to the differences in country coverage in the two sources, the two sets of reports reflect somewhat

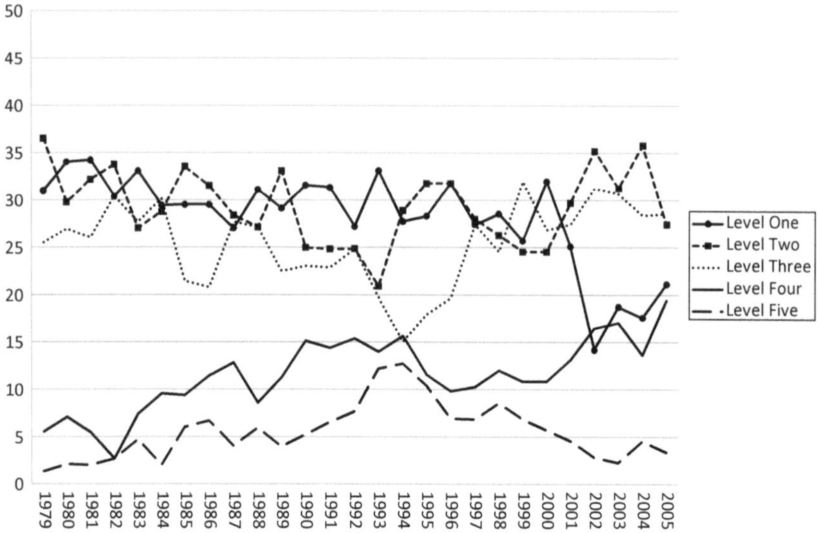

Figure 3.4. Political Terror Scale Based on State Department Reports with Amnesty International Data Filling in Country Gaps, 1979–2005

different mandates, sources of evidence, vetting processes, frameworks, and potential ideological biases (Poe, Carey, and Vazquez 2001). Despite these potential differences, Poe, Carey, and Vasquez (2001) found that most political terror scores were the same regardless of the source report, and when there was a difference, it was typically minor, within one point on the scale. In examining the differences in the scores, the overall trend the authors identified was that the Department of State tended to be somewhat less harsh than Amnesty International in its evaluations. The authors suggest that this result may on the one hand reflect the Department of State's giving greater weight to sovereignty issues or being easier on its allies for security and political reasons, or it may on the other hand reflect Amnesty's role as a human rights NGO whose "very subsistence is gained from publicizing human rights difficulties" (661). They also report that the Amnesty-based scores and the Department of State–based scores have tended to converge over time. While their study ended with 1995 reports, we see from Figure 3.5, which presents the annual means over time, that the convergence continues in the following decade as well.[7] The mean Department of State–based score has risen over time, from 2.09 to 2.5, whereas the mean Amnesty-based score has declined from 2.89 to 2.69. Poe, Carey, and Vasquez attribute the decline in the Amnesty-

Figure 3.5. Mean Repression: Political Terror Scale, 1979–2005

based scores to the eventual inclusion of less repressive countries in their reports, and suggest that while the increase in State Department–based scores may reflect real increases in state levels of repression, they may also reflect improvements in the Department of State reports in response to its critics' claims of biases. Their empirical analyses did find some evidence suggesting a potential bias in the reports in the late 1970s and early 1980s but found that it faded over time; they remain somewhat concerned, however, as they found evidence of a potential new bias in favor of U.S. trade partners (677). These findings, while encouraging overall, suggest that parallel analyses with the measures may be prudent.

Cingranelli and Richard's (1999) Physical Integrity Rights Index captures the same core components of political repression (political imprisonment, torture, disappearance, and killings) that Gibney's Political Terror Scale does, but with some additional advantages, and perhaps a couple of disadvantages as well. In the analyses in this book I have inverted the CIRI Index to represent the level of *repression* of rights rather than the protection of rights. Figure 3.6 presents the annual mean over time. As with the Political Terror Scales, we see substantial variation over the two decades, with a significant spike in the means as the Cold War ends, but once again we see the

Figure 3.6. Mean Physical Integrity Abuse: CIRI Index Inverted, 1981–2005

means at the end of the time frame (3.0) returning to approximately the beginning mean in 1981 (2.91). As noted previously, overall, the CIRI Index correlates highly with the Political Terror Scales.

Figure 3.7 presents the annual means for the Freedom House Civil Liberties Index. We do not observe as much variation in these means as we do with the repression of personal integrity rights, and here we see a rather notable overall downward trend in repression, with the mean in 2005 (3.25) a full point lower than the mean at the beginning of the data set in 1979 (4.27). We must continue to be somewhat cautious about interpreting the trends over time with the Freedom House measure, as we are unable to identify or control for the undocumented methodological changes they have made over time to the index.

Figure 3.8 presents the mean repression scores for freedom of speech and press, freedom of assembly and association, and freedom of religion, with the CIRI measures inverted to reflect repression of these freedoms and with each of the three measures constituting a 3-point scale ranging from 0 to 2. Several interesting trends emerge. First, the most obvious pattern is that repression of religious freedom is consistently higher than repression of the other two sets of freedoms, and although there is some variation over time, there

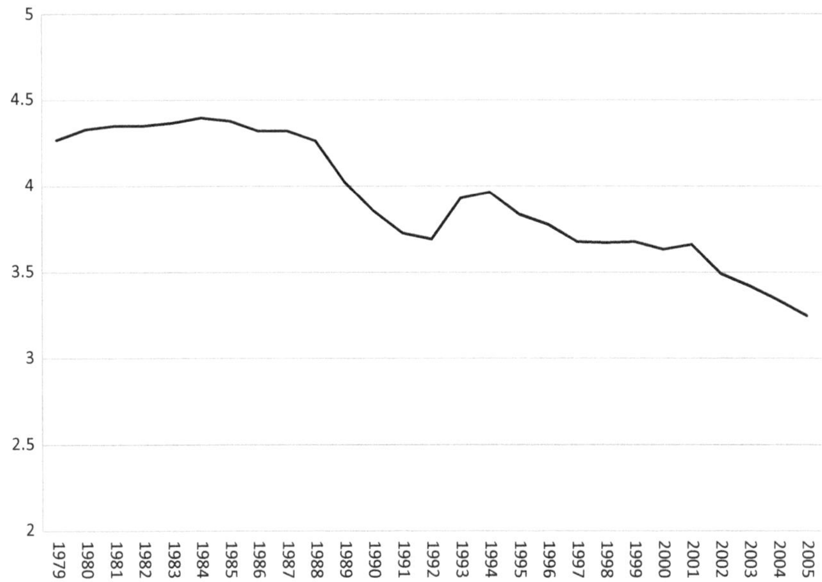

Figure 3.7. Mean Repression of Civil Liberties (Freedom House Index), 1979–2005

Figure 3.8. Mean Repression of Freedom of Speech and Press, Freedom of Association and Assembly, and Freedom of Religion (CIRI), 1981–2005

is virtually no improvement in the entire period. Indeed, in 2005 we see a higher mean of repression (1.40) than in 1981 (1.29). In subsequent chapters we will see that in several ways the repression of freedom of religion is rather distinct from other forms of repression. Second, we see a clear improvement in the level of repression for the other two categories of freedom, beginning with the end of the Cold War and leveling off in the mid-1990s, with an increase in repression of speech/press beginning after 2001, which could be related to the shift in emphasis toward national security priorities following September 11. We do not see the same pattern, however, for freedom of assembly and association, which during most years is repressed less than speech and press freedoms. The comparison of the individual components reveals information that is missing in the broader Freedom House measure of civil liberties. While the repression of assembly/association most closely follows the trend of the Freedom House measure, its trajectory in 2005 is in a different direction, one that may belatedly follow that of repression of speech/press, which deviates significantly from the Freedom House measure after 2001. Interestingly, the Freedom House measure shows no increase whatsoever after September 11, 2001. Obviously, the pattern of repression of religious freedom is lost within the Freedom House measure. In fact, on closer inspection of the Freedom House measure, as currently reported, it remains unclear whether individual religious freedom is even evaluated. The checklist appears to capture only institutional or community religious freedom: "Are religious institutions and communities free to practice their faith and express themselves in public and private?" The same dilemma arises in regard to freedom of speech and expression, which is not identifiable in their question set. As a whole these differences reinforce my choice to use multiple measures of civil liberties, despite the logistical difficulty in reporting results, and the difficulty in synthesizing divergent results across different measurements.

Why States Repress: The Standard Model of Repression

The simple descriptive examination of political repression can reveal only a limited view of global repression, and it raises many questions—such as, why does the level of state repression of human rights not parallel the level of state acceptance of human rights norms in formal treaties, which now approaches universality, or formal commitment in formal bills of rights and other constitutional protections, which also have become the norm? What domestic circumstances drive a state's choice to use these tools of repression? Which domestic institutions and conditions constrain the state's opportunity and/or willingness to make that choice? To what extent do external actors and circumstances constrain or facilitate the state's exercise of coercive behavior? A variety of approaches within political science attempt to explain state abuse of human rights, but none offer an overarching grand theory that synthesizes the theoretical concerns of the various subfields. Again, I do not claim to do so here, nor do I believe it to be a realistic goal. I do believe, however, that the core assumptions of the dominant theories express commonalities that may be incorporated under the organizing concepts of opportunity and willingness that I employ here for structuring the somewhat disparate approaches that attempt to understand political repression or human rights abuse.

The opportunity and willingness framework set forth in Chapter 1 argues that decision makers face a varying array of environmental factors that shape their menu of available of behavioral options. Furthermore, these actors' selection from the menu of options is informed by the actors' own norms or values and shaped by a complex incentive structure, including the consequences and benefits of the options. The framework is appropriate for the soft rationalism of the political repression literature and for the standard model of repression that has emerged. The standard model has typically included domestic and external threats (civil and/or international war), regime types (democracy, autocracy, military, and leftist), and socioeconomic conditions (economic development, population size, and colonial legacy). In the sections that follow I discuss the theoretical expectations briefly here as they have been explored more thoroughly in Chapter 2.

Domestic and External Threats: Civil and International War

Generally, realists and rational functionalists perceive states as rational actors whose behavior is based primarily upon narrow self-interest and is largely a function of the state's calculation of the benefits and costs (Waltz 1979; Keohane 1984). Continuing with the menu metaphor, state decision makers choose from of the option of engaging coercive force and other tools of repression because they see them as the most effective means to achieve their primary goal of staying in power. I assume that the most pervasive environmental factor that increases leaders' willingness to employ one of these tools is a threat to the leaders' rule, whether real or perceived, and that the more serious the threat, the more willing state leaders are to use coercive force to prevent, contain, or punish such threats (Keith and Poe 2004). The repressive tools the regime employs may range from a threat of repression to the actual application of force, each aimed at deterring or stopping actions that challenge the regime and are perceived to be to threats. As Davenport (2007a) notes, state actors carefully weigh the cost, benefits and likelihood of success in engaging these tools or alternative mechanisms of control, as well as assess the odds of achieving their goals with these tools. I believe civil war is the most violent of domestic threats, seeking nothing less than the removal of the current government by extra constitutional means. Presumably, then, it will be perceived by regimes as the most serious of the domestic threats, and thus the benefit of applying repression will be more likely to outweigh costs. In addition, we know that regimes often use the cover of this severe threat to legitimize repression of their opposition, and engage in excessive use of force and target civilian populations on thin excuses of collaboration with insurgents. Examples abound, such as Russian police in Chechnya and the Nepalese Royal Army, in the introductory examples above. Civil war has received the most empirical attention of the various forms of threats, and its presence has been demonstrated to be the strongest of any predictor, in terms of impact, statistical robustness, and consistency, across a variety of measures of repression and other human rights behavior (Poe and Tate 1994; Davenport 1995c; Cingranelli and Richards 1999a; Keith 1999, 2002b, 2004; Poe, Tate, and Keith 1999; Richards 1999; Apodaca 2001; Regan and Henderson 2002; Davenport and Armstrong 2004; Keith and Poe 2004; Bueno de Mesquita et al. 2005; Abouhard and Cingranelli 2006).[8]

- Hypothesis One: The presence of civil war increases the probability of political repression.

Civil War is measured following Small and Singer's (1982) guidelines for identifying instances of civil war: (1) "the government, as the central authority in a country, must be involved as a direct participant in the war" and (2) "there must be effective resistance, that is, either both sides must be 'organized for violent conflict'" or "the weaker side, although initially unprepared [must be] able to inflict upon the stronger opponents at least five percent of the number of fatalities it sustains" (215).

Interstate wars also pose a potential threat, one that varies according to the level of the state's participation in the hostilities and the proximity of the war zone to the state's territory. Political leaders may use the potential threat from an international war as an opportunity to repress their political opposition with the cloak of legitimacy that national security claims provide. For example, in the case of Saddam Hussein's Iraq, we saw the cover or diversion of war used to employ chemical weapons on the Kurdish town of Halabja and to eliminate an innocent ethnic population as the Iran-Iraq war came to an end. The expected nexus between international war and civil conflict was demonstrated by Stohl's early work (1975, 1976) to the extent that international war increased the level of domestic violence. And at least one early study examined the effect of international wars on repression; Rasler's (1986) study of the twentieth-century United States found evidence that administrations did indeed increase levels of repression during wars. Subsequently, large-*N* studies have confirmed the effect of participation in international war on domestic political repression (Poe and Tate 1994; Poe, Tate, and Keith 1999; Cingranelli and Richards 1999a, 1999b), and over time international war has become a key component of the standard model of human rights behavior (Keith 1999, 2002a; Richards 1999; Apodaca 2001; Davenport and Armstrong 2004; Landman 2005; Abouharb and Cingranelli 2006, 2008). As I noted in Chapter 2, the impact of international war is substantially lower than that of civil wars. This finding is somewhat intuitive, for even though external threats such as interstate war are potentially more devastating than civil wars, often the latter are a greater threat to a regime because of proximity and the ability of the opposition to impose damage.

- Hypothesis Two: The presence of international war increases the probability of political repression.

International War is measured following Small and Singer's (1982) guidelines for identifying instances of international war: a nation experiences an international war when it is a participant in a conflict in which more than one national government is directly involved and in which "(1) there was a total of a thousand or more battle deaths suffered by all of the participants in the conflict, [and] 2) the particular country suffered at least a hundred fatalities or had a thousand or more personnel taking part in the hostilities" (50 and 55).

Political scientists have also sought to understand the impact of less severe forms of threat, as well other dimensions of threat, such as the variety of strategies and frequency of conflict, and now have multiple measures potentially capturing the full range of repressive tools that regimes have at their disposal, as well as multiple measures capturing the most significant dimensions of threat. In Chapter 6 I examine more fully the theoretical expectations in regard to a broader range of domestic threats; I explore the robustness of several measures of threat; and I statistically identify dimensions of threat and their the explanatory power in regard to both categories of state repressive behavior.

Regime Characteristics: Democracy, Autocracy, Military Regimes, and Leftist Regimes

As discussed in Chapter 2, a third stream within the rational-actor perspective dismisses the reification of the state and instead recognizes the role of numerous domestic actors and institutions within the state (particularly in democratic regimes) that may affect the regime's menu of acceptable policy options as well as its calculation of costs and benefits related to repression of internationally recognized human rights. Poe, Tate, and Keith (1999) argued that state leaders in democratic regimes have less opportunity and less willingness to employ the tools of repression when faced with threats because of structural constraints and costs, such as a system of checks and balances, the limited nature of power in democratic governments, and the means for citizens to remove abusive regimes associated with democracies (see also Poe and Tate 1994; Davenport 1999). Concomitantly, democratic regimes may be less willing to engage in repressive behavior to deal with threats as these systems provide alternative mechanisms through which conflict can be channeled for possible resolution (Poe, Tate, and Keith 1999; Davenport 2007c). Equally as important, though, is the socialization of democratic polities toward norms such as compromise, toleration, negotiation, and non-violent means of conflict resolution (Poe, Tate, and Keith 1999; 1999).

These general explanations tend to assume a rather monolithic set of democracies, although it should be noted that most empirical human rights studies ultimately test the *level* of democratization rather than assuming a simple dichotomy between democratic and nondemocratic regimes. Most studies also tend to assume a linear association, at least in their empirical models. Recent theoretical and empirical work suggests that these sometimes unstated assumptions do not accurately reflect the true relationship between democracy and repression. Initially, for the sake of replication, I conceptualize and operationalize democracy as originally conceived in the standard model. I recognize that this operationalization may in fact incompletely specify the model. I will immediately turn to the theoretical arguments and empirical explorations of critics of this specification (Gleditsch and Ward 1997; Keith 2002a; Regan and Henderson 2002; Davenport and Armstrong 2004; Bueno de Mesquita et al. 2005) and engage in additional explorations.

It is important to pause here to address specifically the distinction between democracy and human rights, both conceptually and in terms of measurements, so that we do not create a tautology describing or testing this relationship. Poe and Tate (1994) suggest that in order for democracy to "function as an independent explanation for state terrorism and the abuse of personal integrity, it must be defined in terms of procedures and rights that do not themselves preclude repression," and it "must be defined in terms that allow independent operationalization of the concept" (856). Here, I follow Poe and Tate (1994) and other studies of personal integrity abuse and use a definition of political democracy that primarily captures the institutional and structural aspects of democracy that are most appropriate here. Political democracy is defined as "a system of governance in which rulers are held accountable for their actions in the public realm by citizens acting indirectly through the competition and cooperation of their elected officials" (Schmitter and Karl 1991, 76). Political democracy has proven to be one of the more consistent and potent explanators in political repression models; almost four decades of research support the expectation that higher levels of democracy are associated with lower levels of repression, across both categories of repression (for example, Hibbs 1973; Ziegenhagen 1986; Mitchell and McCormick 1988; Henderson 1991; Poe and Tate 1994; Davenport 1995c, 1999, 2007a; Poe, Tate, and Keith 1999; Richards 1999; Zanger 2000; Apodaca 2001; Keith 2002a; Davenport and Armstrong 2004; Bueno de Mesquita et al. 2005; Keith, Tate, and Poe 2009).

- Hypothesis Three: The higher the level of political democracy a regime has achieved, the less likely it is to engage in political repression.

Political Democracy has been measured with a variety of instruments across these studies, with Polity emerging as the dominant measure of democratization, and Freedom House's Political Rights Index being used more as a test of robustness, in part because of the concerns mentioned above in regard to the other Freedom House measure, which apply to this indicator as well. The Polity measure has the advantage of allowing researchers to disaggregate its components. I believe that the Polity IV data (Marshall and Jaggers 2011) allow us to best achieve the conceptual separation we desire, because of the focus on the electoral process of the country's executive. Polity's institutional democracy indicator is an 11-point additive index coded along four dimensions using the following rules:

> *Competitiveness of Political Participation*: competitive (3), transitional (2), and factional (1)
> *Competitiveness of Executive Recruitment*: elective (2) and transitional (1)
> *Openness of Executive Recruitment*: open election (1) or dual (hereditary and election) (1)
> *Constraint on Chief Executive:* executive parity or subordination to legislative or judicial branches (4), intermediate constraints (constraints that fall between parity/subordination and substantial limitations) (3), substantial limitations (2), and intermediate constraints (constraints that fall between substantial limitations and slight to moderate limitations). (Marshall and Jaggers 2007, 14)

The standard model has also included measures that to some extent distinguish among types of autocracy. For example, scholars have examined the role of military regimes (McKinlay and Cohan 1975; Poe and Tate 1994; Poe, Tate, and Keith 1999) and Marxist-Leninist regimes (Mitchell and McCormick 1988; Poe and Tate 1994; Poe, Tate, and Keith 1999). As Poe and Tate (1994) note, the increased willingness of a military regime to employ coercive means against its civilian population is not surprising, as "military juntas are based on force, and force is the key to coercion" (858). And, as Poe, Tate, and Keith (1999) have argued, because the leaders in a military regime have direct control of the instruments of coercion, they will also be likely to face fewer constraints and barriers than other leaders if they choose to act repressively (293). Poe and Tate (1994) caution that "since military rule is by definition antithetical to democracy, it might be that any apparent relationship between military rule and state terrorism is spurious, a result of a failure to control for the democratic/nondemocratic nature of the regime" (858). Davenport (2007b) argues that in "political systems where the agents of repression (i.e., the military) directly wield power, there is a higher likelihood that repressive behavior—especially violent activity—would be applied out of habit, familiarity, an impulse to meet specific organizational norms, and a desire to expand prestige in/control over the political system" (486). However, Davenport points out that there is a significant scholarship that disagrees with some of these assumptions: "Others have noted that the armed forces tend to shy away from their area of expertise and implementing repressive behavior. Indeed, the hesitancy of the 'professional soldier' to interfere in domestic politics because of organizational norms is a constant theme in older research . . . , persisting up to the present" (491 and citations therein). In addition, Davenport argues that a military regime will have less need to resort to "overt manifestations of coercive power" because "such power is signaled by the presence of the military itself" (491).

Despite the strong theoretical arguments that would lead us to expect military regimes to be more repressive than nonmilitary regimes, empirical evidence has been mixed. Poe and Tate (1994) found no such effect; however, Poe, Tate, and Keith (1999) and Keith, Tate, and Poe (2009), which provided larger time frameworks, did find the expected effect, although its impact was somewhat minor. Davenport (2007b), who utilizes a different categorization of military regimes, also fails to find an effect for military regimes in regard to personal integrity abuse but does find evidence that military regimes are *less* likely to restrict the broader civil liberties category of repression (as defined and measured by Freedom House).[9] In explaining these different results Davenport notes: "It seems reasonable to suggest that these political systems reduce civil liberties restrictions because they tend to avoid involving themselves with the political processes which are normally responsible for these repressive activities (i.e., legislatures and courts) . . . and more inclined to use repressive techniques which are more directly within the realm of their expertise—physical violence" (500).

While I find Davenport's explanation plausible, there is evidence of military regimes' curbing freedom of press, detaining protestors, and engaging in lower forms of repression. Take, for example, the rather ironic example of the military government of Myanmar in regard to the referendum on the draft constitution:

> In February the government issued the Referendum Law for the Approval of the Draft Constitution, which provided for a prison term of up to three years and/or a substantial fine for anyone caught campaigning against the referendum. The government used the law to detain many activists peacefully campaigning against the constitution or calling for a boycott. Over 70 were arrested in late April for trying to stage a peaceful demonstration. Journalists and human rights defenders were particularly targeted for their work throughout the year. (Amnesty International 2009)

Amnesty International cites the examples of Saw Wai, a poet, who was arrested and sentenced to two years in prison for "inserting a concealed message in a Valentine's Day poem," and Nay Phone Latt, a blogger, who was arrested and sentenced to twenty years and six months in prison for "images and cartoons that appeared in his blogs" (ibid.).

Davenport's (2007b) use of the Freedom House Civil Liberties Index also makes it somewhat problematic to assume that the measure does not capture physical violence, because the Freedom House survey on civil liberties does include a question about political terror, physical harm, and violence; but, as I noted above, it is difficult to note its location or weight within its scale. Also, as I read Davenport's table, the military regime measure did not have a statistical effect on any of the personal integrity models, a result that parallels some previous findings. I am reluctant to lay this hypothesized relationship to rest or to remove the variable from the standard model just yet. Thus, I continue to explore this hypothesis in this chapter but am cautious about its place in the standard model. I treat Davenport's findings as an alternative hypothesis.

- Hypothesis Four: States with military regimes will be more likely to engage in political repression.
- Alternative Hypothesis Four: States with military regimes will be more likely to engage in personal integrity abuse and less likely to engage in civil liberties restrictions.

Military Regimes is operationalized following Poe, Tate, and Keith (1999), Keith, Tate, and Poe (2009), and others who have used Madani's (1992) classification, which builds upon McKinlay and Cohan (1976), where military regimes are defined as those that had come to power "as a consequence of a successful *coup d'état*, led by the army, navy or air force, [and] that remained in power with a military person as the chief executive, for at least six months in a given year" (61). This operationalization also includes a small number of mixed regimes, "with either a civilian as the chief executive and several military persons in the cabinet or a military head of government who nominated a civilian as the head of government and himself worked behind the scenes" (Madani 1992, 61). The measure is dichotomous, with military regimes coded (1) and all other regimes coded (0).

As noted in Chapter 2, scholars have approached with some caution the expectation that leftist regimes will be more likely to repress than non-Marxist regimes, and, as we will see below, that hesitancy has been justified empirically. In part, the expectation that leftist regimes are more repressive reflects the assumptions of Cold War hardliners but in part the association is linked Marxist-Leninist tenets about the "need for a dictatorship of the proletariat" (Poe and Tate 1994, 858). More recent empirical evidence runs counter to these assumptions, demonstrating that at least in regard to personal integrity rights, Marxist or Marxist-Leninist regimes are likely to repress, perhaps because the exhaustive social control by these regimes negates the need for severe forms of repression or perhaps simply due the afterlife of past repression. Of course the latter explanation would apply across regime types. It is important to note that Davenport (2007b) found that a leftist regime is more likely to *increase* civil liberties restrictions, an important distinction I will return to later in this chapter. Here, I test an alternative hypothesis based on the mixed empirical work, which has been supported somewhat by theoretical (albeit largely post-hoc) expectations.

- Hypothesis Five: States with Marxist or Marxist-Leninist regimes will be more likely to engage in political repression.
- Alternative Hypothesis Five: States with Marxist or Marxist-Leninist regimes will be less likely to engage in political repression.

Marxist or Marxist-Leninist Regimes is operationalized as "those governed by a socialist party or coalition that does not allow effective electoral competition with non-socialist opposition" (Poe and Tate 1994, 858). This measure is a dichotomous variable, with Marxist or Marxist-Leninist regimes coded (1) and all other regimes coded (0).

Socioeconomic Conditions: Economic Development, Population Size, and Colonial Legacy

As discussed in Chapter 2, there are two schools of thought concerning the somewhat indirect relationship between human rights and economic development. The positive model expects that economic liberalization and liberal trade policies in particular, will facilitate economic development, lead to improvements in the political and social conditions for the population, and foster the liberal democracy in developing states. In contrast, the malign perspective argues that more economically developed states will exploit less economically developed states, produce uneven development and diminished socioeconomic growth. And ultimately, the regimes' options are constrained by economic relationships with the developed world, and its decisions are likely to made to benefit MNCs and domestic elites rather than to promote the needs and rights of their own citizens. Ultimately, the two positions disagree on how globalization would affect the cost/benefit structure of using coercive force, and they disagree about whether the values and interests of the general public or those of MNCs and economic elites control the menu of appropriate policy tools and priorities.

Mitchell and McCormick (1988) make a more straightforward scarcity argument: "The poorest countries, with substantial social and political tensions created by economic scarcity, could be most unstable and thus most apt to use repression in order to maintain control" (478). As does Henderson (1991), who argues: "It is only logical to think that, with a higher level of development, people will be more satisfied and, hence, less repression will be needed by the elites" (126). As Poe and Tate (1994) noted, the expected effects of economic growth are more mixed. Since economic growth "expands the resource base, it should reduce the economic and social stresses that lead governments to use terrorism as a policy tool [but] there has also been a strong argument that rapid economic growth is most likely to be a destabilizing force that will, in fact, increase instability and a regime's temptation to resort to coercive means to maintain control" (858). Gurr (1970, 1986) cautioned that rapid economic growth may be destabilizing because it cannot keep up with simultaneously rising expectations and because it inevitably occurs unevenly, often harming the poorer segment of the population. As Henderson notes, the sharpening of class differences within the population may cause the elite to employ tools of repression to quell the protest of the disadvantaged classes.

As with the domestic economic environment, state population size and level of growth are also seen as conditions associated with popular unrest stemming from scarcity within the state. Henderson (1993) argues that "growth in numbers of people can create scarcity—a short-fall between what people need and want and what they have. Under this pressure governments may be pushed in an authoritarian direction. . . . What is worse, government may resort to repression as a coping mechanism" (325). Thus Poe and Tate (1994) assert that a large population may increase the occurrence of repression in at least two ways: (1) as a simple matter of probability, a large number of people increases the number of occasions on which such coercive acts can occur; and (2) by placing stress on national resources and threatening environmental deterioration, further reducing available resources (857). Similarly, Henderson (1993) argues that "the extent of scarcity varies from country to country, but in the more hard-pressed countries, burgeoning demands will keep governments off-balance and will incline them to resort to repression [and] growing populations absorb any economic growth rate that may occur, thus frustrating governments' efforts" (4).

Studies of human rights have demonstrated that economic development is strongly associated with lower levels of state repression (McKinlay and Cohan 1975, 1976; Mitchell and McCormick 1988; Park 1987; Henderson 1991; Poe and Tate 1994; Poe, Tate, and Keith 1999; Richards 1999), and studies of democratization have also demonstrated that countries with greater wealth are more likely to be democratic (for example, Lipset 1959; Prezworksi and Vreeland 2000), and democracy itself is one of the strongest and most consistent predictors of reduced state repression (Apodaca 2001; Bueno de Mesquita et al. 2005; Davenport 1995c, 1999, 2007a; Henderson 1991; Hibbs 1973; Keith 2002a; Mitchell and McCormick 1988; Poe and Tate 1994; Poe, Tate, and Keith 1999; Richards 1999; Zanger 2000; Ziegenhagen 1986). Most of these studies have demonstrated that the size of the effect is not typically substantively significant; coefficients on average approach zero, especially when the models incorporate factors beyond the limited standard model. Many of these variables represent a more viable policy alternative to improve human rights conditions than would the necessary increase in the level of economic development required to produce even a modest improvement (for example, Keith 2002a; Keith, Tate, and Poe 2009).

Over time economic growth has been dropped from many models because of its repeated failure to achieve statistical significance, but I continue to test it here because this time frame represents the largest under study thus far. Population size, typically logged, has consistently been shown to increase levels of repression, but, as with economic growth, population growth has proven to be insignificant as studies of repression have extended over time and have controlled for additional influences. In these initial analyses of the base model, I continue to include each of the economic development and population measures as a core component of the standard model, but recognize the possible limited utility of some of these measures, especially in light of recent trends in the field.

- Hypothesis Six: The higher the level of economic development achieved by a state, the lower the level of political repression exercised by the state.
- Hypothesis Seven: The higher the level of economic growth achieved by a state, the lower the level of political repression exercised by the state.
- Hypothesis Eight: The larger the population size within a state, the higher the level of political repression exercised by the state.
- Hypothesis Nine: The higher the level of population growth in the state, the higher the level of political repression exercised by the state.

Economic Development is operationalized as per-capita GDP and *Economic Growth* is operationalized as percentage growth in GDP per capita, which is consistent with most large-*N* cross-national studies of political repression, regardless of category of repression (for example, Poe and Tate 1994; Poe, Tate, and Keith 1999). *Population Size* is operationalized as the natural logarithm of the total national population, and *Population Growth* as the average percent increase in national population from one year to the next, over the twenty-six-year period of the study.

Finally, over time the inclusion of a control for British colonial experience has become standard in explanatory models of state repression (for example, Mitchell and McCormick 1988; Poe and Tate 1994; Keith 1999; 2002a; Poe, Tate, and Keith 1999; Davenport and Armstrong 2004). Mitchell and McCormick (1988) posited the original argument linking British colonial rule's presumably strong association with postcolonial development of democracy to a relatively greater respect for human rights; in contrast, other colonial experiences were assumed to have introduced a greater degree of hierarchy and authoritarianism and, with it, higher levels of political repression. The results have been inconsistent. For example, the variable was not statistically significant in Poe and Tate's early work (1994), which examined repression in the 1980s, but the variable was statistically significant in all four of the models in Poe, Tate, and Keith (1999), which expanded the data back to 1976 and forward to 1993. However, Keith (2002a) and Keith, Tate, and Poe (2009), which extended the analyses forward to 1996, and which added measures of constitutional protections and institutional provisions, found the measure statistically insignificant. Keith (2004) found some evidence of colonial influences, in that rights-related constitutional provisions performed better in countries with Iberian colonial experience; and Keith and Ogundele (2007) found that in Sub-Saharan Africa former francophone colonies had better human rights protection than anglophone ones and that constitutional protections and institutional provisions of former francophone colonies outperformed those of anglophone ones. I examine British colonial experience in this initial analysis of the standard model, and return to the issue more fully in subsequent chapters, examining other colonial legacies such as the type of legal system and related institutional features.

- Hypothesis Ten: States with British colonial experience will be less likely to engage in political repression.

British Colonial Experience is a dichotomous variable, with countries that were territories of Great Britain at some point during their histories coded (1) and all other countries coded (0).

Analysis of the Standard Model

The time frame of these analyses is 1980–2005 for models employing the Political Terror Scale and 1982–2005 for the models employing CIRI measures.[10] The measures of the dependent variable are ordinal, and thus fail to meet the Ordinary Least Squares (OLS) requirement that variables be measured at the interval level. In previous models my co-authors and I estimated my multivariate model using OLS rather than a multivariate technique such as ordered logit or probit (see Richards, Gelleny, and Sacko 2001; Richards and Kimmelman 1999), which does not assume a dependent variable with equal interval scores. We did so for several reasons: (1) the results produced by ordered logit and OLS for my models are substantively very similar; (2) optimal scaling analyses strongly suggest that the effective level of measurement of our dependent variable is approximately interval; (3) the interpretability advantages of OLS over ordered logit are substantial, particularly for projecting results over time; and (4) OLS results may be more effectively compared with the results of previous research. In this book I follow Neumayer's (2005) dual approach in estimating my models. As Neumayer notes, computing fixed effects in ordered probit or logit models is extremely complex, currently there is not a standard statistical package to estimate such a model, and adding fixed effects by hand leads to biased coefficients and standard errors; thus, he runs parallel estimations using OLS with fixed effects and a standard ordered probit estimator without fixed effects (936–37). I follow this approach and report results from estimating both models.

I ran a series of preliminary analyses that led me to remove the British colonial experience variable from all the models. When the fixed effects were adding to the OLS model, the British colonial experience was thrown from the model for collinearity because there is no within-country variation in this period for colonial experience. In a parallel OLS estimation without fixed effects and in the ordered probit models, the British colonial variable never achieved statistical significance. Thus I removed it from the base model to allow uniform comparison across the models. As already noted, I was increasingly dissatisfied with this simple dichotomy, as other work has demonstrated that the influence is more nuanced (Keith 2004; Keith and Ogundele 2007). In the following chapters I explore measures that may more meaningfully capture the colonial legacy.

Table 3.1 reports the models estimated for repression of personal integrity rights with the results for the models with Department of State-based PTS measure in columns 1 and 2, the Amnesty International–based PTS measure in columns 3 and 4, and the CIRI Index in columns 5 and 6. For each of the analyses I report both the fixed-effects analysis (odd-numbered columns) and then the ordered probit analysis without fixed effects (even-numbered columns). As we look across the four personal integrity models, we see that the models perform quite consistently, with some slight variation in levels of statistical significance, and we see only one variable that does not perform consistently; thus for ease of presentation and interpretation I focus primarily on the State Department–based PTS fixed-effects model in column 1.

The variables and the model generally perform consistently with those of previous studies. The lagged dependent variable in the State Department PTS fixed-effects model produces the largest coefficient (.49), which substantively means that a 1-point increase in the previous year's level of repression would be associated with an increase of approximately half a point on the 5-point scale. As Poe and Tate (1994) emphasized, "such coefficients mean that our country scores on state terrorism are strongly seated characteristics of their political systems that do not change easily or rapidly"; perhaps equally important, "these coefficients provide a mechanism through which the effects of changes in the independent variables at a given time ($time_t$) continue to influence the dependent variables beyond the time of the occurrence of the change" (860).

The presence of civil war continues to have one of the strongest effects on repression across all models, and in the Department of State fixed-effects model I find that the initiation or continuation of a civil war would be associated with an increase in the level of repression by almost half a point (.47) on the 5-point scale, or, in the case of the CIRI fixed-effects model, an almost 1-point (.95) increase on its 9-point scale. As in previous studies, the effect of international war on this form of repression is significantly smaller; in the Department of State fixed-effects model the presence of an international war is associated with an increase in the level of repression, but only by about .15 on the PTS. The difference in magnitude between the effect of international war and civil war is not surprising and reflects the fact that civil wars occur within the state, whereas interstate wars are often fought far away from at least some of the belligerents' states. The performance of both variables strongly demonstrates the influence of environment on a regime's choice to employ repression. In Chapter 6 I examine the influence of structures such as an independent judiciary and the effect of formal protections aimed at regulating state behavior during periods of threat.

The level of democratization performs consistently with previous studies. Again, using the Department of State model as a reference, we see that an improvement of 1 point on the 11-point Polity index would be associated with a decrease in on the PTS measure of .04, which is a rather small effect. Movement from the least democratic to the most democratic, while not highly likely in the real world, could potentially lead to an improvement of close to half a point on the PTS measure. These results held in a parallel analysis using the Freedom House Political Rights Index as a test of robustness.[11] Nonetheless, I choose to stay with the Polity measure for the remainder of the analyses, because of my ability to disaggregate it in the analyses that follow

Table 3.1. Standard Model of Repression of Personal Integrity Rights, 1980–2005

	Personal Integrity Rights Abuse (PTS-SD) 1980–2005		*Personal Integrity Rights Abuse (PTS-AI) 1980–2005*		*Personal Integrity Rights Abuse (CIRI) 1982–2005*	
	Fixed Effects (1)	*Ordered Probit (2)*	*Fixed Effects (3)*	*Ordered Probit (4)*	*Fixed Effects (5)*	*Ordered Probit (6)*
Rights Abuse (*t* – 1) (+)	.49 (.03)***	1.34 (.04)***	.41 (.02)***	1.14 (.04)***	.42 (.03)***	.55 (.02)***
Civil War (+)	.47 (.07)***	.74 (.10)***	.50 (.08)***	.66 (.09)***	.95 (.18)***	.60 (.09)***
International War (+)	.15 (.06)***	.26 .09)***	.13 (.07)*	.21 (.08)***	.22 (.11)**	.22 (.08)***
Political Democracy (–)	–.04 (.01)***	–.06 .01)***	–.04 (.01)***	–.06 (.01)***	–.07 (.02)***	–.06 (.01)***
Military Regimes (+)	.03 (.06)	.01 (.06)	.03 (.04)	.01 (.06)	.22 (.14)*	–.02 (.06)
Marxist or Marxist-Leninist Regimes (+/–)	–.06 (.12)	–.21 (.08)***	–.25 (.07)**	–.26 (.07)***	–.05 (.21)	–.21 (.08)***

Economic Development (–)	–.00002	–.00002	–.00001	.00002	.00006	–.00003
	(.00)***	(.00)	(.00)	(.00)***	(.00)	(.00)***
Economic Growth (–)	–.01	–.01	–.01	–.01	–.003	–.0001
	(.00)***	(.00)***	(.00)***	(.00)**	(.00)	(.00)
Logged Population (+)	.62	.15	.25	.15	.84	.16
	(.10)***	(.00)***	(.11)***	(.01)***	(.22)***	(.01)***
Population Growth (+)	–.04	–.01	–.03	.03	–.06	.03
	(.01)	(.02)	(.02)	(.02)	(.06)	(.02)**
Observations	3301	3301	3301	3301	3024	3024
R^2 /Pseudo-R^2	.76	.46	.70	.40	.73	.30
F /Chi^2	113.46	2166.06	52.18	2065.68	58.72	2750.91
Prob > F / Prob > Chi^2	.0001	.0001	.0001	.0001	.0001	.0001

Fixed-effects and ordered probit estimation with robust standard errors. Standard errors in parentheses. *Significant at the 10 percent level. **Significant at the 5 percent level. ***Significant at the 1 percent level. All tests one-tailed except where no direction predicted (+) predicted positive direction, (–) negative, and (+/–) no predicted direction.

below. Although the effect of democratization may be incompletely specified at this point, my intention here is to confirm the extent to which the results of the standard model expanded over time are consistent with previous studies examining the standard model of repression.

As discussed above, three of the variables have been problematic: British colonial influence, Marxist regime, and military regime. I removed the British colonial measure for the reasons discussed above. The military regime variable consistently produces positive coefficients (with one exception), as expected, but achieves acceptable levels of statistical significance in only one model: the fixed-effects model for the CIRI Index. I am reluctant to discard this measure from the standard model of repression of personal integrity rights and continue to explore this relationship further, particularly in tandem with my subsequent exploration of the measurement of democracy. Subsequently we will see this variable performs much more consistently with theoretical expectations once the model is more correctly specified. The coefficient for the Marxist or Marxist-Leninist regime consistently produces negative coefficients in all six models, and the coefficients are statistically significant in all three probit models and in the fixed-effects model with the Amnesty International–based PTS measure. If we use this model as an example, the coefficient (-.25) suggests that states with a leftist regime will be less likely to repress and a change from a nonleftist to leftist regime would be associated with a reduction in repression by about .25 on the 5-point PTS measure.

The performance of the other four socioeconomic measures is rather mixed. Most notably, population growth fails to achieve statistical significance in all but one model. The coefficients for economic development are statistically significant in only three of six models, and in the models where they do achieve acceptable levels of significance, their substantive impact is quite small, equivalent to zero. For example, in the Department of State fixed-effects model the coefficient is .00001 and substantively suggests that in order to reach an improvement in the human rights scale of even .01, the state would need to experience a $1,000 per-capita increase in GDP, which would be the equivalent of expecting Nepal to double the size of its economy in a single year. We see similar small effects in regard to the population coefficients; for example, a percentage increase in population size would be associated with an increase in the level of repression by .0062. The substantive value of these predictors remains relatively minor, as they have in previous studies. In the subsequent chapters I expand this exploration with additional measures that capture economic liberalization/globalization. The overall fit of the models is good, and the models explain roughly the same amount of variation in state repression as previous studies—with *R*-squareds between .70 and .76.

I next apply the standard model to state restriction of civil liberties. The results are reported in Table 3.2; columns 1 and 2 report the results with the Freedom House measure, and columns 3 through 8 report the results using the individual CIRI measures. As above, for each of the analyses I report both the fixed-effects analysis (odd-numbered columns) and then the ordered probit analysis without fixed effects (even-numbered columns). The model utilizing the Freedom House measure performs quite similarly to the personal integrity model, with two notable exceptions. First, the coefficients for military regimes are negative, as predicted by Davenport (2007b), and they achieve a satisfactory level of statistical significance in the ordered probit model, but not in the fixed-effects model. Second, the coefficients for Marxist or Marxist-Leninist regimes are positive and achieve acceptable levels of statistical significance in both the fixed-effects model and the ordered probit model. As we will see below, this effect holds across all four measures of civil liberties. This result lends strong support to Keith's (2002a) suggestion that in Marxist or Marxist-Leninist regimes, control of society and personal freedoms has often been so complete that the regime might be less likely than its non-leftist counterparts to need to engage in the more severe abuses of personal integrity rights to maintain order. Thus, I do find two significant differences in modeling restrictions of civil liberties and repression of personal integrity rights, both related to regime type. Using the opportunity and willingness framework, these results suggest that factors based in the agent (ideological values of a leftist regime and the norms of a military government) may indeed affect the choice of which tool of repression to utilize, not simply the choice of whether to repress or not.

In addition, I find that the magnitude of some of the coefficients varies quite a bit from the personal integrity abuse models; the presence of civil war has a much smaller effect on this less severe form of repression than it does on the narrower and more egregious set of personal integrity rights abuse; here civil war is associated with a mere .12 increase on a 7-point scale, compared with the .47 increase on the 5-point Political Terror Scale. Again, we must keep in mind the limitations of the Freedom House Civil Liberties Index does to some (unknown) extent capture state-sponsored "political terror" (personal integrity abuse), but we cannot separate it out from the measurement of repression of rights ranging from freedom of press to academic

Table 3.2. Standard Model of Repression of Civil Liberties

	Civil Liberties Restrictions (Freedom House) 1980–2005		*Restriction of Freedom of Speech and Press (CIRI) 1982–2005*		*Restriction of Freedom of Assembly and Association (CIRI) 1982–2005*		*Restriction of Freedom of Religion (CIRI) 1982–2005*	
	Fixed Effects (1)	*Ordered Probit (2)*	*Fixed Effects (3)*	*Ordered Probit (4)*	*Fixed Effects (5)*	*Ordered Probit (6)*	*Fixed Effects (7)*	*Ordered Probit (8)*
Rights Restrictions (*t*–1) (+)	.68 (.02)***	2.00 (.08)***	.23 (.03)***	1.13 (.05)***	.45 (.03)***	1.61 (.06)***	.46 (.03)***	2.22 (.07)***
Civil War (+)	.12 (.05)***	.28 (.09)***	.07 (.04)**	.17 (.09)**	–.02 (.05)	.03 (.10)	–.01 (.04)	–.13 (.12)
International War (+)	–.01 (.06)	.07 (.09)	.05 (.03)*	.18 (.09)**	.04 (.04)	.04 (.10)	.04 (.03)*	.24 (.14)**
Political Democracy (–)	–.09 (.01)***	–.18 (.01)***	–.06 (.01)***	–.16 (.01)***	–.05 (.01)***	–.14 (.01)***	–.01 (.00)***	–.12 (.01)***
Military Regimes (–)	–.11 (.06)**	–.17 (.07)***	.02 (.04)	.02 (.07)	.09 (.05)**	.01 (.08)	–.04 (.03)*	–.22 (.09)***
Marxist or Marxist-Leninist Regimes (+/–)	.33 (.12)***	.29 (.12)***	.28 (.08)***	.54 (.11)***	.24 (.07)***	.46 (.11)***	.06 (.07)	.08 (.14)
Economic Development (–)	–.00001 (.00)***	–.00002 (.00)***	–.00003 (.01)	–.00001 (.00)***	.00001 (.00)	.00003 (.00)	.00001 (.00)	.00006 (.00)

Economic Growth (–)	–.004	–.01	.002	.01	–.01	–.005	.001	.01
	(.00)**	(.00)**	(.002)	(.00)	(.01)**	(.01)	(.01)	(.01)
Logged Population (+)	–.18	.05	.14	.03	–.07	.08	–.10	.10
	(.07)	(.01)***	(.11)	(.01)**	(.08)	(.02)***	(.07)	(.02)***
Population Growth (+)	–.02	.04	–.01	.02	–.01	.01	.0004	–.05
	(.02)	(.02)**	(.01)	(.02)	(.01)	(.02)	(.01)	(.03)
Observations	3377	3377	3045	3045	3045	3045	3045	3045
R^2 /Pseudo-R^2	.95	.68	.59	.40	.75	.53	.62	.54
F/Chi^2	294.02	1409.63	32.61	1771.29	120.40	1691.66	33.89	1361.14
Prob > *F/Chi*^{2}	.0001	.0001	.0001	.0001	.0001	.0001	.0001	.0001

Fixed-effects and ordered probit estimation with robust standard errors. Standard errors in parentheses. *Significant at the 10 percent level. **Significant at the 5 percent level. ***Significant at the 1 percent level. All tests one-tailed except where no direction predicted (+) predicted positive direction, (–) negative, and (+/–) no predicted direction.

freedom, from effective collective bargaining to an independent judiciary, from the right to own property to the right to choose marriage partners, and to protection against political terror and war. Thus, while we can say that a maximum increase in the level of political democratization could decrease the level of repression by almost 1 on the 7-point civil liberties scale, it is difficult to describe substantively what that improvement in rights protection would look like. I seek to address this dilemma with subsequent examination of individual civil liberties. The economic measures continue to perform poorly and inconsistently, even more so than in the personal integrity models: economic growth is statistically significant in only one model and economic development in only three of the eight models. Population growth again fails to perform consistently, and population size is significant only in the non-fixed-effects probit model. The models perform quite satisfactorily, explaining as much as 95 percent of the variation in the fixed-effects model. I turn next to analyses of a narrower set of individual civil liberties.

As we can see in Table 3.2, the model for restrictions on freedom of speech and press performs closely to the broader Freedom House model, and we see only two key differences. Most significantly, the military regime coefficient is positive rather than negative, but it does not achieve high enough levels of statistical significance to be acceptable even if we had not predicted a singular direction. The coefficient for international war achieves statistical significance in both the fixed-effects and ordered probit models. Thus while international war may not affect the broad range of rights captured in the Freedom House measure, it does have a harmful affect on freedom of press and speech. The effect is a rather small: the onset of an international war would be associated with an increase of .05 in the 3-point scale. It is frustrating to be unable to separate out repression of freedom of speech from freedom of press, as it seems likely that freedom of press would be more threatening.

In the model for freedom of assembly and association, I find that not only is international war not statistically significant in either model, but neither is the more severe form of threat, civil war. This finding runs counter to theoretical expectations that during periods when the regime itself is most under threat, civil liberties are most likely to be curbed. This particular finding would imply that public exercise of public assembly and association are less threatening to a regime under threat than is the exercise of freedoms of speech and press. Again, it is unfortunate that we are unable to separate out the effect of association and assembly in these models, as it seems likely that the freedom to assembly would be more immediately threatening to a regime, with the opposition taking to the streets, than freedom of association, which would capture the opposition's ability to participate in organizations and political parties. In both of the assembly/association models, the military regime coefficients are positive again, and here the coefficient in the fixed-effects model achieves an acceptable level of statistical significance. Only the model for religious freedom performs similarly to the Freedom House civil liberties model in that the military regime coefficients are negative and statistically significant. This finding suggests that military regimes may find freedom of religion to be less threatening than other freedoms that more specifically empower the opposition. And in fact the civil war coefficients are not statistically significant in the religious freedom models, a finding that parallels the freedom of association models. On the other hand, international war has a harmful effect and is statistically significant, which parallels the freedom of speech model. The somewhat mixed results across the four civil liberties measures suggest that it would be wise to continue using the separate measures of civil liberties, along with the broader Freedom House measure. In subsequent chapters I will continue to explore these differences as I more fully specify the models to account for formal rights protections and legal institutions.

As we look across these standard models, we see that the model continues to perform quite well across the three personal integrity measures, explaining approximately three-quarters of the variation in state repression of personal integrity rights. Five of the ten variables perform consistently across all measures: lagged repression, civil war, international war, political democracy, and population size. The Marxist or Marxist-Leninist regime measure performs consistently in five of six models. The two economic variables perform consistently across half the models, although the substantive effect of the coefficients is minor. Population growth consistently fails. The military regime variable continues to be problematic, with coefficients that are positive across measures, as expected; however, the coefficients achieve acceptable levels of statistical significance in only one of the models. While overall the standard model performs rather satisfactorily, I believe it is rather narrow, in that its primary focus is on domestic institutions and circumstances. Thus, in the following chapter I examine more transnational influences, such as trade openness, foreign direct investment, and INGOs, as I move into analyses of the impact of law and courts on state repression.

The standard model does not perform as well in regard to the less severe form of political repression—restriction of civil liberties. The performance of the model varies across the different measures of civil liberties. When I limit the analysis strictly to the Freedom House civil liberties measure we see that the model performs quite well, explaining 90 percent of the variation in state restrictions; in the individual models the explanatory power as measured by the R-squared statistic ranges from .59 to .75. The discrepancies between the models of personal integrity abuse and civil liberties restrictions fall across two of the somewhat problematic variables in the model. The leftist regime variable has a positive effect on civil liberties restrictions, a result that fits with Keith's (2002a) explanation above; and the military regime variable has a negative effect in the ordered probit model, a result that fits with Davenport's (2007b) hypothesis. So overall the model is rather satisfactory, but because of the concerns about the content and construction of the Freedom House measure, I examined alternatively three singular civil liberty restrictions. At this point, the model tended to lose its consistency, especially in regard to freedom of religion. Only three of the variables perform consistently: prior restrictions, level of political democracy, and logged population. The Marxist-Leninist variable is consistent across all models in the direction of its coefficient, but the coefficients are not statistically significant in the religious freedom model. The effects of threat are somewhat puzzling, in that civil war has no effect on restrictions of freedom to assemble/associate or on religious freedom; and international war, which we would expect to have a smaller effect, consistently produces positive coefficients, but they achieve statistical significance only in the speech and religious freedom models. I explore the threat dimension more thoroughly in Chapter 6 and attempt to ferret out more of this relationship. The economic and population effects are even more inconsistent in these models. Next, I return to the issue of alternative specifications of democracy.

Gleditsch and Ward (1997) urged scholars to move beyond discrete classification of "democracy" or "autocracy" and to focus more on the subdimensions of the concept of democracy after empirically demonstrating that the components of the Polity measure are primarily driven by its executive constraint dimension, and that the other dimensions, which measure patterns of executive recruitment and the extent and competitiveness of participation dimensions, are "not especially powerful in determining the degree of democracy" (380). Studies of political repression do not use the Polity data as a dependent variable, nor do they typically use the data to divide countries into two discrete categories; instead, as I have done above, I use the index to control for the level of political democracy attained in the country. Nonetheless, Keith (2002a) followed Gleditsch and Ward's suggestion and tested the four components of the Polity democracy measure separately; two of the components produced statistically significant relationships: *Constraint on the Chief Executive* and the *Competitiveness of Political Participation*. While Ward and Gleditsch's analysis revealed that the Polity democracy measure was largely driven by executive constraint, Keith found the competitiveness of political participation to be a more powerful explanator. As a next step in my analyses, I re-estimated the model, disaggregating the democracy measure. My initial analyses found that the competitiveness of executive competition was too highly correlated with executive constraint and competitiveness of competition, and the subsequent preliminary analysis with the subdimension revealed it to be repeatedly insignificant statistically; so I chose to estimate only three of the sub-dimensions within the standard models here. The coefficients and standard errors for the democracy measures are presented in Table 3.3; the other coefficients remained identical with the previous models, so for ease presentation I do not report them here. As with Keith (2002a), I find that executive constraints and competiveness of political participation are the driving influences within the Polity measure on state repression. The two coefficients are statistically significant across all eight models. In these analyses, as in Keith (2002a), the competiveness of political participation produces the largest effect on state repression: a maximum improvement in competiveness of political participation would associated with a .21 decrease in the level of personal integrity abuse, using the Amnesty International–based PTS fixed-effects model as an example. The coefficient of -.05 for executive constraints suggests that a change from no constraints on the executive to a system in which the executive has parity with the legislative or judicial branch would be associated with a .20 change in the level of personal integrity abuse. The coefficient for openness of recruitment is significant only in the Department of State–based models and the civil liberties models.

In the civil liberties fixed-effects model, a maximum change in executive constraint would be associated with a .36 change in the 7-point scale, and a maximum change in the competiveness of political participation would be associated with a .45 change in the scale. A maximum change in the openness of executive recruitment would be associated with a .17 decrease in civil

Table 3.3. Disaggregated Democracy and Political Repression, 1980–2005

	Personal Integrity Rights Abuse (PTS-SD) 1980–2005		*Personal Integrity Rights Abuse (PTS-AI) 1980–2005*		*Personal Integrity Rights Abuse (CIR) 1982–2005*		*Civil Liberties Restrictions (Freedom House) 1980–2005*	
	Fixed Effects (1)	*Ordered Probit (2)*	*Fixed Effects (3)*	*Ordered Probit (4)*	*Fixed Effects (5)*	*Ordered Probit (6)*	*Fixed Effects (7)*	*Ordered Probit (8)*
Constraint on the Chief Executive	–.03 (.02)**	–.04 (.02)***	–.05 (.02)***	–.04 (.02)**	–.09 (.05)***	–.03 (.03)*	–.09 (.02)***	–.26 (.06)***
Openness of Executive Recruitment	–.10 (.07)*	–.09 (.07)*	–.01 (.09)	–.01 (.07)	–.05 (.18)	–.03 (.07)	–.17 (.08)**	–.26 (.06)***
Competitiveness of Political Participation	–.05 (.03)*	–.17 (.03)***	–.07 (.04)**	–.19 (.04)***	–.12 (.07)**	–.21 (.03)***	–.15 (.03)***	–.45 (.06)***

Full standard models estimated. Only disaggregated democracy coefficients reported. *Significant at the 10 percent level. **Significant at the 5 percent level. ***Significant at the 1 percent level.

liberties restrictions. The combined effect associated with a maximum change in these three components of political democracy would be approximately 1 point on the 7-point Freedom House civil liberties scale. The size of the effects is somewhat smaller than those produced by the coefficient for the aggregated measure (.11), with a maximum change producing a decrease of 1.10 points. The combined effect associated with a maximum change in the statistically significant two components of political democracy would be associated with a change of -.41 on the 5-point Amnesty-based PTS scale, and the three components would also be associated with a change of -.41. The size of the associated effects is approximately the same as in the effects of the coefficient for the aggregated measure in these models as well.

The work of Davenport and Armstrong (2004), and subsequently Bueno de Mesquita et al. (2005), suggests that there is also a threshold effect at work in the level of political democracy. I address that possibility next. As noted in Chapter 2, most studies of repression tend to assume a linear association between democracy and repression. Recent theoretical and empirical work suggests that these sometimes unstated assumptions do not accurately reflect the true relationship between democracy and repression. Davenport and Armstrong argue that the relationship between democracy and repression has been misspecified and that a threshold effect is a more accurate characterization. Specifically, Davenport and Armstrong argue that from this perspective, until there is a particular combination of institutions and behavioral factors in place, authorities will not be compelled to respect human rights. Below this critical point, the constraints are not comprehensive or severe enough to deter repressive action, nor are the social control mechanisms well enough situated to provide viable alternatives for state repression. As these institutions and behavioral patterns gain strength beyond some threshold and the country's overall level of democracy increases, however, the repressive behavior used by authorities should decrease. Above the critical point, constraints become too significant to ignore, and democracy functions as an acceptable substitute for influencing citizens (2004, 542).

Davenport and Armstrong's (2004) extensive statistical examination demonstrated that we might best conceptualize democracy in three distinct categories, each of which was shown to have a different effect: (1) no or low level of democracy (values of 0–7 on the Polity Index), which has no effect; (2) an intermediate category (values of 8–9 on the Polity Index), which has some negative effect on state repression; and (3) highest level of democracy (10 on the Polity Index), which has a strong negative effect (548). Davenport and Armstrong conclude that the influence of this trichotomized measure of democracy is linear in nature; however, they caution that "it should not be forgotten that underlying this influence is the non-linear threshold effect" (549). Table 3.4 re-estimates the models utilizing their operationalization of this trichotomy. I score category 1 values as 0, category 2 values as 1, and category 3 values as 2. Re-estimating the model very slightly reduced the size of the other coefficients in the model, with the exception of the military regime variable, whose influence seems to be clarified somewhat with the more appropriate delineation of democracy's influence. Table 3.4 reports only the coefficients for the trichotomized democracy measure, along with those for the military regimes variable. All eight of the democracy coefficients continue to be highly statistically significant, and the size of the coefficients is approximately five times as large, a result that is not surprising given that we have reduced the matrix of the scale from an 11-point scale to a 3-point scale. In the State Department–based PTS fixed-effects model in Table 3.2, we saw that a maximum increase in the level of democracy would produce a .40 change in the level of state repression; this effect assumes a uniform .04 improvement with each step up the democracy scale. Davenport and Armstrong's more appropriately conceptualized measure suggests that only when a state moves across the threshold into level 8 or higher on the democracy scale will we expect the state to have a decrease in repression—a .09 decrease for each unit increase in the 3-point index. Thus, the overall impact of democracy remains somewhat smaller, and its impact begins only when the state crosses the identified thresholds.

In improving the operationalization of the democracy, we clarify the effect of the military regime measure, which presumably no longer shares as much variance with the democracy measure. The coefficients are now highly statistically significant across all six personal integrity abuse models, whereas previously the coefficients were significant in only one of the models. In addition, the size of the military regime coefficients increases substantially in each of these models, usually doubling or even quadrupling in size. Overall, then, the use of the corrected democracy measure not only clarifies our interpretation of democracy's impact; it also refines one of the somewhat problematic specifications of the standard model of repression.

The work of Bueno de Mesquita et al. (2005) simultaneously addresses the aggregation issue demonstrated by Keith (2002a) and the threshold issue demonstrated by Davenport and Armstrong (2004) in regard to democracy's influence on state repression. Their exhaustive analyses continue to dem-

Table 3.4. Trichotomized Democracy and Political Repression, 1980–2005

	Personal Integrity Rights Abuse (PTS-SD) 1980–2005		*Personal Integrity Rights Abuse (PTS-AI) 1980–2005*		*Personal Integrity Rights Abuse (CIRI) 1982–2005*		*Civil Liberties Restrictions (Freedom House) 1980–2005*	
	Fixed Effects (1)	*Ordered Probit (2)*	*Fixed Effects (3)*	*Ordered Probit (4)*	*Fixed Effects (5)*	*Ordered Probit (6)*	*Fixed Effects (7)*	*Ordered Probit (8)*
Trichotomized Democracy	–.19**	–.40***	–.12**	–.38***	–.26***	–.37***	–.20***	–.61***
	(.05)	(.04)	(.05)	(.04)	(.09)	(.04)	(.07)	(.06)
Military Regime	.11***	.11***	.12***	.10***	.34***	.08**	.05	.03
	(.06)	(.05)	(.0)	(.06)	(.13)	(.06)	(.05)	(.07)

Full standard models estimated. Only disaggregated democracy coefficients reported. *Significant at the 10 percent level. **Significant at the 5 percent level. ***Significant at the 1 percent level.

onstrate the significance of the individual components of democracy, and they confirm especially the critical nature of the accountability dimension's effect on state repression posited by the human rights literature. In addition they demonstrate, not surprisingly, that the components of democracy also have a sharp threshold effect, and conclude that "real improvements in human rights do not occur smoothly but reflect a discontinuous step function achieved only when a society becomes fully democratic" (453). While they emphasize that none of the dimensions can be ignored, they note that "not all dimensions of democracy contribute equally to reductions in human rights abuses," and they find, as Keith (2002a) did, that party competition is the most important component in reducing state repression (456). I follow these authors, and re-estimate the model with the disaggregated democracy components, adding threshold dummy variables that delineate whether the state has or has not reached the maximum level of that component. Because the openness of executive recruitment has only values of 0 or 1, we need not create a threshold measure for it.

These models turned out to be somewhat problematic. First, the disaggregated components are highly correlated with the threshold dummy variables, especially when lagged—this collinearity is not surprising, given that the categories are mere 3- or 4-point scales. Second, I found consistent substantive differences between the fixed effects and ordered probit models. For example, in each of the four fixed-effects models, regardless of lags, the party competition threshold is positive and statistically insignificant, and in each of the probit models without fixed effects the coefficient is negative and statistically significant. This effect holds even when only threshold variables and not the disaggregated components are in the models. Table 3.5 reports the model with no lags, as the correlations are within more acceptable ranges when the variables are not lagged. The disaggregated components produce coefficients that perform as they did in the previous models. The executive constraints threshold dummy coefficient is statistically significant in only one model—the Amnesty International ordered probit model without fixed effects. The executive competition threshold dummy coefficient does not achieve statistical significance in any model. As noted above, the party competition dummy coefficients are statistically significant in the probit models only for the personal integrity measures, and the same is true in the civil liberties model. As a whole I believe Davenport and Armstrong's delineation proves more satisfactory than the disaggregated measures and the thresholds for the disaggregated measures. It performs consistently across all models

Table 3.5. Disaggregated Democracy with Threshold Effects and Political Repression, 1980–2005

	Personal Integrity Rights Abuse (PTS-SD) 1980–2005		*Personal Integrity Rights Abuse (PTS-AI) 1980–2005*		*Personal Integrity Rights Abuse (CIRI) 1982–2005*		*Civil Liberties Restrictions (Freedom House) 1980–2005*	
	Fixed Effects (1)	*Ordered Probit (2)*	*Fixed Effects (3)*	*Ordered Probit (4)*	*Fixed Effects (5)*	*Ordered Probit (6)*	*Fixed Effects (7)*	*Ordered Probit (8)*
Constraint on the Chief Executive	–.04 (.03)*	–.06 (.03)**	–.04 (. 03)*	–.04 (.04)	–.09 (.07)*	–.05 (.03)**	–.10 (.03)***	–.22 (.04)***
Openness of Executive Recruitment	–.10 (.08)*	–.11 (.06)**	–.01 (.08)	–.02 (.06)	–.07 (.18)	–.05 (.07)	–.15 (.08)**	–.26 (.07)***
Competitiveness of Political Participation	–.06 (.03)**	–.03 (.04)	–.10 (.04)***	–.10 (.04)***	–.12 (.09)*	–.08 (.04)***	–.17 (.04)***	–.27 (.05)***
Executive Constraint Threshold Dummy	–.02 (.08)	–.10 (.09)	–.10 (.09)	–.23 (.07)***	–.12 (.19)	–.05 (.08)	.07 (.08)	.07 (.11)
Executive Competition Threshold Dummy	.05 (.05)	.16 (.08)	.05 (.06)	.22 (.07)	.10 (.14)	.15 (.07)	–.03 (.05)	–.01 (.08)
Participation Competition Threshold Dummy	.01 (.14)	–.76 (.11)***	.11 (.17)	–.55 (.11)***	–.11 (.20)	–.61 (.10)***	.16 (.09)	–.32 (.12)***

Full standard models estimated. Only disaggregated democracy coefficients reported. *Significant at the 10 percent level. **Significant at the 5 percent level. ***Significant at the 1 percent level.

of both categories of repression, regardless of estimation technique. In the subsequent analyses I use their trichotomous measure in the base model.

Conclusions

In this chapter I have extended the standard model across time, examining almost three decades of state behavior across two categories of repression—the narrower and more egregious personal integrity abuse and the broader, perhaps less severe civil liberties restriction—employing multiple indicators of each of category of rights. While the analyses have demonstrated that the standard model continues to hold quite well for personal integrity abuse, I have clarified some relationships in the personal integrity model. And while the model generally holds for the repression of civil liberties, it does so only with the hypotheses postulated by Keith (2002a) in regard to leftist regimes and Davenport (2007b) in regard to military regimes. This model continues to demonstrate that a government's decisions to employ repression against personal integrity rights are most affected by the threat of civil war, while the decision to repress civil liberties is most influenced by regime type, which can reflect both structural constraints (or lack of constraints) and ideological or normative preferences. Threats do influence both forms of repression, but restrictions on civil liberties are inconsistently influenced by civil war, depending upon the particular type of liberty at stake, and the magnitude of their impact is substantially lower than in personal integrity abuses. International war consistently influences repression of personal integrity rights, but its impact is much smaller than that of civil war, presumably because the theater of international war may be far removed from the belligerent's physical territory, and thus pose a less proximate threat, at least in the short term. The influence of international war on civil liberties restrictions is inconsistent, increasing only the repression of speech/press and freedom of religion. While the impact on speech and press seems logical, its impact on religious freedom and civil war's failure to influence only religious freedom seems somewhat counter to logic, as civil wars would be more likely to trigger to cultural differences. I continue to explore the threat dimension in Chapter 6.

Regime type exerts considerable influence upon state decisions to repress its citizens. Regime type can represent structural features (free and fair elections in democracy) that impose a cost on the selection of some items within the state's menu of policy options, or they can represent a particular set of values through which decisionmakers assess the appropriateness of the behavior to be placed on the menu of options. The finding that military regimes are more likely to employ personal integrity abuse and less likely to employ restrictions on civil liberties supports Davenport's (2007b) overall assessment that military regimes are less likely to repress civil liberties "because they tend to avoid involving themselves with the political processes which are normally responsible for these repressive activities (i.e., legislatures and courts)" but are more likely to "use repressive techniques which are more directly within the realm of their expertise—physical violence" (500), which would clearly include repression of personal integrity rights.

My study sheds some light on the long-standing controversy over whether the inconsistent findings regarding the influence of leftist regimes on political repression reflect a Department of State bias. While it has been argued that "the tenets of Marxist-Leninist theory about the need for a dictatorship of the proletariat" would suggest that Marxist-Leninist regimes may be more inclined toward repression (Poe and Tate 1994, 858), my results support Keith's (2002a) further explanation that in these regimes, control of society and personal freedoms has often been so complete that the regime might be less likely to need to engage in these more severe abuses of personal integrity rights, which is exactly what I find—along with finding that these regimes are more likely to control a broad range of citizen behavior of the sort that might reduce the need to employ more severe forms of repression, such as those measured by personal integrity abuse, which also supports Davenport's (2007b) findings.

In this chapter I have also examined multiple specifications of democracy. Davenport and Armstrong's (2004) trichotomous measure, which ultimately reflects the threshold effect they found, performs most consistently, demonstrating a moderate effect in every single model I tested, regardless of the type of repression or the estimation method. Keith's (2002a) disaggregated specification performed consistently across all models, but ultimately does not account for a threshold effect. When Bueno de Mesquita et al.'s (2005) threshold dummy variables were utilized in conjunction with the disaggregated components, less than half of the threshold effects were statistically significant. In subsequent chapters I employ in the base model the more consistently performing trichotomous measure, which seems to clarify the relationship of military regimes. As for the standard set of indicators that delineate economic development or resource constraints, these factors continue to be somewhat inconsistent in terms of statistical significance, but not enough to dismiss completely, despite the minimal substantive impact of some. The population indicators clearly suggest that regimes consistently respond to resource constraints in regard to repression of personal integrity rights, although the influence is less clear in regard to civil liberties restrictions, once fixed effects are controlled. Economic development and growth produce such minimal and inconsistent effects that I am tempted to drop them from the model, but ultimately I consider that them to be a significant potential control. I have dropped the British colonial variable from the model because of its consistent failure. Instead I will attempt to examine the impact of a legal system, which may better capture a substantive dimension of colonial legacy.

The standard model captures a significant but limited set of factors related to both agent and structure that constrain or facilitate a regime's decision to repress or that delineate between the choices of the appropriate form of repression to employ. The model has significant limitations, despite its strong explanatory power. It focuses primarily on domestic factors and includes only one factor that represents the international context and none that represent potentially important transnational influences, such as trade or foreign investment, embeddedness in global society, state formal commitment to international law or domestic law, or the role of INGOs. The model also fails to account for other domestic institutions, such as the judiciary, which when independent may potentially constrain a regime's resort to repression. In addition, the factors demonstrated to influence state level and type of repression in the standard model are largely difficult to manipulate, at least in the short term. In the next chapter I turn specifically to the role of the judiciary in facilitating or constraining a state's choice to repress its citizens.

Chapter 4

Political Repression and the Role of the Judiciary

The independence of the judiciary was largely undermined by the order by General Musharraf in January 2000 that Pakistani judges take a fresh oath of loyalty to his administration. In May 2000, the Supreme Court, reconstituted after the dismissal of six judges who refused the oath, upheld General Musharraf's military coup of 1999, under the doctrine of state necessity. (Seiderman 2002, 270)

Despite political progress [in the Democratic Republic of Congo] towards a democratic state based on the rule of law, ongoing violence has hampered the effectiveness of the judicial system. A new Transitional Constitution providing for the independence of the judiciary was promulgated on 4 April 2003. However, the judiciary's situation is still worrying, since impunity is the norm, and corruption and interference by the executive are widespread. In 2003 and 2004, 1,700 magistrates were intermittently on strike demanding the effective independence of the judiciary. Attacks against lawyers have continued to occur regularly. (Ibid., 1)

Judicial institutions in Sierra Leone are moribund or almost completely ineffective as a consequence of a

> devastating civil war dating from 1991. Judges are poorly resourced and often ill-trained. The expectations for State institutions which arose following the 1999 peace agreement by rebels and pro-governmental forces in 1999 have yet to be realized. (Ibid., 321)

> With his accession to power as Amir [of Bahrain] in March 1999, Sheikh Hamad began an unprecedented process of political reform. In a 2001 open national referendum, the population voted overwhelmingly in favour of a new National Charter calling for the establishment of a constitutional monarchy, respectful of the principles of separation of powers and the rule of law, and the establishment of a Constitutional Court. The National Charter also provides for a legislative system consisting of two chambers, including one with legislative attributes, to be elected directly and freely by the citizens by 2003. The most remarkable development related to the judiciary in Bahrain was the abolition of both the Decree Law on State Security Measures and the State Security Court Measures. In 2000, a Supreme Council of the Judiciary was established for the first time. (Ibid., 41)

Increasing attention is given to the concept of judicial independence by international lawyers, academics, and aid organizations interested in the rule of law, democratization, and/or states' human rights behavior. This association between an independent judiciary and rights protection is not a new one. Alexis de Tocqueville in his *Democracy in America* noted that an independent judiciary empowered with judicial review is "one of the most powerful barriers erected against the tyranny of political assemblies" (1966, 261). The current focus on judicial independence and rights protection has largely stemmed from the renewed emphasis on constitutionalism in the democratizing world of the post-Cold War era. As Russell (2001) notes, within the general trend toward liberal democracy in the world today, judicial independence is viewed as an "essential feature of liberal democracy" (2); and as Ginsburg (2003) notes, the power of judicial review now forms part of the "script" of modernity, like presidencies and legislatures (26).[1] This connection with rights protection is accepted by many scholars, such as Ackerman (1991), who argues that an independent judiciary is "the ultimate guarantor of constitutionalism," and by organizations such as the American Bar Association, whose Code of Judicial Conduct states that an "independent and honorable judiciary is indispensable to justice in our society" (as cited in Ramseyer 1994, 721). Larkins (1996) goes even further, arguing that judicial independence is "not meaningful if the courts cannot exercise it to check the arbitrary or unjust exercise of power by political and social actors" (611). In addition, the United States Agency for International Development (USAID 2002) links U.S. democracy and governance assistance to the promotion of rule-of-law principles, which include respect for human rights protected in part through judicial independence. More broadly, international legal scholars such as Steiner and Alston (1996) recognize that an independent judiciary is "the essential guardian of the rule of law" (711); and international financial institutions such as the Inter-American Development Bank argue that "without judicial independence, there is no rule of law" (Jarquin and Carillo 1998, vii). Most of these expectations are based on the assumption that an independent judiciary should be able to withstand incursions upon fundamental rights because (1) the courts' authority and institutional well-being are formally delineated and protected, (2) the courts have some ability to review the actions of other agencies of government, and (3) judges' jobs are constitutionally secured.

These expectations are not universal. There are skeptics (especially in regard to Latin American and African courts) who doubt that judges on the bench will be inclined or able to challenge a dictatorial regime, and skeptics who fear that an overly independent judiciary can be as abusive in its exercise of power as the legislative or executive branches (for example, Moderne 1990; Frühling 1993; Prempeh 1999; Prillaman 2000; Mutua 2001; Russell 2001; Hilbink 2007). Some skeptics point to our "propensity to confuse legal prerequisites with reality" (Clark 1975, 426–27) or point out that while formal judicial or legal systems may be "universalistic and egalitarian," true commitment to equality under the law is actually quite superficial (Rosenn 1987, 35). Other skeptics include rational-choice proponents such as Ramseyer (1994; see also Ramseyer and Rasmussen 2003), who counters such optimism by observing that "independent judiciaries are not common to freedom-loving countries everywhere," and in fact, he argues, they "are not as likely as we hope," because the willingness of the legislature to keep the judiciary independent depends upon the expected electoral fortunes of politicians in power (722). Scholars within the strategic approach, such as McNollgast (2006) and Tiede (2006), argue that "judicial independence is not the automatic result of constitutional or statutory provisions that establish tenure for judges, nor is judicial independence limited by checks and balances or legal traditions," but "rather, judicial independence waxes and wanes with changes in the political composition" of the branches of government (McNollgast 2006, 108). Historian Bernard Schwartz's cautionary assessment of the rule of law in the U.S. context reflects the broader skepticism in the global context, especially in regard to formal mechanisms of judicial independence:

> [We] too often forget that the rule of law draws only limited strength from judicial guarantees; it must have its roots far deeper than a formal fundamental document and decisions of judges enforcing it. Our public law depends for its efficacy on popular acceptance of its basic presuppositions. Acceptance, rather than formal legal machinery, is the decisive force in the law's implementation. With Learned Hand in a famous passage, we may "wonder whether we do not rest our hopes too much upon constitutions, upon laws and upon courts. These are false hopes, believe me, these are false hopes." (1993, 126)

Scholars such as Russell (2001) do not dismiss the realism espoused by skeptics but rather argue that none of it justifies abandoning the principle or ideal of judicial independence. Instead Russell declares that "the job of the political scientist who believes in liberal democracy is to figure out what kinds of independence it is most essential to maintain" (11). I take on Russell's challenge in this chapter, and seek to determine the dimensions of judicial independence that matter most in reducing the likelihood of state repression of human rights, and to determine the conditions under which they work best.

Social scientists who study state repression have only lately examined the issue of the judiciary's role in curbing political repression as an empirical one. The small body of large-*N* cross-national research examining the role of courts has produced mostly mixed results, which suggest that the optimistic expectations may be somewhat naïve but not totally without substance (Blasi and Cingranelli 1996; Keith 2002b, 2004; Howard and Carey 2004; Apodaca 2004; Powell and Staton 2009; Keith, Tate, and Poe 2009). The most pessimistic findings have been those on the effect of formal provisions of judicial independence on personal integrity rights (Keith, Tate, and Poe 2009); however, other studies have demonstrated more optimistic results in regard to a broader set of civil liberties (Keith 2002b) and basic needs rights (Apodaca 2004). With only a few exceptions have these studies of repression examined the actual achieved levels of judicial independence rather than mere formal promises. Cross (1999) found that *de facto* judicial independence decreased the likelihood of unreasonable searches and increased the protection of political rights. Unfortunately, his measure of judicial independence is the subjective rating of the late Charles Humana, which provides no replicable operationalization of the concept of judicial independence. In addition, the study is limited to a small, not fully representative sample of countries. Howard and Carey (2004) present the first systematic replicable measure of *de facto* judicial independence that is available for the global set of countries, and their findings, while limited to seven years, support those of Cross (1999), suggesting that higher levels of judicial independence are associated with higher levels of political rights. None of these studies has been able to control for the possibility that many of the factors associated with state use of political repression are likely to be those associated with the dependent variable—adopting constitutional provisions for judicial independence or achieved levels of judicial independence. In other words, it is not possible to determine whether the effects of formal judicial independence on state repression found in Cross' study were the result of the conditions or circumstances that made the state likely to adopt constitutional provisions in the first place or whether they were the consequence of formal independence itself. I follow Abouharb and Cingranelli (2008) and model these selection effects in my analyses.

In this chapter I empirically test competing approaches that seek to explain why states adopt formal provisions of judicial independence. I then examine the question whether these formal provisions affect the levels of achieved judicial independence, controlling for selection effects. I believe these are the first systematic cross-national empirical examinations of either of these questions. Next I create explanatory models of state repression that examine the effect of achieved judicial independence, while controlling for selection effects. I also examine the role of civil society groups and their interaction with the judiciary in forming "judicial networks," as suggested by Moustafa's (2007) work. And I investigate the cultural influence of legal systems, as well as other potential colonial legacies. I find substantial evidence to suggest that the optimists' expectations concerning judicial independence are not misplaced in regard to either form of political repression. Judicial independence matters.

Conceptualizing Judicial Independence

Some scholars, even those who deem judicial independence to be an essential feature of liberal democracy, argue that there is little agreement on just what this condition is or on what kind or how much of it is required for a liberal democratic regime (Russell 2001, 1). Others such as Larkins (1996) claim that judicial independence "may be one of the least understood concepts in the fields of political science and law." Larkins also points out that "on some level, as Theodore Becker (1970) noted more than thirty-five years ago, we all know what it means, yet its full significance, intricacies, and implications still seem beyond our reach" (607). Kornhauser (2002) goes so far as to argue that "the confusion over the meaning of judicial independence cannot be eliminated," and thus "judicial independence is not a useful, analytic concept" (45). I do not accept this extreme assertion but rather believe that despite the variation in definitions or conceptualization of the elements of judicial independence, there is significant agreement on its basic principles. Indeed, globally there has been substantial movement, as I will show below, toward formally adopting these principles.

In the political science and law literature there is substantial conceptual overlap in defining judicial independence, with most scholars building upon Becker's 1970 definition:

> (a) the degree to which judges believe they can decide and do decide consistent with their own personal attitudes, values and conceptions of the judicial role (in their interpretation of the law), (b) in opposition to what others, who have or are believed to have political or judicial power, think about or desire in like matters, and (c) particularly when a decision adverse to the beliefs or desires of those with political or judicial power may bring some retribution on the judges personally or on the power of the court. (144)

Rosenn (1987) suggests that Becker's definition needs further refinement and recommends broadening its scope and simplifying the language. He then offers his revised definition of judicial independence: "the degree to which judges actually decide cases in accordance with their own determination of the evidence, law and justice, free from coercion, blandishments, interference, or threats of government authorities or private citizens" (7). The definition put forth by Ferejohn, Rosenbluth, and Shipan (2004) is similar to Becker's and Rosenn's; they say: "We take judicial independence to mean court autonomy from other actors," and they further delineate it, saying that "to the extent that a court is able to make decisions free of influence from other political actors, and to pursue its goals without having to worry about the consequences from other institutions, it is independent" (3). Other scholars (such as Cameron 2002; McNollgast 2006; Tiede 2006; Powell and Staton 2009) argue that the conceptualization of judicial independence should extend beyond the decision-making stage to include the *implementation* of judicial policy without undue interference from other political actors.

Some scholars define judicial independence by specifically parsing the definition into categories or its core dimensions. Rosenn's (1987) examination of Latin American judiciaries produces two broad but somewhat overlapping categories: protection of the judicial decision-making process from outside pressures and protection of the personal independence of the judge. He identifies the common structural measures that seek to insure independence in each of the categories. Dimensions of judicial independence related to protecting the integrity of judicial decisions include (1) guaranteed noninterference with judicial proceedings, (2) jurisdictional monopoly (no special tribunals), (3) requirement of a reasoned opinion, and (4) requirement of public trials. Measures protecting personal independence include (1) irreducibility of salaries, (2) guaranteeing the judiciary a fixed percentage of the budget, (3) protected tenure in office, (4) specified and transparent selection and reappointment processes, (5) protected transferability of judges, (6) avoidance of conflicts of interest, and (7) judicial immunity.

Larkins (1996) defines judicial independence as "the existence of judges who are not manipulated for political gain, who are impartial toward the parties of a dispute, and who form a judicial branch which has the power as an institution to regulate the legality of government behavior, enact 'neutral' justice, and determine significant constitutional and legal values" (611). He posits three dimensions similar to Rosenn's: impartiality,[2] insularity, and scope of authority (609). The first two he identifies from within the literature and notes that they are obviously linked to the goal of the judiciary's being a neutral third party: (1) impartiality requires that judges base their decisions on law and facts, not on a predilection toward one of the litigants (Fiss 1993; Shapiro 1981); and (2) political insularity requires that judges not be used as tools to further political aims or punished for preventing their realization (Clark 1975; Rosenn 1987; Fiss 1993). He notes that impartiality is difficult to identify and that political insularity is typically achieved through widely accepted formal and structural safeguards such as life tenure and protected salary. He adds a third component: the scope of the judiciary's authority as an institution, which he describes as "the relationship of the courts to other parts of the political system and society and *the extent to which they are collectively seen as a legitimate body for the determination of right and wrong, legal and illegal*" (610).[3]

Russell (2001) also synthesizes the literature, noting that in political science, judicial independence basically encompasses two concepts: the autonomy of judges, both collectively and individually from other institutions and individuals; and judicial behavior, by which he means the individual judge's capacity for independent thought and judgment (6). He notes that the two concepts are closely related in that one is the means to the other; we want judges to enjoy a high measure of autonomy so that they can think and act independently rather than being controlled or influenced by other actors (6). Russell ultimately argues that judicial independence does not refer to a single lack of dependence but, rather, is best understood as two-dimensional, having both an external dimension (all those forces outside the judiciary itself that can encroach on the autonomy of the judiciary collectively or individually) and an internal dimension (sources of influence and control within the judiciary itself). He also argues that in terms of the sources of dependency, external controls and influences must be distinguished from those that are internal, and that in terms of the targets of influence or control, the individual judge must be distinguished from the judiciary as a collective whole or institution. He confirms that the external dimension is the most widely recognized dimension, as it embraces the principle of separation of powers (11).

While the dimensions of judicial independence conceptualized by each of these scholars and others do not fit together perfectly, we can see a common-core across them that allows us to identify two somewhat overlapping sets of distinctions. The first is the distinction between (1) institutional (or collective) independence from the other branches or private and public actors and (2) the independence of individual judges from the same influences. The independence of the individual judges is further distinguished by the source of influences or dependence, which can lie in either external sources (other branches or outside actors) or internal sources within the judiciary itself.

The next task is to identify the principal elements or standards that would be closely linked to the concept of judicial independence and that yield suggestions as to how the concept can be effectively operationalized. International organizations such as the International Bar Association and the United Nations have set forth minimum standards or basic principles of judicial independence, which I believe represent substantial consensus in the international legal community on the priorities for shaping structural safeguards for the judiciary.

Elements of Judicial Independence

The International Bar Association adopted a set of minimum standards in 1983. The New Delhi standards, as they are called, set forth only *minimum expectations* rather than ideals, as Justice King (1984) notes. They identified essential standards for personal and substantive independence of the individual justice and, to a lesser degree, standards for collective and institutional independence. They included such standards as guaranteed terms and protected salaries and fiscal autonomy for the judicial branch. More usefully, the United Nations General Assembly adopted in 1985 a set of basic principles that I argue now best represent international consensus on what the basic elements of judicial independence are or should be; therefore, I base my measures on these conceptualizations. The UN recommendations are outlined in two documents: *Basic Principles on the Independence of the Judiciary* (1985) and the 1995 report by Dato' Param Cumaraswamy, the UN special rapporteur on the independence of judges and lawyers. Both documents explicitly call for formal enshrinement of the principles of judicial independence in written constitutions or law.

The UN Basic Principles are as follows:

1. The independence of the judiciary shall be guaranteed by the State and enshrined in the Constitution or the law of the country. It is the duty of all governmental and other institutions to respect and observe the independence of the judiciary.

2. The judiciary shall decide matters before them impartially, on the basis of facts and in accordance with the law, without any restrictions, improper influences, inducements, pressures, threats or interferences, direct or indirect, from any quarter or for any reason.
3. The judiciary shall have jurisdiction over all issues of a judicial nature and shall have exclusive authority to decide whether an issue submitted for its decision is within its competence as defined by law.
4. There shall not be any inappropriate or unwarranted interference with the judicial process, nor shall judicial decisions by the courts be subject to revision. This principle is without prejudice to judicial review or to mitigation or commutation by competent authorities of sentences imposed by the judiciary, in accordance with the law.
5. Everyone shall have the right to be tried by ordinary courts or tribunals using established legal procedures. Tribunals that do not use the duly established procedures of the legal process shall not be created to displace the jurisdiction belonging to the ordinary courts or judicial tribunals.
6. The principle of the independence of the judiciary entitles and requires the judiciary to ensure that judicial proceedings are conducted fairly and that the rights of the parties are respected.
7. It is the duty of each Member State to provide adequate resources to enable the judiciary to properly perform its functions. (United Nations 1985)

The special rapporteur's principles are as follows:

(1) All necessary measures should be taken to respect, protect, and promote the independence of judges.

(2) In particular, the following measures should be taken:

  (a) The independence of judges should be guaranteed pursuant to the provisions of the Convention and the constitutional principles, for example by inserting specific provisions in the constitutions or other legislation or incorporating the provisions of this recommendation in internal law. Subject to the legal tradition of each State, such rules may provide, for instance, the following:

    (i) decisions of judges should not be subject to any revision outside any appeals procedures as provided by law;

(ii) the terms of office of judges and their remuneration should be guaranteed by law;
(iii) no organ other than the courts themselves should decide on its own competence, as defined by law;
(iv) with the exception of decisions on amnesty, pardon or similar, the Government or the administration should not be able to take any decision which invalidates judicial decisions retroactively;

(b) The executive and legislative powers should ensure that judges are independent and that steps are not taken which could endanger the independence of judges.

(c) All decisions concerning the professional careers of judges should be based on objective criteria and the selection and career of judges should be based on merit, having regard to qualifications, integrity, ability and efficiency. The authority taking the decision on the selection and career of judges should be independent of government and administration. In order to safeguard its independence, rules should ensure that, for instance, its members are selected by the judiciary and that the authority decides itself on its procedural rules.

However, where the constitutional or legal provisions and traditions allow judges to be appointed by government, there should be guarantees to ensure that the procedures to appoint judges are transparent and independent in practice and that the decisions will not be influenced by any reasons other than those related to the objective criteria mentioned above. These guarantees could be, for example, one or more of the following:
(i) special independent and competent body to give the Government advice which it follows in practice; or
(ii) the right for an individual to appeal against a decision to an independent authority; or
(iii) the authority which makes the decision safeguards against undue or improper influences.

(d) In the decision-making process, judges should be independent and be able to act without any restrictions, improper influence, inducements, pressures, threats or interferences, direct or indirect, from any quarter or for any reason. The law should provide for sanctions against persons seeking to influence judges in any such manner. Judges should have unfettered freedom to decide cases impartially, in accordance with their conscience and their interpretation of the facts, and in pursuance of the prevailing rules of the law. Judges should not be obliged to report on the merits of their cases to anyone outside the judiciary.

(e) The distribution of cases should not be influenced by the wishes of any party to a case or any person concerned with the results of the case. Such distribution may, for instance, be made by drawing lots or a system for automatic distribution according to alphabetical order or some similar system.

(f) A case should not be withdrawn from a particular judge without valid reasons, such as cases of serious illness or conflict of interest. Any such reasons and the procedures for such withdrawal should be provided for by law and may not be influenced by any interest of the Government or administration. A decision to withdraw a case from a judge should be taken by an authority which enjoys the same judicial independence as judges.

(3) Judges, whether appointed or elected, shall have guaranteed tenure until a mandatory retirement age or the expiry of their term of office, where such exists. (United Nations 1995, 9–10)

There is considerable overlap in the principles discussed in these two documents, but the UN's Basic Principles appear to be broader than the special rapporteur's principles. They go beyond listing the formal attributes of an independent judiciary to prescribing certain actions that the judiciary *should* take—specifically, that the judiciary should ensure fair trials and should protect individual rights. For now I limit my analysis to the key formal provisions that the UN suggests will produce an independent judiciary.

Merging the two sets of UN principles produces the following criteria for an independent judiciary:

1. (a) Terms of office and (b) remuneration are constitutionally guaranteed, regardless of whether judges are appointed or elected.
2. The decisions of judges are not to be subject to any revision outside any appeals procedures as provided by law.
3. The courts have exclusive authority to decide on their own competence, as defined by law—their decisions are made without any restrictions,

improper influences, inducements, pressures, threats, or interference, direct or indirect, from any quarter or for any reason.

4. The courts have jurisdiction over all issues of a judicial nature. This criterion seems to relate to the criterion that everyone shall have the right to be tried by ordinary courts or tribunals using established legal procedures. This criterion could be condensed to the requirement that civilians not be tried in military courts or exceptional courts.
5. The courts must have adequate resources.
6. The executive and legislative powers should ensure that judges are independent and that steps are not taken that could endanger the independence of judges. This criterion could be condensed to the formal separation of powers of the branches of government.
7. The selection and career of judges should be based on merit: qualifications, integrity, ability, and efficiency. The authority taking the decision on the selection and career of judges should be independent of government and administration. If the constitutional or legal provisions and traditions allow judges to be appointed by government, there should be guarantees to ensure that the procedures to appoint judges are transparent and independent in practice and that the decisions are based on the above criteria.

The first element seeks to protect individual judges from possible professional and personal retribution from the other branches of government. It also attempts to limit improper influences generally that might interfere with judicial impartiality. The next two elements, finality of decisions and exclusive authority, are aimed at safeguarding judges' ability to carry out their functions fully without incursions from other state actors, and the elements are intended to enhance the probability that judicial decisions will not be hollow attempts to protect human rights. The fifth element, fiscal autonomy, is directed both at protecting the courts from the financial retribution of an abusive regime and at ensuring that the court has adequate resources to fully carry out its functions. The sixth element, formal separation of powers, further removes judicial power from arbitrary abuses of the other branches, since under such a structure the judiciary's power is a constitutional grant of power rather than a grant of power from the state that could be removed at will. The final element, enumerated qualifications, is directed at establishing institutional professionalism and impartiality. This provision should lead to the presence of judges who are competent and who have been socialized to the norms of judicial independence, which should make them more willing and able to withstand incursions from other branches upon human rights. I conclude that these seven elements represent from a theoretical perspective the best guide to operationalizing international and academic consensus about what constitutes judicial independence.[4]

Like Russell (2001) and the UN, I believe that one of the most fundamental ways to protect judicial independence is through formalized constitutional guarantees, and we would agree that newly emergent democracies would be well advised to write strong principles of judicial independence into their constitutions along with a catalog of fundamental rights (Russell 2001, 22–23). I, too, recognize that constitutional language may be valuable from a symbolic and educational perspective and agree with Siegan (1994) that constitutions are potentially "the most important legal document for a nation that subscribes to the rule of law" because they define the relationship between the nation's people and their government (72) and because they impose constraints upon government and protect the individual's freedoms from arbitrary or abusive state action (see Andrews 1964; Finer 1974; Stotzky 1993; Siegan 1994; Elster 1993).[5] In the next section, I address specifically the theoretical expectations concerning states' motivation to adopt formal provisions for an independent judiciary and then empirically examine these before moving on to examine whether these promises are likely to be translated into practice.

Why Do States Adopt Formal Provisions for an Independent Judiciary?

The U.S. founding fathers recognized the potential of an independent judicial branch as a restraint against tyranny of the majority. In *Federalist* No. 78, Hamilton argued that courts were designed as an intermediary body between the people and the legislature, acting to keep a potentially overzealous legislature within the limits of its assigned powers. These expectations have survived over time and two centuries later reflect the assessment of the international community, represented by the United Nations, which has declared judicial independence to be a human rights priority (United Nations 1996).

Legal scholars perceive a broader function. Russell (2001) argues that a judiciary's essential function in a liberal democracy derives from two "closely related social needs": "First, in a civil society, we want some of our relations with each other and with our government to be regulated by reasonably well-defined laws setting out mutual rights and duties. Second, when disputes arise about these legal rights and duties, we want a mutually acceptable third-party adjudicator to settle the dispute" (9). Today judicial independence, as Tiede (2006) notes, is frequently touted as "the lynchpin of a democratic society and the rule of law," with foreign donors providing "vast amounts of money to help establish judicial independence in emerging democracies" (129). USAID more specifically declares in its *Guidance for Promoting Judicial Independence and Impartiality:* "In democratic, market-based societies, independent and impartial judiciaries contribute to the equitable and stable balance of power within the government. They protect individual rights and preserve the security of person and property. They resolve commercial disputes in a predictable and transparent fashion that encourages fair competition and economic growth. They are key to countering public and private corruption, reducing political manipulation, and increasing public confidence in the integrity of government" (2002, 4).

The world society approach would predict this convergence toward the norm of judicial independence and its perceived role of guarantor rights. The approach generally posits that "many features of the contemporary nation-state derive from worldwide models constructed and propagated through global cultural and associational processes" (Meyer et al. 1997, 144–45). Go (2003) notes that the approach "suggests that all states have constitutions, and constitutions come in a very similar package, because the larger system dictates that they should" (72). Thus, legitimacy of the state may hinge upon its adoption of "standard sociopolitical forms" such as constitutions (Boli-Bennet 1987; Go 2003) or its participation in international human rights regimes that have institutionalized world norms of human rights behavior (Wotipka and Ramirez 2007; Hafner-Burton and Tsutsui 2005). The perspective posits three mechanisms through which states are influenced by the world society: (1) world meetings, conferences, and conventions in which the standards are articulated; (2) norms cascades through which states are influenced by the behavior of states globally and within their regions; and (3) embeddedness in the broader world, from which they learn the appropriate state identity and behaviors (Wotipka and Ramirez 2007, 314–15 and citations therein). In regard to mechanism (1) the United Nations clearly promulgated a set of international standards and explicitly called for states to formal enshrinement of these through written constitutions or domestic law. From the world society approach I derive four hypotheses that I examine in this chapter.

- Hypothesis One: As more states within the global set of countries incorporate constitutional provisions for judicial independence, the likelihood increases that other states will adopt similar provisions.
- Hypothesis Two: As more states within a region incorporate constitutional provisions for judicial independence, the likelihood increases that other states within that region will adopt similar provisions.
- Hypothesis Three: States will be more likely to adopt formal provisions for judicial independence following the promulgation of three international documents setting standards for judicial independence: (1) the Delhi standards passed by the International Bar Association in 1983; (2) the UN's *Basic Principles on the Independence of the Judiciary* adopted in 1985; and the 1995 report by Dato' Param Cumaraswamy, the UN special rapporteur on the independence of judges and lawyers.
- Hypothesis Four: The more the state is embedded in the international community, the more likely it will be to adopt formal provisions for judicial independence.

Several rational-choice-based theories espouse an electoral logic to explain state decisions to write new or revised constitutional provisions for judicial independence: Ramseyer's (1994) electoral market logic, Ginsburg's (2003) insurance theory, and Hirschl's (2004) hegemonic preservation theory. Ramseyer (1994) argues that political support for an independent judiciary depends on two conditions: (1) whether the ruling party expects elections to continue indefinitely, and, (2) if they expect that elections will continue, then whether the ruling party expects to continue to win the elections indefinitely (722). Ramseyer posits that when conditions are such that the ruling regime is no longer likely to continue winning elections, the regime will support an independent court in order to protect its policies. Thus, ultimately, for Ramseyer "judicial independence may be a matter of electoral exigency" (746). Ginsburg's insurance theory (2003) follows a similar logic in regard to the power of judicial review. He specifically asks why constitutional drafters, who are presumably self-interested politicians, would choose to empower the judiciary with judicial review. He argues that the answer "depends on the prospective power positions of constitutional designers in the postconstitutional government" (24). He contrasts the incentives facing a ruling regime in a state with a dominant single party that is likely to hold onto its power in the new system, with the incentives of a ruling regime within a state with many political parties competing for power. He concludes that in the first state there is little incentive to empower a neutral third body to resolve constitutional disputes, whereas in the second state, the regime faced with the prospect of losing power would value limited government and want an alternative forum in which the opposition or losing party can challenge the majority's policies. Thus, he makes a general prediction that "explicit constitutional power of and access to judicial review will be greater where political forces are diffused than where a single dominant party exists at the time of constitutional design" (25).

Ginsburg also argues that new democracies and regimes in transition face more uncertainty than do established democracies or autocracies; electoral outcomes are harder to predict in new democracies, and transitioning regimes by definition face significant and uncertain changes in the party system and institutional structures. He concludes that "uncertainty increases demand for the political insurance that judicial review provides . . . insurance for the past against the future" (2003, 30–31). For example, he finds that the constitutional reforms initiated in 1987 in Korea were negotiated among three political parties of roughly equal power, and that in "situations of such uncertainty, all parties had an incentive to set up a strong, accessible constitutional court, and the drafters adopted the German model" (249). Similarly, Magaloni (2008) concludes that "a powerful Supreme Court in Mexico could only come about when power became diffused and the ruling party could no longer anticipate with certainty that it would hold power in the future" (182). For Ginsburg, then, the spread of judicial review around the globe "does not merely reflect a norm among constitution drafters, but a response to the problems of electoral uncertainty that they face" (31). Ginsburg's insurance theory does not predict that judges will actually follow the founders' wishes and protect the rights of the political minority, but rather recognizes the potential agency cost in that judges may impose their own preferences. Thus, he cautions that like insurance, judicial review merely serves as a risk-reduction device, which generally is never foolproof.

While Ginsburg's insurance theory specifically addresses the creation of a system of judicial review, I believe it may also have a viable application to the creation of an independent judiciary, which would seem to be a necessary condition for the exercise of judicial review as a form of political insurance for the opposition or political minorities. Hirschl's (2004) hegemonic preservation theory posits that leaders whose control of the majority decision-making process is threatened by a peripheral group will transfer power to the judiciary "to secure their policy preferences even when majoritarian decision-making processes are not operating to their advantage" (95). Ginsburg and Moustafa (2008) note that in both Hirschl's hegemonic preservation theory and Ginsburg's insurance theory, "ruling parties who will soon be displaced by their opponents have an incentive to empower the judiciary because they believe the regime and its institutions will continue without them" (12).[6] I derive three hypotheses from these electoral logic theories, which I examine in this chapter:

- Hypothesis Five: States with competitive political participation or political fragmentation will be more likely to adopt or maintain constitutional provisions for judicial independence.
- Hypothesis Six: New democracies will be more likely to adopt or maintain constitutional provisions for judicial independence.
- Hypothesis Seven: States in transition will be more likely to adopt or maintain constitutional provisions for judicial independence.

In regard to the "credible commitment problem" in the economic sphere, states may signal to potential investors the seriousness of their commitment to the rule of law and economic liberalism with the explicit promulgation of constitutional rights (property rights, in particular) and with the establishment of an autonomous judiciary to serve as a neutral forum to handle disputes arising over the violation of property rights and other government actions (for example, Milgrom, North, and Weingast 1990; Olson 1993; Weingast 1995, 1997). As Ginsburg and Moustafa (2008) note, "the global trend toward economic liberalization in recent decades has encouraged and facilitated the establishment or reform of more robust judicial institutions" (9). They cite as examples the World Trade Organization (WTO) regime, "which specifically requires states to provide judicial or quasi-judicial institutions in trade-related arenas: a network of bilateral investment treaties promises neutral dispute resolution to reassure investors"; and multilateral lending institutions, such as the World Bank and Inter-American Development Bank, which "expend vast resources to promote judicial reform in developing countries" (9). Shapiro (2008) observes that "an international epistemic community of investment bankers and lawyers acting through entities ranging from American law schools to the World Bank has been busy trying to persuade the world that one key to national economic success is the 'rule of law' enforced by independent judiciaries" (327), and he concludes that even authoritarian regimes "anxious to attract foreign investment . . . can be persuaded to institutionalize relatively independent and effective courts to assure investors of legal protections" (330).

As we saw Chapter 2, the positive perspective of economic liberalism expects that economic liberalization generally, and liberal trade policies in particular, will facilitate economic development, lead to improvements in the political and social conditions for the population, and foster the liberal democracy in developing states. Harrelson-Stephens and Calloway (2003) argue that the economic interdependences lead to the diffusion of broader values, including those of human rights, and thus improved human rights is a spillover effect from international trade (145). From this perspective the diffusion of values associated with economic development and liberal trade policies that shape the demands of the public are likely to include the norm of an independent tribunal as guardian of these rights. Thus, from two different perspectives we would expect to see evidence of increasing provision for judicial independence as the level of economic development and economic liberalization increases within a state.

- Hypothesis Eight: Economic liberalization within a state will increase the likelihood that the state will adopt or maintain constitutional provisions for judicial independence.
- Hypothesis Nine: Economic development within a state will increase the likelihood that the state will adopt or maintain constitutional provisions for judicial independence.

This perspective is not without its critics. As we saw in Chapter 2, the dependency theory critique of liberal economic theory argues generally that more economically developed states exploit less economically developed states, a phenomenon that leads to uneven development and hinders the socioeconomic growth of states whose economies are vulnerable to the demands of multinational corporations and multilateral lending institutions. Ultimately, the less economically developed state's options are constrained, and its policies are shaped to benefit the interests of multinational corporations and domestic elites rather than those of its citizens. Thus, economic liberalization would not be likely to lead to the dividends suggested above, and might decrease the probability of meaningful reform, such as establishing a truly independent judiciary, particularly if its independence could threaten the regime's economic self-interest. As we saw in Chapters 2 and 3, empirical studies have generated some evidence to support an alternative hypothesis to the liberalization hypotheses above.

- Alternative Hypothesis Eight: Economic liberalization within a state will decrease the likelihood that the state will adopt or maintain constitutional provisions for judicial independence.
- Alternative Hypothesis Nine: Economic development within a state will decrease the likelihood that the state will adopt or maintain constitutional provisions for judicial independence.

I believe the examination of these hypotheses will improve our substantive and empirical understanding of why states adopt provisions for judicial independence and will more fully inform our understanding of the effect of judicial independence on political repression. I next turn to my measurement of formal, or *de jure,* judicial independence.

Measuring Formal Judicial Independence

I have constructed seven ordinal measures for constitutional provisions that reflect the seven international principles of judicial independence I described earlier. Since it is possible that a constitution may meet a criterion to some degree but not fully, I have coded the variables as follows:

No provision (0): No constitution or constitution does not provide this element.
Qualified provision (1): Constitution provides for this element to a limited degree or provides for this element vaguely but not fully.

Explicit and full provision (2): Constitution provides for this element fully and explicitly.

In addition, for two measures I defined a fourth code, (-1), for constitutional provisions that explicitly deny an international principle of judicial independence. The nine measures are:

Guaranteed Terms: The constitution guarantees terms of office, regardless of whether appointed or elected, and restricted removal of judges. This measure reflects the first part of the first merged UN element above.
Finality of Decisions: The decisions of judges are not subject to revision outside appeals procedures provided by law. This measure reflects the second merged UN element.
Exclusive Authority: The courts have exclusive authority to decide on their own competence, as defined by law—their decisions are made without any restrictions, improper influences, inducements, pressures, threats, or interference, direct or indirect, from any quarter or for any reason. This measure reflects the third merged UN element.
Ban Against Exceptional or Military Courts: The courts have jurisdiction over all issues of a judicial nature (civilians are tried by ordinary courts or tribunals, not by military or exceptional courts). This measure reflects the fourth element above. It includes an additional score beyond (0), (1), and (2). Constitutions are coded (-1) if they explicitly condone trying civilians in military courts or allow the formation of exceptional courts. I give these constitutions a negative score because not only do the constitutions specifically fail to ban these types of courts (which would have earned a score of 0), but also they go so far as to explicitly *legitimize* the use of such courts.
Fiscal Autonomy: The courts are fiscally autonomous. Their salaries and/or their budgets are protected from reduction by the other branches. This measure reflects the fifth merged element and the second part of the first element.
Separation of Powers: The courts are housed in a separate branch from the executive and legislative powers. This measure reflects the sixth merged element.

> *Enumerated Qualifications:* The selection and career of judges are based on merit (qualifications, integrity, ability, efficiency). This measure reflects the seventh merged element.

Two Additional Elements: In addition to the seven elements that emerge from the United Nations' principles I consider two more questionable elements: hierarchical system and judicial review. Neither of these elements would have the level of consensus for their inclusion that the above elements have. In part, my inclusion of these elements as potential indicators of formal judicial independence rests upon my commitment to building on prior work in this area, and in particular the work of Blasi and Cingranelli (1996), which develops one of the first indicators of judicial independence. Their index is composed of eight factors that overlap substantially with my list of principles based on the UN recommendations: (1) the judiciary is housed in a separate branch; (2) the judiciary is fiscally autonomous; (3) the judiciary has the power of judicial review of the actions of the legislative and executive branches; (4) judges have life tenure (at least for the highest-level judges); (5) judges are protected by restricted removal procedures; (6) the judiciary is organized in a hierarchical system; (7) public hearings are required; and (8) the judiciary is composed of professional judges.

The most notable difference between the UN principles and Blasi and Cingranelli's index is the political scientists' inclusion of judicial review, which is not specified in the United Nations' lists. In fact authorities disagree as to whether judicial review is a power that contributes to an independent judiciary or whether an independent judiciary is a necessary component for the real exercise of judicial review (contrast Blasi and Cingranelli 1996 with Rosenthal 1990). However, in the international community and to some extent in the United States as well, judicial review is linked to rights protection by an independent judiciary. For example, Keck (2002) suggests that in the United States "the very mission of an independent Supreme Court [has] come to be identified—in the minds of ordinary citizens and the justices themselves—with the enforcement of rights-based limits on political action," and "for the justices to abandon this role would be to call into question the very justification for their office" (135). International proponents of constitutional or judicial review have long expected this independent, rights-protective role for the judiciary, especially in periods of crisis or instability (for example, Becker 1970; International Commission of Jurists 1983; Caine

1987–88; Chowdhury 1989; Maduna 1989; Ackermann 1989; Stotzky 1993; Garro 1993).

The second notable difference between Blasi and Cingranelli's index and the UN principles is the scholars' inclusion of the requirement for a hierarchical system in which the judiciary is structured in multiple tiers, with the highest-level court exercising final control/review of lower court decisions. In theory this structural arrangement could ensure that the decisions of lower-level judges, who are arguably more susceptible to corruption or other outside influence, are subject to review by the higher courts. Compared to higher court judges, lower court judges are presumably more numerous, less qualified at least in terms of experience, less socialized to judicial norms, and less well paid and hence more susceptible to bribery. Thus an effective judicial hierarchy would potentially strengthen overall independence vis-à-vis external actors. Additionally, this dimension would seem to strengthen judicial impartiality and the stability of the courts' jurisprudence. At the same time, a hierarchical system potentially weakens the independence of these lower court judges to the extent that career advancement, remuneration, or the security or amenability of the work environment is dependent upon higher-level judges. Russell (2001) notes that judicial independence can be threatened not only from outside, but also from within by senior judges using administrative controls (see also Guarnieri and Pederzoli 2002; Ramseyer and Rasmussen 2003). Certainly Prillaman's (2000) work and that of other Latin Americanists would suggest that a hierarchical structure can be abused, especially in systems that lack transparency in their selection processes and personnel decision making. Rosenn (1987), on the other hand, argues that judicial independence is not necessarily inconsistent with judiciaries in which senior judges make decisions regarding lower court judges' promotion, transfers, and salaries, presumably on the basis of judicial performance (5). Later in this chapter I conduct analyses of *de facto* judicial independence and examine the impact of these provisions on *de facto* judicial independence. I include the following two measures separately in my analyses:

> *Judicial Review:* Courts exercise judicial or constitutional review of legislative and executive branches.[7] I recorded a (-1) for constitutions in which courts were explicitly forbidden to exercise judicial or constitutional review.

Hierarchical System: Courts are structured in multiple layers, with the highest-level court exercising final control/review of lower court decisions.

Trends over Time

In this section I present a simple descriptive analysis of the trends in states' constitutional commitment to the core elements of judicial independence. First, Figure 4.1 shows the seven provisions as a bundle, demonstrating the annual mean in a 16-point additive index. For the first decade of this period the mean provision is 4 points, and we see a strong upward trend beginning in 1990 and 1991 with the end of the Cold War and the beginning of the wave of new constitution writing. The trend levels off in 1996 and continues across the period, ending with a mean of 6.6, which is well below the midpoint of the index.

States vary substantially in their adoption of the various provisions, so in Figure 4.2 I present the mean level of constitutional provision for the

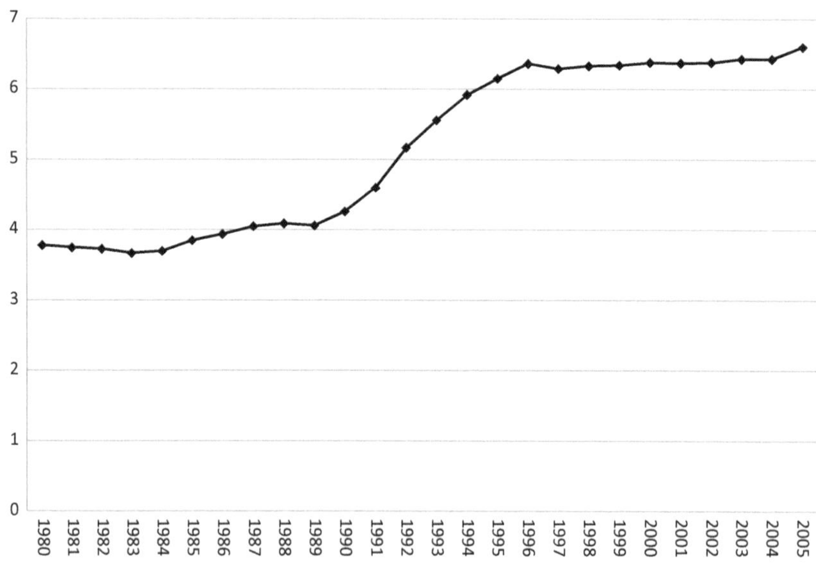

Figure 4.1. Mean Score on a 16-Point Index of Formal Judicial Independence, 1980–2005

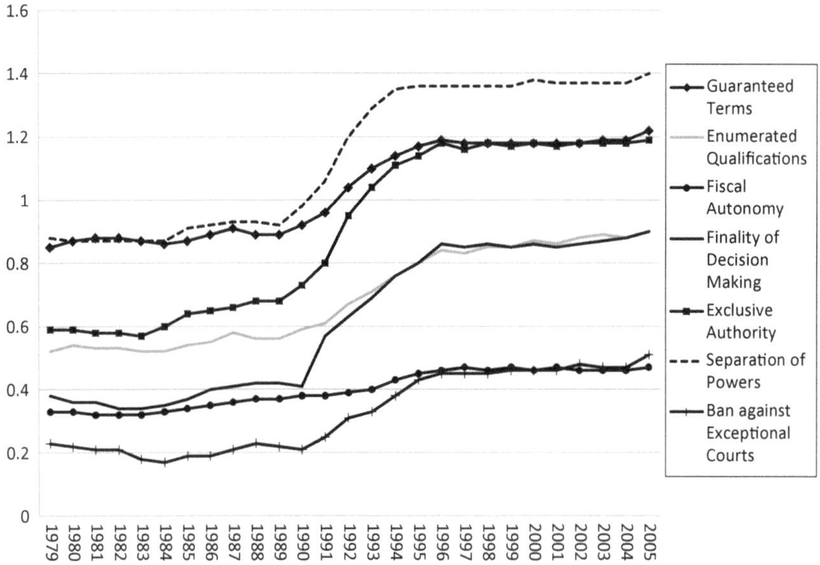

Figure 4.2. Mean Constitutional Provision for Basic Elements of Judicial Independence, 1979–2005

seven basic elements of judicial independence. Several patterns emerge. First, each of the means increases during the wave of constitution writing by newly independent states at the end of the Cold War, and then tapers off by the end of the period, 2005. Second, provision for separation of powers consistently remains the strongest, with a mean of 1.4. Third, we see the other six provisions fall into parallel pairs that converge by 1996. Provision for enumerated terms of office and provision for exclusive judicial authority have the second-highest means, achieving approximately 1.20 by 2005. Thus, for these three measures the mean in 2005 falls between full and qualified provision. The second pair (enumerated qualifications and finality of decision making) consistently earns means about .30 lower than the first pair and achieves a mean of .90 by 2005, which approximates a mean of qualified provision. The last pair (provision for fiscal autonomy and bans of exceptional courts) achieves means that reach only .50 by 2005. The mean for a ban against exceptional courts is driven down (by .07) because of the (-1) coding of countries that explicitly allow exceptional courts (only 318 observations out of 4,364). Overall, these patterns do suggest some degree of convergence, as Go (2003) would predict.

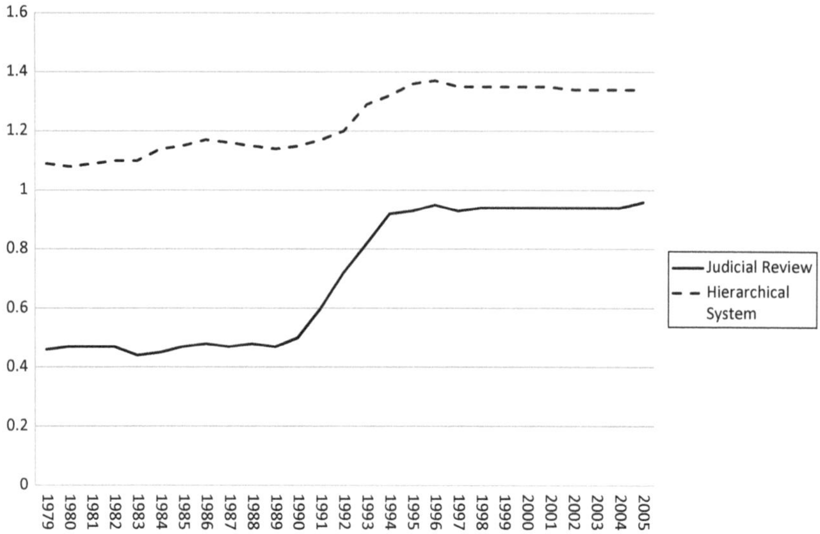

Figure 4.3. Mean Constitutional Provision for Judicial Review and Hierarchical Systems, 1979–2005

In Figure 4.3 I present the means over time for the two additional constitutional provisions. As with the previous seven provisions, we see a similar increase in the mean level following the end of the Cold War, with the provision for judicial review experiencing a much steeper increase. The provision for a hierarchical system begins with a higher mean (1.09) than any of the seven provisions for judicial independence and ends with a mean (1.34) approximately equal to those for the provisions for guaranteed terms and for exclusive judiciary authority. The provision for judicial review begins with a mean of .46 in 1979 and ends with a mean of .96, a result suggesting that on average states have at least qualified provision for judicial review. I next turn to operationalizing my concepts and presenting the sixteen measures to be employed in the model to test these hypotheses.

Operationalizing the Hypotheses

Dependent Variable: Formal Judicial Independence is operationalized as a 16-point additive index of the seven provisions of formal judicial independence. The index ranges from -1 to 14.

Global and Regional Norms: Norms-based perspectives, such as the world society approach, share a common problem in that norms are impossible to observe directly, and it is difficult to measure their influence without creating serious circularity. As Goodliffe and Hawkins (2006) note, "operationalizing norms is a tricky business. . . . norms are difficult to identify and their influence is hard to track" (361). Thus, empirical studies have typically relied on indirect surrogates, which have included cumulative participation in human rights treaties (as an indicator of diffusion of particular international norms) and have examined the global community of states and/or regional communities of states as potential venues of norm diffusion. To operationalize the effect of the pressure of international norms, I follow Goodliffe and Hawkins (2006) and Simmons (2000) and create measurements of global and regional commitments to formal judicial independence (see also Wotipka and Ramirez 2007). Specifically, I create an additive index of seven indictors of formal judicial independence to create a 16-point index that ranges from -1 to 14. I then create annual measures of the average commitment scores of the global set of countries and an annual measure of the average commitment scores for each geographical region. For the judicial review model, I also create an annual measure of the average commitment scores for each geographical region.

Dummy Variables for International Standards: I create three dummy variables depicting the years in which three international documents were promulgated that set standards for judicial independence: (1) the New Delhi standards passed by the International Bar Association in October 1982 (King 1982), (2) the UN's *Basic Principles on the Independence of the Judiciary* (1985), and the 1995 report by Dato' Param Cumaraswamy, the UN special rapporteur on the independence of judges and lawyers.

Embeddedness: I follow the treaty commitment/compliance literature (for example, Hafner-Burton and Tsutsui 2005; Landman 2005; Goodliffe and Hawkins 2006; Wotipka and Ramirez 2007) and use (1) the number of international governmental organizations (IGOs) of which the country is a member and (2) the number of international nongovernmental organizations (INGOs) (Landman 2005, see 177–88, for further discussion of the measurements).

Competitive Political Participation: To operationalize competitive political participation I employ Polity's (Marshall and Jaggers 2011) *Competitiveness of Political Participation*, as described in Chapter 3. I also tested several measures to capture political fragmentation using three measures from the World Bank's Database of Political Institutions: (1) measure that captures the total vote share of all opposition parties; (2) measures of whether the opposition party has an absolute majority in (a) the house or (b) the senate; and (3) their combined measure of whether the opposition has an absolute majority in the house and/or the senate (Beck, Keefer, and Clarke 2010). None of the measures achieved acceptable levels of statistical significance.

New Democracies: I follow Simmons (2000) and Goodliffe and Hawkins (2006) and utilize Polity's (Marshall and Jaggers 2011) "Democracy" measure and create a dummy variable that denotes a country as a new democracy when it first achieves a score of 7 or above. The country remains a new democracy until it either drops below 7 on the scale or stays at 7 or above for at least ten years.

States in Transition: I employ a dummy variable using the Polity data set, which identifies countries in transition.

Economic Development and Liberalization: I employ four measures to capture economic development and economic liberalization. First, I create a measure *Trade Openness* using the Penn World Table 6.3 version of "openk," which is defined as exports plus imports divided by real GDP per capita, of which I take the natural log. Second, I create a dummy variable that denotes *Membership in the WTO.* I considered countries to be members of the WTO for their beginning year if they had been members for at least six month. Third, I include the World Bank measure of *Foreign Direct Investments,* net inflows as a percentage of GDP. Fourth, I include the World Bank measure of *Per-Capita GDP* (constant 2000 $).

Analysis

As in Chapter 3, in estimating the models I conduct parallel analyses following Neumayer's (2005) dual approach. I use ordered probit estimation because all the dependent variables are ordered ordinal variables rather than continuous cardinal variables. However, using ordered probit means that I cannot include country fixed effects in the model. As Neumayer notes, computing fixed effects in ordered probit or logit models is extremely complex, there is not currently a standard statistical package to estimate such a model, and adding fixed effects by hand leads to biased coefficients and standard errors. (936). Thus, he runs parallel models, one using OLS with fixed effects and the second a standard ordered probit estimator without fixed effects (937). I follow this approach and report results from estimating both models in Table 4.1. The odd-numbered columns are fixed-effects models, and

Table 4.1. Model of Commitment to Judicial Independence, 1980–2005

	Formal Judicial Independence 16-Point Index 1980–2000		*Formal Judicial Independence 16-Point Index 1980–2005*	
	Fixed Effects (1)	*Ordered Probit (2)*	*Fixed Effects (3)*	*Ordered Probit (4)*
Formal Judicial Independence (*t*–1) (+)	.77 (.02)***	.75 (.06)***	.79 (.02)***	.83 (.07)***
New Delhi Standards (+)	.02 (.07)	.06 (.07)	.04 (.07)	.05 (.08)
UN Basic Principles (+)	.04 (.15)	.09 (.13)	.06 (.15)	.10 (.15)
Special Rapporteur's Report (+)	.18 (.12)*	.20 (.13)*	.21 (.12)**	.25 (.14)**
Global Norms (+)	.11 (.05)**	.08 (.04)**	.08 (.04)**	.06 (.03)**
Regional Norms(+)	.17 (.05)***	.07 (.02)***	.16 (.04)***	.06 (.01)***
IGOs (+)	.001 (.00)	.001 (.00)	—	—
Logged INGOs (+)	.15 (.33)	.04 (.09)	—	—
Party Competition (+)	.14 (.10)*	.002 (.02)	.11 (.07)*	.001 (.01)
New Democracy (+)	.05 (.12)	.04 (.03)*	.02 (.07)	.05 (.03)**
Regime In Transition (+)	.06 (.47)	.21 (.45)	.02 (.44)	.21 (.44)
Logged Trade (+/–)	–.12*** (.04)	–.08 (.05)*	–.09 (.04)***	–.07 (.04)**
WTO Member (+/–)	–.18 ** (.08)	–.30 (.07)***	–.18 (.07)***	–.27 (.06)***
Net FDI (+/–)	–.003 (.003)	–.01 (.01)***	–.001 (.001)	–.01 (.001)***
Logged GDP (+/–)	–.001 (.001)	–.0001 (.001)	–.001 (.001)	–.001 (.001)

(continued)

Table 4.1 (*continued*)

	Formal Judicial Independence 16-Point Index 1980–2000		*Formal Judicial Independence 16-Point Index 1980–2005*	
	Fixed Effects (1)	*Ordered Probit (2)*	*Fixed Effects (3)*	*Ordered Probit (4)*
Observations	2295	2295	2813	2813
R^2 /Pseudo-R^2	.92	.44	.93	.47
F /Chi^2	223.14	426.43	306.44	442.55
Prob > F / Prob > Chi^2	.0001	.0001	.0001	.0001

All independent variables are lagged one year. Fixed-effects and ordered probit estimation with robust standard errors. Standard errors in parentheses. *Significant at the 10 percent level. **Significant at the 5 percent level. ***Significant at the 1 percent level. All tests one-tailed except where no direction predicted: (+) predicted positive direction, (–) negative, and (+/–) no predicted direction.

the even-numbered models are ordered probit without fixed effects. In addition I ran parallel analyses because two of the independent variables (IGOs and INGOs) are restricted in the time frame to 1979–2000. Thus I estimate one model with these two variables restricted to the smaller time frame and then reestimate the model without these two variables for 1980–2005. I report the results for both periods even though the results are largely unchanged in the model with the longer period and no measures for IGOs and INGOs (some of the coefficients in the latter model achieve somewhat higher levels of statistical significance, and a few coefficients are slightly larger).[8]

It is not surprising that the level of formal provision for judicial independence in the prior year produces the largest coefficients in the models (.77 and .79 in the fixed-effects models). This finding suggests that formal judicial independence is a strongly seated characteristic of a political system that does not change easily or rapidly. The first two hypotheses are strongly supported across all four models: as the world society approach predicts, both global norms and regional norms are positively associated with constitutional provisions for judicial independence. If we take the first fixed-effects model (column 1) as an example, we see that a one-unit increase in the global mean would be associated with a .11 increase in the judicial independence index and similarly a .17 increase in regard to the region's mean. A maximum increase in the global mean from -1 to 15 would be associated with a 1.54 increase in the index, and a maximum increase in the regional mean would be associated with a 2.38 increase in the mean. Such leaps in standards are not likely in the real world; in my data set the biggest increase in the global norm/mean is approximately .5 (from 1992 to 1993), and the overall increase across the twenty-seven-year period is 3 points. Nonetheless, both global and regional norms clearly influence the presence of these constitutional provisions. The third hypothesis derived from the world society approach, which posits the influence of promulgation of international standards, receives only moderate support; neither the United Nations Basic Principles nor the Delhi Standards have a statistically significant effect; however, the UN special rapporteur's report is associated with a moderate impact (coefficients of .18 and 21 in the fixed-effects model) comparable to that of the regional norms. Of course, any dummy variable that represents a particular year is a rather inelegant measure, and we have to accept that the measure may be capturing other influences.

Despite predictions by both the world society approach and the transnational network approach, the fourth hypothesis receives no statistical support in these analyses: neither a state's level of participation in IGOs nor the presence of INGOs within the state is associated with the adoption of formal provisions for judicial independence. The models produce somewhat mixed results in regard to the insurance theory hypothesis, with the competitiveness of participation variable producing statistically significant and positively signed coefficients in the fixed-effects model but not in the ordered probit models. The new democracy measure produces statistically significant and positively signed coefficients in the ordered probit models but not in the fixed-effects models. And the measure of states in transition is not statistically significant in any of the models. Each of the indicators of economic liberalization is negatively associated with formal judicial independence, a result that supports the malign perspective of economic liberalization, and each of the coefficients achieves acceptable levels of statistical significance except for the FDI coefficients in the fixed-effects models. Economic development also produces negative coefficients and fails to achieve acceptable levels of statistical significance in any model.

The overall performance of the models is strong, with R-squares ranging from .92 to .93 in the fixed-effects models and pseudo R-squares ranging from .44 to .47. As a whole these analyses suggest that state commitment may be influenced by the diffusion of norms globally and regionally, but I see no evidence of diffusion of norms through embeddedness in the international system. And I find no evidence that states' commitment to formal judicial independence is influenced by the transnational network of INGOs. I do, however, find significant, if somewhat inconsistent, support for the electoral logic hypotheses. Finally, not only do I find no support for the economic liberalization theory; instead I find support for its critics' position that globalization and liberalization do not always produce the expected dividends and rather impose a cost. This evidence fits with the extensive research of Abouharb and Cingranelli (2008), which examines the effect of IMF and World Bank structural adjustment programs and finds that the programs had a harmful rather than beneficial effect on political stability and a wide range of rights. I continue to find evidence of this harmful association throughout the remainder of the analyses, whether in regard to state commitment to formal human rights norms or in regard to state use of repression. And it holds in the next analysis as I turn to the question of whether these formal institutions are likely to produce the promised independent judiciary—in other words, whether *de jure* independence will lead to *de facto* independence.

Does *De Jure* Independence Lead to *De Facto* Independence?

Constructivists would expect that the norms and obligations set forth in constitutional provisions would be honored by national governments. Henkin (1979) argues that while governments may sometimes violate their legal obligations, it has long been observed most governments keep most of their commitments most of the time. Chayes and Chayes (1993) also argue that governments take their commitments seriously and make a good-faith effort to comply in the spirit of *pacta sunt servanda* (agreements are to be kept and honored) where "compliance is the normal organizational presumption" (179). Others argue that governments and their citizens may hold metabeliefs about the legitimacy of the rule of law and see such compliance with commitments as being integral to the state's identity as a legitimate nation-state (Finnemore and Sikkink 1998, 903–4). These expectations lead us to the following hypothesis:

- Hypothesis One: Formal provisions for judicial independence will lead to higher levels of *de facto* judicial independence.

While the world society perspective would predict that global norms will be diffused among states over time, leading to more states' adopting constitutions and provision for strong judicial independence, the logic of the perspective leads to the possibility that as the weight of these norms grows in defining legitimate or deviant governments, the more likely states are to adopt the formal provision without the willingness or capacity to implement the promised institutions, thus leading to a decoupling between promise and practice. As Hafner-Burton and Tsutsui (2005) point out, the adoption of such norms may often be "a symbolic gesture to signal that the government is not a deviant actor" and therefore will not necessarily lead to compliance with the formal commitments; thus the formal commitment is "often loosely coupled with the relevant practice" (1383). They argue that, in the context of international human rights treaties, as "the legitimacy of a treaty grows to the extent that nonratifying states look like deviants, governments are more likely to ratify without willingness or capacity to comply with the provisions, thus increasing the likelihood of decoupling" (1383). Some empirical evidence supports this expectation, and indeed ratification of treaties is often associated with worse human rights behavior (for example, Keith 1999; Hathaway 2002; Hafner-Burton and Tsutsui 2005; but see Landman 2005). Thus, formal provisions of judicial independence may also be associated with lower levels of achieved judicial independence, which suggests an alternative hypothesis:

- Alternative Hypothesis One: Adoption of constitutional provisions may lead to a decoupling effect in which the provisions have no effect or a negative effect on achieved judicial independence.

While the world society approach would caution that these formal provisions might be adopted or maintained as simple "veneers of legal legitimation," Ginsburg and Moustafa (2008), like other scholars such as Risse, Ropp, and Sikkink (1999), posit that regimes may get caught in their own rhetoric (6). Specifically, they argue that "the more a regime relies on rule of law rhetoric, the greater the opportunity for litigants and judges to expose the shortcomings of the government" and its failure to comply with its promises (7). More specifically Moustafa (2007) argues that the judiciary and activists can form "judicial support networks" composed of "institutions and associations, both transnational and domestic, that facilitate the expansion of judicial power by actively initiating litigation and/or supporting the independence of the judicial institutions if they come under attack" (13). These expectations lead to my second hypothesis:

- Hypothesis Two: The greater the level of NGO participation in a state, the more likely the judiciary is to be independent in practice.

In regard to *de facto* independence I return to the economic liberalism perspective and the global trend toward economic liberalization. According to Ginsburg and Moustafa (2008), this trend has encouraged and facilitated not just the establishment of formal promises of judicial independence but also the association of liberalization with the establishment of reform toward more robust judicial institutions. Like Powell and Staton (2009), I believe that the credible commitment argument would predict some degree of compliance with the commitment, at least in the short term; otherwise why would the formal commitment constitute a *credible* commitment to the interested parties (150)? Here, as above, I also assume that the diffusion of values associated with liberalized trade and the increased public demands associated with economic development will also include expectations for an independent judiciary as guardian of these rights. However, the malign perspective of economic liberalization, as well as the evidence presented above, justifies positing an alternative hypothesis:

- Hypothesis Three: The greater the level of economic liberalization and economic development, the more likely the judiciary is to be independent in practice.
- Alternative Hypothesis Three: The greater the level of economic liberalization and economic development, the less likely the judiciary is to be independent in practice.

I also believe that other domestic conditions affect the likelihood of judicial independence, especially perceived or real domestic threats. Prillaman's (2000) analysis of Latin American courts demonstrates that one of the foremost impediments to judicial independence is a declaration of a state of emergency, such as in El Salvador, which resulted in Duarte's "Decree Law 507 of December 1980—that destroyed any façade of judicial independence by suspending all guarantees of civil liberties and due process" and in which "military judges were empowered to conduct all investigations in secret" (41–42). Similarly,

Prillaman documents the destructive effect military coups may have on judicial independence, such as in Argentina. Following the military coup in 1976 the junta dismissed all Supreme Court judges in the provinces, suspended tenure of all federal judges, and required all judges to swear to uphold the decrees declared by the junta and to swear that their allegiance was to goals of the regime rather than to the constitution (32, n26). He also observes that military governments, which want to maintain the façade of judicial independence but which do not want to be constrained by an independent judiciary, will often purge the courts; he notes that the Argentine Supreme Court has been replaced en masse six times and that on two other occasions all but one of the judges were purged (20; see also Rosenn 1987, 27). Similarly, Rosenn (1987) points to the military regime in Uruguay, a country that had "previously enjoyed a well-deserved reputation for judicial independence"; the military regime in 1977 "promulgated an astounding Institutional Act that overtly abolished the independence of the judiciary" (23). Pahl (1993) documents the impact of state-of-siege legislation in Colombia, which established special secret courts that eventually became permanent institutions. Over time the jurisdiction expanded from drug cases to cases of political crime such as rebellion, sedition, and other acts of violence committed with criminal intent. Prillaman notes the frequency of this method of reducing institutional independence by bypassing the ordinary court system and creating "more malleable institutions such as special tribunals that can be brought under the executive branch through the ministries of justice or interior" (2000, 20). For example, numerous special tribunals created by the Sandinistas in Nicaragua were exclusively empowered to rule on issues such "counterrevolutionary activities," were under the direct control of the Ministry of the Interior, and ultimately answered only to the president, with no appeal to the Supreme Court (20). Similarly, during the 1980s in Chile, Prillaman finds that 95 percent of all criminal cases were tried in military courts (140). Rosenn (1987) demonstrates a similar path in Brazil, where civilians were tried by military tribunals for national security crimes and were often tortured with impunity offered by the military courts (25). I derive two additional hypotheses that I examine here:

- Hypothesis Four: States experiencing threats will be likely to maintain a judiciary that is independent in practice.
- Hypothesis Five: In states with military regimes, it will be less likely that the judiciary will be independent in practice.

I believe that even well-intentioned regimes that are willing to comply with their formal commitments may lack the economic resources, the technical capabilities, and underlying infrastructure to implement the promised formal institution of judicial independence (see Epp 1998; Prillaman 2000; Sherif and Brown 2002; An-Na'im 2003). In his edited volume of African case studies, An-Na'aim (2003) reports that all courts included in the study lacked sufficient resources (23). For example, Nigerian courts lacked basic material and even rudimentary equipment, such as typewriters and stationery, and "as a result of the severe financial constraints and the low level of professionalism generally, court personnel, including magistrates, extort money from litigants" (23). He found that across the board African courts lacked adequate courtroom facilities, access to court reporters, and personnel to meet their overcrowded dockets (23). USAID (2002) notes that "judiciaries with inadequate resources usually cannot offer the salaries, benefits, and pensions needed to attract and retain qualified candidates, and, in some cases, to diminish the likelihood of corruption" (25). While detailing a long list of ways in which the lack of adequate resources affects judicial independence, USAID notes that the effect is more direct when judiciaries must to turn to entities outside the judiciary to supplement an inadequate budget (25). I therefore hypothesize that not only will lower economic wealth act to constrain the likelihood of *de facto* independence, but also other resource constraints, such as population size, will lower the possibility of achieved independence.

- Hypothesis Six: The lower the economic wealth of a state, the less likely the judiciary is to be independent in practice.
- Hypothesis Seven: The greater the population constraint of a state, the less likely the judiciary is to be independent in practice.

I also believe that the separation of powers and strategic approaches inform our question of whether formal provisions are likely to lead to achieved judicial independence. These perspectives would caution against the likelihood that *de jure* judicial independence would affect *de facto* independence. Ferejohn (1999) argues that the independence of the judiciary "is dependent upon the willingness of the popular branches to refrain from using their ample constitutional powers to infringe on judicial authority" (382). And in the context of the United States, he argues that the willingness to refrain usually holds because "the diversity and heterogeneity of American political parties usually makes it difficult to form constitutional majorities capable of infringing on judicial powers" (382). He further argues that rare periods of party unity are dangerous times for the independence of the judiciary. Similarly, Ferejohn, Rosenbluth, and Shipan (2004) argue that political fragmentation gives the judiciary more space to take more independent action, as politicians are able to take steps to curb the courts through legislative overrides and constitutional revision only to the extent that they form a sufficiently coherent and disciplined group. They note that a coherent legislative majority can influence outcomes of judicial action in a variety of ways. For example, the U.S. Congress can widely influence the review of agency action: "It can give the authority for review to one court rather than another; indicate that certain actions are not reviewable by the courts; specify the grounds on which courts can make decisions; determine whether the courts must defer to agency expertise; and set deadlines for action" (8). Unified governments also have greater potential to pass laws or to amend the constitution to limit the courts' independence by restricting its jurisdiction, removing protections of tenure and salary, and restricting budgetary autonomy. The work of McNollgast (2006) and Tiede (2006) also suggests that formal provision for elements of judicial independence, such as protected tenure and fiscal autonomy, will not necessarily result in *de facto* judicial independence. McNollgast emphasizes the dependency of the judiciary in that it cannot enforce it orders or opinions without the assistance or acquiescence of the other branches. Russell (2001) also cautions that even if the structures for judicial independence are fully implemented, the judiciary ultimately is maintained by the state and renders decisions that must be backed up by "the coercive arm of the state" (10). McNollgast ultimately argues that judicial independence is better conceptualized as a "strategic interaction" among political actors that is not fixed but rather fluctuates with the political composition of the main branches of government (109). Thus we can derive the following hypothesis:

- Hypothesis Eight: States with high degrees of political fragmentation will be more likely to achieve *de facto* judicial independence.

Finally, I consider the impact of colonial legacies, as well as types of legal systems, which in many states are directly linked to prior colonial experience. Carey (2002) maintains that the imposition of foreign legal systems on indigenous legal systems not only has led to dual and conflicting legal (and political) cultures but also has contributed to the perceived illegitimacy of legal decisions and institutions in many postcolonial states (65–66). However, several distinctions have been made between the English common law and French civil law systems. It can be argued, for example, that the underlying principle of separation of powers is seen somewhat differently by judges in civil law and common law countries. Common law countries, especially the United States, see judges as balancing the power of the other branches of government. By contrast, the original idea of separation of powers in France was to assign different roles to legislation and to judges, with the latter only applying the law. Other characteristics associated with common law include predictability of results (through the principle of *stare decisis*) and the desire to treat equally everyone who faces the same or similar legal problems, as opposed to the civil system, in which a judge is not legally bound by the previous decision of a higher court in an identical or similar case and is quite free to ignore such a decision. More importantly, in regard to human rights, Joireman (2004) posits that adopting English common law leads to stronger rule of law than does adopting continental civil law; but he argues this to be true only in those countries that have been colonized. Moderne (1990) specifically argues that judicial independence and constitutionalism will be less prevalent in francophone than anglophone Africa. He believes the francophone states have had less exposure to U.S. constitutionalism and that the "dual link of common language and French metropolitan training enjoyed by a majority of Francophone African elites has influenced the new states' judicial models" (335). He also notes that anglophone states may have a longer history with judicial independence as a result of the independence of the African colonial judiciary under the British prior to independence. When political power was transferred in these countries, Moderne argues, the "constitutional guarantee of judicial independence was considered to be of the utmost importance" (328–29).

- Hypothesis Nine: States with British colonial experience will be more likely than those with francophone colonial experience to foster an independent judiciary.

Rosenn (1987) makes a similar connection in regard to Latin American states, which are heirs to the civil law tradition in which judges historically have been weak figures. He argues: "Unlike his common law counterpart, a civil law judge does not have the power to punish the defiance of his orders by jailing the recalcitrant party for contempt of court. Civilians have tended to regard judges as expert technicians whose sole function is to apply the law to the facts. An independent role for the judge in civil law tradition has long been denied" (33). He argues that while most Latin American countries have "grafted the institution of judicial review on this civil law trunk," most judges are ill prepared to take the political role that this function assumes, since they are "career judges with no independent base and contacts and with relatively narrow experience" and ultimately lack not just the experience but the temperament that this role would require (33). Ginsburg and Moustafa (2008) note that the "rapid spread of the civil law model historically was not merely the result of colonial diffusion, in which colonizers simply reproduced the legal institutions of the mother country," but rather "in many cases, the civil law model was purposefully adopted independent of colonial imposition because it provided a better system through which rulers could constrain, if not prevent judge-made law" (19). While the differences between these two systems are "often overstated and even less meaningful over time as more civil law countries adopt procedures for judicial review of legislation, civil law judges may be relatively more constrained than their common law counterparts as a formal matter" (19). I take these arguments to form a broader hypothesis in regard to the common law–civil law differences:

- Hypothesis Ten: Countries with civil law systems will be less likely than countries with common law systems to have an independent judiciary.

Finally, I argue that democracies generally tend to keep the promises they make (for example, Dixon 1994; Leeds 1999; Simmons 2000; Landman 2005; Powell and Mitchell 2007; Powell and Staton 2008) because their constituents have access to majoritarian political institutions to punish their representatives and the regime in power for not complying (Poe and Tate 1994; Keith 1999, 2002a; Poe, Tate, and Keith 1999). In other words, elections "provide the tools for the public to hold government officials accountable for their actions" (Keith 2002a, 122).

- Hypothesis Eleven: The higher the level of political democracy a state achieves, the more likely the state's judiciary is to be independent.

I believe the examination of these hypotheses will improve our substantive and empirical understanding of why states adopt provisions for judicial independence or the power of judicial review. I next turn to the issue of measuring achieved or *de facto* judicial independence.

Measuring Behavioral (*De Facto*) Judicial Independence

As Howard and Carey (2004) note, prior to their work there had not been a systematic replicable measure of judicial independence available for the global set of countries that went beyond formal provisions. A few studies have used or created subjective ratings for a significant albeit nonrandom cross-section of countries; however, as I noted above, these evaluations are generally not replicable (for example, Johnson 1976; Cross 1999; La Porta et al. 2004). I agree with Howard and Carey that it should be possible to create a measure that is replicable and valid and that the U.S. Department of State's annual country reports on human rights practices offer the best resource to code judicial independence for the global set of countries. I also share their concern that the reports are potentially thinner in their reporting of judicial independence backward in time and have kept this in mind in my coding and analyses. Another caveat I have tried to keep in mind in creating the judicial independence measure is that it is a measure of judicial independence *as reported* by the Department of State. As such, the scores represent the considered judgment of Department of State field officers who have been charged by Congress and their superiors with delivering annual assessments for the countries where they are stationed regarding human rights practices (and judicial independence) as conceptualized under international law. Just how "expert" their assessments are might be debated.[9] Nevertheless, I would strongly defend these assessments as providing the best data source currently available for evaluating levels of judicial independence for the global set of nations across a significantly long period. I recognize that some scholars would express concern that one of my key dependent variables, the Political Terror Scale (PTS), is based solely on the same source as measure of *de facto* judicial independence. Thus it remains even more important that we conduct parallel analysis using the Amnesty International–based PTS measure as well the Freedom House civil liberties measure. The Cingranelli and Richards (CIRI) Index is based on both the Amnesty International and Department of State reports, with the Amnesty International reports controlling.

In constructing my measure of behavioral judicial independence I used Howard and Carey (2004) as a reference point. They described their measure, which they were able to create for ten years, as follows: "Our full, or high, independence measure corresponds to judiciaries that function in practice independent of the executive and legislature, are relatively free from corruption and bribery, and afford basic criminal due process protections to criminal defendants. Our middle measure of independence corresponds to judiciaries that have one, but not both, of these two characteristics, or that have partial measures of both" (287–88). Howard and Carey code the two measures as independent dichotomous variables; presumably the default or reference category is those without judicial independence. While I applaud Howard and Carey's measure of judicial independence, I find it less than ideal for my purposes here because one of its three components considers whether the state provides due process protections to criminal defendants. This component seems at best indirectly related to consensus definitions of judicial independence, and it appears to conflate independence and impartiality, which I prefer not to do. In addition, my strong interest in subsequently exploring the potential influence of judicial independence on human rights leads me to be very sensitive to possible overlaps between operationalizations of independent variables used in human rights models and dependent variables such as the PTS and CIRI measures of personal or physical integrity abuse. These dependent variables assess the degree of abusive or politically motivated state behavior, including imprisonment, torture, disappearance, and extrajudicial killings, which seem by their very nature to deny the basic due process rights included in Howard and Carey's operationalization of judicial independence. Therefore, I am reluctant to follow Howard and Carey's operationalization because ultimately I want a measure that would be fully independent of human rights protection variables. In creating my "behavioral" or *de facto* judicial independence indicator, I first compiled a document containing all portions of the Department of State country reports that dealt with the judiciary for the entire set of countries for two sample years, 2003 and 1993. I then read this compilation to ascertain what coding specificity was possible given the level of detail reported across countries for the two sample years. While it might be desirable to create a richer measure than the Howard and Carey indicator, the level of information in the reports simply did not promote confidence that I could do so for the entire set of countries, a conclusion that I assume Howard and Carey reached as well.

From my reading of these reports I created a measure that captured my conceptualization of judicial independence, one that I believe is appropriate for the data available in the Department of State reports, and that closely reflects the language of the Department of State assessments themselves.[10] I created a trichotomous measure that assigns scores as follows:

> *Fully Independent Judiciary (2):* The judiciary is reported as "generally independent" or is independent in practice, with no mention of corruption or outside influence.
> *Somewhat Independent Judiciary (1):* The judiciary is reported to be somewhat independent in practice, with reports of (some) pressure from the executive "at times" or with occasional reports of corruption.
> *Nonindependent Judiciary (0):* The judiciary is reported as not being independent in practice; is reported to have significant or high levels of executive influence or interference; or is reported to high levels of corruption. See the appendix at the end of the chapter for country excerpts and examples of the coding.

Using these definitions, I had two research assistants code all countries for the years 2003 and 1993. Their independently coded scores produced a reliability coefficient of .91. I then coded the Department of State reports backward in time, so that I could assess initially whether the reports were becoming too thin as we moved back into the 1980s. Coders were instructed not to force the coding if the reports became insufficiently detailed to determine the appropriate score, and we reemphasized this message as the coding moved to earlier years. While I cannot be sure that coders always explicitly noted that the information present in a report was insufficiently detailed to allow a confident coding, for the years 1981–1984, the four years for which I expected information to be least adequate, they did do so, and reported insufficient information in less than 1 percent of the country-years.

Trends over Time

Figure 4.4 presents the annual means for the *de facto* or behavioral measure of judicial independence. In order to compare the mean level of *de facto* independence with *de jure* independence I take the additive index of the seven constitutional provisions and then convert the index to a three-point scale to allow us to compare the level of formal achievement with actual achievement of judicial independence in same line graph. An interesting pattern

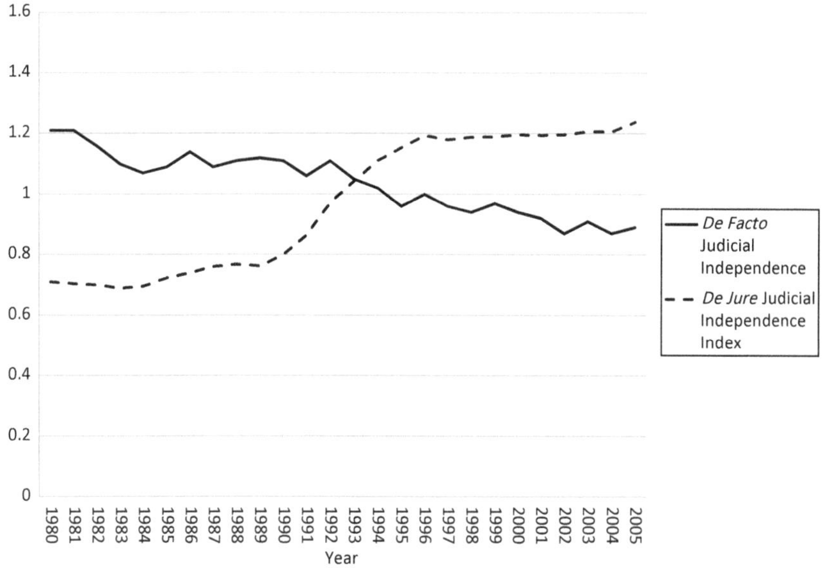

Figure 4.4. Mean Level of *De Facto* Judicial Independence Compared Against *De Jure* Index, 1980–2005

emerges that provides strong evidence of decoupling with the post-Cold War constitutions. Prior to 1993 we see a higher mean level of *de facto* judicial independence than formal judicial independence (as much as .50) during a significant portion of this period. Following 1993 we see a growing gap between practice and promise.

Figure 4.5 presents the percentage of countries that fall into each of the *de facto* judicial independence categories so that we can see composition within the categories and movement across the categories as well. Prior to 1995, fully independent judiciaries was actually the modal category, ranging from almost 50 to 40 percent until 1993 when the percentages began to slowly decline to the mid to low 30s. The midlevel category of "somewhat independent" judiciaries has seen some variation but has largely remained between 20 and 30 percent of the states. Prior to the post-Cold War constitution writing, the lowest category and midlevel category of independence/remained fairly equal in terms of proportions of states failing with the two categories. In 1992 we see the percentage of "not independent" states increase until it becomes the modal category in 1995. Thus while the global script may call for constitutional provision for judicial independence, these formal promises appear to remain unfulfilled, and

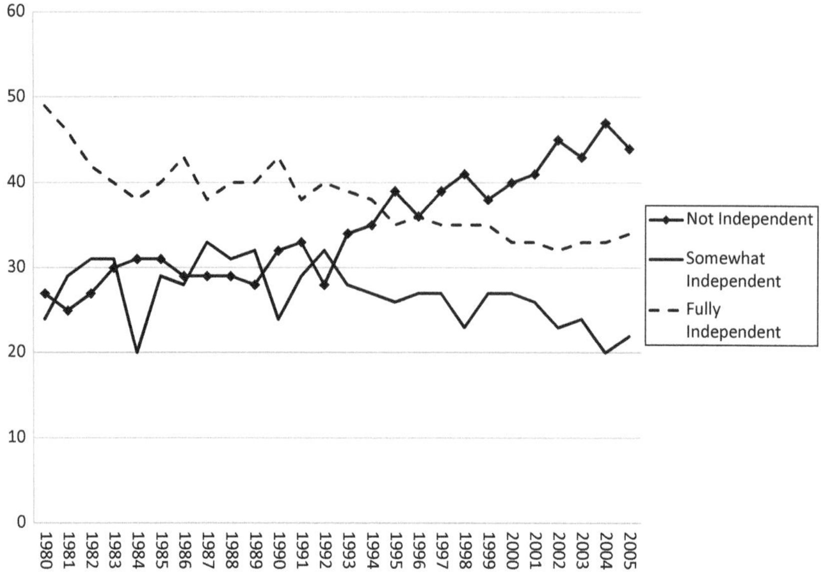

Figure 4.5. Percentage of Countries in Each Category of Judicial Independence, 1980–2005

globally we find the judiciaries on average to be less independent now than they were twenty-five years ago. Obviously, this simple bivariate line graph only begins to tell the story. I examine the relationship more rigorously in the section that follows. I now turn to operationalizing my concepts and presenting the measures to be employed in the models to test these hypotheses.

Operationalizing the Hypotheses

Dependent Variable: The dependent variable is *De Facto Judicial Independence* as measured above.

Formal (De Jure) *Judicial Independence:* This measure is operationalized as a 16-point additive index of the seven provisions of formal judicial independence. The index ranges from -1 to 14.

Constitutional Provision for Judicial Review and Hierarchical System: I also include separate measures for constitutional provision for judicial review and for a hierarchical system as operationalized above.

Embeddedness: I use the two measures described above.

Economic Development and Liberalization: I employ the same four measures described above.

Domestic and Internal Threats: In this model I examine three types of threats. *Civil war,* which is measured, following Small and Singer's (1982) guidelines for identifying instances of civil war: (1) "the government, as the central authority in a country, must be involved as a direct participant in the war," and (2) "there must be effective resistance, that is, either both sides must be 'organized for violent conflict' or the weaker side, although initially unprepared, [must be] able to inflict upon the stronger opponents at least five percent of the number of fatalities it sustains" (215). *International war,* which is measured following Small and Singer's guidelines for identifying instances of international war: a nation experiences an international war when it is a participant in a conflict in which more than one national government is directly involved and in which "(1) there was a total of a thousand or more battle deaths suffered by all of the participants in the conflict, [and] (2) the particular country suffered at least a hundred fatalities or had a thousand or more personnel taking part in the hostilities" (50 and 55). To capture the presence of an armed insurgency I utilize Poe et al.'s (2000) measure, *Organized Violent Rebellion,* which is operationalized as a situation in which a substantial organized movement seeks to alter the governmental system, bringing about a significant change in the constitution or other political institutions through armed attacks, including terrorist activities, guerrilla movements, and most attempted coups, but not full-scale civil war.

Military regimes: I operationalize military regimes following Poe, Tate, and Keith (1999), Keith, Tate, and Poe (2009), and others who have used Madani's (1992) classification, which builds upon McKinlay and Cohan (1975), where military regimes are defined as those that have come to power "as a consequence of a successful *coup d'état,* led by the army, navy or air force, that remained in power with a military person as the chief executive, for at least six months in a given year" (Madani 1992, 61; see McKinlay and Cohan 1975, 1). This operationalization also includes a small number of mixed regimes "with either a civilian as the chief executive and several military persons in the cabinet or a military head of government who nominated a civilian as the head of government and himself worked behind the scenes" (Madani 1992, 61). The measure is dichotomous, with military regimes coded (1) and all other regimes coded (0).

Population Constraints: Population constraints are operationalized as the natural logarithm of the total national population. I lag this variable one year.

Political Fragmentation: I test several measures to capture political fragmentation using three measures from the World Bank's Database of Political Institutions: (1) measure that captures the total vote share of all opposition parties; (2) measures of whether the opposition party has an absolute majority in (a) the house or (b) the senate; and (3) their combined measure of whether the opposition has an absolute majority in the house and/or the senate (Beck, Keefer and Clarke 2010).

Colonial Experience and Legal System: I create two dummy variables to indicate former British colonies and francophone colonies (colonies of France and Belgium). I create two dummy variables for (1) any state with a civil law system and (2) any state with a common law system.

Political Democracy: I utilize Davenport and Armstrong's (2004) trichotomous operationalization of Polity and Keith's (2002a) disaggregated sub-dimensions of Polity, as operationalized in Chapter 3.

Selection Effects: As noted at the beginning of this chapter, there is a strong possibility that many of the factors associated with state fulfillment of a constitutional promise are likely to be those associated with the behavioral practice itself. Thus, we would be unable to separate out whether effects of formal promises of judicial independence (*de jure*) on actual achieved (*de facto*) judicial independence were the result of the conditions or circumstances that made the state likely to adopt constitutional provisions for judicial independence in the first place or whether they were the consequence of formal independence itself. I follow Abouharb and Cingranelli's (2007, 84–87) two-step approach in dealing with this issue. First, I estimated the model of state adoption of constitutional provisions for judicial independence in the section above, and then I linked the equation predicting *de facto* judicial independence by generating probabilities from the equation predicting adoption of *de jure* judicial independence and adding them into the *de facto* equation as my selection effects.

Analysis

I undertook a series of initial analyses with my model. First, I estimated the models utilizing a variety of lags of the formal measure; the contemporaneous effect was consistently the strongest in terms of impact and statistical significance. Table 4.2 reports the results of my first set of models, without controlling for democracy. Table 4.3 presents the analysis testing the two key measures of democracy. As in the previous tables, the odd-numbered columns report the fixed-effects models, and the even-numbered columns report the ordered probit models. The first two columns include the period 1980–2005 minus the IGO and INGO measures (which are time-restricted), and the second two columns report the analysis for the period 1980–2000 with the IGO and INGO measures included.

In Table 4.2 we see that the models for the two periods perform virtually the same, even with addition of the IGO/INGO measures in one set of models. The largest predictor of judicial independence is past achievement of judicial independence: coefficients of .46 and .43 in the fixed-effects models suggest that a 1-point increase over the previous year's level of independence will be associated with an almost .5 increase in the 3-point scale. As with the *de jure* independence model, these scores suggest that *de facto* judicial independence is a strongly seated characteristic of a state's political system that does not change easily or rapidly. Despite the apparent gap between promise and practice that we saw in the descriptive analyses above, the formal commitments do affect the level of actual judicial independence in practice, if rather moderately. The measure of formal commitment to judicial independence produces a coefficient of .02 that is statistically significant in all four models. In the fixed-effects models the coefficients can be interpreted to mean that a 1-unit increase in a 14-point additive index would be associated with a .02 increase in the 3-point scale, a result that is rather limited substantively; however, a maximum increase from no provision of judicial independence to full provision of judicial independence would be associated with a .39 increase in *de facto* judicial independence. In these models I also tested the two somewhat controversial constitutional provisions separately but found neither judicial review nor hierarchical systems to be statistically significant. None of three indicators of economic liberalization is statistically significant. The model suggests no support for the hypothesis or the alternative hypothesis in regard to economic liberalization. I do, however, find evidence that judicial independence is dependent in part on the availability of resources for institution building and support—logged per-capita GDP is significant in all four models, but the impact is quite small: a percentage increase in the per-capita GDP would be associated with an increase in the level of judicial independence by .001 in each of the fixed-effects models. The resource constraint hypothesis is supported in that the population is statistically

Table 4.2. Model of *De Facto* Judicial Independence, 1980–2005

	1980–2005 (without IGO/INGO)		*1980–2000 (with IGO/INGO)*	
	Fixed Effects (1)	*Ordered Probit* (2)	*Fixed Effects* (3)	*Ordered Probit* (4)
De Facto Judicial Independence$_{t-1}$ (+)	.46 (.03)***	1.71 (.06)***	.43 (.03)***	1.56 (.06)***
Formal Judicial Independence (+)	.02 (.01)*	.01 (.01)**	.02 (.01)**	.02 (.01)**
Selection Effects (+)	.00 (.01)	.01 (.02)	.01 (.01)	.01 (.02)
Judicial Review Provision (+)	–.07 (.04)	–.09 (.04)	–.06 (.04)	–.05 (.04)
Hierarchical System Provision (+/–)	.03 (.04)	.01 (.03)	.02 (.04)	.01 (.04)
Trade$_{t-1}$ (+/–)	–.001 (.001)	–.001 (.001)	–.001 (.001)	–.001 (.001)
WTO Member$_{t-1}$ (+/–)	–.02 (.02)	–.06 (.05)	.003 (.03)	–.01 (.07)
Net FDI$_{t-1}$ (+/–)	.001 (.00)	.001 (.00)	.001 (.00)	.01 (.01)
Logged Per Capita GDP$_{t-1}$ (+)	.08 (.04)**	.20 (.03)***	.10 (.05)**	.21 (.03)***
Logged Population $_{t-1}$ (–)	–.54 (.10)***	–.04 (.02)**	–.58 (.13)***	–.05 (.02)***
Organized Violent Rebellion (–)	.01 (.02)	.01 (.06)	.02 (.03)	.03 (.07)
Civil War (–)	–.09 (.05)**	–.13 (.10)*	–.09 (.06)*	–.19 (.11)**
International War (–)	–.07 (.04)*	–.06 (.12)	–.08 (.05)*	–.08 (.05)*
Military Regime (–)	–.09 (.05)**	–.003 (.08)	–.13 (.05)***	–.08 (.08)
Political Fragmentation (+)	.001 (.001)	.01 (.001)***	.001 (.001)	.01 (.001)***
British Colony	—	.21 (.06)***	—	.28 (.07)***
IGO Membership	—	—	.001 (.001)	.01 (.001)***

Table 4.2 (*continued*)

	1980–2005 (without IGO/INGO)		1980–2000 (with IGO/INGO)	
	Fixed Effects (1)	*Ordered Probit* (2)	*Fixed Effects* (3)	*Ordered Probit* (4)
Logged INGO Membership	—	—	–.04 (.05)	.07 (.03)***
Observations	2884	2884	2337	2337
R^2 /Pseudo-R^2	.73	.50	.70	.47
F /Chi^2	29.26	1392.04	20.14	1181.11
Prob > F / Prob > Chi^2	.0001	.0001	.0001	.0001

Fixed-effects and ordered probit estimation with robust standard errors. Standard errors in parentheses. *Significant at the 10 percent level. **Significant at the 5 percent level. ***Significant at the 1 percent level. All tests one-tailed except where no direction predicted (+) predicted positive direction, (–) negative, and (+/–) no predicted direction.

significant in all four models, but the impact here is also quite small: in the fixed-effects model a percentage increase in population size is associated with an increase in the level of judicial independence by .01, with rounding.

More significantly in terms of substantive effect, I find that two of the three forms of threat, civil war and international war, are negatively associated with judicial independence and achieve statistical significance in seven of the eight models. The coefficients suggest that the onset of civil war or international war is associated with a moderate decrease in judicial independence of close to .1 in the judicial independence index. Violent domestic rebellions, which do not rise to the level of civil war, fail to achieve statistical significance; this result suggests that the overall independence of the judiciary is not diminished when the state faces violent threats of a more limited nature. I tested the robustness of this finding by substituting other measures of violent domestic threats such as coups, event counts of guerrilla warfare, and revolutions—none of which achieved statistical significance. Clearly, judicial independence suffers during times of threat, but the good news seems to be that the threats must rise to a fairly significant level for an observable effect generally. The hypothesis that military regimes will be more likely to curb judicial independence is supported in both fixed models (coefficients of -.09 and -.13) but not in the non-fixed-effects model. I engaged

Table 4.3. Model of *De Facto* Judicial Independence Testing Trichotomous Measure of Democracy, 1980–2005

	1980–2005 (without IGO/INGO)		*1980–2000 (with IGO/INGO)*	
	Fixed Effects (1)	*Ordered Probit (2)*	*Fixed Effects (3)*	*Ordered Probit (4)*
De Facto Judicial Independence$_{t-1}$ (+)	.46 (.03)***	1.61 (.06)***	.42 (.03)***	1.48 (.06)***
Formal Judicial Independence (+)	.02 (.01)**	.01 (.01)**	.02 (.01)**	.01 (.01)**
Selection Effects (+)	01 (.01)	.01 (.02)	.01 (.01)	.01 (.02)
Provision for Judicial Review (+)	–.06 (.04)	–.08 (.04)	–.06 (.04)	–.05 (.05)
Provision for Hierarchical System (+/–)	.03 (.04)	–.01 (.03)	.01 (.04)	–.01 (.04)
Trade$_{t-1}$ (+/–)	–.001 (.001)	–.001 (.001)	–.001 (.001)	–.001 (.001)
WTO Member$_{t-1}$ (+/–)	–.02 (.02)	–.20 (.06)***	.01 (.03)	–.01 (.001)
Net FDI$_{t-1}$ (+/–)	.001 (.00)	–.01 (.00)***	.001 (.00)	–.01 (.00)
Logged Per Capita GDP$_{t-1}$ (+)	.07 (.03)**	.11 (.03)***	.12 (.05)***	.11 (.03)***
Logged Population$_{t-1}$ (–)	–.54 (.10)***	–.06 (.02)***	–.57 (.13)***	–.07 (.02)***
Organized Violent Rebellion (–)	.01 (.02)	.02 (.06)	.02 (.03)	.05 (.07)
Civil War (–)	–.07 (.05)**	–.06 (.10)	–.06 (.06)	–.15 (.11)*
International War (–)	–.06 (.04)*	–.05 (.11)	–.05 (.05)	–.09 (.08)
Military Regime (–)	–.07 (.05)**	.06 (.08)	–.10 (.05)***	–.04 (.08)
Government Fragmentation (+)	.001 (.001)	.01 (.001)***	.001 (.001)	.01 (.001)***
British Colony	—	.34 (.07)***	—	.38 (.07)***

Table 4.3 (*continued*)

	1980–2005 (without IGO/INGO)		*1980–2000 (with IGO/INGO)*	
	Fixed Effects (1)	*Ordered Probit (2)*	*Fixed Effects (3)*	*Ordered Probit (4)*
IGO Membership	—	—	.001 (.001)	.01 (.001)***
Logged INGO Membership	—	—	–.06 (.04)	.04 (.03)
Trichotomous Measure of Democracy	.08 (.05)*	.55 (.05)***	.10 (.07)*	.50 (.06)***
Observations	2764	2764	2245	2245
R^2 /Pseudo-R^2	.74	.52	.71	.50
F /Chi^2	25.56	1470.22	18.00	1228.18
Prob > F / Prob > Chi^2	.0001	.0001	.0001	.0001

Fixed-effects and ordered probit estimation with robust standard errors. Standard errors in parentheses. *Significant at the 10 percent level. **Significant at the 5 percent level. ***Significant at the 1 percent level. All tests one-tailed except where no direction predicted (+) predicted positive direction, (–) negative, and (+/–) no predicted direction.

in preliminary tests of the four measures of government fragmentation and ultimately decided upon the indicator of the vote share held by opposition parties. The government fragmentation hypothesis is supported in part: the coefficients in the model controlling for fixed effects are not statistically significant; however, in the ordered probit model the coefficients achieve a high level of statistical significance, but the coefficients approximate zero.

The measure for British colonial experience is dropped from the fixed-effects model because of collinearity, but in the model without fixed effects the British colonial experience coefficient is associated with higher levels of judicial independence. When I substitute French colonial experience for British colonial experience I find that the coefficient is negative, but it would be statistically significant only at the .13 level. I also substitute my legal system type measures for the colonial legacy measures, assuming that they represent a more direct test of the institutional structure. I ran the model with the common law system dummy variable and then with the civil law system dummy variable. Both coefficients were statistically significant in the ordered probit models but the invariant dummy variables are dropped from the fixed-effects models. I find evidence that supports the claim that common law systems will be more independent than their civil law counterparts: the civil law system measure produces a coefficient of -.10, which is significant at the .05 level, and the common law measure produces a much larger coefficient of .35, which is statistically significant at the .001 level. Finally, in the two models with measures of IGO participation and INGO presence, the coefficients (.01 and .07) are statistically significant in the ordered probit model, but not in the fixed-effects model. Overall, I find that formal provisions for judicial independence have a moderate influence on achieved judicial independence, and that several environmental factors influence the level of independence that courts enjoy. I deliberately did not model democracy in these first models, to allow us to establish systematically a base model before testing the various specifications of democracy. Next I move on to the analysis examining the impact of democratization on judicial independence.

I test the two specifications of democracy from Chapter 3: the trichotomous measure of level of democracy and the disaggregated components. The analysis with trichotomous measures is reported in Table 4.3. Adding democracy to the models produces a couple of significant changes, but largely the model performs the same as in the previous analysis. The coefficient for formal provision for judicial independence remains the same size and achieves acceptable levels of statistical significance in all four models. Once democracy is controlled for, we see that the negative coefficients for FDI and WTO membership gain statistical significance in the non-IGO/INGO ordered probit model. More importantly, civil war and international war lose their statistical significance in all but one (international war) or two (civil war) of the four models, a result suggesting that the accountability features of democracy may decrease the likelihood that a regime will take advantage of a domestic crisis to curb the judiciary. Finally, when controlling for level of democracy, INGO membership loses its statistical significance, but IGO participation remains statistically significant. We have to be somewhat cautious in comparing these models, as this INGO/IGO model extends only to 2000, and thus the model lacks five years that the other models cover. In regard to the democracy measure, I find the coefficients to be statistically significant in all four models. If we use the fixed-effects model in column 1 as an example, we see that a 1-unit increase would be associated with a .08 increase in judicial independence or a maximum increase of .16 for a maximum in the level of democracy, a relatively minor impact.

In Table 4.4 I tested the second democracy measure, the disaggregated components, which allow us to test separately two components of the Polity democracy measure that may be particularly important to the realization of judicial independence: constraints on the executive and party competition. Of the three components I examine, these two are statistically significant in all four models. The coefficients in fixed-effects models suggest that a change from no constraints on the executive to a system in which the executive has parity with the legislative or judicial branches is associated with a .16 or .24 change in the level of judicial independence. As in the base repression models of Chapter 3, party competition produces the largest effect of the two components: a maximum improvement in competiveness of political participation is associated with a .15 increase in the level of judicial independence. This model performs almost identically with the models in Table 4.3 except that in the ordered probit models, the coefficients for formal judicial independence lose their statistical significance once we control for these components of democratization. In the fixed-effects models the coefficients for formal judicial independence retain their statistical significance. To further examine the relationship between these provisions and party competition and executive constraints, I re-estimated the models, including interactive terms for the democracy components and the formal index. The interactive terms produce positive coefficients that are statistically significant at .0001 in all four models. Table 4.5 reports the coefficients for the constitutive terms and interaction terms. The base model performs the same, so for ease of presentation I do not report those coefficients. The interaction terms tell us that the formal provisions for judicial independence are associated with an increase in achieved levels of judicial independence when constraints are placed on the executive and when parties are competitive within the state. However, the coefficient for the formal provisions do not achieve statistical significance; this result tells us that formal provisions absent competitive parties and executive constraints have no influence on the actual level of judicial independence. The constitutive terms "Executive Constraint" and "Party Competition" produce negative coefficients that are highly statistically significant, a result suggesting that when the formal provisions are not present in the constitutions, the components of democratization reduce the likelihood of judicial independence.

I next estimated the model with interaction terms testing the assumption that the effect of the provisions on judicial independence would be conditional on circumstances such as domestic threat, economic conditions, and embeddedness; however, I found that none of the interactions achieved statistical

Table 4.4. Model of *De Facto* Judicial Independence Testing Disaggregated Measure of Democracy, 1980–2005

	1980–2005 (without IGO/INGO)		*1980–2000 (with IGO/INGO)*	
	Fixed Effects (1)	*Ordered Probit (2)*	*Fixed Effects (3)*	*Ordered Probit (4)*
De Facto Judicial Independence$_{t-1}$ (+)	.45 (.03)***	1.62 (.06)***	.41 (.03)***	1.48 (.06)***
Formal Judicial Independence (+)	.01 (.01)*	.001 (.01)	.02 (.01)**	.01 (.02)
Selection Effects (+)	.01 (.01)	.01 (.02)	.01 (.01)	.01 (.02)
Provision for Judicial Review (+)	–.07 (.04)	–.09 (.04)	–.06 (.04)	–.05 (.05)
Provision for Hierarchical System (+/–)	.02 (.04)	–.02 (.04)	.01 (.04)	–.02 (.04)
Trade$_{t-1}$ (+)	–.001 (.001)	–.001 (.001)	–.001 (.001)	–.001 (.001)
WTO Member$_{t-1}$ (+)	–.02 (.03)	–.22 (.06)***	.01 (.03)	–.12 (.08)
Net FDI$_{t-1}$ (+)	.001 (.001)	–.01 (.00)***	.001 (.00)	–.01 (.00)*
Logged Per Capita GDP$_{t-1}$ (+)	.09 (.04)**	.17 (.03)***	.14 (.05)***	.13 (.03)***
Logged Population$_{t-1}$ (–)	–.62 (.11)***	–.05 (.02)***	–.66 (.13)***	–.07 (.02)***
Organized Violent Rebellion (–)	.01 (.02)	.01 (.07)	.02 (.03)	.01 (.07)
Civil War (–)	–.07 (.05)	–.08 (.11)	–.06 (.07)	–.14 (.12)
International War (–)	–.06 (.04)*	–.03 (.12)	–.07 (.05)*	–.09 (.11)
Military Regime (–)	–.01 (.05)	.21 (.08)	–.03 (.05)	.10 (.08)
Government Fragmentation (+)	.001 (.001)	.002 (.001)*	–.001 (.001)	.002 (.001)**
British Colony	—	.38 (.07)***	—	.41 (.07)***

Table 4.4 (*continued*)

	1980–2005 (without IGO/INGO)		*1980–2000 (with IGO/INGO)*	
	Fixed Effects (1)	*Ordered Probit (2)*	*Fixed Effects (3)*	*Ordered Probit (4)*
IGO Membership	—	—	.001 (.001)	.01 (.001)***
Logged INGO Membership	—	—	–.06 (.04)	.02 (.03)
Constraint on the Chief Executive	.04 (.02)**	.13 (.03)***	.06 (.02)***	.13 (.03)***
Competitiveness of Political Participation	.05 (.03)**	.19 (.05)**	.05 (.04)*	.16 (.05)***
Openness of Executive Recruitment	.01 (.06)	.10 (.09)	–.02 (.08)	.09 (.09)
Observations	2728	2728	2214	2214
R^2 /Pseudo-R^2	.74	.52	.71	.50
F /*Chi*²	25.09	1444.73	18.72	1218.99
Prob > *F* / Prob > *Chi*²	.0001	.0001	.0001	.0001

Fixed-effects and ordered probit estimation with robust standard errors. Standard errors in parentheses. *Significant at the 10 percent level. **Significant at the 5 percent level. ***Significant at the 1 percent level. All tests one-tailed except where no direction predicted (+) predicted positive direction, (–) negative, and (+/–) no predicted direction.

significance. The judicial independence index remained statistically significant in the models. Overall, the models suggest that the level of judicial independence fostered or allowed in a state is dependent upon a variety of circumstances well beyond mere formal promises. The formal promises increase the level of judicial independence, but the effect is minimal in terms of size, and becomes inconsistent across methods of estimation, once core components of democratization are controlled. The provisions perform consistently when the trichotomous measure of democracy is utilized; however, the relationship appears to be more complicated, as the analysis of disaggregated factors demonstrated. The formal provisions' influence is dependent upon the presence of legislative checks on the executive as well as a competitive party system. Thus, I conclude that formal provisions alone offer only a weak

Table 4.5. Model of *De Facto* Judicial Independence Testing with Interaction Effects for Disaggregated Measure of Democracy, 1980–2005

	1980–2005 (without IGO/INGO)		*1980–2000 (with IGO/INGO)*	
	Fixed Effects (1)	*Ordered Probit* (2)	*Fixed Effects* (3)	*Ordered Probit* (4)
Formal Judicial Independence (+)	.01 (.01)	.001 (.01)	.01 (.01)	.01 (.02)
Interaction: Constraint on the Chief Executive and Formal Judicial Independence	.11 (.02)***	4.62 (.13)***	.11 (.02)***	4.59 (.16)***
Interaction: Competitiveness of Political Participation and Formal Judicial Independence	.24 (.03)***	8.55 (.26)***	.26 (.04)***	8.38 (.26)***
Constraint on the Chief Executive	–.06 (.02)***	–4.54 (.13)***	–.06 (.02)***	–4.53 (.13)***
Competitiveness of Political Participation	–.19 (.04)***	–8.51 (.27)***	–.22 (.05)***	–8.53 (.27)***
Observations	2728	2728	2214	2214
R^2 /Pseudo-R^2	.81	.73	.79	.71
F /Chi^2	62.70	7416.34	48.17	5491.82
Prob > F / Prob > Chi^2	.0001	.0001	.0001	.0001

influence on the *de facto* level of independence, which appears to be influenced more by a broader set of electoral conditions, resource capabilities and constraints, and to some extent violent threats to the regime. In the next section I turn to the question of whether achieved levels of judicial independence reduce the probability that a regime will choose to employ tools of repression.

The Judiciary and State Repression

The domestic institutions and democratic peace literatures argue that state institutions and structures can both facilitate and constrain state use of repression. As I noted in Chapter 2, this rational-actor perspective dismisses the assumption of a unitary state actor and instead recognizes the role of numerous domestic actors and institutions within the state, particularly in democratic regimes, which is likely to affect the regime's menu of acceptable policy options or to influence its calculation of the costs and benefits associated with compliance or noncompliance with formal rights commitment. Opportunity is constrained because the structure and nature of democratic governments make extensive use of repression more difficult to arrange. Willingness is dampened because democracy "provides citizens (at least those with political resources) the tools to oust potentially abusive leaders from office before they are able to become a serious threat" (Poe and Tate 1994, 855); thus the cost of repression is increased (Davenport 1999). From the perspective of domestic legal institutions it is not just democratic electoral processes but also the legal institutions associated with democratic systems that can potentially provide the public and other political actors with the tools and venues through which they can hold the regime accountable should it fail to keep its formal commitments, both domestic (Keith 2002a) and international (for example, Keith 1999; Neumayer 2005; Hathaway 2007; Powell and Staton 2009). Larkins (1996) emphasizes the unique role of the courts, especially in transitional democracies: "The judicial branch, after all, is the institution normally charged with the enforcement of the constitution, rights, and other democratic procedures in constitutional democracies. Ideally, through the application of judicial or constitutional review, judges can not only mediate conflicts between political actors but also prevent the arbitrary exercise of government power" (606).

An independent judiciary, in particular, should be able to protect against the regime's abuse of its authority and "should be able to withstand incursions upon rights because (1) the courts' power and fiscal well-being are protected, (2) the courts have some ability to review the actions of other agencies of government, and (3) the judges' jobs are constitutionally protected" (Keith, Tate, and Poe 2009, 649). Powell and Staton (2009) posit that in states in which the courts are effective, the use of repression may lead to rights claims in which the regime may incur a loss of resources as punishment for violating its obligations (154). Not only may the regime incur a loss of resources, but such litigation also introduces potential reputational costs. Thus, the increased potential cost of repression may affect the regime's cost/benefit calculation in its decision whether to employ coercive force against its citizens. In addition, NGOs may initiate human rights litigation and form with courts what Moustafa (2007) refers to as "judicial support networks," which consist of domestic and transnational institutions and associations that support the judiciary's independence and power, thus intertwining the fate of the judicial independence and the legal recourse to rights (Ginsburg and Moustafa 2008, 13). These expectations lead us to predict that higher levels of judicial independence will be associated with lower levels of state repression.

- Hypothesis: States with higher levels of judicial independence will be less likely to engage in political repression.

These expectations are in part built upon the assumption that judges will be rights-friendly and produce liberal-democratic jurisprudence; but, as Prempeh (1999) notes, actual decisions of the courts, even structurally independent courts, sometimes take a different course (136). He points to the Ghanaian Supreme Court under the liberal fourth republican constitution that went into effect in January 1993. The justices on the bench were much more disposed toward a jurisprudence of executive supremacy than a jurisprudence of constitutionalism. Furthermore, he argues that "for the better part of its life, the African state—and for that matter, the African judiciary—has paid homage to a jurisprudence of executive supremacy, with regrettable consequences for civil liberties and personal freedoms across the continent" (140). He posits that "a judiciary habituated by custom, training, and experience to this way of thinking learns, quite naturally, to be excessively deferential to the state and all manner of public authority," and thus "such a judiciary reckons its institutional role primarily as one of maintaining 'law and order,' and not as protecting freedom or restraining government" (140). Russell's (2001) cautionary assessment parallels Prempeh's; he cautions that judges "come to their work with predispositions based on their pre-judicial experience and affiliation" and these predispositions are not easily shed (10). More specifically, Rosenn (1987) argues: "Latin American culture and political tradition are heavily authoritarian. The pattern of executive domination is not accidental. Rather it reflects the Roman law tradition of granting autocratic powers to the emperors and *paterfamilias*, the corporativism and patrimonialism of colonial rule, and the hierarchical structure of the Catholic church. Despite extensive constitutional rhetoric, the principle that the government should be subjected to the rule of law does not come naturally to most of Latin America" (34).

Thus, regardless of structural provision for or actual achievement of judicial independence, judges are likely to have a belief system that mirrors the larger political culture.[11] Hilbink's (2007) work suggests more specifically that in the case of the Chilean judiciary, the institutional structure and the ideology of the judiciary explains how the judiciary "so easily ignored [their constitutional] oath and supported, sometimes passively, other times actively, the illiberal, antidemocratic, and *anti-legal* agenda of the military government" (3). She argues that the personal views of the judges are not sufficient explanation of the courts' behavior, but rather the strong institutional "antipolitics" conception of the role of judiciary meant that "publicly challenging the validity of the regime's laws and policies in the name of liberal-democratic values and principles was viewed as unprofessional 'political' behavior, which threatened the integrity of the judiciary and the rule of law" (7). The hierarchical institutional structure of the Chilean judiciary allowed the Supreme Court control over discipline and promotion across ranks, and thus, as Hilbink points out, judges who wanted to succeed professionally learned that their best strategy was "to eschew independent and innovative interpretation in favor of conservative rulings that would please the high-court justices" (6). Thus, I find significant expectations that judicial independence will not lead to less state repression of rights to support the null hypothesis:

- Null Hypothesis: States with higher levels of judicial independence will not be less likely to engage in political repression.

In the section that follows I describe the full model of political repression, which controls for the effect of the type of legal system as well as colonial legacies.

Models of Political Repression

Dependent variables: I continue to examine measures of rights repression in this chapter as I did in Chapter 3, including the three measures of repression of personal integrity rights (the CIRI Index and the two PTS measures) and civil liberties (the Freedom House measure) and CIRI's individual measures of repression of freedom of speech, association, and religion. These variables are operationalized fully in Chapter 3.

De Facto *Judicial Independence:* I employ the measure as operationalized above.

Selection Effects: See the preceding section for a full description.

Judicial Review: I employ the formal measure of judicial review, as operationalized above.

Standard Model and Additional Control Variables: I incorporate the above variables within the revised standard model I estimated in Chapter 3. The model includes a lagged dependent variable, measures for civil and international war, military and Marxist/Marxist-Leninist regimes, logged population size, and per-capita GDP. I also test the two alternative measures of democracy: Davenport and Armstrong's (2004) trichotomous operationalization of Polity and Keith's (2002a) disaggregated sub-dimensions of Polity. These measures are operationalized in Chapter 3. I add two measures of economic liberalization: trade and FDI, as operationalized above. In these models I also attempt to refine the measure of colonial experience by replacing the standard British colonial legacy measure with indicators of legal system type. I follow Keith and Ogundele (2007) and use five categories derived from the divisions created by the University of Ottawa Law School's World Legal System project: Civil Law Systems, Common Law Systems, Customary Law Systems, Muslim Law Systems, and Mixed Systems.[12]

Finally, I control for state level of commitment to the ICCPR and to the Convention Against Torture (CAT). I follow Landman (2005) in operationalizing treaty commitments, and in fact I use his data, updating and extending it to 2005. I code countries that have ratified the treaty (or protocol) (2), have become signatories (1), and have not signed the treaty (0). As discussed above, controlling for reservations is increasingly important. Again, I use Landman's weighted measure that accounts for reservations, and I extended the data forward in time. Landman operationalizes as follows:

(4) Given to countries that have no reservations with regard to said treaty, interpretive declarations that do not modify obligations, or nonsubstantial declarations.
(3) Given to countries whose reservations could have some but not major impact on their obligations.
(2) Given to countries whose reservations have a noticeable effect on their obligations under the treaty to a whole article, nullifying or leaving open the possibility not to abide by a whole article.

(1) Given to countries whose reservations can have significant and severe effects on the treaty obligations. (42)[13]

Countries that are not signatories are coded (0). Of particular importance in regard to the ICCPR, Landman notes that "reservations that could allow for violation of nonderogable rights, particularly those accepted as customary international law (e.g., torture) or fundamental principles such as nondiscrimination" are coded (1) (176). Of particular relevance to the CAT, Landman notes that reservations that subject "the whole treaty or [limit] fundamental elements, such as the definition of torture or cruel, inhuman, or degrading treatment or punishment, to religious or national legislation" would be coded (1) (176). As discussed in Chapter 2, the compliance literature lacks consensus on the effect of treaty membership on political repression. Realists posit that treaties are cheap talk and that state compliance with a treaty will dissipate once the state's interest comes into conflict with the legal obligation (Hoffmann 1956; Waltz 1979; Mearsheimer 1994). Constructivists are generally more optimistic about state compliance due to norms diffusion (Cole 2005; Wotipka and Ramirez 2007) or the continuing pressure of transnational networks of INGOs (Keck and Sikkink 1998; Risse, Ropp, and Sikkink 1999); however, the world society approach does suggest a possible decoupling between promises and practice (Hafner-Burton and Tsutsui 2005). Thus I examine the effect of the treaties with a two-tailed test, with the exception of the Optional Protocol, which has been demonstrated to be more strongly linked to improved rights behavior (for example, Keith 1999).

Analysis

First, I estimate the models of political repression of physical integrity rights using the standard model identified in Chapter 3. I employ the trichotomous measure of democracy as the base model and then run parallel analyses to test for possible differences with disaggregated measures. Table 4.6 presents the results for the former model. The results for the standard model are essentially identical with the performance in Chapter 3. The coefficients for the democracy measure are somewhat smaller once the effect of *de facto* judicial independence is controlled, and the military regimes coefficient loses its statistical significance in one of the six models. The coefficients for *de facto* judicial

Table 4.6. Standard Model of Repression of Personal Integrity Rights with Judicial Independence, 1980–2005

	Personal Integrity Rights Abuse (PTS) 1980–2005		*Personal Integrity Rights Abuse (AI) 1980–2005*		*Personal Integrity Rights Abuse (CIRI) 1982–2005*	
	Fixed Effects (1)	*Ordered Probit (2)*	*Fixed Effects (3)*	*Ordered Probit (4)*	*Fixed Effects (5)*	*Ordered Probit (6)*
Rights Abuse (*t*–1) (+)	.48 (.02)***	1.28 (.04)***	.41 (.02)***	1.10 (.04)***	.41 (.03)***	.52 (.02)***
De Facto Judicial Independence (–)	–.12 (.03)***	–.25 (.03)***	–.09 (.03)***	–.14 (.03)***	–.26 (.06)***	–.19 (.03)***
Selection Effects: Judicial Independence (+)	–.01 (.02)	–.02 (.03)	–.01 (.02)	–.03 (.04)	–.03 (.04)	–.05 (.03)*
Formal Judicial Review (+/–)	–.05 (.03)*	–.01 (.02)	–.03 (.03)	–.03 (.02)	–.13 (.07)*	–.001 (.02)
Civil War (+)	.47 (.07)***	.74 (.10)***	.51 (.09)***	.66 (.10)***	.97 (.19)***	.62 (.09)***
International War (+)	.14 (.06)***	.27 (.10)***	.12 (.07)*	.23 (.08)***	.18 (.12)**	.23 (.08)***
Trichotomous Measure of Democracy (–)	–.07 (.05)*	–.31 (.05)***	–.13 (.06)***	–.32 (.04)***	–.22 (.11)**	–.29 (.04)***
Military Regimes (+)	.10 (.06)**	.09 (.06)*	.10 (.06)**	.08 (.06)*	.31 (.13)***	.06 (.06)

Marxist or Marxist-Leninist	.03	–.15	–.15	–.17	–.08	–.12
Regimes (+/–)	(.11)	(.08)**	(.13)	(.07)***	(.20)	(.09)*
Economic Development (–)	–.00001	–.00002	–.00002	–.00002	–.00004	–.00001
	(.002)	(.00)	(.00)	(.00)***	(.00)	(.00)***
Economic Growth (–)	–.01	–.01	–.01	–.01	–.002	–.001
	(.00)***	(.00)***	(.00)***	(.00)**	(.01)	(.01)
Logged Population (+)	.46	.15	.09	.16	.58	.16
	(.10)***	(.01)***	(.12)	(.02)***	(.23)***	(.01)***
Population Growth (+)	–.04	–.002	–.04	.02	–.06	.03
	(.01)	(.02)	(.02)***	(.02)*	(.05)	(.02)**
Observations	3187	3187	3187	3187	2933	2933
R^2 /Pseudo-R^2	.77	.47	.70	.40	.74	.31
F /Chi^2	77.41	2120.12	40.28	1983.44	41.83	2728.10
Prob > F / Prob > Chi^2	.0001	.0001	.0001	.0001	.0001	.0001

Fixed-effects and ordered probit estimation with robust standard errors. Standard errors in parentheses. *Significant at the 10 percent level. **Significant at the 5 percent level. ***Significant at the 1 percent level. All tests one-tailed except where no direction predicted (+) predicted positive direction, (–) negative, and (+/–) no predicted direction.

independence are highly statistically significant across all six models, even while controlling for selection effects. The coefficients in the fixed-effects models range from -.09 (Amnesty International–based PTS measure) to -.19 (CIRI index). Using the State Department PTS model as an example, we see that a one-unit increase in judicial independence would be associated with a decrease in the level of personal integrity abuse by .12, while a maximum increase would be associated with a .24 decrease, a result that is quite a bit higher than a maximum increase in the level of democracy (.14). In the model utilizing the CIRI index, a maximum change in judicial independence would be associated with a .38 decrease in the 9-point repression index, which is about two-thirds the size of the impact associated with a maximum increase in democracy. I also tested the formal provision of judicial review in the model; the results are mixed, producing negative coefficients in all six models; but only two of the six coefficients are statistically significant.

Next I re-estimated the model, employing the disaggregated measures of democracy. For ease of presentation, in Table 4.7 I report only the key coefficients of interests, since the results for the remainder of the model remained identical. All six coefficients for *de facto* judicial independence retain their high level of statistical significance and are approximately the same size as in the previous model. When I control the components of democracy, there are some changes in the effect of judicial review. In the original model only two coefficients were statistically significant, and they produced negative coefficients; in this model those two coefficients lose their statistical significance, and two different coefficients are statistically significant but positive. Thus, the influence of judicial review on repression remains quite inconsistent and sensitive to the delineation of democracy, a result which suggests that judicial review is more likely to facilitate rights protection when there are legislative constraints on the executive and when political parties are fully competitive. The coefficients for executive constraint are statistically significant in the three fixed-effects models but not in the ordered probit models. Before I controlled for judicial independence in the model, the coefficients in all six models were statistically significant. The competitiveness of political participation retains its statistical significance in all six models. None of the coefficients for openness of executive recruitment achieves statistical significance.

Table 4.8 presents the civil liberties model with the two different operationalizations of democracy. Once again, I find all the coefficients for *de*

Table 4.7. Disaggregated Democracy and Repression of Personal Integrity Rights with Judicial Independence, 1980–2005

	Personal Integrity Rights Abuse (PTS) 1980–2005		*Personal Integrity Rights Abuse (AI) 1980–2005*		*Personal Integrity Rights Abuse (CIRI) 1982–2005*	
	Fixed Effects (1)	*Ordered Probit (2)*	*Fixed Effects (3)*	*Ordered Probit (4)*	*Fixed Effects (5)*	*Ordered Probit (6)*
De Facto Judicial Independence	–.11	–.25	–.07	–.15	–.23	–.20
	(.03)***	(.04)***	(.03)***	(.03)***	(.03)***	(.03)***
Formal Judicial Review	–.04	.04	–.01	.06	–.11	.02
	(.03)	(.03)*	(.03)	(.02)***	(.07)	(.02)
Constraint on the Chief Executive	–.03	–.002	–.06	–.01	–.09	.003
	(.02)*	(.02)	(.02)***	(.02)	(.05)**	(.02)
Openness of Executive Recruitment	–.07	–.04	.02	.02	.001	–.001
	(.07)	(.07)	(.08)	(.07)	(.18)	(.07)
Competitiveness of Political Participation	–.04	–.20	–.08	–.21	–.08	–.20
	(.03)*	(.03)***	(.04)***	(.06)***	(.07)	(.03)***
Observations	3149	3149	3149	3149	2928	2928
R^2 /Pseudo-R^2	.76	.47	.70	.40	.74	.31
F /Chi^2	67.17	2192.21	33.82	1970.02	41.29	2728.33
Prob > F / Prob > Chi^2	.0001	.0001	.0001	.0001	.0001	.0001

Table 4.8. Standard Model of Repression of Civil Liberties with Judicial Independence, 1980–2005

	1980–2005 (with trichotomous democracy)		*1980–2005 (with disaggregated democracy)*	
	Fixed Effects (1)	*Ordered Probit (2)*	*Fixed Effects (3)*	*Ordered Probit (4)*
Rights Abuse (*t*–1) (+)	.72 (.02)***	2.04 (.08)***	.67 (.02)***	2.01 (.09)***
De Facto Judicial Independence (+/–)	–.12 (.02)***	–.21 (.04)***	–.10 (.02)***	–.20 (.04)***
Selection Effects: Judicial Independence (+)	–.01 (.01)	–.03 (.04)	–.01 (.01)	–.04 (.04)
Formal Judicial Review (+/–)	–.10 (.03)***	–.05 (.03)**	–.07 (.03)***	–.01 (.03)
Civil War (+)	.15 (.04)***	.21 (.09)***	.13 (.05)***	.26 (.10)***
International War (+)	–.04 (.05)	–.02 (.09)	–.03 (.05)	.11 (.10)
Trichotomous Measure of Democracy (–)	–.20 (.05)***	–.58 (.06)***	—	—
Constraint on the Chief Executive	—		–.10 (.02)***	–.20 (.03)***
Openness of Executive Recruitment	—		–.12 (.08)*	–.21 (.08)***
Competitiveness of Political Participation	—		–.14 (.03)***	–.36 (.04)***
Military Regimes (–)	.05 (.05)	.01 (.07)	–.09 (.06)*	–.19 (.08)***
Marxist or Marxist-Leninist Regimes (+/–)	.41 (.11)***	.41 (.13)***	.32 (.12)***	.37 (.14)***
Economic Development (–)	–.001 (.00)*	–.001 (.00)**	–.001 (.00)**	–.001 (.00)*
Economic Growth (–)	.004 (.01)**	.01 (.005)**	.002 (.01)	–.01 (.005)*
Logged Population (+)	–.37 (.08)	.02 (.02)*	–.26 (.07)	.05 (.01)*
Population Growth (+)	–.02 (.01)	.06 (.02)	–.01 (.01)	.04 (.02)**

Table 4.8 (*continued*)

	1980–2005 (with trichotomous democracy)		*1980–2005 (with disaggregated democracy)*	
	Fixed Effects (1)	*Ordered Probit (2)*	*Fixed Effects (3)*	*Ordered Probit (4)*
Observations	3262	3262	3220	3220
R^2 /Pseudo-R^2	.86	.68	.91	.69
F /Chi^2	252.15	1533.98	261.37	1453.42
Prob > F / Prob > Chi^2	.0001	.0001	.0001	.0001

Fixed-effects and ordered probit estimation with robust standard errors. Standard errors in parentheses. *Significant at the 10 percent level. **Significant at the 5 percent level. ***Significant at the 1 percent level. All tests one-tailed except where no direction predicted (+) predicted positive direction, (–) negative, and (+/–) no predicted direction.

facto judicial independence to be statistically significant, even controlling for selection effects. Using the fixed models as a point of reference, we can see that a maximum increase in *de facto* judicial independence would be associated with a .24 or .20 decrease in the 7-point index of repression of civil liberties. Provision of judicial review produces negative coefficients in all four models; three achieve acceptable levels of statistical significance. These results suggest that judges may be more likely to employ the power of judicial review to protect citizens against less egregious forms of repression, but when the form of repression is more severe, such as in personal integrity abuse, judges appear to be less willing or less effective in exercising the power consistently to protect rights. A maximum increase in provision for judicial review would be associated with a .30 decrease in repression in the fixed-effects model with the trichotomous measure of democracy; the size of the impact is slightly less than that of a maximum change in democracy (.40). The coefficient is slightly lower in the model disaggregated democracy.

The coefficients for the trichotomous measure of democracy achieve acceptable levels of statistical significance, as do all the disaggregated measures of democracy. When we compare these models, which include the judicial independence measures, with the standard model in Chapter 3, we find that military regime type is no longer statistically significant except in the models employing the disaggregated measure; whereas leftist regime type continues to produce a strong positive effect on repression of civil liberties in all four models. The rest of the model performs similarly to the model in Chapter 3.

My next step was to expand the standard model of repression. First I tested the hypothesis that "judicial networks" would decrease the level of repression, but I found no evidence of such effect in any of the models. I next engaged in a series of preliminary analyses examining various combinations of dummy variables delineating legal system type. Since these measures are invariant, they are thrown out of the fixed-effects model. In none of the ordered probit models did the legal system type achieve acceptable levels of statistical significance, so I dropped these measures from the repression models. In the last set of models I test additional measures for economic liberalization, including net FDI and trade openness. I also examine the effect of INGOs, and I further expand the model to test the impact of membership in the ICCPR, its Optional Protocol, and the CAT, controlling for reservations made to the treaty. I tested the ICCPR and the CAT with two-tailed tests because the literature predicts both a positive and a negative effect (Keith 1999; Hathaway 2002; Hafner-Burton and Tsutsui 2005). I tested the more stringent Optional Protocol because the literature supports this effect (Keith 1999). Initial analysis found none of the treaty membership variables to be statistically significant, so I added interaction effects between the INGOs and treaty membership with the expectation that membership in the treaty would have more of an effect with the presence of INGOs to hold the regime accountable (see Risse, Ropp, and Sikkink 1999). This final model is limited to 1980–2000 because of INGO data limitations; therefore, the models are not directly comparable to the first analysis. I believe that the benefit of empirically testing the INGO effect offsets the loss of five years.

The last set of analyses is presented in Table 4.9 (repression of personal integrity) and Table 4.10 (repression of civil liberties). Trade openness and FDI have no effect on personal integrity abuse in any of the six models, nor does the level of INGO presence in the state, with one exception—the ordered probit model for the CIRI index. The effect of treaty membership is rather thin and inconsistent. In no model does membership in the CAT or the Optional Protocol achieve statistical significance. The coefficients for ICCPR membership are statistically significant in four of the six models. In the two PTS fixed-effects models and the two fixed-effects civil liberties models, the coefficients are positive, and in addition the interaction between INGOs and the ICCPR is negative and statistically significant, a result suggesting that membership has a harmful effect except when INGOs are present. In the ordered

Table 4.9. Expanded Model of Repression of Personal Integrity Rights with Judicial Independence, 1980–2000

	Personal Integrity Rights Abuse (PTS) 1980–2000		*Personal Integrity Rights Abuse (AI) 1980–2000*		*Personal Integrity Rights Abuse (CIRI) 1982–2000*	
	Fixed Effects (1)	*Ordered Probit (2)*	*Fixed Effects (3)*	*Ordered Probit (4)*	*Fixed Effects (5)*	*Ordered Probit (6)*
Rights Abuse (*t*–1) (+)	.41	1.20	.31	1.04	.35	.48
	(.04)***	(.05)***	(.03)***	(.04)***	(.03)***	(.02)***
De Facto Judicial Independence (–)	–.11	–.23	–.08	–.14	–.32	–.21
	(.04)***	(.04)***	(.04)***	(.04)***	(.09)***	(.04)***
Selection Effects: Judicial Independence (+)	–.04	–.09	–.01	–.01	–.02	–.01
	(.02)**	(.04)**	(.02)	(.04)	(.04)	(.04)
Formal Judicial Review (+/–)	–.09	.02	–.02	–.03	–.13	.03
	(.04)**	(.04)	(.04)	(.02)	(.09)*	(.03)
Civil War (+)	.53	.69	.58	.69	1.00	.62
	(.11)***	(.12)***	(.11)***	(.11)***	(.23)***	(.10)***
International War (+)	.11	.22	.05	.19	.18	.24
	(.08)**	(.13)***	(.09)	(.12)***	(.15)	(.11)**
Trichotomous Measure of Democracy (–)	–.13	–.37	–.06	–.29	–.25	–.29
	(.08)*	(.06)***	(.07)	(.06)***	(.14)**	(.05)***
Military Regimes (+)	.05	.10	–.01	.02	.27	.04
	(.08)	(.06)*	(.08)	(.07)	(.17)*	(.07)

(continued)

Table 4.9 (*continued*)

	Personal Integrity Rights Abuse (PTS) 1980–2000		*Personal Integrity Rights Abuse (AI) 1980–2000*		*Personal Integrity Rights Abuse (CIRI) 1982–2000*	
	Fixed Effects (1)	*Ordered Probit (2)*	*Fixed Effects (3)*	*Ordered Probit (4)*	*Fixed Effects (5)*	*Ordered Probit (6)*
Marxist or Marxist-Leninist Regimes (+/–)	.10 (.14)	–.13 (.10)	–.06 (.17)	–.19 (.10)**	–.12 (.32)	–.19 (.10)**
Economic Development (–)	–.00001 (.00)***	–.00002 (.00)	–.00001 (.00)**	–.00002 (.00)***	.00004 (.00)	–.00001 (.00)***
Economic Growth (–)	–.01 (.00)***	–.02 (.01)***	–.01 (.00)***	–.02 (.00)**	–.01 (.01)	–.01 (.004)*
Logged Population (+)	.15 (.23)	.15 (.02)***	.03 (.23)	.16 (.02)***	.23 (.42)	.15 (.02)***
Population Growth (+)	–.04 (.01)	.02 (.02)	–.04 (.01)***	.02 (.02)*	–.09 (.06)*	.03 (.02)**
Trade (+/–)	.003 (.02)	.05 (.04)	.003 (.02)	.02 (.04)	.04 (.04)	.06 (.04)
FDI (+/–)	.001 (.002)	.001 (.02)	.003 (.002)	.002 (.01)	.002 (.01)	.001 (.01)

Logged INGO Presence (–)	.19	–.01	.12	.02	.17	–.06
	(.09)	(.04)	(.09)	(.04)	(.16)	(.04)**
ICCPR Membership (+/–)	.17	–.21	.23	–.10	.16	–.26
	(.08)**	(.11)**	(.09)***	(.11)	(.23)	(.09)***
Optional Protocol Membership (–)	.01	.32	–.09	.27	–.25	.13
	(.09)	(.10)	(.12)	(.09)	(.24)	(.09)
CAT Membership (+/–)	–.09	–.06	–.07	–.11	–.04	–.04
	(.07)	(.10)	(.07)	(.09)	(.13)	(.09)
Interaction INGO-ICCPR (–)	–.03	.03	–.04	–.01	–.03	.04
	(.01)***	(.01)	(.01)***	(.02)	(.04)	(.02)
Interaction INGO-Optional Proto (–)	.002	–.06	.02	–.05	.04	–.03
	(.01)	(.02)***	(.02)	(.02)***	(.04)	(.01)**
Interaction INGO-CAT (–)	–.09	.01	.01	.02	.01	.04
	(.07)	(.02)	(.02)	(.02)	(.02)	(.02)
Observations	1955	1955	1955	1955	1913	1913
R^2 /Pseudo-R^2	.70	.48	.65	.41	.66	.30
F /Chi^2	25.54	1346.12	13.48	1394.28	14.51	1962.66
Prob > F / Prob > Chi^2	.0001	.0001	.0001	.0001	.0001	.0001

Table 4.10. Expanded Model of Repression of Civil Liberties with Judicial Independence, 1980–2000

	1980–2000 (with trichotomous democracy)		*1980–2000 (with disaggregated democracy)*	
	Fixed Effects (1)	*Ordered Probit (2)*	*Fixed Effects (3)*	*Ordered Probit (4)*
Rights Abuse (*t*–1) (+)	.67 (.03)***	1.86 (.10)***	.61 (.10)***	1.83 (.10)***
De Facto Judicial Independence (+/–)	–.18 (.04)***	–.32 (.05)***	–.15 (.04)***	–.32 (.05)***
Selection Effects: Judicial Independence (+)	.003 (.02)	–.01 (.05)	–.01 (.02)	–.04 (.05)
Formal Judicial Review (+/–)	–.13 (.04)***	–.05 (.03)	–.11 (.04)***	–.01 (.04)
Civil War (+)	.19 (.06)***	.29 (.10)***	.19 (.07)***	.36 (.11)***
International War (+)	.03 (.07)	.26 (.15)**	.07 (.07)	.41 (.13)***
Trichotomous Measure of Democracy (–)	–.25 (.07)***	–.56 (.07)***	—	—
Constraint on the Chief Executive	—		–.10 (.03)***	–.16 (.04)***
Openness of Executive Recruitment	—		–.27 (.12)**	–.36 (.10)***
Competitiveness of Political Participation	—		–.18 (.05)***	–.37 (.06)***
Military Regimes (–)	.06 (.09)	.03 (.09)	–.13 (.09)*	–.23 (.09)***
Marxist or Marxist-Leninist Regimes (+/–)	.37 (.15)***	.41 (.18)**	.28 (.16)*	.41 (.19)**
Economic Development (–)	.001 (.00)	–.001 (.00)***	–.001 (.00)**	–.001 (.00)***
Economic Growth (–)	.002 (.01)	.01 (.007)*	.001 (.01)	–.01 (.01)
Logged Population (+)	–.52 (.19)	.02 (.02)	–.35 (.18)	.05 (.02)***

Table 4.10 (*continued*)

	1980–2000 (with trichotomous democracy)		*1980–2000 (with disaggregated democracy)*	
	Fixed Effects (1)	*Ordered Probit (2)*	*Fixed Effects (3)*	*Ordered Probit (4)*
Population Growth (+)	–.01	.06	–.01	.03
	(.02)	(.03)**	(.01)	(.03)
Trade (+/–)	–.02	–.06	–.01	–.05
	(.01)	(.04)	(.02)	(.04)
FDI (+/–)	–.001	.001	–.001	.001
	(.002)	(.004)	(.001)	(.004)
Logged INGO Presence (–)	.01	–.08	.01	–.05
	(.05)	(.05)**	(.05)	(.05)
ICCPR Membership (+/–)	.12	–.12	.12	–.09
	(.06)*	(.12)	(.06)**	(.12)
Optional Protocol Membership (–)	.03	.19	–.01	.26
	(.11)	(.10)	(.10)	(.10)
CAT Membership (+/–)	–.07	–.12	–.06	–.13
	(.07)	(.09)	(.07)	(.10)
Interaction INGO-ICCPR (–)	–.02	.02	–.02	.01
	(.01)**	(.02)	(.01)*	(.02)
Interaction INGO-Optional Proto (–)	–.004	–.04	–.01	–.04
	(.02)	(.02)***	(.02)	(.02)***
Interaction INGO-CAT (–)	.01	.02	.01	.02
	(.01)	(.02)	(.01)	(.02)
Observations	2002	2002	1975	1975
R^2 /Pseudo-R^2	.74	.66	.85	.68
F /Chi^2	97.64	1039.09	92.63	1013.14
Prob > F / Prob > Chi^2	.0001	.0001	.0001	.0001

Fixed-effects and ordered probit estimation with robust standard errors. Standard errors in parentheses. *Significant at the 10 percent level. **Significant at the 5 percent level. ***Significant at the 1 percent level. All tests one-tailed except where no direction predicted (+) predicted positive direction, (–) negative, and (+/–) no predicted direction.

probit models the interaction effects fail to achieve statistical significance, but the negative ICCPR coefficients do, as does the interaction terms for INGOs and the Optional Protocol. I explore these results further in Chapter 5.

Conclusions

In this chapter I addressed three core questions in regard to judicial independence: Why do states adopt formal provisions of judicial independence? Does formal commitment make a difference in achieved levels of judicial independence? Does the achieved level of judicial independence reduce the level of state repression of personal integrity rights and civil liberties restrictions? Each question informs the next. If the choice to adopt or maintain provisions of judicial independence merely reflects the need to make commitments *appear* credible in order to satisfy the concerns of potential investors or the demands of opposition groups or INGOs, then we would expect little congruence between the promises and the actual behavior. The evidence in this chapter suggests overall that the promises are not "cheap talk," nor is there evidence of a decoupling effect posited by some scholars applying the world society approach once we move beyond bivariate analysis. This is not to say that I believe that no countries do make empty promises of judicial independence for state legitimacy or material interest, but rather I suggest that generally states do not engage in these empty promises, or, if they do, they may be caught in their own rhetoric and eventually provide some level of judicial independence. The choice to adopt provisions for judicial independence appears to reflect the diffusion of norms, both globally and regionally, and follows the promulgation of the final sets of standards set forth through the United Nations. While this evidence of diffusion of norms supports the world society approach, I find no evidence that state embeddedness in the international community influences the incorporation of these standards into state constitutions, nor do I find an observable influence of a transnational network. I am somewhat cautious about these particular findings, since my time frame ends in 2000 because of the lack of IGO/INGO data.

The dominant theories within the comparative courts literature regarding judicial independence and/or judicial review find substantial support when applied to my formal provisions model. Regimes facing electoral uncertainty (because the state is newly democratizing or because of the emergency of strong multiparty competition) appear to adopt or maintain constitutional provisions for judicial independence in order to foster the possibility of having an alternative forum in which they may influence policy should they lose control of the regime through elections or in which their political and civil rights may be protected against the new majority. Subsequent evidence in the chapter suggests that the judiciary as insurance may pay off, at least in regard to repression of core freedoms and personal integrity rights. Economic liberalism completely fails to influence the adoption of provisions for judicial independence, and instead, all three indicators of economic liberalism and globalization are associated with *less*, not more, formal protections. This evidence parallels the large body of evidence that Abouharb and Cingranelli (2008) produced in regard to the IMF and World Bank structural adjustment programs; their evidence strongly suggested that the ameliorative effects of economic liberalization were not just overstated but rather the effects in reality were contrary to rights provision. I continue to find this effect across all analyses in all chapters of this book, in regard to both constitutional promises and political repression, and thus this work strongly supports the position taken by critics of globalization and economic liberalism.

Formal commitment to judicial independence is not simply an empty gesture—constitutional provisions do indeed influence actual levels of achieved judicial independence across the global set of states, even when controlling for selection effects and other factors. While my analysis demonstrates that formal judicial independence is a strongly seated characteristic of a political system that does not change easily or rapidly, I do find that the achieved level of judicial independence is influenced by a variety of factors. Economic resources matter. The greater the state's economic wealth, the more likely the state is to foster independence in the judiciary, and the more resource constraints there are, as measured by population size, the less likely the state will be to provide for an independent judiciary. While resources matter, economic liberalization is not associated with actual fulfillment of judicial independence. There is some evidence that embeddedness in the global society increases judicial independence, in that a state's participation in IGOs is associated with increased levels of judicial independence; but the presence of INGOs does not make a difference. Threats such as civil war and international war do affect a regime's willingness to allow judicial independence, but the effect largely disappears once we control for legislative constraints on the executive and for party competition. The influence of the formal provisions ultimately depended upon these components of democratization, whose positive influence on judicial independence was also dependent upon the formal provisions. Democracy produces the strongest effect next to military regimes, which are considerably less likely to allow for an independent judiciary generally.

I acknowledge that the work of Pereira (2008) suggests that military regimes under some circumstances may support the independence of the courts; here I simply suggest that overall military regimes are less likely to do so than nonmilitary regimes. Finally, I do find evidence to support Ferejohn, Rosenbluth, and Shipan (2004), who argue that courts are more able to act independently when the ability of other politicians to engage in court curbing action is constrained by political fragmentation. Some environmental factors, such as colonial legacy and type of legal system, which are largely invariable across time, fail to influence judicial independence in most models. However, I do find some support that states with previous British colonial experience or common law systems are more likely to have independent judiciaries than are states with civil law systems. As a whole I would conclude, not surprisingly, that formal provisions by themselves alone only weakly influence the actual independence of the judiciary, which ultimately is also influenced more by a broader set of electoral conditions, resource capabilities, and constraints, and to some extent by violent threats to the regime.

My primary interest in judicial independence was to examine its effect on political repression, while controlling for factors that may similarly influence both a state's decision to adopt formal provisions and its decision to allow the fulfillment of these provisions. Clearly, similar influences are at work in regard to each of these behaviors; thus I control for selection effects in each of my models. Even when controlling for selection effects I find that the achieved level of judicial independence in a state does in fact reduce the likelihood of repression of personal integrity rights and civil liberties restrictions. Thus judicial independence seems to have earned its place as an "essential feature of liberal democracy" and an "essential guardian of the rule of law," although these roles are also shared by democratic institutions, especially by competitive party systems. Nonetheless, I do find that in regard to repression of personal integrity the influence of judicial independence outweighs that of democratization but is substantially less than the impact of civil war. However, in the case of civil liberties restrictions, while the impact of judicial independence is relatively large, the level of democratization slightly outweighs its influence on judicial independence. On the other hand, its influence surpasses that of civil war in regard to repression of this broader set of rights, which presumably affects a larger segment of the population than does personal integrity abuse. The evidence lends overwhelmingly support to the domestic institutions arguments that an independent judiciary can increase the material and reputational costs to regimes employing coercive force against their citizens to such an extent that regimes' use of these tactics would deterred or reduced. An independent rights-supporting judiciary may over time also socialize both the public and the regime toward a rights consciousness that under most circumstances may remove the tools of repression from the menu of appropriate policy options. I am unable to test these mechanisms directly, but I believe that the evidence I present here should provide impetus for future large-*N* cross-national studies of repression. The results have strong implications for actors and institutions within the international community that support the development of democratic institutions and the reform of judicial or legal systems more specifically. Efforts to entrench an independent judiciary formally in a documentary constitution are not futile; however, they are not sufficient. Ultimately, the impact of the formal provisions is dependent upon core components of pluralistic democratization such as fostering a competitive party system and establishing legislative checks on the executive branch. Judicial independence is unlikely to be fully realized unless the state has sufficient resources to fund the infrastructure and institutional access to the public that allow the judiciary to function effectively, to attain legitimacy in the broad public, and to serve as that ultimate guarantor of rights that the world increasingly expects of it.

Appendix: Examples of Judicial Independence Language and Country Ratings in U.S. Department of State Human Rights Reports (2002)

The following excerpts provide examples of the language the Department of State uses in its assessment of judicial independence, generally in its first summative evaluation of the country. Additional information in support of the assessment sometimes follows in the same section or in the "Right to Public and Fair Trial" section.

Benin: coded as (1) somewhat independent

The Government generally respected the constitutional provision for an independent judiciary; however, the executive has important powers in regard to the judiciary, and the judiciary was inefficient and susceptible to corruption at all levels. The Constitution provides for an independent judiciary, and the Government generally respected this provision in practice; however, the executive branch has important powers with regard to the judiciary, and the judiciary remained inefficient in some respects and susceptible to corruption at all levels.

Botswana: coded as (2) fully independent

The Government generally respected the constitutional provisions for an independent judiciary. The judicial system did not provide timely fair trials due to a serious and increasing backlog of cases. . . .

The Constitution provides for an independent judiciary, and the Government generally respected this provision in practice.

Marshall Islands: coded as (0) not independent

The Constitution provides for an independent judiciary; however, judges are appointed by the Cabinet, and past governments have attempted to influence the judiciary. The Government generally respected the human rights of its citizens, and the law and the judiciary provide effective means of dealing with individual instances of abuse. Actions to improve the Attorney General's office and the independence of the judiciary improved the human rights situation.

Solomon Islands: coded as (1) somewhat independent

The Constitution provides for an independent judiciary; however, prior to RAMSI's arrival, the judiciary was hampered by police ineffectiveness, lack of resources, and threats against judges and prosecutors. . . .

The Government did not encourage any judicial or independent investigation of human rights abuses that occurred during the conflict, which contributed to a climate of impunity. The judicial system functioned poorly during the first half of the year due to the ongoing violence and a lack of resources.

Bulgaria: coded as (0) not independent

The Constitution provides for an independent judiciary; however, the judiciary suffered from corruption and wide-ranging systemic problems. The judiciary continued to struggle with wide-ranging systematic problems and suffered from serious corruption.

Austria: coded (2) as independent

The judiciary is independent.

Chapter 5

Constitutional Provisions for Human Rights as Protection Against Political Repression

> The Constitution [of Ethiopia] prohibits arbitrary arrest and detention; however, the Government frequently did not observe these provisions in practice. (U.S. Department of State 2003)

> The Constitution [of the Maldives] provides for freedom of assembly "peaceably and in a manner that does not contravene the law"; however, the Government imposes limits on this right in practice. The Home Ministry permits public political meetings during electoral campaigns, but limits them to small gatherings on private premises. (U.S. Department of State 2001)

> The Constitution [of Mozambique] expressly prohibits such practices; however, police continued to commit serious abuses, and torture, beatings, death threats, physical and mental abuse, and extortion remained problems. (U.S. Department of State 2003)

> The Constitution [of Syria] provides citizens with the right to express opinions freely in speech and in writing; however, the Government restricts these rights significantly in practice. The Government strictly controls dissemination of information and permits no written or

> individual criticism of the President, the President's family, the Ba'th Party, the military, or the legitimacy of the regime. (U.S. Department of State 1999)

> The Constitution [of the Kyrgyz Republic] provides for the right of association; however, at times local authorities inhibited this right in practice. (U.S. Department of State 2001)

> The Constitution [of Turkey] prohibits such practices; however, members of the security forces continued to torture, beat, and otherwise abuse persons regularly. Despite the Government's cooperation with unscheduled foreign inspection teams, public pledges by successive governments to end the practice, and government initiatives designed to address the problem, torture continued to be widespread, particularly in the southeast. (Ibid.)

> The Constitution [of Cuba] recognizes the right of citizens to profess and practice any religious belief, within the framework of respect for the law; however, in law and in practice, the Government places restrictions on freedom of religion. (U.S. Department of State 1999)

As noted throughout this book, a global script for state legitimacy appears to have emerged, one that calls for a written constitution or the equivalent, with an embedded bill of rights, democratic processes and institutions, and, increasingly, some form of judicial review or restraint on state power to protect political and human rights. Much of the constitution writing in the last half of the twentieth century resulted from the transition of almost 100 former colonies to independence, and, as Go (2003) notes, most of these states have rewritten their original postcolonial constitutions at least once. These documents accounted for roughly two-thirds of all the world's constitutions by the 1970s, and by the 1990s, postcolonial constitutions, combined with those of former Soviet countries and other secessionist states, accounted for more than four-fifths of the constitutions of the world (Beer 1992). Most relevant to this chapter, all but 10 percent of the currently existing postcolonial constitutions have rights provisions in a section devoted to rights under a separate title (Go 81). Hirschl (2000) reports more broadly that "nearly every recently adopted constitution or constitutional revision contains a bill of rights" (92). This movement toward constitutional provision for a bill of fundamental rights parallels the movement toward formal commitment to international human rights norms, which, as noted in Chapter 1, now approaches near universality: each of the core conventions composing the international human rights regime claims state parties representing from 75 to 99 percent of the global set of states.

While these patterns are undeniable, one does not have to read many Department of State reports before coming across familiar phrases such as "the constitution provides for . . . *however in practice* . . ." or "the constitution prohibits . . . *but in practice* . . ." that repeatedly suggest the limitations of these formal commitments in curbing political repression. As Shapiro (2008) cautions, "written constitutions with some sort of bill of rights have become almost like national flags as an integral symbol of national sovereignty for all states, including authoritarian regimes that have no other intention than waving them in the international arena" (330). Thus, the skepticism of this current decade—that constitutions may not matter where they are most needed—reflects a similar skepticism two decades ago that many of constitutions of world are "worthless scraps of paper" (Howard 1991, 3). This skepticism has been largely supported empirically; in the last decade a growing body of literature has demonstrated a clear gap between law and practice in regard to constitutional provisions for rights (for example, Blasi and Cingranelli 1996; Davenport 1996; Keith 2002a; Keith, Tate, and Poe 2009) and international human rights treaties (for example, Keith 1999; Hathaway 2002; Hafner-Burton and Tsutsui 2005). Not only have studies demonstrated that international human rights treaties and at least some constitutional provisions for human rights do not have the intended effect; they have also demonstrated that some formal protections are often associated with higher levels of repression (for example, Keith 1999; Hafner-Burton and Tsutsui 2005; Keith, Tate, and Poe 2009), a result suggesting a decoupling effect between promise and practice (Hafner-Burton and Tsutsui 2005). In other words, as the norm requiring written bills of rights increasingly distinguishes between legitimate and deviant governments, states may become more likely to adopt rights provisions without the willingness or capacity to deliver on these promises, thus potentially creating not only a gap between promise and practice, but also a negative association between practice and promise. Not all the empirical news has been bad; there is some evidence that a few constitutional provisions for rights matter: freedom of press (Davenport 1996 found an effect on negative sanctions, but Keith 2002a found no effect on personal integrity rights) and the rights to a public trial and a fair trial (Keith 2002a). Landman's (2005) exhaustive study of the international human rights regime found evidence to suggest that some of these treaties can make a difference under certain circumstances, as did Simmons' (2009) subsequent work.

The empirical studies of the effect of constitutional rights provisions have suffered several limitations. The time framework of these studies has typically included only the first few years of the post–Cold War era, which experienced a significant wave of constitution writing. Extending the period under examination to 2005 allows me to examine an additional decade in which many of the newly independent states have had time to develop and consolidate their new political institutions—of particular interest, their judicial system. Most existing studies have examined one category of repression and ignored the other. In this chapter I examine the promise of five core individual freedoms and four core due process rights and their effect on both categories of political repression (repression of personal integrity rights and repression of civil liberties). In addition I examine the effect of the formal promises on the realization of the particular promised freedoms, such as speech, press, association, assembly, and religion. Previous empirical studies have also not been able to control for the possibility that many of the factors associated with the dependent variable, state repression, are likely to be also associated with the independent variable—the promulgation of constitutional provisions for human rights. In this chapter I again engage in a two-step process that I believe allows me to examine these relationships more rigorously. First, I create models to empirically test competing approaches explaining why states adopt constitutional protection of core rights. I believe that this is the first systematic large-*N* cross-national empirical examination of this question and that it is a crucial one both theoretically and statistically. Second, I examine the effect these formal provisions have on the level of state repression, controlling for selection effects created from the first model. I make several additional improvements to the model of repression; most important, I am able to model the effect of an independent judiciary. I also examine the interaction of these formal commitments with those made in international human rights treaties. And I examine the role of civil society groups and their interaction with an independent judiciary in forming "judicial networks" that may facilitate the translation of formal rights into practice. I turn first to the question of why states make formal commitments to fundamental rights in constitutional documents.

Constitutional Commitment to Human Rights

I examine two types of constitutional protections that are expected to reduce the likelihood of one or both types of state repression: (1) the core individual freedoms associated with constitutional liberalism: speech, assembly, association, press, and religion; and (2) four key due process protections that directly relate to personal integrity abuse: writ of habeas corpus (the prisoner's right to be promptly informed of the charges), protection against arbitrary arrest, prohibition against torture or cruel and unusual punishment, and the guarantee of a fair and public trial. Both sets of constitutional protections are key elements in the internationally recognized minimum standards for human rights in the International Covenant on Civil and Political Rights (ICCPR). The theoretical justification for each set of constitutional provisions is somewhat different. The constitutional provisions for individual freedoms should allow persons the legitimacy to openly criticize and challenge the regime or the status quo through a broad range of individual and collective behaviors without facing the threat of coercive state action. Or, conversely, they should give citizens recourse to a legal remedy if the regime does engage in repressive behavior, which ultimately raises the potential material and reputational costs to the regime in selecting repression as a policy tool. In addition, as Poe and Tate (1994) suggest, these types of freedoms may also influence repression of personal integrity rights in that they "may make it easier for citizens and opposition leaders to publicize attempts at repression, thereby bringing down on would-be abusive leaders the weight of majority or world opinion" (123–24). Constitutional provisions for due process ensure protection against arbitrary government action that directly relates to the right of personal integrity—the right not to be arbitrarily imprisoned, tortured, killed, or disappeared. The writ of habeas corpus protects individuals against arbitrary or political imprisonment to the extent that the government is required to present evidence promptly and sufficient to justify holding a prisoner and to make known the charges leveled against a prisoner—obviously precluding the phenomenon of disappearances and limiting arbitrary political imprisonment. The promise of a fair and public trial should make it more difficult for regimes to hold secret trials in which persons can be convicted for political reasons or on trumped-up charges. Public trials also facilitate the dissemination of information, allowing the press and public opinion to function as curbs on repressive behavior in both categories. The ban on torture, when practiced, directly eliminates one component of personal integrity abuse and should decrease the number of extrajudicial killings, which sometimes result from torture.

Even though my primary interest lies in examining the effect of constitutional rights provisions on political repression, I turn first to the issue of why states choose to adopt or maintain these provisions. I am motivated by two reasons: (1) I believe it may shed theoretical light on a state's subsequent choice of whether to employ tools of repression that would violate these promises, and (2) the analysis will facilitate our ability to test and control for selection effects in our repression models. Bills of rights today constitute a core part of the global script for statehood. Just as a state's legitimacy or "good nation" identity is increasingly linked to a formal commitment to international human rights norms through treaty law (Cole 2005; Wotipka and Ramirez 2007), I believe that this status is also increasingly linked to a state's formal commitment in domestic constitutional law to these human rights norms. I posit that these domestic commitments are influenced by the same three mechanisms articulated by world society scholars studying treaty commitment: (1) world meetings and conferences in which the human rights standards are articulated, (2) norms cascades through which states are influenced by the behavior of states globally and within their regions, and (3) embeddedness in the broader world, from which they learn the appropriate state identity and behaviors (see Wotipka and Ramirez 2007, 314–15). Specifically, in regard to mechanism (1), I believe that the World Conference on Human Rights in 1993, in Vienna, Austria, in which representatives of 171 states adopted by consensus the Vienna Declaration and Programme of Action, represents the strongest declaration of the universality of human rights and, of equal importance, represents the strongest level of consensus achieved in regard to the meaning and nature of human rights and fundamental freedoms (see DeLaet 2006, 10–12). The language of the Vienna Declaration unequivocally states that "the universal nature of these rights and freedoms is beyond question" and that "while the significance of national and regional particularities and various historical, cultural, and religious backgrounds must be borne in mind, it is the duty of the States, regardless of their political, economic, and cultural systems, to promote and protect all human rights and freedoms" (United Nations 1993, section 1, paragraph 5). The first step in the Programme of Action urges states to incorporate these standards into domestic law as well as to strengthen domestic institutions such as the judiciary: "The World Conference on Human Rights urges Governments to incorporate standards as contained in international human rights instruments in domestic legislation and to strengthen national structures, institutions and organs of society which play a role in promoting and safeguarding human rights" (section 83). I derive the following four hypotheses from this approach:

- Hypothesis One: As more states within the global set of countries incorporate constitutional provisions for core human rights, the likelihood increases that other states will adopt and/or maintain similar provisions.
- Hypothesis Two: As more states within a region incorporate constitutional provisions for the core human rights, the likelihood increases that other states within that region will adopt and/or maintain similar provisions.
- Hypothesis Three: States will be more likely to adopt and/or maintain formal provisions for core human rights in response to the Vienna Declaration.
- Hypothesis Four: The more the state is embedded in the international community, the more likely it will be to adopt and/or maintain formal provisions for core human rights.
- Hypothesis Five: States that have committed to the ICCPR will be more likely to adopt and/or maintain formal provisions for core human rights.

The transnational advocacy networks perspective (Keck and Sikkink 1998; Risse, Ropp, and Sikkink 1999) posits that international human rights norms are diffused through networks of transnational and domestic actors who "bring pressure 'from above' and 'from below' to accomplish human rights change" (Risse and Sikkink 1999, 18). Risse, Ropp, and Sikkink (1999) specifically posit a five-phase spiral model that assumes that (1) repression triggers activation of a transnational network that invokes human rights norms and applies pressure on the repressive state to make concessions; (2) the repressive state denies the validity of the human rights norms as a subject for international jurisdiction and asserts instead the norm of nonintervention; (3) the regime eventually makes some tactical concessions to the transnational network;

(4) the regime becomes trapped in its own rhetoric and concessions, which can lead to either the opposition's bringing about a regime change or a process of gradual liberalization in which the regime accepts international norms (ratifies treaties and institutionalizes norms domestically in constitutions or domestic law); and (5) ultimately we may see rule-consistent behavior as a result of the regime's acceptance of the validity of the human rights and increased scrutiny and pressure by domestic and transnational actors. Therefore, I expect that pressure from international non-governmental organizations (INGOs) will increase the probability of adopting and maintaining constitutional provisions. This expectation parallels my fourth hypothesis to the extent that embeddedness is typically measured by the INGO membership.

- Hypothesis Six: The stronger the INGO presence in a state, the more likely the state will be to adopt and/or maintain formal provisions for core human rights.

In Chapter 4 I examined the rational-choice-based theories that espouse an electoral logic to explain state decisions to write new or revised constitutional provisions for judicial independence (Ramseyer 1994; Ginsburg 2003; Hirschl 2004), which I believe have a logical extension in regard to constitutional provision for rights protections. Ultimately, each of the three theories posits that ruling regimes in systems with competitive party systems can no longer safely predict that they will be the party that wins control of the government, and thus will seek to protect their policies or preferences by providing an alternative forum to the majoritarian institutions in which the former ruling state actors may challenge the current government. More broadly, such a regime is likely to favor limited government in the face of this uncertainty. And I would further argue that the regime would favor strong future due process rights that would be necessary in order to be able to effectively press claims in a court of law. In addition, just as Moravcsik (2000) has argued that states facing political uncertainty are likely to commit to international human rights treaties to "lock in" the benefits of human rights norms, the logic would seem to follow in regard to constitutional commitments to individual human rights norms. Ginsburg (2003) (as well as Moravcsik) argues that new democracies and regimes in transition face more uncertainty than do established democracies or autocracies; electoral outcomes are harder to predict in new democracies, and transitioning regimes by definition face significant and uncertain changes in the party system and institutional structures. Thus, for these regimes constitutional promises for due process and basic freedoms may also serve as "insurance for the past against the future." I make three additional hypotheses:

- Hypothesis Seven: States with competitive political party systems will be more likely to adopt or maintain constitutional provisions for core human rights.
- Hypothesis Eight: New democracies will be more likely to adopt or maintain constitutional provisions for core human rights.
- Hypothesis Nine: Regimes in transition will be more likely to adopt or maintain constitutional provisions for core human rights.

Finally, I return to the economic liberalization hypotheses discussed in Chapter 4 in regard to judicial independence. I continue to explore both the positive and malign perspective of economic liberalization and globalization. The positive perspective would expect that an interdependent economy and trade would indirectly encourage states to adopt or maintain constitutional provisions for core rights. Liberal trade policies would be expected not only to facilitate economic development, but also to contribute to an improvement in social and political conditions in less economically developed states, which would in turn over time lead to the emergence of a middle class that increasingly makes rights demands upon its government, and arguably these demands for core rights would be likely to include formal enumeration of the rights in a written constitution that carries the weight of paramount law. Also, as Harrelson-Stephens and Calloway (2003) argue, just as trade relationships promote the diffusion of wealth, technology, investment, and capital, interdependence leads to the diffusion of values, including those of human rights, and thus improved human rights is a spillover effect from international trade. This diffusion of values may include those associated with legitimate statehood, such as a written constitution, with an embedded bill of rights and an independent judiciary.

- Hypothesis Ten: Economic liberalization and economic development will increase the likelihood that a state will adopt or maintain constitutional provisions for core rights protections.

As we saw in Chapter 4, this perspective is not without its critics, who argue generally that more economically developed states exploit less economically developed states, a phenomenon that leads to uneven development and hinders the socioeconomic growth of the states whose economies are vulnerable to the demands of multinational corporations (MNCs) and multilateral lending institutions. Further, critics argue that the integration of developing countries into the global economy leads to exploitation through "cheap labor, minimal skill transmissions, restrictions on technology transfers, and on long-term commitments to stay and invest," and thus "foreign capital reinforces and strengthens repression in developing countries" (Apodaca 2001, 591). Ultimately, the options of the less economically developed state are constrained, and its policies are shaped to benefit the interests of MNCs and domestic elites rather than those of its citizens. Thus, economic liberalization would not be likely to lead to the dividends suggested above, and might decrease the probability of meaningful reform, such as establishing core freedoms that would allow the opposition to engage in speech and activities that threaten political stability and the regimes' economic self-interest, or establishing core due process rights that might hamper the regime's efforts to prosecute those that pose a threat to its political and economic stability. Empirical evidence supports an alternative hypothesis to the liberalization hypothesis above.

- Alternative Hypothesis Ten: Economic liberalization and economic development will decrease the likelihood that a state will adopt or maintain constitutional provisions for core rights protections.

I believe the examination of these hypotheses will improve our substantive and empirical understanding of why states adopt provisions for core individual freedoms and due process rights, which will more fully inform our understanding of the influence of constitutional provisions on both categories of political repression. I next turn to the measurement of constitutional provision of these freedoms and rights.

Measuring Constitutional Promises

Constitutional Provisions for Fundamental Freedoms: I operationalize the extent to which constitutions provide for the following five fundamental freedoms by coding their presence in the text of national constitutions: (1) freedom of speech, (2) freedom of association, (3) freedom of assembly,

(4) freedom of religion, and (5) freedom of press. I coded the presence of each freedom as (2) explicitly mentioned in the constitution; (1) explicitly mentioned but with (an) exception(s) or qualification(s), such as a public interest clause; or (0) not mentioned in the constitution. The data sources for the constitutional variables are Blaustein (1971–1993) and Flanz (1997–2009), both of which are updated annually.

Constitutional Provisions for Due Process Protections: I operationalize the extent to which constitutions provide for the following four due process protections by coding their presence in the text of national constitutions: (1) right to the writ of habeas corpus, (2) right to a public trial, (3) right to a fair trial, and (10) a ban against torture or cruel and usual punishment. I coded the presence of each right as (2) explicitly mentioned in the constitution; (1) explicitly mentioned but with (an) exception(s) or qualification(s), such as a public interest clause; or (0) not mentioned in the constitution. The data sources for the constitutional variables are the same as above.

Trends in Constitutional Provision for Fundamental Freedoms and Due Process

Figure 5.1 presents the annual means for each of the five fundamental freedoms. Several patterns emerge from the data. First, we can see an overall increase in the mean level of constitutional protection of each of these freedoms over the twenty-six-year period, not surprisingly beginning with the wave of constitution writing following the breakup of the Soviet Union. The trend clearly fits the observation of an emerging global norm for providing such freedoms, at least formally, and supports Go's (2003) prediction of a convergence. The measure is a 3-point index from 0 to 2; thus, while four of the measures achieve a mean approaching 1 point, a score of 1 point on the scale represents only qualified protection of these freedoms, not a full guarantee. Second, a clear and consistent rank-ordering of these freedoms is apparent, with provision for freedom of the press consistently achieving a mean that is .20 to .30 less than the other freedoms, even after the end of the Cold War. This difference suggests that regimes may consider formally empowering the press as a riskier endeavor than giving citizens individual freedoms. Freedom of speech is consistently more strongly or more frequently protected than freedom of assembly, a result that is not surprising, since freedom of assembly would protect active

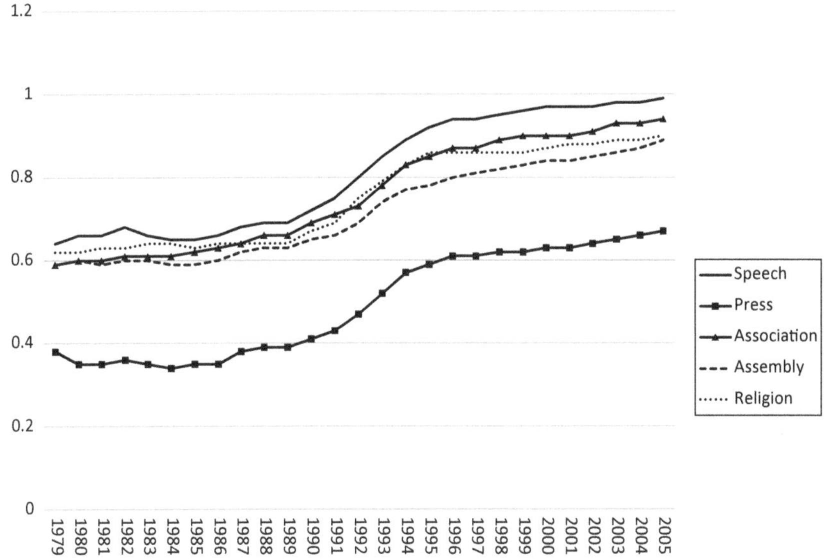

Figure 5.1. Mean Constitutional Provision for Five Freedoms, 1979–2005

behavior beyond mere speech. Many constitutions place specific limitations on the right to assemble, such as the U.S. Constitution, which limits the freedom by specifying "peaceably." The annual means for freedom of association and religion fall between those for speech and assembly.

We see much more variation in regard to constitutional provision for the four due process rights. Figure 5.2 depicts the annual means for these measures. As with the fundamental freedoms, we can see an increase over time in the annual means for each of the due process measures, which once again begins with the wave of constitution writing at the end of the Cold War. Provision for fair trial is consistently the least provided-for protection, and even at the end of my period it achieves a means of only .58 on the 3-point scale. Provision for a public trial is consistently approximately .20 higher than fair trail until 2003, when the mean provision of fair trial begins to increase. The annual means of the constitutional ban on torture and provision for writ of habeas corpus (or similar protections against arbitrary arrests) are nearly identical and consistently higher than the trial means until 1991, when the annual mean for the ban against torture begins increasing beyond that of the provision for habeas corpus, reaching 1.14 at the end of the period, 2005.

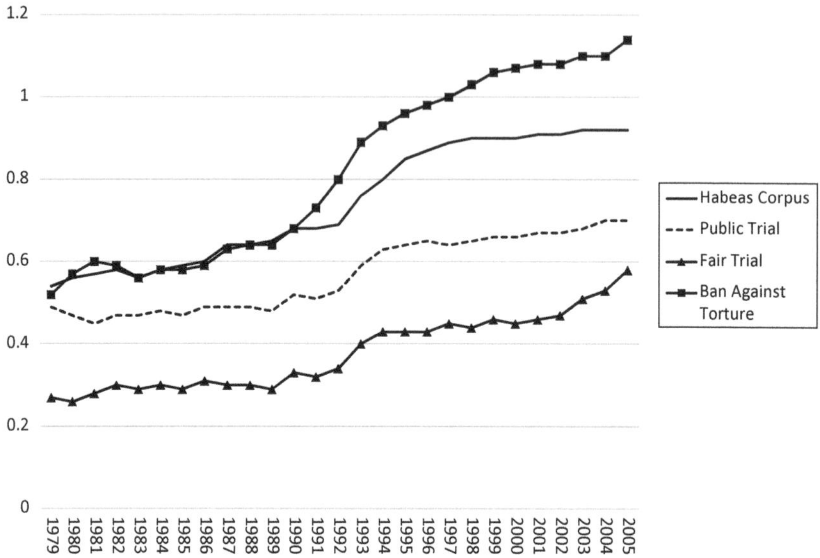

Figure 5.2. Mean Constitutional Provision for Due-Process Rights, 1979–2005

The increase follows closely upon the entry into force of the Convention Against Torture. As we will see below, I do find evidence of an association between membership in the CAT and constitutional bans on torture. I now turn to operationalizing the concepts and presenting the measurements I utilize in this chapter's models.

Operationalizing the Hypotheses

Dependent Variables: I run three different models: one for the formal provision of fundamental freedoms, one for the formal provision of due process rights, and one that combines the provision of fundamental freedoms and due process rights. The *Personal Freedoms Index* is operationalized as an 11-point additive index of the five provisions of fundamental freedoms. The index ranges from 0 to 10. The *Due Process Index* is operationalized as a 9-point additive index of the four due process provisions. The index ranges from 0 to 8. *Constitutional Provision for Fundamental Freedoms* is operationalized as an 11-point additive index of the five provisions of fundamental freedoms. The index ranges from 0 to 10. The *Bill of Rights Index* is operationalized as a 19-point index of the combined freedoms and due process rights. The index ranges from 0 to 18.

Global and Regional Norms: These two annual measures are described fully in Chapter Four.

Dummy Variable for International Human Rights Conference: I create a dummy variable for 1993, the year of the World Conference on Human Rights in Vienna.

Embeddedness: I use the two measures presented in Chapter 4.

Treaty Commitments and Reservations: I include a control measure in the model for state treaty commitments as operationalized in Chapter 4.

Competitive Political Participation or Political Fragmentation: I use the same four measures described in Chapter 4.

New Democracies and States in Transition: These two measures are operationalized as in Chapter 4.

Economic Liberalization: I employ the same four measures operationalized in Chapter 4.

Analysis

I estimate commitment models for the bill of rights index, the personal freedom index, and the due process index. For each of these indices I estimate two models: one that includes the INGO and IGO measures but extends only through 2000 because of data limitations (reported in Table 5.1) and one that covers the broader period 1980–2005 (reported in Table 5.2). Table 5.1 reports the model for the full nineteen-point bill of rights index in the first two columns, followed by the personal freedoms index and then the due process index. As in the previous chapters I report the fixed-effects models in odd-numbered columns and the non-fixed-effects probit models in the even-numbered columns. The first hypothesis receives support in only one of the six models. Global norms are associated with higher commitment only in the non-fixed-effects personal freedoms model. Regional norms, however, are associated with higher commitment in both models of the full bill of rights. In the analysis of the two separate indices, the regional norms variable achieves statistical significance only in regard to the due process rights index (non-fixed-effects model). Thus the second hypothesis receives full support

Table 5.1. Model of Commitment to Individual Freedoms and Due Process, 1980–2000

	Bill of Rights Index		*Personal Freedoms Index*		*Due Process Index*	
	Fixed Effects (1)	*Ordered Probit (2)*	*Fixed Effects (3)*	*Ordered Probit (4)*	*Fixed Effects (5)*	*Ordered Probit (6)*
Freedoms/Rights (*t*–1) (+)	.76	.69	.78	1.16	.80	1.45
	(.03)***	(.06)***	(.03)***	(.09)***	(.03)***	(.12)***
Global Norms (+)	–.08	–.02	–.03	.17	–.07	–.10
	(.07)	(.03)	(.11)	(.08)**	(.07)	(.07)
Regional Norms (+)	.13	.09	–.06	.01	–.04	.06
	(.06)***	(.01)***	(.06)	(.02)	(.05)	(.02)***
Vienna Declaration (+)	.06	.02	.04	.05	.06	.08
	(.14)	(.13)	(.07)	(.13)	(.06)	(.13)
IGOs (+)	–.001	–.002	–.001	–.001	–.001	–.003
	(.002)	(.01)	(.001)	(.01)	(.001)	(.01)
Logged INGOs (+)	.16	.02	.15	.06	.08	.03
	(.08)*	(.01)*	(.06)***	(.02)***	(.04)***	(.01)***
Membership: ICCPR (*t*–1) (+)	.19	.02	.09	.04	.10	.03
	(.07)***	(.01)**	(.03)***	(.02)**	(.03)***	(.01)***
Party Competition (*t*) (+)	.44	.09	.24	.10	.17	.10
	(.16)***	(.02)***	(.08)***	(.03)***	(.06)***	(.03)***

New Democracy (*t*) (+)	.07	.06	.06	.04	.02	.01
	(.07)	(.03)**	(.04)***	(.04)	(.03)	(.03)
Logged Trade (+/–)	–.003	.01	–.003	.03	–.001	.02
	(.03)	(.03)	(.02)	(.03)	(.01)	(.04)
WTO Member (+/–)	–.11	–.14	–.02	–.18	.04	–.07
	(.08)	(.05)***	(.06)	(.06)***	(.05)	(.06)
Net FDI (+/–)	–.003	–.003	–.001	–.003	–.001	–.001
	(.00)	(.001)**	(.001)	(.002)	(.001)	(.002)
Logged GDP (+)	–.09	–.07	–.03	–.08	–.08	–.05
	(.22)	(.02)***	(.09)	(.03)***	(.11)	(.03)**
Observations	2418	2418	2418	2418	2418	2418
R^2 /Pseudo-R^2	.90	.42	.90	.53	.92	.56
F /Chi^2	260.04	595.47	225.18	359.85	325.77	383.80
Prob > F / Prob > Chi^2	.0001	.0001	.0001	.0001	.0001	.0001

All independent variables are lagged two years except where noted. Fixed-effects and ordered probit estimation with robust standard errors. Standard errors in parentheses. *Significant at the 10 percent level. **Significant at the 5 percent level. ***Significant at the 1 percent level. All tests one-tailed except where no direction predicted (+) predicted positive direction, (–) negative, and (+/–) no predicted direction.

Table 5.2. Model of Commitment to Individual Freedoms and Due Process, 1980–2005 (without INGO and IGO measures)

	Bill of Rights Index		*Personal Freedoms Index*		*Due Process Index*	
	Fixed Effects (1)	*Ordered Probit (2)*	*Fixed Effects (3)*	*Ordered Probit (4)*	*Fixed Effects (5)*	*Ordered Probit (6)*
Freedoms/Rights (*t*–1) (+)	.78 (.03)***	.73 (.06)***	.78 (.03)***	1.25 (.10)***	.82 (.03)***	1.52 (.12)***
Global Norms (+)	–.03 (.05)	–.001 (.03)	–.03 (.11)	.13 (.06)***	.01 (.04)	–.02 (.05)
Regional Norms (+)	.13 (.06)***	.09 (.01)***	–.06 (.06)	.01 (.02)	–.01 (.04)	.07 (.02)***
Vienna Declaration (+)	.06 (.14)	.05 (.13)	.04 (.07)	.07 (.14)	.07 (.06)	.10 (.13)
Membership: ICCPR (+)	.16 (.06)***	.03 (.01)**	.09 (.03)***	–.04 (.02)	.08 (.03)***	.03 (.01)***
Party Competition (*t*) (+)	.34 (.13)***	.07 (.02)***	.24 (.08)***	.10 (.03)***	.13 (.05)***	.08 (.03)***
New Democracy (*t*) (+)	.07 (.05)*	.05 (.03)**	.06 (.04)***	.03 (.03)	.02 (.03)	.01 (.03)
Logged Trade (+/–)	–.01 (.03)	.01 (.03)	–.003 (.02)	.03 (.03)	–.01 (.02)	.02 (.03)

WTO Member (+/–)	–.11	–.11	–.02	–.13	.03	–.04
	(.08)	(.05)**	(.06)	(.05)***	(.04)	(.05)
Net FDI (+/–)	–.003	–.003	–.001	–.003	–.001	–.001
	(.00)	(.001)**	(.001)	(.002)	(.001)	(.001)
Logged GDP (+/–)	–.05	–.07	–.03	–.07	–.02	–.05
	(.18)	(.02)***	(.09)	(.03)***	(.08)	(.02)***
Observations	2791	2791	2791	2791	2791	2791
R^2 /Pseudo-R^2	.91	.44	.91	.55	.93	.58
F /Chi^2	341.06	563.27	271.77	318.84	412.38	347.35
Prob > F / Prob > Chi^2	.0001	.0001	.0001	.0001	.0001	.0001

All independent variables are lagged two years except where noted. Fixed-effects and ordered probit estimation with robust standard errors. Standard errors in parentheses. *Significant at the 10 percent level. **Significant at the 5 percent level. ***Significant at the 1 percent level. All tests one-tailed except where no direction predicted (+) predicted positive direction, (–) negative, and (+/–) no predicted direction.

only when progress toward formally adopting the rights is conceptualized as a broad bundle of rights.

The Vienna Declaration has no observable effect on the formal provisions. Support for the fourth hypothesis is dependent upon the conceptualization of state embeddedness. State participation in IGOs produces no statistically significant evidence of the hypothesized diffusion of norms in any of the six models. On the other hand, a strong INGO presence is associated with higher formal commitment, and produces statistically significant coefficients in all six models, but the effects are quite small. A percentage increase in the number of INGOs would be associated with a .002 increase in the bill of rights index and the personal freedoms index with rounding and would be associated with a .001 increase in the due process index. The INGO measure is not just an indicator of state of embeddedness in the world society approach; it also reflects the transnational network hypothesis that the presence of INGOs represents the potential to bring both outside and inside pressure to bear against a regime to extract concessions such as formal promises. As a final measure of embeddedness, I included an indicator of a state's level commitment to the ICCPR. States that are parties to the ICCPR are more likely to adopt or maintain constitutional protections for core human rights. Each of the coefficients is positive and statistically significant, as expected. If we look at the bill of rights model as an example, we see that a 1-point increase in the level of commitment to the ICCPR in the previous year would be with a .19 increase in the level of state commitment to the broad bundle of rights and freedoms, and a maximum increase in level of commitment would be associated with a .76 increase.

The seventh hypothesis, that states with competitive political party systems will seek a form of political insurance through a constitutional bill of rights, receives the strongest support, producing positive coefficients that are statistically significant in all six models. The coefficient in the bill of rights index model (.44) is the largest produced in any model, excluding the lagged dependent variable. This coefficient suggests that a maximum change in party competitiveness would be associated with a 1.32 increase in the level of commitment to fundamental rights and freedoms (on a 19-point scale). In regard to the personal freedoms index, a maximum change would be associated with a .72 increase in the 11-point index of rights and a .51 increase in the 9-point due process index. The other two political insurance hypotheses produce weak results. The new democracy measure produces positive coefficients in all six models, but only two achieve acceptable levels of statistical significance: the ordered probit model for the bill of rights index and the fixed-effects model for the personal freedoms index. The transitions measure is deleted from the models because of high collinearity in all six models. The indicators of economic liberalization and development produce negative coefficients in each of the models, but they do not achieve statistical significance in any fixed-effects model, and the trade indicator fails to achieve statistical significance in any model; however, GDP produces negative coefficients that are statistically significant in each of the ordered probit models, and WTO membership and FDI produce negative coefficients that are statistically significant in the model employing the overall bill of rights index. In the other ordered probit models only WTO membership is statistically significant, and only in the personal freedoms model. Thus, overall we continue to see a general failure of economic liberalism to produce a beneficial effect on rights commitment and see some evidence of the harmful effect its critics fear. The second set of models, which includes the longer time period but drops the INGO/IGO measures, produces nearly identical results, with only two exceptions: the new democracy coefficient in the bill of rights fixed-effects model achieves statistical significance, and one of the model produces an ICCPR coefficient that is negative (non-fixed-effects personal freedoms model).

The overall performance of the commitment models is quite good. For example, the *R*-squares on the fixed-effects models range from .90 to .93, and pseudo-*R* squares on the ordered probit models range from .42 to .58, with full twenty-six year period models (with no INGO/IGO measures) performing slightly better. Overall, I find only moderate support for the normative approaches but consistent support for the transnational network theory. I find strongest support for the insurance theory in regard to the role of competitive party systems; the support is mixed in regard to new democracies. I find no support for economic liberalization theory but rather find some evidence to support its critics, just as I did in regard to commitment to formal judicial independence. I turn now to a more significant question for my study—whether these provisions will actual translate into state practice.

Translating Constitutional Promises into Practice

The potential value of written constitutions, especially those with embedded bills of rights, has long been recognized. As Madison put it, "political truths declared in that solemn manner . . . become incorporated with the national sentiment, and counteract the impulses of interest and passion" (1788). Scholars have posited that they are more than mere codes "which govern the allocation of functions, powers and duties" of government officials; they "set forth moral prescriptions and political, social and economic aspirations" (Finer 1974, 145–47). They are "the goals, ideals, and the moral standards by which they want others, including their own posterity, to judge the community" (Murphy 1993, 10). They "articulate the ideals or intentions of the communities they serve" and "provide standards against which the governors can be measured by the governed and by themselves" (Andrews 1964, 21, 24). They greatly extend the reach of the rule of law and provide individual protection from the overextension of governmental power, providing new duties and standards of justice and fairness that both politicians and bureaucrats are now required to meet; and more importantly, they represent "catalogues of very important interests and activities over which the individual rather than the state has been given final control" (Beatty 1994, 16). From an international law perspective, "when international norms are integrated in the constitutional bill of rights, they are elevated to the category of constitutional norms at the domestic level" and thus "become norms of paramount hierarchy in the country" (Mondlane 2003, 191). Other scholars argue that a bill of rights "may promote the development of a 'rights consciousnesses in popular culture'" and "encourage individuals to interpret harms to their interests as violation of 'rights' and, because of this changed consciousness, constitutional rights may become rallying points for social movements and popular pressure on government" (Epp 1998, 13). Returning to the opportunity and willingness framework, bills of rights (particularly in tandem with a judiciary empowered with judicial review) could potentially change the menu of appropriate choices, change the costs of inappropriate choices, and influence the values through which the regime will evaluate the choices. Core theoretical perspectives disagree somewhat over this expectation.

As observed in Chapter 4, constructivists would expect that the norms and obligations set forth in constitutional provisions would be honored by national governments who take their formal commitments seriously or at least make a good-faith effort to comply with them (Chayes and Chayes 1993). Other scholars argue that governments and their citizens may hold metabeliefs about the legitimacy of the rule of law and see such compliance with legal commitments as being integral to the state's identity as a legitimate nation-state (Finnemore and Sikkink 1998, 903–4). I believe these expectations hold in regard to constitutional commitments. These expectations to lead us to the following hypothesis:

- Hypothesis One: Formal provisions for core human rights will increase the odds that these rights will be achieved in practice.

And while as discussed above the world society perspective would expect that global norms would be diffused among states over time, leading to more states' adopting constitutions and specific enumeration of these rights, the logic of the perspective does lead to the possibility that as the weight of these norms grows in defining legitimate or deviant governments, the more likely states are to make formal promises without the willingness or capacity to implement them, thus leading to a decoupling between promise and practice. As noted already, some empirical evidence supports this expectation, and indeed some constitutional commitments and treaty commitments have been associated with worse human rights behavior (for example, Keith 1999; Hathaway 2002; Keith 2002a; Hafner-Burton and Tsutsui 2005). Thus, constitutional provisions for core human rights may also be associated with lower levels of achieved human rights, and I posit an alternative hypothesis:

- Alternative Hypothesis One: Adoption of the constitutional rights provisions may lead to a decoupling effect in which the provisions have no effect or even a negative effect on the level of human rights achieved in the state.

We return again to the transnational advocacy networks perspective discussed above (Keck and Sikkink 1998; Risse, Ropp, and Sikkink 1999), which posits that international human rights norms are diffused through networks of transnational and domestic actors. The spiral model that assumes that regimes may become entrapped by their tactical concessions, which may take the form of constitutional promises—promises that may simply reflect instrumental motivations such as avoiding material sanctions or reputational costs. According to the model, once governments stop denying the validity of the human rights norm and start "talking the human rights talk," not only do they become entrapped in their own rhetoric, eventually the logic of arguing takes over and evolves into a true dialogue between the norms-violating government, which is kept in the dialogue by reputational concerns, and the

INGOs and other critics (Risse, Ropp, and Sikkink 1999, 27–28). Some regimes, faced with a "fully mobilized domestic opposition linked up with transnational networks for whom rights have achieved consensual status," start a process of gradual liberalization that moves the regime to formally accept international norms through ratification of human rights treaties and institutionalizing the norms domestically in constitutions or domestic law (Risse, Ropp, and Sikkink 1999, 28–29). Ultimately the model posits that we may see rule-consistent behavior resulting from both the regime's acceptance of the validity of the human rights and the increased scrutiny and pressure of domestic and transnational actors. Risse, Ropp, and Sikkink engage in an extensive set of case studies, and they find variation as to when and to what extent countries incorporate human rights norms into domestic law; but they do not find "a single case in which a sustained improvement of human rights conditions was not preceded by the country's move toward the rule of law" and incorporation of international human rights norms into domestic institutions and law (249). Therefore, we would expect that pressure from INGOs will increase both the probability of adopting and maintaining constitutional provisions, as we saw above, but also that they will play a role in translating the promises into practice; which gives us our second hypothesis:

- Hypothesis Two: The stronger the presence of INGOs, the greater the likelihood that constitutional provisions will be translated into achieved rights.

While we may not be able to claim that an independent judiciary is "the ultimate guarantor of constitutionalism" (Ackerman 1991), the analysis in Chapter 4 does produce significant and consistent support for the hypothesis that an independent judiciary is strongly associated with less political repression of a variety of rights. The evidence supports expectations that an independent judiciary may serve as an "essential guardian of the rule of law" (Steiner and Alston 1996, 711) and as "powerful barriers against the tyranny of political assemblies" (de Tocqueville 1966, 261).

- Hypothesis Three: The more independent the judiciary, the more likely it will be that states comply with their constitutional promises of core rights.

I test these hypotheses in a series of analyses employing the standard model of repression from the previous two chapters.

Models of Political Repression

Dependent Variables: I continue to examine measures of rights repression in this chapter as I did in Chapter 3, including the three measures of repression of personal integrity rights (the CIRI Index and the two PTS measures) and civil liberties (the Freedom House Civil Liberties Index and the CIRI individual measures of repression of freedom of speech, association, and religion). These variables are operationalized fully in Chapter 3.

Formal Provision of Fundamental Freedoms and Due Process Rights: In the models below I test the constitutional provisions as additive indices described in the section above and as individual provisions.

INGO Presence: I use the number of international non-governmental organizations *(INGOs)* (Landman 2005). I include an interactive term for the interaction between the presence of INGOs and the constitutional provision.

De Facto *Judicial Independence:* I employ the measure as operationalized in Chapter 4.

Selection Effects: As I noted in Chapter 4, there is a strong possibility that many of the factors associated with the adoption of constitutional provisions are potentially those associated with my dependent variable, state repression. Thus, I would be unable to separate out whether any observed effects of the provisions on state repression were the result of the conditions or circumstances that made the state likely to adopt the provisions in the first place or whether they were the consequence of the provisions themselves. As in Chapter 4, I follow Abouharb and Cingranelli's (2008, 84–87) two-step approach in dealing with this issue. First, I estimated the model of state adoption of formal provisions in the section above and then I linked the equation predicting state repression by generating probabilities from the equation predicting constitutional adoption of the provisions and adding them into the equations for political repression as selection effects. I also continue to control for selection effects with judicial independence.

Standard Model: I incorporate the variables above into the revised standard model I estimated in Chapter 3. The model includes a lagged dependent variable, measures for civil and international war, military and Marxist/

Marxist-Leninist regimes, logged population size, per-capita GDP, and Davenport and Armstrong's trichotomous operationalization of Polity. I continued to test measures of colonial legacy and legal system type, but because the variables continued to be dropped from the fixed-effects models for collinearity and continued to be statistically insignificant in the non-fixed-effects models, I dropped the measures from subsequent analysis.

Analysis

I ran two sets of analysis: one that focuses on repression of personal integrity rights and one that focuses on repression of civil liberties. I ran each of these analyses in the expanded standard model of repression I utilized in Chapter 4. Because of the large number of models run in this chapter, I reduce the tables to simply report the key variables of interest (the constitutional indices and judicial independence), because the standard model continues to perform consistently across chapters, and this reduction of information allows us more easily to compare the key variables of interest. I ran preliminary models with interaction terms for the constitutional measures and judicial independence (full period) and with interaction terms for the constitutional measures and INGO presence (truncated period). None of the interactions with INGOs was statistically significant, so I did not include them in the final models. The interactions with judicial independence were statistically significant in regard to the due process index and the individual freedoms index; therefore, I ran them in the final models. Table 5.3 reports the key coefficients from three personal integrity models. In the model with the full bill of rights index we see that this broad index produces negative coefficients that achieve statistical significance in three models—the Department of State fixed-effects models and both of the CIRI effects models; however, the coefficients are quite small (-.01 to -.03). Using the CIRI fixed-effects model as an example, a maximum increase in the bill of rights index would be associated with a .54 decrease in the 9-point CIRI index of political repression. Judicial independence continues to produce strong coefficients across all six models. The broad bill of rights index includes my measures of personal freedoms, and these rights may be less directly related to personal integrity rights than to due process rights; therefore, I expect that when we separate out the due process rights from the broader index, we will be more likely to observe a significant effect.

The due process model is presented in the middle of Table 5.3. Here we find evidence of an interactive effect with judicial independence in three of the four PTS models. The interactive terms suggest that the due process provisions are associated with less repression of personal integrity rights when the judiciary is independent. The statistically significant constitutive terms for judicial independence can be interpreted to mean that judicial independence has a beneficial effect even without the due process clauses present. The failure of the constitutive due process coefficients to achieve statistical significance suggests that the provisions without an independent judiciary have no effect. There is one exception: the due process coefficient in the Amnesty-based PTS model suggests that provisions under these circumstances (without an independent judiciary) may even be associated with higher levels of repression. Since only one of six coefficients achieves statistical significant, we must be cautious in accepting this result.

The coefficients reported in Table 5.3 are the core coefficients of interest from the model examining the four individual provisions of due process, controlling for judicial independence and interaction effects between the provisions and the judiciary. Both the coefficient for the provision for the ban against torture and the interactive term with judicial independence fail to produce statistically significant coefficients across all six models. The fair trial provision produces negative coefficients that achieve acceptable levels of statistical significance in the Amnesty-based PTS and CIRI models. The interactive term with judicial independence and fair trial is insignificant in all six models. The coefficients in the two fixed-effects models suggest that a maximum increase in the provision for fair trial would be associated with a .20 decrease in the PTS scale and a .32 decrease in the CIRI index. The habeas corpus measure produces two statistically significant positive coefficients; however, in the Department of State PTS model the interaction term is statistically significant, a result suggesting that when the judiciary is independent, the right to habeas corpus reduces the probability of repression. However, when the judiciary is not independent, the provision has a harmful effect. The public trial coefficients are positive and statistically significant in the CIRI models, as are the interaction terms for the public trial provisions and judicial independence. These results suggest that when the judiciary is independent, the right to public trials is associated with less repression, but that when the judiciary is not independent, the provision has a harmful effect. Thus as a whole the due process protections perform weakly in regard to personal integrity rights, except in the presence of an independent judiciary or

Table 5.3. Coefficients for Rights Index with Judicial Independence Estimated in Standard Model of Repression of Personal Integrity Rights, 1980–2005

	Personal Integrity Rights Abuse (PTS-SD) 1980–2005		*Personal Integrity Rights Abuse (PTS-AI) 1980–2005*		*Personal Integrity Rights Abuse (CIRI) 1982–2005*	
	Fixed Effects (1)	*Ordered Probit (2)*	*Fixed Effects (3)*	*Ordered Probit (4)*	*Fixed Effects (5)*	*Ordered Probit (6)*
BILL OF RIGHTS MODEL						
Bill of Rights Index (+/–)	–.01 (.00)**	.01 (.01)	–.002 (.01)	.01 (.01)	–.03 (.01)***	–.01 (.01)*
De Facto Judicial Independence (–)	–.11 (.03)***	–.25 (.03)***	–.09 (.03)***	–.14 (.03)***	–.24 (.06)***	–.19 (.03)***
DUE PROCESS MODEL						
Due Process Index (+/–)	–.003 (.02)	.04 (.02)	.02 (.01)	.04 (.02)***	–.04 (.03)	–.01 (.02)
De Facto Judicial Independence (–)	–.10 (.03)***	–.21 (.05)***	–.06 (.03)**	–.07 (.04)***	–.21 (.09)***	–.18 (.04)***
Interaction: Due Process Index and Judicial Independence (–)	–.01 (.01)	–.02 (.01)*	–.02 (.01)**	–.03 (.01)***	.02 (.02)	–.01 (.01)
INDIVIDUAL PROVISIONS MODEL						
Fair Trial (–)	–.06 (.06)	–.07 (.07)	–.10 (.06)**	–.10 (.07)***	–.16 (.13)*	–.10 (.05)**

Public Trial (–)	.04	.05	.05	.10	.09	.12
	(.07)	(.06)	(.08)	(.05)	(.18)	(.06)
Habeas Corpus (+/–)	–.05	.10	.01	.11	–.07	.01
	(.05)	(.05)**	(.06)	(.05)***	(.12)	(.05)
Torture (+/–)	.03	.02	.07	.01	.00	–.03
	(.04)	(.05)	(.05)	(.04)	(.09)	(.04)
De Facto Judicial Independence (–)	–.09	–.21	–.06	–.08	–.20	–.18
	(.04)***	(.05)***	(.03)**	(.04)**	(.09)**	(.04)***
Interaction Fair Trial and Judicial	.02	.04	–.01	–.01	–.02	.05
Independence (–)	(.04)	(.05)	(.04)	(.05)	(.06)	(.04)
Interaction Public Trial and Judicial	.00	–.08	.00	–.11	.01	–.13
Independence (–)	(.04)	(.04)	(.04)	(.05)***	(.07)	(.04)***
Interaction Habeas Corpus and Judicial	–.03	–.05	–.03	–.03	–.02	–.01
Independence (–)	(.03)	(.03)*	(.03)	(.04)	(.06)	(.03)
Interaction Torture and Judicial	–.01	.02	–.01	.04	–.03	.03
Independence (–)	(.03)	(.04)	(.03)	(.03)	(.06)	(.03)

Full standard models estimated. Only constitutional and judicial independence coefficients reported. *Significant at the 10 percent level. **Significant at the 5 percent level. ***Significant at the 1 percent level.

in the specific case of provision for fair trial. Judicial independence continues to have an independent effect even in the absence of the due process provisions. These results provide a more nuanced picture than previous work, suggesting that the independent judiciary may be a necessary foundation for these rights to be effective generally. Such a relationship is not surprising; in fact it is rather surprising that the conditional relationship is not observable across all the models.

I next turn to the models of repression of civil liberties. I ran two sets of analyses here, one utilizing the aggregate Freedom House measure (reported in Table 5.4) and one set utilizing the CIRI individual measures inverted to represent repression of (1) freedom of speech and press, (2) freedom of association and assembly, and (3) freedom of religion (reported in Tables 5.5 and 5.6). As with the previous analysis, I ran the standard models first without interaction terms, and then ran analyses with interaction terms for the provisions/indices with judicial independence. None of the interaction terms was statistically significant, so I did not include them in the final models reported here. As a whole we see that the constitutional provisions perform much better in the civil liberties model than they did in the personal integrity models. In Table 5.4, the Freedom House models using the broad bill of rights index are reported in the first two columns, the models using the personal freedoms index are reported in third and fourth columns, and the models using the due process index are reported in the last two columns. Across the table as a whole, each of the three rights indices is statistically significant in each model. The coefficients are moderate in size: a maximum increase in the bill of rights index would be associated with a decrease of .36 in the 7-point civil liberties repression measure, a decrease of .30 in regard to the personal freedoms index, and a decrease of .27 in regard to the due process index. Judicial independence continues to maintain its influence.

In the bottom half of the table I report the core coefficients of interest from the models, rerun to include the presence of INGOs. As with the previous analysis, I ran preliminary models with interactive terms between INGOs and the rights indices, but the interactions and constitutive terms were not statistically significant, so I did not include the interaction terms in the final model. While the presence of INGOs was not significantly related to the more severe reform of repression—personal integrity rights abuse—here we do find that they are negatively associated with the less egregious category repression—civil liberties measured broadly—but the coefficients are statistically significant only in the non-fixed-effects models. The effect of INGOs

Table 5.4. Coefficients for Rights Index with Judicial Independence Estimated in Standard Model of Repression of Freedom House Civil Liberties, 1980–2005

	Freedom House Civil Liberties					
	Bill of Rights Index		*Personal Freedoms Index*		*Due Process Index*	
	Fixed Effects (1)	*Ordered Probit (2)*	*Fixed Effects (3)*	*Ordered Probit (4)*	*Fixed Effects (5)*	*Ordered Probit (6)*
Rights Index (+/–)	–.02	–.02	–.03	–.02	–.03	–.03
	(.005)***	(.01)***	(.01)***	(.01)**	(.01)***	(.01)***
De Facto Judicial Independence (–)	–.11	–.20	–.11	–.20	–.11	–.20
	(.02)***	(.04)***	(.02)***	(.04)***	(.02)***	(.04)***
1982–2000 Controlling for INGOs						
Rights Index (+/–)	–.02	–.02	–.04	–.02	–.01	–.04
	(.01)***	(.01)***	(.01)***	(.01)**	(.01)	(.01)***
Natural Log of INGOs Presence (–)	–.02	–.06	–.02	–.06	–.02	–.07
	(.03)	(.02)***	(.03)	(.02)***	(.03)	(.02)***
De Facto Judicial Independence (–)	–.15	–.26	–.15	–.26	–.14	–.26
	(.03)***	(.04)***	(.03)***	(.04)***	(.03)***	(.04)***

Full standard models estimated. Only constitutional and judicial independence coefficients reported. *Significant at the 10 percent level. **Significant at the 5 percent level. ***Significant at the 1 percent level.

Table 5.5. Coefficients for Rights Indices and Provisions with Judicial Independence Estimated in Standard Model of Repression of Individually Measured Civil Liberties, 1982–2005

	Repression of Freedom of Speech and Press		*Repression of Freedom of Assembly and Association*		*Repression of Freedom of Religion*	
	Fixed Effects (1)	*Ordered Probit (2)*	*Fixed Effects (3)*	*Ordered Probit (4)*	*Fixed Effects (5)*	*Ordered Probit (6)*
FREEDOMS INDEX MODELS						
Personal Freedoms Index (+/–)	–.04 (.01)***	–.07 (.01)***	–.05 (.01)***	–.08 (.01)***	–.01 (.01)	–.02 (.02)
De Facto Judicial Independence (–)	–.09 (.02)***	–.24 (.04)***	–.06 (.02)***	–.16 (.04)***	–.01 (.01)	–.20 (.05)***
INDIVIDUAL PROVISIONS MODELS						
Freedom of Religion (+/–)	—	—	—	—	–.02 (.03)	–.10 (.06)***
Freedom of Association (+/–)	—	—	–.08 (.08)	–.36 (.09)***	—	—
Freedom of Assembly (+/–)	—	—	–.11 (.09)	.003 (.09)	—	—
Freedom of Speech (+/–)	–.26 (.07)***	–.25 (.07)***	—	—	—	—
Freedom of Press (+/–)	.07 (.06)	.02 (.05)	—	—	—	—
De Facto Judicial Independence (–)	–.09 (.02)***	–.25 (.06)***	–.06 (.02)***	–.16 (.04)***	–.01 (.01)	–.20 (.04)***

Full standard models estimated. Only constitutional and judicial independence coefficients reported. *Significant at the 10 percent level. **Significant at the 5 percent level. ***Significant at the 1 percent level.

Table 5.6. Coefficients for Rights Indices and Provisions with Judicial Independence and INGOs Estimated in Standard Model of Repression of Individually Measured Civil Liberties, 1982–2000

	Repression of Freedom of Speech and Press		*Repression of Freedom of Assembly and Association*		*Repression of Freedom of Religion*	
	Fixed Effects (1)	*Ordered Probit (2)*	*Fixed Effects (3)*	*Ordered Probit (4)*	*Fixed Effects (5)*	*Ordered Probit (6)*
FREEDOMS INDEX MODEL						
Personal Freedoms Index (+/–)	–.05 (.01)***	–.08 (.01)***	–.06 (.01)***	–.09 (.02)***	–.01 (.01)	–.02 (.02)
Natural Log of INGOs Presence (–)	.02 (.04)	–.02 (.02)	.06 (.04)	–.01 (.03)	–.03 (.03)	–.09 (.03)***
De Facto Judicial Independence (–)	–.11 (.02)***	–.24 (.04)***	–.07 (.02)***	–.19 (.05)***	–.01 (.01)	–.20 (.05)***
INDIVIDUAL PROVISIONS MODEL						
Freedom of Religion (+/–)	—	—	—	—	–.01 (.01)	–.10 (.06)***
Freedom of Association (+/–)	—	—	–.09 (.08)	–.44 (.10)***	—	—
Freedom of Assembly (+/–)	—	—	–.14 (.09)*	.04 (.11)	—	—

(continued)

Table 5.6 (*continued*)

	Repression of Freedom of Speech and Press		*Repression of Freedom of Assembly and Association*		*Repression of Freedom of Religion*	
	Fixed Effects (1)	*Ordered Probit (2)*	*Fixed Effects (3)*	*Ordered Probit (4)*	*Fixed Effects (5)*	*Ordered Probit (6)*
Freedom of Speech (+/–)	–.30 (.09)***	–.25 (.07)***	—	—	—	—
Freedom of Press (+/–)	.07 (.07)	.02 (.05)	—	—	—	—
Natural Log of INGOs Presence (–)	.02 (.04)	.03 (.04)	.05 (.04)	.01 (.03)	.03 (.04)	–.08 (.04)***
De Facto Judicial Independence (–)	–.09 (.02)***	–.25 (.06)***	–.08 (.02)***	–.19 (.05)***	–.01 (.01)	–.20 (.06)***

Full standard models estimated. Only constitutional and judicial independence coefficients reported. *Significant at the 10 percent level. **Significant at the 5 percent level. ***Significant at the 1 percent level.

remains substantively small, approximating zero in these models; a percentage in the number of INGOs would be associated with only a .001 decrease in repression. The judiciary maintains its effect, even with INGOs added to the model. As a whole the indices of freedoms are much more powerfully associated with lessening repression of the broader civil liberties, which is expected given that the promised rights are more closely matched to the measure of repression—civil liberties restrictions.

Next we move from the broad categories of civil liberties repression to examine repression of specific individual freedoms: speech and press, assembly and association, and religion. These results are reported in Table 5.5 (1982–2005, without IGO and INGO measures) and Table 5.6 (1982–2000, with IGO and INGO measures). As in the tables above, in Tables 5.5 and 5.6 I present only the coefficients of interest because the base model continues to perform consistently with the previous analyses: speech and press models are reported in columns 1 and 2, assembly and association in columns 3 and 4, and religion in columns 5 and 6. In the top half of Table 5.5 I present the coefficients for the personal freedoms index model, and in the bottom half I present the coefficients from the models estimated with the appropriate individual provisions separated out of the index and estimated in the matching freedoms model. For example, I estimate the impact of freedom of association provisions and freedom of assembly provisions on the repression of freedom of association and assembly, as measured by the CIRI three-point scale.

Table 5.5 shows that the individual freedoms index is translated into less repression of freedom of speech and press, as well lower levels of restrictions on freedom of association and assembly. All four coefficients are statistically significant and produce fairly strong effects. Using the fixed-effects models as examples, we would expect that a maximum increase in the 11-point scale of rights would be associated with a decrease in the 3-point repression of speech/press scale by .40 and would be associated with a decrease in the 3-point repression association/assembly scale by .50. However, the coefficients for the personal freedoms index are not statistically significant in either of the repression of religious freedom models. And for the first time, judicial independence loses its effect in one of the models, the fixed-effects religious repression model. I return to this association momentarily. my next analysis shifts into an examination of the impact of individual promises of repression of the specific promised right. Here we find that the specific promise of religious freedom is associated with less religious repression and achieves acceptable levels of statistical significance in the non-fixed-effects model but not in the fixed-effects model. Again the coefficient for judicial independence fails to achieve acceptable levels of statistical significance in this model. These results provide some evidence that translation of a formal promise of free exercise of religion into actual freedom faces more significant cultural hurdles, and the results also suggest that the judicial arena may not be immune to those cultural influences.

The individual provisions for assembly and association perform rather weakly, with only the promise of freedom of association achieving statistical significance, and even then in only one model. The promise of freedom of speech appears to be the core constitutional promise in this bundle of rights. It achieves statistical significance in both models, and produces strong coefficients. A maximum change (from no provision to full provision) in the provision of freedom of speech would be associated with a .52 decrease in the 3-point repression of speech/press scale. Freedom of press is not statistically significant in either model. I do not believe we can discount the effect of the bundled set of rights on actual state practice, even if individually some of the provisions fail to perform consistently. It is likely that their combined effect has some influence as well. As with the previous models in preliminary analyses, I examined interactive effects with judicial independence and the provisions and found none of the interactions to be statistically significant, so I did not include them in the final models. I next re-estimated my models employing measures to capture the presence of INGOs. As with the previous models, I engaged in preliminary analysis to test for interactive effects, but the interaction models did not produce statistically significant results, and thus I did not include interactive terms in the final models. I do find in the INGO models some changes from the non-INGO models, albeit minor ones. I report the core coefficients in the INGO models in Table 5.6. The models using the personal freedoms index are reported in the top half of the table. The presence of INGOs noticeably produces a coefficient statistically significant in only one of the personal freedoms index models—interestingly, it is in the religious freedoms non-fixed-effects model—and controlling for the INGO effect reduces the statistical significance of the freedoms index below that which would be considered acceptable. It had achieved statistical significance before the INGO measure was added. Moving to the individual provisions analyses, again the presence of INGOs is again statistically significant only in the religious freedoms non-fixed-effects model; however, here the individual provision for religious freedom retains its statistical significance. Controlling for the presence of INGOs, while statistically insignificant itself, does pull the coefficient for the provision of freedom of assembly into an acceptable range of statistical significance. While overall the presence of INGOs is marginal, its effect is most felt in the area of repression (religious freedom) that is only weakly affected by constitutional protections and an independent judiciary.

Conclusions

In this chapter I addressed two core questions: Why do states adopt constitutional provisions for individual rights and freedoms? Does formal commitment make a difference in actual state behavior? In other words, to what extent do the promises lessen state repression of these promised rights? The world society approach predicted that most states would have similar constitutional "packages" because the larger system dictates that they should in order to achieve good state status (Go 2003), and my descriptive analysis confirmed that bills of rights constitute a core part of this package. I extended the world society approach to predict that domestic rights commitments are influenced by the same three mechanisms articulated by world society scholars studying treaty commitment; however, I found rather mixed evidence. I found no evidence of a global norms cascade but did find consistent evidence of a regional diffusion, at least in regard to the broader bundle of rights, and some evidence of a regional effect on due process rights. I found no evidence that embeddedness in the broader world, as measured by IGO participation, influences formal commitment but did find strong, consistent evidence that the increased presence of INGOs does influence formal commitment to rights. This evidence also supports the transnational network theory. These results run somewhat contrary to those I found in regard to state commitment to formal judicial independence in Chapter 4. There both regional and global norms strongly and consistently influenced commitment, but INGOs had no demonstrable effect on commitment to judicial independence. It is possible that while the transnational networks may appreciate the potential rights-protective role of an independent judiciary, they may be more motivated to influence the discourse and formal commitment to fundamental rights, rather than expend limited resources to enhance the independence of an institution that in many states has not played a rights-protective role but rather has legitimized the abuses of authoritarian regime.

I also examined the expectation that regimes facing electoral uncertainty would seek to "lock in" the benefits of formal rights. I found strong and consistent evidence across all three indices that regimes with strong party competition are more likely to adopt and maintain the constitutional freedoms, and I found moderate evidence of the same effect in regard to new democracies. This evidence parallels that found for state adoption and maintenance of formal provisions for judicial independence. While the application of the positive perspective of economic liberalization predicted that an interdependent economy and trade would indirectly encourage states to adopt or maintain constitutional provisions for core rights, I found no evidence of this "dividend" but instead, as in Chapter 4, continued to find consistent evidence that supported the malign perspective that economic liberalism is not likely to lead to these dividends and actually decreases the probability of meaningful reform. Finally, I found that prior commitment to the ICCPR was consistently associated with higher levels of constitutional commitment across each category of rights under study here. Overall, these results suggested optimism that the formal commitments would be translated into action, given the role of norms and prior treaty commitment to international human rights norms, and the potential ongoing role that INGOs and a competitive party system would continue to play in committed states.

The optimistic perspective of these formal commitments recognizes the potential that these formal constitutional provisions would allow persons the legitimacy to openly criticize and challenge the regime without the threat or application of coercive state action, and that the formal guarantee of rights would provide recourse to a legal remedy, and impose material and reputational costs to the regime were it to engage in repression, thus over time discouraging the regime from selecting this costly policy tool. Thus, I argued from my opportunity and willingness framework that bills of rights or particular formalized freedoms potentially change the menu of appropriate choices, change the costs of inappropriate choices, and influence the values through which the regime will evaluate the choices. Overall, the evidence suggests that the formal commitments are much more likely to curb repressive state behavior in regard to the broader set of civil liberties than in regard to the more egregious repression of personal integrity rights. While I find that due process rights do lessen the probability of personal integrity abuse, the formal provisions, not surprisingly, were largely dependent upon the presence of an independent judiciary. Individually, the due process protection appeared to be largely driven by provision for fair trials and public trials. The provision for fair trials operated on repression independent of judicial independence, whereas the public trial provision was dependent upon the level of judicial independence. This relationship clearly merits future study, particularly further delineation of fair trial protection beyond the explicit enumeration of a "right to a fair trial." And in regard to public trial provision it would be fruitful to study the connection between public trials provisions in bills of rights that enumerate a right to public trial and provisions in judicial sections of constitutions that require the judiciary to hold trials in public.

I found overwhelming evidence that the formal commitment to individual freedoms and rights decreased the probability of broad civil liberties restrictions, whether examining the provisions as a bundle of nine rights or as the two categories, due process rights and fundamental individual freedoms. I found that the influence of these rights was independent of the presence of INGOs and the judiciary's independence. I also found evidence that the personal freedoms index reduced the likelihood of repression of two sets of individual freedoms (speech and press, assembly and association) but not the third, freedom of religion. Concomitantly, I found that religious repression was the one form of repression not consistently influenced by judicial independence, a result suggesting that the translation of a formal promise of religious freedom to the actual free exercise of religious faces more significant cultural hurdles than the other freedoms, and suggests that the judicial arena may not immune to those cultural influences in regard to this freedom. I did find one encouraging link in regard to religious freedom: while the presence of INGOs has no effect on repression of the other four freedoms, I did find evidence that broader INGO presence decreased the likelihood of repression of religious freedom. Thus their effect was evident where it is perhaps most needed, in the area of repression that is only weakly affected by constitutional protections and an independent judiciary.

As a whole the evidence in this chapter suggests that despite the somewhat pessimistic findings of earlier studies of constitutional provisions for rights, optimists are fairly justified in their expectation that such provisions are more than mere window dressing and more than mere codes that "govern the allocation of functions, powers and duties" of government officials (Finer 1974, 145–47). Instead they appear, especially in the case of civil liberties, to enumerate "the goals, ideals, and the moral standards by which [states] want others, including their own posterity, to judge the community" (Murphy 1993, 10). And the evidence does suggest that although provisions may indeed extend the reach of the rule of law and provide individual protection from the overextension of governmental power, it appears that the standards of justice and the level of protection of the individual are thinner in regard to personal integrity rights. Given the egregious nature of even low levels of personal integrity abuse, it is perplexing that the potential "rights consciousness" that develops around a bill of rights would not extend as readily or consistently to forms of repression such as torture, killing, and disappearance. It may be that the state is more likely to employ this form of repression during periods of threat, and that the threat itself or the claim of national security may provide a cloak of legitimacy for the state to engage without sanction in these more egregious acts. I turn to that question as we move into the next chapter.

Chapter 6

Constitutional Protections and Repression When Regimes Are Threatened

> The Egyptian government's renewal of the emergency law today for two more years breaches again its 2005 promise to end the state of emergency and repeal the law. The government said that it would limit the use of the emergency law to terrorism and drug-related crimes, subject to judicial supervision, a promise it has previously made and then broken, most recently in February 2010. In fact, security officials continue to use the emergency law to detain people in cases that have nothing to do with terrorism and instead target political dissent. The law has been used repeatedly against members of the Muslim Brotherhood, activists and bloggers. (Human Rights Watch 2010)

> King Gyanendra of Nepal today dismissed the government, assumed direct power, and declared a nation-wide state of emergency. This action plunges the country deeper into crisis and puts the Nepalese people at even greater risk of gross human rights abuses. Widespread human rights abuses have taken place during the nine-year conflict in Nepal between government forces and the Communist Party of Nepal (CPN) (Maoist) rebels. Political leaders have been placed under arrest and communications links within Nepal and with the outside

> world have been severed. All independent Nepali media have been closed down and state owned radio announced that a number of rights—including freedom of movement and freedom of assembly—have been suspended. (Human Rights Watch 2005)

> In a national atmosphere of revenge, when many basic rights as guaranteed by the Zambian constitution were suspended, Amnesty International believes that police and security officers tortured at least six individuals suspected of involvement in the coup attempt. Other human rights violations were allowed to take place—such as prolonged administrative detentions that violated the right to fair trial, the suppression of legitimate and peaceful opposition political activity, and severe curtailment of citizens' freedoms of expression, assembly and association—under a state of emergency that appeared to be unnecessary. How was the torture and other human rights violations allowed to happen? Amnesty International believes the flouting of the Constitution's procedural guarantees governing detentions under a state of emergency; the Government of Zambia's abuse of repressive laws dating back to the colonial era; the lack of safeguards in the legal system; and the limited powers of the HRC [United Nations Human Rights Commission] facilitated the violation of human rights, including the use of torture during incommunicado detention that lasted for days, sometimes weeks. (Amnesty International 1998)

In this chapter I examine the role that domestic threats to a state play in the government's choice to employ tools of repression, especially when the threats involve violence. As Finn (1991) notes, political violence merits special attention, not just because it is "among the most frequent and severe of constitutional emergencies, but because it is best suited to exposing the limitations of constitutionalism" (6). As the three excerpts above illustrate, constitutional promises of human rights protection are most at risk of abuse during these periods, when a regime may respond in disproportionate measure, ignore constitutional rights, and use the opportunity to punish and quell its opposition, all under a claim of legitimacy that it is simply protecting the security of the state and broader public's safety. Violent threats to states are one of most studied factors associated with political repression, and their effect on state use of repression has been demonstrated more consistently over time than any other circumstance, except regime type, which typically pales in the magnitude of impact relative to that of domestic violence (for example, Davis and Ward 1990; Alfatooni and Allen 1991; Poe and Tate 1994; Davenport 1995c, 1996; Gartner and Regan 1996; Cingranelli and Richards 1999a; Richards 1999; Poe, Tate, and Keith 1999; Poe et al. 2000; Apodaca 2001; Regan and Henderson 2002; Davenport and Armstrong 2004; Keith and Poe 2004; Bueno de Mesquita et al. 2005; Abouhard and Cingranelli 2006). State claims of threats to national security are not without some basis; globally states have faced a fairly constant level of threat over the last thirty years. Figures 6.1 and 6.2 present the annual mean level of several forms of domestic threats, as well as international war, from 1979 through 2005. The means for the dichotomous measures presented in Figure 6.1 can be translated to the proportion of states facing each form of threat, which multiplied by one hundred gives the percentage of states experiencing that particular threat.

Figure 6.1 shows that the most violent form of domestic threat, civil war, remains fairly constant over time; however, violent rebellion (which includes armed attacks, including terrorist activities, guerrilla movements, and most attempted coups, but not full-scale civil war) has gradually declined since the end of the Cold War but surges somewhat around 2003. In most years, 20 to 30 percent of states face rather severe forms of violence, even if the violence falls short of civil war. The most prevalent threat, not surprisingly, is organized nonviolent protest; we see a significant surge during the transitional decade following the dissolution of the Soviet Union, with the means gradually falling within the prior range beginning in 1997. Clearly, these numbers are affected by instability in the former Soviet republics or Soviet Bloc states; in 2004 seventeen of these states experienced protest: Albania, Macedonia, Croatia, Bosnia, Bulgaria, Moldova, Romania, Russia, Latvia, Lithuania, Ukraine, Belarus, Armenia, Georgia, Azerbaijan, Tajikistan, and Kazakhstan. The frequency of unarmed rebellions shows a similar surge and returns to slightly lower means than in the early 1980s.

Figure 6.2 presents means for event counts of threats. While there is variation over time and we can identify a few significant spikes, most of the annual

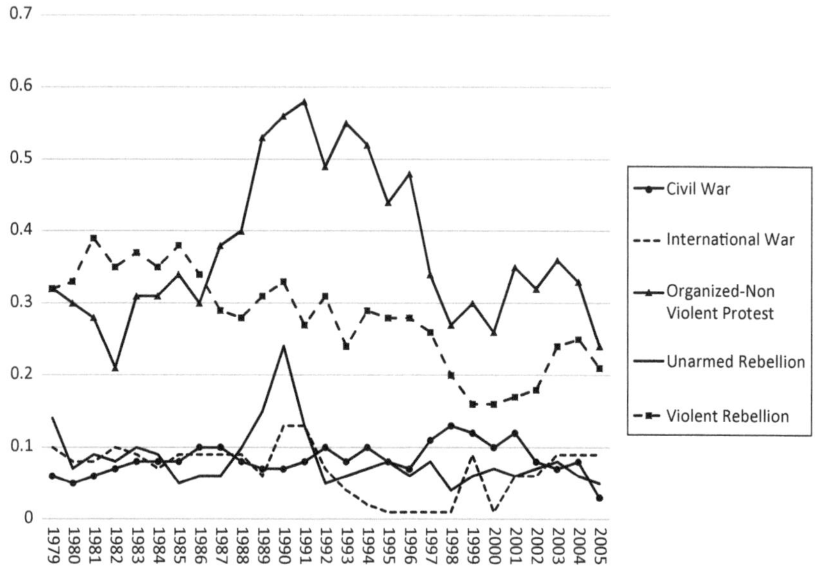

Figure 6.1. Mean Level of Presence of Threat (Dichotomous Measure), 1979–2005

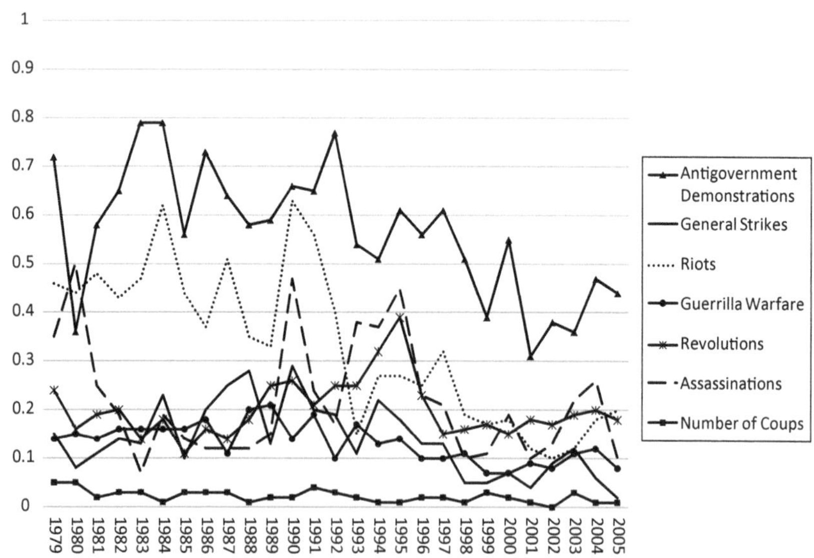

Figure 6.2. Mean Level of Threat (Event Counts), 1979–2005

means stay within a fairly consistent range, with one significant exception: the mean level of riots declines and then spikes with the end of the Cold War, and makes a significant downward trek after 1997, ending .26 lower than it began in 1979. This graph tends to overstate somewhat the presence of threat. The data represent 4,440 country-years, and in 60 percent of those country-years there was no incident of any level of domestic threat measured here, and in 69 percent of country-years there were no violent threat events. In regard to the threats captured in Figure 6.1, in 43 percent of the country-years there were no threats experienced, and in 64 percent of the country-years there were no violent forms of threat experienced.

Legal scholars, however, note the surprising and persistent frequency of states resorting to declarations of states of emergency in response to domestic threats; accordingly, they have devoted substantial effort to trying to identify and promote the appropriate legal standards and safeguards to protect human rights during states of emergency or states of exception that are declared in response to domestic threats (Higgins 1976–77; Buerganthal 1981; Hartman 1981; Questiaux 1982; Daes 1983; Cea 1987; Chowdhury 1989; Grossman 1990; Frühling 1993; Fitzpatrick 1994a, 1994b; Henkin and Hargrove 1994). Many of the declared states of emergency have been strongly associated with human rights abuse ranging from a disproportionate use of force to arbitrary imprisonment and torture of political opponents to widespread extrajudicial killings. However, as the International Commission of Jurists (ICJ) notes, "A state of emergency need not entail gross or excessive violations of human rights. The state of emergency is the counterpart in international law of self-defense in penal law. That it may be necessary to suspend respect for certain human rights in order to prevent the nation from falling into chaos is universally admitted" (1983, 413). The ICJ further notes that "recourse to a state of emergency corresponds to a certain respect for legalism, or at least the desire to demonstrate such respect" and therefore a formal declaration of a state of emergency may be a step in the direction of preventing gross violations of human rights (413–14). Out of concern for the human rights and legal protection of citizens living under states of emergency, the ICJ undertook a comprehensive study in parallel with a UN special rapporteur, Nicole Questiaux, who had been charged to prepare a report on "The Question of the Human Rights of Any Person Subjected to Any Form of Detention and Imprisonment." The study led the ICJ to call for states to adopt constitutional safeguards to protect against human rights abuse during states of emergency. Such provisions, it argued, serve two functions. On the one hand, for regimes that resort to emergency clauses in good faith, it is possible to know in advance the extent and limit of their emergency powers through "rules that are given the highest position in the hierarchy of domestic law" (432). On the other hand, for regimes not disposed to respect the limits of their authority, the provisions provide objective criteria by which the government's conduct can be evaluated. Ultimately the provisions "represent a freely determined national consensus on the degree of dissent which may be tolerated, the values which are so fundamental that they may in no circumstances be violated, and on the limits to the power of a legitimate government" (432). Specifically, the ICJ recommends that state constitutions clearly set out the conditions under which states of emergency may be declared and exercised so that (1) regimes that resort to emergency clauses in good faith will know in advance the extent and limit of their emergency powers; and (2) regimes that are not disposed to respect the limits of their authority may be judged according to the extent to which they live up to these specific rules. The ICJ further recommends that constitutions specify that emergency measures may not affect those rights recognized as nonderogable in international law, and that they should spell out the effects of states of emergency on the rights of citizens, as well as the powers of the various branches of government. Finally, the ICJ recommends that constitutions enumerate and define situations that justify departure from the normal legal order and establish a procedure for declaring a state of emergency that (1) gives primary responsibility to the legislature, (2) specifies the duration of the emergency, and (3) periodically reviews the need for its continuation.

A comparable set of recommended constitutional provisions regulating states of emergency was adopted by consensus by another group of international lawyers and law scholars, the International Law Association (ILA), following six years of study by a special subcommittee and an additional two years of revision (see Lillich 1985, 1072): the Paris Minimum Standards of Human Rights Norms in a State of Emergency (Minimum Standards). The Minimum Standards, which drew in part upon the work of the ICJ, restates that constitutions should require that states of emergency be extendable only with the legislature's approval; but the standards add the additional protection that the legislature should not be dissolved during the emergency; and the requirement that if the state is a party to a regional or international treaty, the declaration of the state of emergency must be subject to judicial or other review (Chowdury 1989, 13–15). The United Nations Commission on Human Rights, in agreement with these organizations, takes the position that explicitly and clearly defining limitations on constitutional rights is better than leaving the question of acceptable restrictions open to interpretation by omitting any constitutional discussion of limits. If limits are specifically enumerated, it is thought, regimes will have only specified circumstances under which they can legitimately suspend constitutional rights.

While the delineation of these standards has achieved a high degree of consensus among international lawyers and their associations, assessments of the standards' application in the real world have been decidedly pessimistic. For example, Grossman's (1990) analysis of Latin American constitutions reveals that while most of these constitutions do have emergency clauses that are supposed to apply only in relatively restricted circumstances (in the case of a possible foreign attack or internal disorder that endangers the constitution), under these declared emergencies constitutional rights are broadly suspended. Grossman finds it difficult to assess how much the different constitutional provisions matter but fears that the emergency provisions provide a "rationalization for deprivation of human liberties" (188). Cea (1987) notes that the Chilean constitution gives the president unilateral powers to declare a state of siege or martial law "nearly at will," the power to monitor the behavior of judiciary, and the power to suspend most civil liberties (665). Haile (1996) reports that in Ethiopia, under constitutional provision, most rights are derogable during a declared state of emergency.

The ICJ and legal scholars express concern about the institutionalization of states of emergency, noting that Syria has "been under a continuous series of emergencies since the end of the Ottoman rule in 1920" (1983, 415). They also note that the people of Uruguay have become "accustomed to the emergency regime to the point that it has become the normal machinery of government" (ibid.). Frühling (1993) also expresses concern over what he terms to be excessive authorization of the derogation of rights in Latin American constitutions. Specifically, he points to Paraguay, a country that has allegedly been under siege for over forty years. Egypt provides a similar example; its state of emergency has been renewed every three years since 1981, when Anwar Sadat was assassinated, and in fact the country has been under a state of emergency since the 1967 Six Day War, with the exception of only eighteen months in 1980–81. The UN special rapporteur on human rights in Egypt has criticized the state for the abuses made in the name of national security and the wide discretion allowed to officers in the state security apparatus who "in practice enjoy carte blanche in deciding on whom to arrest" (Amnesty International, March 10, 2010). Amnesty International asserts that in

Egypt "emergency powers have long been used to prosecute political opponents, journalists, secularists, intellectuals, Islamists, women, religious minorities, gays and just about any group outside of the control of the regime" (ibid.). As my introductory example notes, these powers have even been used to persecute bloggers.

The International Commission of Jurists' report (1983) represents the first systematic effort to survey constitutional provision for state of emergency clauses. The ICJ asserts that almost all constitutions contain provisions that deal with states of emergency; its survey of thirty-four countries reveals that twenty of these have some constitutional provision for states of emergency, another five have constitutional and legislative provisions, and six have legislative provisions for states of emergency. The report also highlights the significance of this issue, noting that in 1983 states of emergency existed in approximately one-fifth of the world's nations. Davenport's (1996) study is the first systematic empirical test of the effects of constitutional provisions for states of emergency. He measured whether or not a state of emergency clause was included in the constitution and whether there were limitations placed on the emergency powers. Davenport was agnostic as to the intent underlying the general state of emergency clause, noting that the clauses could "capture a legitimate attempt at sanctioning government behavior within certain circumstances ('constitutional promise') or they might represent the government's general attempt at circumventing nonrepressive governance ('constitutional threat')" (638). Ultimately, he expected that restrictions on emergency powers would lower the odds of repression. His analysis demonstrated a negative association between the presence of a general state of emergency clause and political repression, but he found no relationship in regard to the restrictions during the emergency periods. Subsequent analyses (Keith and Poe 2004; Keith, Tate, and Poe 2009) have demonstrated that particular emergency clauses may be problematic, at least under some circumstances—specifically, duration and derogation clauses. Other clauses that either prohibit dissolving the legislature or empower the legislature's role vis-à-vis the executive are found to lessen the odds of political repression. I address these clauses more specifically in the sections below. These studies have suffered the same limitations I have discussed in previous chapters, and again I seek to improve our theoretical and empirical understanding of the provisions' relationship to repression by first understanding why countries adopt or maintain these provisions. I then am able to assess more rigorously the constitutional provisions' effects by modeling selection effects, capturing the effects of the judiciary, INGOs, economic liberalization, and membership in the International Covenant on Civil and Political Rights (ICCPR), as well as derogations made to it.

Constitutional Regulation of States of Emergency

In the previous two chapters I have discussed a variety of perspectives that inform our understanding of why states adopt constitutional provisions that reflect international standards for human rights or judicial independence, and my empirical examinations have supported some explanations more than others. I believe that the decision to adopt constitutional provisions for states of emergency will largely be affected by the same factors. As I have discussed these perspectives more fully in the previous chapters, I will summarize them here and focus on their implications for state of emergency clauses, as well as discuss three additional hypotheses. While constitutional bills of rights and provisions for an independent judiciary clearly are a part of the global script for state legitimacy, and are increasingly prevalent in newly promulgated constitutions, I will demonstrate below that constitutional provisions to regulate human rights during states of emergency do not appear to be as core a part of the script as the other features are, a finding that runs counter to the ICJ's general assessment. Still, I argue that strong international norms regarding the derogation of human rights during emergencies have emerged since the ICCPR went into force, and they consolidated into a set of minimum standards during the mid-1980s through the efforts of international groups such as the International Lawyers Association and the International Commission of Jurists, as discussed above. The ILA and ICJ standards specifically call for the adoption of constitutional provisions that regulate states of emergency. While I do not have as strong expectations in regard to commitment to these types of clauses as the others under study, I do believe that the world society's assumption that "all states have constitutions, and constitutions come in a very similar package, because the larger system dictates that they should" (Go 2003, 72) would apply here as well, perhaps with a smaller degree of convergence.

I continue to examine this approach's hypothesis that these constitutional commitments will be influenced by the mechanisms of world society, specifically, I believe that that two events may have served as mechanism through which standards are articulated: the sixty-first conference of the

International Law Association, held in Paris from August 26 to September 1, 1984, which produced the Paris Minimum Standards of Human Rights Norms in a State of Emergency; and the International Commission of Jurists report and recommendations, *States of Emergency: Their Impact on Human Rights,* which was submitted to a UN subcommission in March 1983.[1] I derive the following five hypotheses from this approach:

- Hypothesis One: As more states within the global set of countries incorporate constitutional state of emergency provisions, the likelihood increases that other states will adopt and/or maintain similar provisions.
- Hypothesis Two: As more states within a country's region incorporate constitutional state of emergency provisions, the likelihood increases that other states within that region will adopt and/or maintain similar provisions.
- Hypothesis Three: States will be more likely to adopt and/or maintain constitutional state of emergency provisions following the 1984 conference of the International Law Association and the 1983 report by the ICJ.
- Hypothesis Four: The more the state is embedded in the international community, the more likely it will be to adopt and/or maintain constitutional state of emergency provisions.
- Hypothesis Five: States that have committed to the ICCPR will be more likely to adopt and/or maintain constitutional state of emergency provisions.

As discussed in previous chapters, the transnational advocacy networks perspective (Keck and Sikkink 1998; Risse, Ropp, and Sikkink 1999) posits that international human rights norms are diffused through networks of transnational and domestic actors who "bring pressure 'from above' and 'from below' to accomplish human rights change" (Risse and Sikkink 1999, 18) to both adopt and adhere to formal commitments to international human rights norms. Thus, in the previous analysis I have expected that pressure from INGOs will increase the probability of adopting and maintaining constitutional provisions. This expectation parallels the fourth hypothesis above to the extent that embeddedness is typically measured by INGO membership.

- Hypothesis Six: The stronger the INGO presence in a state, the more likely the state will be to adopt and/or maintain constitutional state of emergency provisions.

From a realist perspective states facing a strong domestic threat such as an armed insurgency or civil war will have a negative incentive to adopt constitutional provisions for states of emergency that might restrict their ability to deal with such threats in a timely manner and limit the methods they deem necessary or most appropriate to protect national security or public safety. On other hand, states may adopt these clauses, even if they potentially limit the regime's menu of options, because the mere ability to declare constitutionally a state of emergency may provide the regime a cover of legitimacy to engage in some repressive behaviors and to downplay those behaviors that "cross the line" in regard to international standards or the formal commitment the state has made. We know that states that have made derogations to the ICCPR engage in repression of personal integrity rights—rights which may not be derogated under the ICCPR (Keith 1999). I examine these expectations empirically.

- Hypothesis Seven: States facing an armed insurgency or engaging in civil war will be less likely to adopt or to maintain constitutional state of emergency provisions.
- Alternative Hypothesis Seven: States facing an armed insurgency or engaging in civil war will be more likely to adopt or to maintain constitutional state of emergency provisions.

We saw strong evidence in Chapter 4 to support the rational choice-based theories that espouse an electoral logic to explain state decisions to write new or revised constitutional provisions for judicial independence (Ramseyer 1994; Ginsburg 2003; Hirschl 2004). In Chapter 5 I posited a logical extension in regard to constitutional provision for rights protections, and once again found strong support for the hypotheses derived from the theories. As I noted previously, ultimately each of the three theories posits that ruling regimes in systems with competitive political participation or political fragmentation can no longer safely predict that they will be the parties that win control of the government, and thus will seek to protect their policies or preferences by providing an alternative forum to the majoritarian institutions in which the former ruling state actors may challenge the current government. More broadly, a regime will be likely to favor limited government in the face of this uncertainty, and would favor more explicit delineation of checks on the regime's power, perhaps especially in regard to states of emergency that potentially could be faked or exaggerated to provide the regime with a cover of legitimacy in repressing minority opposition. And just as Moravcsik (2000) has argued that states facing political uncertainty are likely to commit to international human rights treaties to "lock in" the benefits of human rights norms, the logic would seem to follow in regard to constitutional commitments to individual human rights norms in times of emergency. Ginsburg (as well as Moravcsik) argues that new democracies and regimes in transition face more uncertainty than do established democracies or autocracies; electoral outcomes are harder to predict in new democracies, and transitioning regimes by definition face significant and uncertain changes in the party system and institutional structures. Thus constitutional regulation of states of emergency may at least indirectly also serve as "insurance for the past against the future." I make three additional hypotheses:

- Hypothesis Eight: States with competitive political party systems will be more likely to adopt or maintain constitutional provisions for states of emergency.
- Hypothesis Nine: New democracies will be more likely to adopt or maintain constitutional provisions for states of emergency.
- Hypothesis Ten: Regimes in transition will be more likely to adopt or maintain constitutional provisions for states of emergency.

Finally, I return to the economic liberalization hypotheses discussed in Chapters 4 and 5. I continue to explore both the positive and malign perspective of economic liberalization and globalization. The positive perspective would expect that an interdependent economy and trade may indirectly encourage states to adopt or maintain constitutional provisions that reflect international standards. Citizen demands associated with a growing middle class and the diffusion of human rights norms associated with trade relationships would include constitutional provision for rights and limitation of powers during the periods of emergency, when citizens are more likely to become the targets of repression. States may also deal with the credible commitments problem in this manner, signaling to potential investors the seriousness of their commitments even during times of crisis (Milgrom,

North, and Weingast 1990; McChesney 1991; Olson 1993; Weingast 1995, 1997). This signal could work in two directions. First, the state would signal its willingness to bind itself to the rule of law even when it might feel most compelled to violate the norms; and second, the state could signal to investors that while it might be somewhat constrained in its ability to deal with a crisis, it would be able to react within legitimate constraints to deal with the crisis, maintain or restore stability, and ultimately protect the investors' resources. Economic liberalization may influence state adoption of rights provisions from another direction as well.

As we saw in previous chapters, the so-called malign perspective of economic liberalism casts doubts on most of these assumptions and instead argues that economic liberalization would not be likely to lead to theory's expected dividends, and instead may decrease the probability of meaningful reform, such as establishing limitations on the state's ability to deal with its economic self-interest during times of emergency. Empirical studies, as well as the analyses in these chapters, have generated enough evidence to support an alternative hypothesis to the liberalization hypotheses above.

- Hypothesis Eleven: Economic liberalization and economic development within a state will increase the likelihood that the state will adopt or maintain constitutional state of emergency provisions.
- Alternative Hypothesis Eleven: Economic liberalization and economic development within a state will decrease the likelihood that the state will adopt or maintain constitutional state of emergency provisions.

I believe the examination of these hypotheses will improve our substantive and empirical understanding of why states adopt state of emergency provisions, which will more fully inform our understanding of these constitutional provisions' influence on both categories of political repression. I next turn to my measurement of constitutional state of emergency provisions.

Measuring Constitutional Provision for States of Emergency

On the basis of the international recommendations of the ICJ and the ILA I created the following indicators of constitutional regulation of states of emergency or national crisis:

Legislative Declaration: This variable is coded (2) responsibility for declaring the state of emergency is given explicitly to the legislative branch; (1) states of emergency (declared by the executive) are explicitly subject to confirmation by the legislature; (0) no mention of who has the power to declare such a state; and (-1) the executive branch is explicitly given the power to declare a state of emergency with no mention of a role for the legislature or courts.

Ban against Dissolving the Legislature: This variable is coded (2) the legislature may not be dissolved during the emergency or meets "by right"; (1) vague provision for legislature meeting but no explicit prohibition against dissolving the legislature (that is, may say that the legislature can prolong length of session or can reconvene); (0) no mention of dissolving legislature in regard to states of emergency; and (-1) automatically suspends the legislature during a state of emergency or gives the executive explicit power to do so.

Duration of the State of Emergency: This variable is coded (2) duration of the emergency is specified for a set period, and extensions are subject to legislative approval; (1) duration is specified or legislative approval is specified but not both; and (0) no mention of duration or extension process.

List of Nonderogable Rights: This is a dichotomous (or binary) variable coded (1) constitutions give a list of nonderogable rights or include a statement that certain rights/freedoms cannot be revoked during states of emergency; and (0) otherwise.

Trends in Constitutional Provision for States of Emergency

Figures 6.3 and 6.4 present the annual means for each of the four provisions. The figures also present the mean number of states whose constitutions refer to states of emergency in any manner. Figure 6.3 presents the means of the variables in their original metric, and Figure 6.4 presents the means of the measures converted to a 2-point scale so that the trends of the means are based on the same metric. Several patterns emerge from the data. First, we can see the same pattern we have seen in each of analyses in the previous chapters: constitutional provision for states of emergency experiences a surge during the post-Cold War wave of constitution writing that levels off in the mid to late 1990s. Second, the percentage of states with constitutional provisions for states of emergency increases from 55 percent in 1979 to 74 percent in 2006. The means of three of the four clauses go up approximately .30 over time, while the mean for provision of a list of nonderogable rights

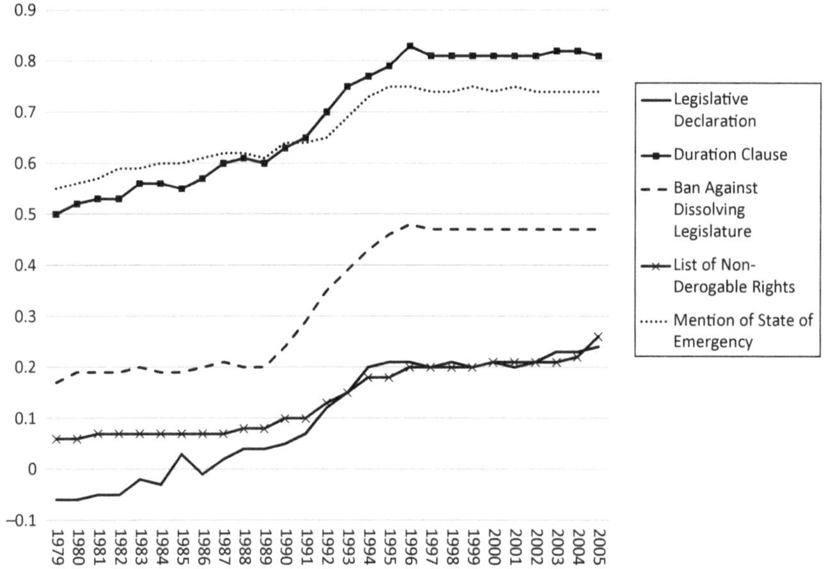

Figure 6.3. Mean Constitutional Provision for States of Emergency, 1979–2005

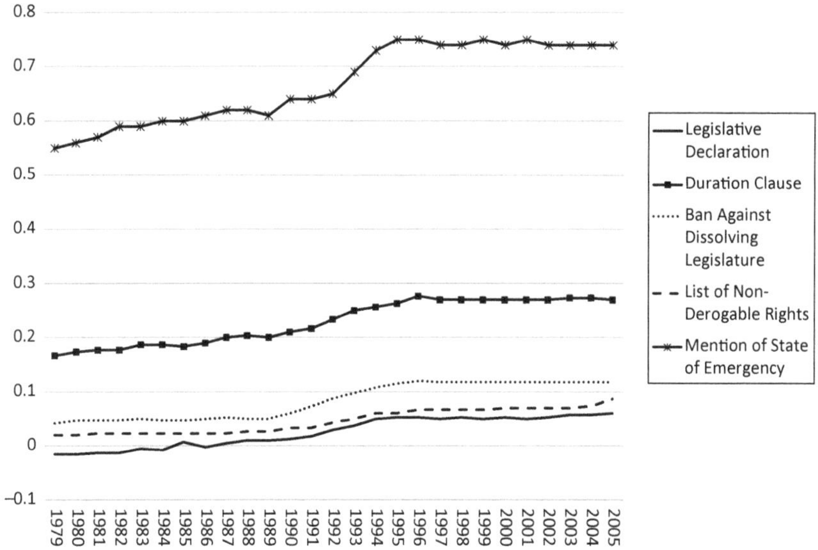

Figure 6.4. Mean Constitutional Provision for States of Emergency, Converted to 2-Point Scales, 1979–2005

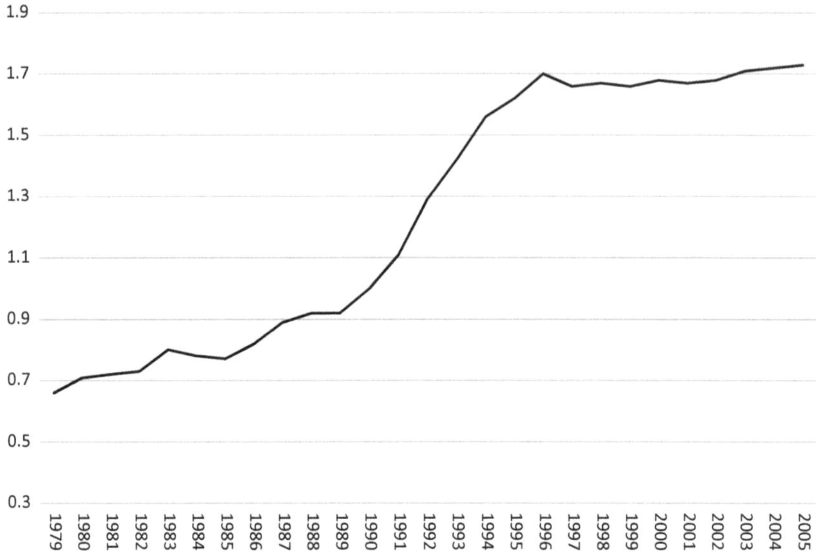

Figure 6.5. Mean Constitutional Provision for States of Emergency: 9-Point Index, 1979–2005

goes up by only .20. Third, provision for limited duration of states of emergency is the most prevalent of the four clauses over the entire period, beginning with a mean provision of .50 and ending with a mean provision of .81. Provision for legislative declaration is the least prevalent, beginning with a mean of only -.06 and ending with a mean of .26. This provision has a possible code of (-1), as does the ban against dissolving the legislature, which begins with a means of .17 that increases over time to .47 in 2005.

Following my practice in previous chapters, I created an additive index of the four provisions that represents the overall formal commitment to state of emergency standards. Figure 6.5 presents that trend over time. The most significant pattern that emerges is an overall low level of formal commitment to these standards that runs counter to the world society's convergence expectations; in 1979 the mean commitment is only two-thirds of 1 point in a 9-point scale, with the steep increase in formal commitment during the post-Cold War constitution writing period that tapers off rather quickly in 1995–96 and stays at approximately 1.75 points, a result that remains quite low given the 9-point scale. Finally, we can see some evidence of an increase in 1986, prior to the end of the Cold War, which may reflect the

Paris Minimum Standards as hypothesized under the world society approach. I turn next to testing that hypothesis and others.

Operationalizing the Hypotheses

Dependent Variable: I create a 9-point additive index of the four provisions of core recommended protections. The index ranges from 0 to 8.

Global and Regional Norms: These two annual measures are described fully in Chapter Four.

Dummy Variables for ILA Conference and ICJ report: I create a single dummy variable depicting the years 1983–1984, which demark the sixty-first conference of the International Law Association, which produced Paris Minimum Standards of Human Rights Norms in a State of Emergency, and the International Commission of Jurists' report and recommendations, *States of Emergency: Their Impact on Human Rights.*

Embeddedness: I use the two measures presented in Chapter Four.

Treaty Commitments and Reservations: I include a control measure in the model for state treaty commitments as operationalized in Chapter 4.

Competitive Political Participation or Political Fragmentation: I use the same four measures described in Chapter 4.

New Democracies and States in Transition: These two measures are operationalized as in Chapter 4.

Economic Liberalization: I employ the same four measures operationalized in Chapter 4.

Armed Insurgency and Civil War: To capture the presence of an armed insurgency I utilize Poe et al.'s (2000) organized *Violent Rebellion* measure, which is operationalized as a situation in which a substantial organized movement seeks to alter the governmental system, bringing about a significant change in the constitution or other political institutions, through armed attacks, including terrorist activities, guerrilla movements, and most attempted coups, but not full-scale civil war. Civil war is operationalized in Chapter 3.

Analysis

I first engaged in a series of preliminary analyses to identify the appropriate lags for the independent variables; the appropriate lags are reported in the tables below. As in Chapters 4 and 5, I estimated two models: first examining the full period under study (1980–2005) without the IGO/INGO measures, and then re-estimating the model with these two additional measures, a task that reduces the period to 1980–2000 because of data limitations. Table 6.1 presents the results of the models. Since the two sets of models perform almost identically, I deal with the first set of models and then compare the differences in the second set. My analysis of the first four hypotheses provides moderate support for the world society approach. The promulgation of the ILA/ICJ standards is not statistically significant; however, the global norms measures are statistically significant in both models while the regional norms are not. In the fixed-effects models participation in the ICCPR is associated with higher levels of state of emergency provision (coefficient of .02), a result that can be interpreted to mean that a change from being a nonparty to the ICCPR to being a party state with no reservations would be associated with a .08 increase in the 9-point provision index, a small impact relatively speaking. The domestic threat hypothesis receives strong support in that the presence of civil war decreases the likelihood of adopting or maintaining state of emergency provisions in all six models, but the impact is rather small—the onset of a civil war would be associated with a .05 decrease in the provision index, using the fixed-effects models as examples. The less severe form of threat, violent opposition, produces no statistically significant effect. The insurance or lock-in theories receive substantial support: both the competitiveness of political participation and new democracy status increase the likelihood of provision in each of the models. These hypotheses had mixed results in the judicial independence commitment in that the coefficients were either statistically significant in either the fixed-effects model or the probit model but not in both models. And in the bill of rights models, the party competition measures performed consistently across all models, but the new democracy coefficients performed somewhat inconsistently.

Just as we saw in Chapter 5, the coefficient for party competition is the largest produced in the fixed-effects models (.11), excluding the lagged dependent variable. This coefficient suggests that a maximum change in party competitiveness would be associated with a .33 increase in the level of commitment to state of emergency protection on the 9-point index. As in the previous analysis, the dummy variable for transitional regimes was deleted from the fixed-effects model for collinearity and failed to achieve statistical significance in the ordered probit models. As in Chapters 4 and 5, I find that all the coefficients for measures of economic liberalization and development

Table 6.1. Model of Commitment to State of Emergency Protections (9-Point Index), 1980–2005

	1980–2005 (without INGO/ IGO measures)		*1980–2000 (with INGO/ IGO measures)*	
	Fixed Effects (1)	*Ordered Probit (2)*	*Fixed Effects (3)*	*Ordered Probit (4)*
Formal State of Emergency Index (*t*–1) (+)	.82 (.01)***	2.10 (.15)***	.80 (.02)***	1.99 (.15)***
Paris Minimum Standards/ICJ Report (*t*) (+)	–.03 (.04)	–.11 (.10)	–.02 (.04)	–.07 (.11)
Global Norms (*t*–2) (+)	.07 (.05)**	.12 (.07)**	–.02 (.06)	.10 (.09)
Regional Norms (*t*–1) (+)	.01 (.05)	–.16 (.07)	.01 (.05)	–.17 (.08)
Membership: ICCPR (*t*–1) (+)	.02 (.01)**	.01 (.02)	.06 (.02)***	.01 (.02)
IGOs (*t*–2) (+)	—	—	–.001 (.001)	–.001 (.001)
Logged INGOs (*t*–2) (+)	—	—	.09 (.03)***	.06 (.03)**
Civil War (*t*–2) (–)	–.05 (.04)*	–.10 (.07)**	–.07 (.05)*	–.09 (.07)*
Violent Rebellion (*t*–2) (–)	.001 (.02)	.03 (.06)	–.01 (.02)	.04 (.06)
Party Competition (*t*) (+)	.11 (.04)***	.07 (.02)***	.12 (.04)***	.08 (.02)***
New Democracy(*t*) (+)	.03 (.02)*	.05 (.04)*	.05 (.03)**	.07 (.04)**
Logged Trade(*t*–2) (+/–)	–.01 (.01)	–.01 (.02)	–.01 (.01)	–.001 (.03)
WTO Member (*t*–2) (+/–)	–.06 (.02)***	–.07 (.05)*	–.06 (.02)***	–.09 (.05)*
Net FDI (*t*–2) (+/–)	–.001 (.001)*	–.004 (.002)***	–.001 (.001)	–.01 (.001)***
Logged GDP (*t*–2) (+/–)	–.01 (.05)	–.08 (.03)***	–.04 (.06)	–.08 (.03)***

(*continued*)

Table 6.1 (*continued*)

	1980–2005 (without INGO/ IGO measures)		*1980–2000 (with INGO/ IGO measures)*	
	Fixed Effects (1)	*Ordered Probit (2)*	*Fixed Effects (3)*	*Ordered Probit (4)*
Observations	2768	2768	2398	2398
R^2 /Pseudo-R^2	.94	.66	.93	.64
F /*Chi*^{2}	389.01	426.42	259.90	428.73
Prob > *F* / Prob > *Chi*^{2}	.0001	.0001	.0001	.0001

Fixed effects and ordered probit estimation with robust standard errors. Standard errors in parentheses. *Significant at the 10 percent level. **Significant at the 5 percent level. ***Significant at the 1 percent level. All tests one-tailed except where no direction predicted: (+) predicted positive direction, (–) negative, and (+/–) no predicted direction.

produce negative rather than positive coefficients. Logged trade is not statistically significant in any of the models, the WTO membership measure is in all four models, and the indicator is in three of four models. The GDP measure produces statistically significant coefficients in the ordered probit models but not in the fixed-effects models. Overall, these results suggest that critics of economic liberalization and globalization have valid substantive concerns, at least in terms of short-term, indirect effects. The consistency of these findings across a variety of constitutional provisions gives further credence to the malign perspective.

The second set of analyses confirms each of these findings, except for one significant difference. In the shorter period, as the INGO and IGO measure is added, the global norms measure loses its statistical significance. The IGO measure does not achieve statistical significance, but the INGO measure does. Thus, the embeddedness hypothesis is supported only to the extent that the presence of INGOs captures the concept; participation in IGOs appears to have no influence on the adoption and maintenance of these human rights norms in constitutions, nor on any of the other provisions studied in this book. The INGO association also provides support for the transnational network hypothesis, which overlaps with the world society approach in its prediction. The role of INGOs in state commitment is consistent whether in relation to constitutional provision for core human rights or for states of emergency protections. I next turn to the question of whether these provisions reduce or increase the likelihood of repression.

State Repression, Threats, and Constitutional Protections

As Keith and Poe (2004) note, the human rights literature has consistently demonstrated that "the most pervasive factor that increases leaders' willingness to repress is a *threat to the leaders' rule*, whether real or perceived" (1075) (for example, Davis and Ward 1990; Alfatooni and Allen 1991; Poe and Tate 1994; Davenport 1995c, 1996; Gartner and Regan 1996; Cingranelli and Richards 1999; Richards 1999; Poe, Tate, and Keith 1999; Poe et al. 2000; Apodaca 2001; Regan and Henderson 2002; Davenport and Armstrong 2004; Keith and Poe 2004; Bueno de Mesquita et al. 2005; Abouhard and Cingranelli 2006). Davenport (2007c) refers to this long-standing and consistent finding as "the Law of Coercive Responsiveness": "when challenges to the status quo take place, authorities generally employ some form of repressive action to counter or eliminate the behavioral threat" (7). As a whole, these studies have suggested that the greater the level of threat a government faces, the greater the willingness of the regime to employ tools of repression. Conceptualization of threat, however, varies within the human rights literature.

Davenport (1995c), drawing upon a substantial body of conflict literature, conceptualizes three attributes of domestic conflict: violence, strategic variety, and cultural limits. He argues that violent forms of dissent represent the greatest threat to a regime and may trigger repressive state action for two reasons. First, he argues that the use of violent strategies may lead to the deaths of citizens, create social chaos, and eventually provoke others into antigovernment behavior simply because it can no longer protect them, and thus the regime will have an incentive to deter or limit these possible outcomes (687). Second, he argues that such threats allow the regime a potential claim of legitimacy in responding to actions that are or *can be portrayed as* being dangerous or threatening to other citizens' lives, and thus the regime would face less resistance from the population if it resorts to repressive action. The second attribute, variety of strategies, increases the perceived magnitude of the threat to the regime, increases the level of resources required to deal with a broad set of activities, and stretches thin the regime's ability to regulate the antigovernment behavior, as it has to find a variety of responses appropriate to respond to different strategies and to protect different targets (688). Finally, Davenport argues that cultural limits to dissident behavior may trigger a repressive response by regimes when the behavior moves beyond the cultural norm of behavioral deviance in a state (689). His empirical analyses largely support his hypotheses. Gartner and Regan (1996) focus on government leaders' perception of the credibility and magnitude of the threat facing their regime, and more specifically Regan and Henderson (2002) "conceptualise threat in terms of the demands on a regime by opposition groups" (122). They further argue that "the greater the disparity between the opposition's demands and the status quo position of the ruling party, the more difficult it is to bridge the policy distance between the two groups" thus "when the demands are sufficiently strong and the ruling party refuses to accede them, there is an increased likelihood of violent political instability and its counterpart: political repression" (122). Regan and Henderson find that the level of threat has the greatest impact on state level of repression, even over regime type.

Building upon these studies, Poe et al. (2000) and Keith and Poe (2004) argue that regimes consider three dimensions or three cues of threat behavior that allow the government to distinguish between more serious and less serious forms of threat: (1) whether the event is staged by an organized opposition, which may pose a more serious threat than a spontaneous event because of the potential for prolonged action and the potential that the group could become a real contender for power rather than one that spontaneously occurs in reaction to a proximate trigger; (2) the nature and extent of the grievance or goals of the opposition group, arguing that a group that "seeks a substantial alteration in the very nature of the political system that brought the existing regime to power would tend to be much more threatening, other factors being equal, than an opposition effort with much narrower and less encompassing goals" (Poe et al. 2000, 32); and (3) the presence of violence, which by disrupting public order and the stability of the regime itself makes it the most important factor affecting the regime's perception of threat. Their empirical results support these hypotheses. Following Poe et al. (2000), I suggest the following hypotheses:

- Hypothesis One: The greater the level of threat, the more likely the regime will be to engage in political repression.
- Hypothesis Two: Violent threats are more likely to be associated with political repression than nonviolent threats.

- Hypothesis Three: Threats targeted at substantial alteration of the political system are more likely to be associated with political repression than threats associated with less extensive goals.

As observed in Chapters 4 and 5, constructivists would expect that the norms and obligations set forth in constitutional provisions would be honored by national governments because of the general norm of keeping commitments and honoring agreements or metabeliefs that link the state's identity and legitimacy to compliance with legal commitments. I believe this expectation also holds in regard to these constitutional commitments. Thus, as in the previous chapters, I advance the following hypothesis:

- Hypothesis Four: Constitutional state of emergency provisions will decrease the odds that the state will engage in political repression during periods of domestic or external threat.

While the world society perspective would expect that global norms would be diffused among states over time, leading to more states' adopting constitutions and specific enumeration of these rights, the logic of the perspective also leads to the possibility that as the weight of these norms grows in defining legitimate or deviant governments, states are more likely to make formal promises without the willingness or capacity to implement them, thus leading to a decoupling between promise and practice. As I have noted already, empirical evidence supports this expectation, and indeed some constitutional commitments and treaty commitments have been associated with worse human rights behavior (for example, Keith 1999; Hathaway 2002; Keith 2002a; Hafner-Burton and Tsutsui 2005). Thus, constitutional provisions for core human rights may also be associated with lower levels of achieved human rights, and I test an alternative hypothesis:

- Alternative Hypothesis Four: Adoption of constitutional rights provisions may lead to a decoupling effect in which the provisions have no effect or a negative effect.

Keith and Poe (2004) suggest that state of emergency provisions will have a stronger effect when the regime is faced with violent threats and threats that seek to bring about broad institutional change. Their empirical analyses strongly supported their hypotheses. I extend the hypothesis here:

- Hypothesis Five: Constitutional state of emergency provisions will decrease the odds that the state will engage in political repression during periods of domestic or external threat targeted at institutional change.

At this point I need to address some of the problems that have been identified empirically in regard to state of emergency clauses; these problems suggest alternative hypotheses in regard to two of the clauses under study here. As Grossman (1990), Frühling (1993), Haille (1996), and the ICJ (1983) point out, while the constitutional emergency clauses may be intended to *limit* incursions upon human rights during a crisis, observations would suggest that they frequently have the opposite effect. One of the constitutional clauses under study is the provision of a list of rights that may not be derogated as a result of the emergency; the very presence of such a list implies of course that at least some other rights may justifiably be denied because of the special circumstances. It seems likely that the assumption that some rights may be denied during an emergency provides regimes with an opening to abuse other rights and perhaps even provides them with a cover of legitimacy that facilitates their denial of human rights, even those that are nonderogable. The International Covenant on Civil and Political Rights (ICCPR) has a similar clause in Article IV that enables state parties to ignore some of their human rights commitments during "a time of public emergency which threatens the life of the nation." The standard of threat is quite high and certain articles of the treaty may not be derogated, such the articles protecting the right to life, freedom of thought, conscience, and religion, prohibition of torture, and prohibition of slavery. Empirically, numerous violations of nonderogable rights have been found (Fitzpatrick 1994a, 1994b; Sieghart 1983; Keith 1999). Keith (1999) found that even though these derogations should legally suspend only a limited set of rights, the derogations do significantly increase the probability of personal integrity abuse, which includes such behavior as torture, disappearances, and political killings, behavior that is *not* legally derogable. In fact, when controlling for derogations, the states that were not parties to the treaties had better human rights scores than the states which were. Thus, it may also be the case that the presence of an emergency clause that lists nonderogable rights will have the unexpected consequence of actually increasing the probability of human rights abuse by providing a cloak of legitimacy for the regime's abuse.

The second problematic provision is the duration clause, which sets a time limit on states of emergency and requires states to renew their declarations. I believe this provision may lead to the unintended consequence of encouraging the extension of states of emergency. Clearly, the purpose of the provision is to prevent situations in which a state of emergency is allowed to continue for so long that a permanent state of emergency evolves, such as has occurred in Uruguay, where a state of emergency that was declared in July 1979 continues (based on declarations filed in United Nations; see United Nations 1987). For example, during the 1980s, Peru, whose constitution limits states of emergency to sixty days and then requires a new declaration, existed in what could be described as a permanent state of emergency, extending its state of emergency over thirty times between 1983 and 1987 (based on declarations filed with the United Nations; see United Nations 1987). Between June 1984 and July 1985, El Salvador made fourteen extensions to its state of emergency by legislative decree (based on declarations filed with the United Nations; see United Nations 1987). Pakistan, under General Zia-ul-Haq in the late 1970s and 1980s, is another example of institutionalized state of emergency, despite constitutional provisions that are meant to prevent such effects (Chowdury 1989, 51–53). Empirical evidence has demonstrated these unintended consequences in regard to both of these clauses (Keith, Tate, and Poe 2009), although Keith and Poe (2004) found some evidence that the nonderogable rights clause functioned as expected—but only during periods of civil war. The theoretical caution, as well as the empirical evidence, suggests an alternative hypothesis in regard to these two clauses.

- Hypothesis Six: Duration clauses and nonderogable rights clauses will be associated with higher levels of repression.

In Chapter 5 I discussed the transnational advocacy networks perspective (Keck and Sikkink 1998; Risse, Ropp, and Sikkink 1999), which posits that international human rights norms are diffused through networks of transnational and domestic actors who pressure regimes to adopt international norms formally as well as to comply with these commitments. I expect that during times of threat, the transnational networks will be especially watchful of the state and will apply pressure both "from above and below" to ensure that the regime acts within the internationally accepted parameters of state behavior during periods of threat, especially in regard to human rights, and that the network will pressure a regime with constitutional commitments to honor those commitments. Thus I expect that the presence of INGOs will decrease the odds of repression when the regime is under threat, especially if the regime has formally adopted states of emergency provisions.

- Hypothesis Seven: The stronger the presence of INGOs, the less likely the regime will be to engage in political repression.
- Hypothesis Eight: The stronger the presence of INGOs, the more likely it is that constitutional state of emergency provisions will be associated with less repression.

In Chapter 4 I explored the expectation of many scholars that an independent judiciary is the ultimate guarantor of constitutionalism and protector against tyranny of the majority. I found consistently strong evidence to support this hypothesis in Chapters 4 and 5. The ICJ and ILA standards expect that an independent judiciary and a judiciary empowered with judicial review will play a critical role during states of emergency; therefore, I also include the following two hypotheses:

- Hypothesis Nine: The more independent the judiciary, the more likely it is that state of emergency clauses will reduce political repression during times of threat.
- Hypothesis Ten: States in which the judiciary has the power of judicial review will be less likely to engage in repression when the regime is under threat.

Finally, I turn to the role of state commitment to international human rights norms through participation in international human rights treaties, in particular membership in the International Covenant on Civil and Political Rights (ICCPR). The compliance literature disagrees on the effect of state membership in international human rights treaties. Realists perceive states as unitary rational actors that primarily behave on the basis of self-interest, and thus they would argue that decisions by a state on whether to adhere to international human rights norms or to engage in repression would largely be a function of the state's calculation of the benefits and costs accrued to it by engaging the various choices, and thus any observed compliance with international norms or treaties simply reflects a convergence of interests that will dissipate once the state's material interests conflict with its normative commitments (Hoffmann 1956; Waltz 1979; Mearsheimer 1994). They argue that the formal mechanisms for monitoring and enforcing human rights treaty commitments are deliberately weak, thus allowing states to engage in cheap talk with little or no direct costs, especially as these treaties lack the potential effects of market forces, reciprocal benefits, or potential retaliation from other state parties that typically motivate compliance with international financial agreements (Neumayer 2005). At the same time regimes may face domestic circumstances that make compliance with international norms too costly, even for well-intentioned states, particularly in the face of perceived or real internal threats.

On the other hand, norms-based approaches argue that transnational or international interaction and socialization drive both state commitment to and compliance with international human rights treaties, rather than rationalist calculations. These perspectives emphasize the transformative power of international normative discourse on human rights and the role of activism by transnational actors (international organizations and nongovernmental actors) who support local efforts to press for human rights commitment and who also, through repeated interactions with state actors, socialize states to accept new norms. As discussed above and in Chapters 4 and 5, constructivists expect that the legal obligations states commit to will be honored by national governments because of the general norm of honoring agreements or metabeliefs that link the state's identity and legitimacy to compliance with its legal commitments. The world society perspective posits an integrated cultural system that "promulgates cognitive frames and normative prescriptions that constitute the legitimate identities, structures, and purposes of modern nation-states" (Cole 2005, 477) and that the proliferation of human rights treaties codifying human rights norms, states' legitimacy, or their "good nation" identity is increasingly linked to the formal acknowledgment of these norms (Cole 2005; Wotipka and Ramirez 2007). The logic of the perspective leads to the possibility that as the weight of these norms grows in defining legitimate or deviant governments, states are more likely to make formal promises without the willingness or capacity to implement them, especially during times of threat, which may lead to a decoupling effect. In addition the transnational advocacy networks perspective expects that under pressure a regime eventually will make tactical concessions to the transnational network which may include the regime accepting international norms (ratifies treaties and institutionalizes domestically). Eventually the regime's acceptance of the validity of the human rights norms, along with increased scrutiny under the monitoring and reporting mechanisms of the treaties, may lead to rules-compliant behavior. In the model of state constitutional commitment to the international norms regarding states of emergency, we saw that commitment to the ICCPR increased the odds that states will adopt and maintain state of emergency provisions. And in the previous chapters I find evidence to support this expectation as well. These perspectives provide us with the following hypothesis:

- Hypothesis Twelve: States that are parties to the ICCPR will be less likely to engage in political repression than nonparty states.

I test these hypotheses in a series of analyses employing the standard model of repression from the previous two chapters, and then I examine the conditional effects hypothesized in this section.

Models of Political Repression

Dependent Variables: I continue to examine measures of rights repression in this chapter as I did in Chapter 3, including the three measures of repression of personal integrity rights (the CIRI Index and the two PTS measures) and civil liberties (the Freedom House Index) and CIRI's individual measures of repression of freedom of speech, association, and religion. These variables are operationalized fully in Chapter 3.

Threats: I utilize three standards-based measures of domestic threat, as well as the traditional measures of civil war and international war described and employed in the previous three chapters. The three standards-based measures are those developed in Poe et al. (2000) as a substitute for the traditionally employed events-based data that are often plagued by problems of imperfect and incomplete information. *Organized Nonviolent Protest* is operationalized as a situation in which a mostly unarmed opposition regularly confronts the regime over one or more of its policies using demonstrations, riots, and other unconventional forms of political participation to express disagreement. *Organized Nonviolent Rebellion* is operationalized as a situation in which an unarmed opposition pushes for significant change in the constitution or other political institutions through unconventional means not involving organized violent activities. *Organized Violent Rebellion* is operationalized as a situation in which a substantial organized movement seeks to alter the governmental system, bringing about a significant change in the constitution or other political institutions, through armed attacks, including terrorist activities, guerrilla movements, and most attempted coups, but not full-scale civil war. These data are coded using the *Europa Handbook* and *The Political Handbook of the World.*

Formal Provision for States of Emergency: In the models below I test the constitutional provisions individually.

INGO Presence: I use the number of international nongovernmental organizations (INGOs). The source of these data is Todd Landman's treaty data base (Landman 2005).

De Facto *Judicial Independence:* I employ the measure as operationalized in Chapter 4. I also continue to employ the selection effects from Chapter 4.

Judicial Review: I employ the formal measure of judicial review, as operationalized in Chapter 4.

ICCPR Membership and Derogations: Participation in the ICCPR follows the operationalization utilized in Chapter 4. I also control for state derogations to the ICCPR, which are coded, following Keith (1999), as a dichotomous measure for periods under the state has filed a derogation, with the United Nations delineating the period of the derogation and the conditions justifying it.

Standard Model: I incorporate these variables into the revised standard model I estimated in Chapter 3. The model includes a lagged dependent variable, measures for civil and international war, military and Marxist/Marxist-Leninist regimes, logged population size, and per-capita GDP. I test the two alternative measures of democracy: Davenport and Armstrong's (2004) trichotomous operationalization of Polity (Marshall and Jaggers 2011) and Keith's (2002a) disaggregated sub-dimensions of Polity. These measures are operationalized in Chapter 3.

Analysis

I engage in a series of analyses to test these hypotheses, eventually estimating models that are conditional upon different levels of threat and estimating models with hypothesized conditions and interactions. First I estimated a set of base models that controls for a variety of domestic threats and participation in the international human rights regime—first with the additive state of emergency index and then with the individual provisions. Because of space constraints I report only the analysis of the individual provisions, which are theoretically more interesting because of the conflict in directional expectations for some of the measures. When I estimated the models with the state of emergency index I found the index to be statistically significant in all three fixed-effects personal integrity models but not in the non-fixed-effects models. This same pattern held in models estimating freedom of speech/press and association/assembly. The opposite pattern held in regard to the general measure of civil liberties, and the index had no effect on religious freedom regardless of the model. These results suggest moderate evidence that state of emergency clauses as a bundle of provisions may indeed have a beneficial effect, reducing the likelihood of state repression of both personal integrity rights and civil liberties.

Tables 6.2 through 6.4 report the results of the same base model, using the individual components of the state of emergency index, which offers additional insights into the relationship of these provisions and repression. First, I examine the personal integrity models reported in Table 6.2. I find overwhelming support for the hypotheses in regard to threat. Overall, as the level of threat moves from nonviolent forms to violent forms we see that the size of the coefficients more than doubles in the case of violent opposition and increases tenfold in the case of civil war. Nonviolent protest produces positive coefficients in all six models, but it is the only threat measure that performs inconsistently in terms of statistical significance. The coefficients achieve acceptable levels of statistical significance in four of the models but fail in the two Amnesty International–based models. The impact of these threats is rather small; for example, the coefficients in the Department of State fixed-effects model (.04) and the CIRI fixed-effects model (.16) suggest that the presence of nonviolent protest would only be associated with an increase of repression of less than a .1-point or .2-point increase in 5- and 9-point scales. The size of the coefficients grows and the consistency of statistical significance improves (five of six models) as we move to the other category of nonviolent threat, organized nonviolent rebellion, which is distinguishable from organized nonviolent protest in that its goals are more far-reaching, seeking to change the political system rather than simply seeking change in policies or particular leaders. These results support my third hypothesis. As we move to violent rebellion, which captures armed attacks, including terrorist activities, guerrilla movements, and most attempted coups, but not full-scale civil war, we see the size of the coefficients more than double in size

Table 6.2. Model of Repression of Personal Integrity Rights with State of Emergency Provisions and Judicial Independence, 1980–2005

	Personal Integrity Rights Abuse (PTS-SD) 1980–2005		*Personal Integrity Rights Abuse (PTS-AI) 1980–2005*		*Personal Integrity Rights Abuse (CIRI) 1982–2005*	
	Fixed Effects (1)	*Ordered Probit (2)*	*Fixed Effects (3)*	*Ordered Probit (4)*	*Fixed Effects (5)*	*Ordered Probit (6)*
Rights Abuse (*t*–1) (+)	.42 (.03)***	1.22 (.05)***	.35 (.03)***	1.01 (.04)***	.36 (.03)***	.49 (.02)***
Legislative Checks on Declaration (–)	–.05 (.03)*	–.02 (.02)	–.03 (.04)*	–.02 (.02)	.01 (.07)	–.01 (.02)
Duration Clause (+/–)	–.01 (.06)	.11 (.03)***	–.08 (.06)	.05 (.03)**	–.22 (.13)**	.05 (.03)**
Ban against Dissolving Legislature (–)	.05 (.07)	–.11 (.04)***	.08 (.07)	–.12 (.04)***	.21 (.12)	–.09 .03)***
List of Nonderogable Rights (+/–)	–.09 (.08)	.16 (.07)***	–.09 (.12)	.10 (.06)	–.10 (.20)	.08 (.05)
Selection Effects: Commitment to States of Emergency Provisions (+)	.001 (.03)	.001 (.04)	.01 (.02)	.04 (.04)	–.01 (.04)	–.01 (.03)
De Facto Judicial Independence (–)	–.09 (.03)***	–.30 (.04)***	–.07 (.03)***	–.18 (.04)***	–.26 (.06)***	–.24 (.03)***
Selection Effects: Commitment to Judicial Independence Provisions (+)	.001 (.02)	.02 (.04)	.01 (.02)	–.05 (.04)	–.01 (.04)	–.04 (.03)
Formal Judicial Review (+/–)	–.06 (.04)	–.02 (.02)	–.01 (.05)	–.04 (.03)	–.13 (.10)	–.01 (.02)

(continued)

Table 6.2 (*continued*)

	Personal Integrity Rights Abuse (PTS-SD) 1980–2005		*Personal Integrity Rights Abuse (PTS-AI) 1980–2005*		*Personal Integrity Rights Abuse (CIRI) 1982–2005*	
	Fixed Effects (1)	*Ordered Probit (2)*	*Fixed Effects (3)*	*Ordered Probit (4)*	*Fixed Effects (5)*	*Ordered Probit (6)*
Level of Commitment to the ICCPR: Minus Derogators (–)	–.02 (.01)**	–.02 (.01)**	–.01 (.00)*	–.02 (.01)**	–.01 (.02)	–.02 (.01)*
Level of Commitment to the ICCPR Optional Protocol (–)	.01 (.01)	–.01 (.01)	.01 (.02)	–.04 (.01)***	.01 (.03)	–.02 (.01)**
Level of Commitment to the CAT (+/–)	.01 (.01)	.03 (.02)**	–.001 (.01)	.04 (.02)**	.01 (.02)	.03 (.01)**
Organized Nonviolent Protest (+)	.04 (.03)*	.11 (.05)***	.02 (.02)	.05 (.05)	.16 (.06)***	.14 (.04)**
Organized Nonviolent Rebellion (+)	.06 (.05)	.14 (.08)***	.08 (.06)*	.15 (.09)**	.19 (.10)**	.20 (.08)***
Organized Violent Rebellion (+)	.16 (.03)***	.33 (.06)***	.18 (.04)***	.35 (.05)***	.38 (.07)***	.32 (.05)***
Civil War (+)	.46 (.08)***	.87 (.11)***	.53 (.09)***	.80 (.11)***	.97 (.19)***	.67 (.09)***
International War (+)	.12 (.07)**	.23 (.11)***	.07 (.07)	.12 (.09)*	.11 (.11)	.17 (.08)**
Trichotomous Measure of Democracy (–)	–.04 (.06)	–.31 (.05)***	–.08 (.06)*	–.29 (.05)***	–.19 (.12)**	–.27 (.04)***

Military Regimes (+)	.06	.11	.03	.02	.28	.07
	(.06)	(.06)**	(.07)	(.07)	(.14)**	(.06)
Marxist or Marxist-Leninist	.07	–.01	–.11	.02	.12	–.01
Regimes (+/–)	(.12)	(.10)	(.15)	(.09)	(.15)	(.10)
Economic Development (–)	–.00001	–.00001	–.00001	–.00001	–.00001	–.00001
	(.00)	(.00)***	(.00)*	(.00)***	(.00)**	(.00)
Economic Growth (–)	–.01	–.01	–.01	–.01	–.002	–.01
	(.00)***	(.00)***	(.00)***	(.00)***	(.01)	(.01)
Logged Population (+)	.42	.15	.17	.15	.57	.15
	(.13)***	(.02)***	(.15)	(.02)***	(.28)**	(.02)***
Population Growth (+)	–.03	–.004	–.04	.02	–.06	.03
	(.02)	(.02)	(.02)	(.02)	(.05)	(.02)
Observations	2789	2789	2789	2789	2720	2720
R^2 /Pseudo-R^2	.63	.48	.76	.40	.72	.31
F /Chi^2	30.12	1844.90	19.71	1811.23	23.76	2521.68
Prob > F / Prob > Chi^2	.0001	.0001	.0001	.0001	.0001	.0001

Fixed effects and ordered probit estimation with robust standard errors. Standard errors in parentheses. *Significant at the 10 percent level. **Significant at the 5 percent level. ***Significant at the 1 percent level. All tests one-tailed except where no direction predicted (+) predicted positive direction, (–) negative, and (+/–) no predicted direction.

Table 6.3. Model of Repression of Freedom House Civil Liberties with State of Emergency Provisions and Judicial Independence, 1980–2005

	1980–2005 (without INGO measure)		*1980–2000 (with INGO measure)*	
	Fixed Effects (1)	*Ordered Probit (2)*	*Fixed Effects (3)*	*Ordered Probit (4)*
Rights Abuse (*t*–1) (+)	.71 (.02)***	2.05 (.08)***	.69 (.02)***	1.93 (.09)***
Legislative Checks on Declaration (–)	.04 (.03)	–.01 (.03)	.04 (.03)	.001 (.03)
Duration Clause (+/–)	–.05 (.04)	–.01 (.03)	–.09 (.04)*	–.01 (.03)
Ban against Dissolving Legislature (–)	–.05 (.04)	–.02 (.03)	–.04 (.05)	–.01 (.04)
List of Nonderogable Rights (+/–)	–.04 (.07)	–.10 (.06)	–.03 (.10)	–.04 (.07)
Selection Effects: Commitment to States of Emergency Provisions (+)	–.03 (.01)	–.05 (.04)	–.02 (.02)	–.05 (.04)
De Facto Judicial Independence (–)	–.12 (.02)***	–.25 (.04)***	–.15 (.03)***	–.29 (.05)***
Selection Effects: Judicial Independence Provisions (+)	–.01 (.01)	–.02 (.04)	–.02 (.01)	.04 (.04)
Formal Judicial Review (+/–)	–.05 (.04)	–.02 (.03)	–.05 (.04)	–.03 (.04)
Level of Commitment to the ICCPR: Minus Derogators (–)	–.02 (.01)***	–.03 (.01)***	–.03 (.01)***	–.02 (.01)**
Level of Commitment to the ICCPR Optional Protocol (–)	–.01 (.01)	–.03 (.01)***	.01 (.02)	–.01 (.02)
Organized Nonviolent Protest (+)	–.03 (.02)	–.10 (.05)	–.06 (.02)	–.15 (.05)
Organized Nonviolent Rebellion (+)	.01 (.04)	–.05 (.09)	.01 (.05)	–.06 (.10)
Organized Violent Rebellion (+)	.06 (.02)***	.21 (.06)***	.04 (.03)**	.17 (.06)***

Table 6.3 (*continued*)

	1980–2005 (without INGO measure)		*1980–2000 (with INGO measure)*	
	Fixed Effects (1)	*Ordered Probit (2)*	*Fixed Effects (3)*	*Ordered Probit (4)*
Civil War (+)	.15 (.04)***	.18 (.09)**	.14 (.05)***	.14 (.09)*
International War (+)	–.05 (.05)	–.02 (.10)	.06 (.07)	.20 (.12)**
Trichotomous Measure of Democracy (–)	–.20 (.05)***	–.58 (.06)***	–.21 (.07)***	–.57 (.08)***
Military Regimes (+)	.02 (.05)	.04 (.07)	–.001 (.07)	.06 (.08)
Marxist or Marxist-Leninist Regimes (+/–)	.43 (.12)***	.44 (.13)	.44 (.13)***	.43 (.14)
Economic Development (–)	–.00001 (.00)	–.00001 (.00)***	–.00001 (.00)	–.00001 (.00)***
Economic Growth (–)	–.003 (.002)*	–.01 (.00)***	–.002 (.003)	–.01 (.00)*
Logged Population (+)	–.25 (.09)	.02 (.02)	–.18 (.13)	.03 (.02)**
Population Growth (+)	–.01 (.01)	.05 (.02)**	–.01 (.01)	.05 (.02)***
Logged INGOs (–)			–.01 (.03)	–.05 (.02)***
Observations	3245	3245	2528	2528
R^2 /Pseudo-R^2	.92	.68	.95	.67
F /*Chi*^{2}	162.70	1607.32	107.12	1288.24
Prob > *F* / Prob > *Chi*^{2}	.0001	.0001	.0001	.0001

Fixed effects and ordered probit estimation with robust standard errors. Standard errors in parentheses. *Significant at the 10 percent level. **Significant at the 5 percent level. ***Significant at the 1 percent level. All tests one-tailed except where no direction predicted (+) predicted positive direction, (–) negative, and (+/–) no predicted direction.

Table 6.4. State of Emergency Provisions Estimated in Standard Model of Repression of Individually Measured Civil Liberties, 1982–2005

	Repression of Freedom of Speech and Press		*Repression of Freedom of Assembly and Association*		*Repression of Freedom of Religion*	
	Fixed Effects (1)	*Ordered Probit (2)*	*Fixed Effects (3)*	*Ordered Probit (4)*	*Fixed Effects (5)*	*Ordered Probit (6)*
Rights Abuse (*t*–1) (+)	.22 (.03)***	1.17 (.05)***	.44 (.03)***	1.66 (.06)***	.45 (.03)***	2.19 (.07)***
Legislative Checks on Declaration (–)	.04 (.03)	.04 (.03)	–.01 (.03)	.05 (.03)	–.02* (.07)	.01 (.03)
Duration Clause (+/–)	–.09 (.04)**	–.06 (.03)**	–.05 (.04)	–.06 (.03)**	.02 (.02)	–.03 (.04)
Ban against Dissolving Legislature (–)	–.13 (.05)***	–.01 (.04)	–.09 (.05)**	–.07 (.04)**	–.04 (.04)	–.03 (.05)
List of Nonderogable Rights (+/–)	.17 (.07)	–.06 (.07)	–.01 (.07)	–.09 (.07)	.06 (.06)	–.02 (.10)
Selection Effects: Commitment to States of Emergency Provisions (+)	.02 (.01)	.07 (.04)**	.01 (.01)	.08 (.05)**	–.01 (.01)	–.03 (.05)
De Facto Judicial Independence (–)	–.11 (.02)***	–.27 (.04)***	–.07 (.03)***	–.18 (.04)***	–.02 (.01)**	–.20 (.05)***
Selection Effects: Commitment to Judicial Independence Provisions (+)	.01 (.02)	.03 (.04)	.01 (.01)	.01 (.04)	.01 (.01)	.02 (.06)

Formal Judicial Review (+/–)	–.05 (.04)	–.06 (.03)**	–.06 (.03)**	–.08 (.03)**	–.04 (.03)	.01 (.04)
Level of Commitment to the ICCPR: Minus Derogators (–)	–.01 (.01)	–.01 (.01)	–.02 (.00)**	–.01 (.01)	–.01 (.00)**	.01 (.02)
Level of Commitment to the ICCPR Optional Protocol (–)	.01 (.01)	–.02 (.02)	.01 (.01)	–.01 (.02)	.01 (.01)	–.04 (.02)**
Organized Nonviolent Protest (+)	–.01 (.02)	–.09 (.05)	–.01 (.02)	–.07 (.06)	–.01 (.01)	–.11 (.07)
Organized Nonviolent Rebellion (+)	.03 (.03)	–.01 (.09)	–.02 (.04)	–.14 (.10)	–.02 (.02)	.04 (.12)
Organized Violent Rebellion (+)	–.05 (.02)	.16 (.06)**	–.03 (.02)	–.02 (.06)	–.04 (.02)	–.12 (.08)
Civil War (+)	.12 (.04)***	.11 (.09)	.05 (.06)	.05 (.10)	–.01 (.04)	–.13 (.13)
International War (+)	.04 (.04)	.18 (.11)**	–.06 (.04)*	–.02 (.10)	.04 (.03)*	.24 (.15)**
Trichotomous Measure of Democracy (–)	–.14 (.05)***	–.43 (.05)***	–.10 (.04)**	–.50 (.06)***	–.02 (.02)	–.43 (.08)***
Military Regimes (+)	.09 (.05)**	.23 (.07)***	.17 (.05)***	.20 (.08)***	–.01 (.03)	–.03 (.09)
Marxist or Marxist-Leninist Regimes (+/–)	.44 (.08)***	.73 (.12)***	.30 (.09)	.53 (.13)***	.10 (.06)	.24 (.15)**

(continued)

Table 6.4 (*continued*)

	Repression of Freedom of Speech and Press		*Repression of Freedom of Assembly and Association*		*Repression of Freedom of Religion*	
	Fixed Effects (1)	*Ordered Probit (2)*	*Fixed Effects (3)*	*Ordered Probit (4)*	*Fixed Effects (5)*	*Ordered Probit (6)*
Economic Development (–)	–.00001	–.00001	–.00003	–.00001	–.00001	–.00001
	(.00)	(.00)	(.00)*	(.00)***	(.00)	(.00)***
Economic Growth (–)	–.01	.01	–.003	–.01	.01	–.01
	(.00)*	(.00)**	(.00)**	(.00)**	(.01)	(.01)
Logged Population (+)	.09	.001	–.05	.06	.07	.09
	(.11)***	(.02)	(.09)	(.02)***	(.06)	(.03)***
Population Growth (+)	–.003	.06	–.01	.04	–.01	–.01
	(.01)	(.02)**	(.02)	(.02)**	(.01)	(.03)
Observations	2939	2939	2939	2939	2939	2939
R^2 /Pseudo-R^2	.59	.39	.75	.53	.62	.53
F /Chi^2	24.07	1766.29	56.39	1679.33	19.80	1314.52
Prob > F / Prob > Chi^2	.0001	.0001	.0001	.0001	.0001	.0001

Fixed effects and ordered probit estimation with robust standard errors. Standard errors in parentheses. *Significant at the 10 percent level. **Significant at the 5 percent level. ***Significant at the 1 percent level. All tests one-tailed except where no direction predicted (+) predicted positive direction, (–) negative, and (+/–) no predicted direction.

and achieve high levels of statistical significance in all six models. The onset of such violent threat would be associated with an increase of .16 or .18 in the Political Terror Scale and .38 in the CIRI index. The presence of civil war continues to produce the largest coefficients, even surpassing the impact in previous levels of state repression, which traditionally is the largest effect in all empirical models of repression.

The individual state of emergency provisions perform rather inconsistently across the personal integrity models. The provision for legislative checks on declarations of states of emergency produces small negative coefficients that achieve statistical significance in the two fixed-effects PTS models, while the ban against dissolving the legislature produces negative coefficients that achieve statistical significance only in the three ordered probit models, not in the fixed-effects model. The duration clauses, which I tested without a predicted direction (and the more stringent two-tailed test), produces positive coefficients that achieve acceptable levels of statistical significance in all three ordered probit models, but then produces a negative coefficient in the CIRI fixed-effects model. Indeed the coefficients in all the fixed-effects models are negative but achieve appropriate levels of statistical significance only in the CIRI model. The list of nonderogable rights has the unexpected harmful effect identified in previous work; however, in this model, with its extended period and additional controls for conditions such as judicial independence, the coefficient is statistically significant in only one of the six models. I continue to explore these relationships in subsequent models that are conditioned on the level of threat.

Judicial independence continues to produce moderate-size coefficients that are statistically significant across all six models. In these models, I also tested the impact of state membership in the ICCPR, its Optional Protocol, and the Convention Against Torture (CAT). When I initially tested the impact of the ICCPR, it produced positive rather than negative coefficients. I then estimated the models controlling for state parties to the treaty that had derogated from the treaty—zeroing out those states during years in which they had derogated from the treaty. I then re-estimated the models, which are the model presented in Table 6.2. The operationalization of ICCPR membership minus derogators produces negative coefficients that are statistically significant in five of the six models; the coefficients are rather small in all the models. Clearly, the presence of derogators makes a difference. I ran an alternative model as well, in which I tested derogators as a separate measure. Its coefficients were statistically significant in all six models and moderate in size. For example, in the fixed-effects model, a derogation to the ICCPR would be associated with a .18 increase in the Department of State PTS model, a .16 increase in the Amnesty PTS model, and a .21 increase in the CIRI index model. Commitment to the Optional Protocol is statistically significant in only two of the six models, and commitment to the CAT produces positive coefficients in three of six models, suggesting a decoupling effect.

The compliance literature has suggested that INGOs play a strong role in compliance with international treaty commitments, so I also tested interactive terms in regard to the ICCPR commitment and the presence of INGOS, but the interaction was not statistically significant in any of the personal integrity models, and as we will see below it was statistically significant in only one of the eight civil liberties. As in the previous models of personal integrity repression, I also ran models testing the impact of INGOs, and again none of the coefficients achieved acceptable levels of statistical significance. In addition, I also tested interactions between judicial independence and the provisions, but none of the interactions was statistically significant.

Next I turn to the repression of civil liberties. Table 6.3 reports the results with the Freedom House civil liberties measure; the first two columns report the longer period without the INGO measure, and the last two columns have the truncated period with the INGO measure. In the first set of models we see evidence that the ban against dissolving the legislature is associated with lower levels of repression, but its effect is limited to the fixed-effects model. The list of nonderogable rights performs as the ICJ/ILA would predict—decreasing the level of repression—but once again the coefficient achieves acceptable levels of statistical significance in only one of the two models. The measure does retain its statistical significance in the truncated period with the INGO measure, but the coefficient for the ban against dissolving the legislature does not. The measure for INGO participation is statistically insignificant, so the loss of effect for the ban may be due to the truncated period. The judicial independence measures continue to perform well. The ICCPR measure is statistically significant in all models, and the Optional Protocol measure is significant in ordered probit models but not in the fixed-effects models. The threat measures perform rather differently here, with none of the coefficients for the nonviolent forms of threat achieving acceptable levels of significance in any model. The coefficients for violent rebellion and even civil war are appreciably smaller in magnitude than in the personal integrity abuse model. The presence of civil war is associated with a .20 increase in the

7-point civil liberties repression index, compared to .46 and .53 in the two 5-point PTS fixed-effects models. Clearly, the clauses have less effect on the broader set of civil liberties, but in regard to these rights, their effect is constantly associated with less repression, whereas the effect on personal integrity abuse was mixed. I return to these findings in the next section, where the models are conditioned on the level and type of threat.

Table 6.4 reports the models estimated for repression of the individual freedoms. The freedom of speech/press and freedom of association/assembly models perform more similarly than the religious freedom model, so I will discuss them first. The ban against dissolving the legislature has the most consistent effect, producing coefficients that are statistically significant in three of the four models. We would expect that as a state went from having a constitutional provision that specifically allowed the legislature to be dissolved during emergencies to explicitly banning such a practice, we would see a .39 and .27 decrease in the 3-point repression of speech/press and association/assembly indices. The duration clause produces slightly smaller negative coefficients that are statistically significant in three of the four models. Only one of the state of emergency provisions is statistically significant in the religious freedom model (the legislative check in the non-fixed-effects model), a result that seems somewhat intuitive, as the exercise of religious freedom would in most cases not be directly related to oppositional threats as freedom of speech and assembly might be. I explore this dimension more in the following section.

Judicial independence continues to produce strong coefficients that reach high levels of statistical significance in all six models, including the religious freedom models. In these analyses a judiciary empowered with judicial review produces negative coefficients that are statistically significant in the two assembly/association models and the non-fixed-effects speech/press model. The effect was not statistically significant in regard to the more severe forms of repression, personal integrity abuse. I explore this relationship more below as well. Commitment to the ICCPR is statistically significant in only two of the six models, and commitment to the Optional Protocol is significant in only the religious freedom fixed-effects model, and once again, the coefficients are quite small. Threat continues to play an even smaller role in the repression of these three sets of civil liberties than it did in regard to the broader set of civil liberties, with nonviolent threats having no impact, and even violent threats producing little observable impact: civil war is statistically significant in only one of six models, and violent rebellion in only one model. The threats effect tends to be more observable in the aggregate than in individual forms of repression, and its influence is most strongly linked to the more severe form of repression. This leads us to the next set of analyses, which conditions the models on type or level of threat.

Previous research (Keith and Poe 2004) has demonstrated that the clauses behaved somewhat differently in regard to personal integrity when conditioned on the level of threat: (1) the ban against dissolving the legislature had no effect regardless of the threat condition; (2) the legislative declaration and list of nonderogable rights performed as predicted by the ILA/ICJ in states experiencing civil war; (3) limited duration clause and nonderogable rights performed contrary to the ILA/ICJ expectations (a) when states were experiencing rebellions short of civil war and (b) when states were experiencing violent threats (civil war and violent rebellion). In the following analysis I condition the models on the set of conditions presented in Tables 6.5 through 6.8, beginning with highest level of threat to the lowest level of threat. I estimate the same base model/controls as I did in Tables 6.2 through 6.4. The models continue to control for levels of threat other than those on which the models are conditioned. For example, in the first analysis only states experiencing civil wars are included in the analysis, but in the model for these states that are experiencing civil war I control for other types of threats within the state (such as nonviolent protest).

In the following tables I present only the coefficients for the state of emergency provisions so that we may compare across forms of repression as well across the two methodogical estimations; the fixed-effects models are presented in the top half of the tables, with the ordered probit (non-fixed-effects) models presented in the lower half. I also report the judicial independence coefficients, as I find some variation in conditioning the models on threat level present.

Table 6.5 presents the analysis of countries experiencing civil war. The results of the fixed-effects model perform somewhat similarly to the full personal integrity abuse analysis in that the legislative declaration variable in the State Department PTS model and the duration clause in the CIRI index model maintain their statistical significance; however, the measure for legislative declaration loses its statistical significance in the Amnesty PTS model. The size of the influence of these protections increases significantly when the analysis is limited to countries experiencing civil war—the coefficient for legislative declaration here is -.26 compared to -.05 in the full State

Table 6.5. State of Emergency Coefficients from Conditional Threat Models: Countries Experiencing Civil War

	PTS–SD	*PTS–AI*	*CIRI Index*	*FH Civil Liberties*	*Speech/ Press*	*Association/ Assembly*	*Religion*
Fixed-Effects Models							
Legislative Checks on Declaration (–)	–.26 (.21)*	–.23 (.22)	–.25 (.25)	.13 (.28)	.06 (.16)	–.24 (.06)***	.15 (.10)
Duration Clause (+/–)	.02 (.15)	–.12 (.23)	–.77 (.37)*	.06 (.15)	–.43 (.08)***	–.04 (.09)	.07 (.08)
Ban against Dissolving Legislature (–)	.15 (.27)	.26 (.39)	.96 (.20)	–.03 (.12)	.20 (.19)	–.16 (.10)*	.07 (.09)
List of Nonderogable Rights (+/–)	– .47 (.36)	–.24 (.42)	–.50 (.45)	.11 (.22)	.14 (.21)	.29 (.25)	.31 (.14)**
De Facto Judicial Independence (–)	–.001 (.09)	–.02 (.10)	–.45 (.16)***	–.14 (.06)***	–.06 (.06)	–.11 (.10)	.03 (.04)
Ordered Probit							
Legislative Checks on Declaration (–)	–.12 (.09)*	–.08 (.08)	.14 (.09)	–.12 (.10)	.04 (.11)	–.13 (.12)	.06 (.15)
Duration Clause (+/–)	–.15 (.11)	–.10 (.11)	.04 (.12)	.08 (.13)	–.25 (.13)**	.18 (.14)	.28 (.15)
Ban against Dissolving Legislature (–)	–.04 (.13)	–.13 (.13)	.06 (.12)	.07 (.13)	.06 (.15)	–.40 (.15)***	–.45 (.21)***
List of Nonderogable Rights (+/–)	–.50 (.23)***	–.66 (.24)***	–.50 (.21)***	–.10 (.22)	.07 (.20)	.77 (.24)***	1.22 .38***
De Facto Judicial Independence (–)	.20 (.13)*	.14 (.12)	–.22 (.12)**	–.43 (.15)***	–.17 (.15)	–.25 (.20)*	.05 (.20)

Full standard models estimated. Only constitutional provision and judicial independence coefficients reported. Fixed effects and ordered probit estimation with robust standard errors. Standard errors in parentheses. *Significant at the 10 percent level. **Significant at the 5 percent level. ***Significant at the 1 percent level. All tests one-tailed except where no direction predicted (+) predicted positive direction, (–) negative, and (+/–) no predicted direction.

Department PTS analysis, and similarly the coefficient for the duration clause is -.77 compared to -.22 in the full CIRI index analysis. The ordered probit models, which do not control for fixed effects, produce much more variation from personal integrity analysis of all countries. When limiting the analysis to states with civil wars, only the nonderogable rights measure produces consistent larger negative coefficients, as the ICJ and ILA would expect, and the coefficients are statistically significant in all three personal integrity abuse models. The duration clause and the ban against dissolving the legislature lose their statistical significance when states are limited to those experiencing civil war. The legislative declaration provision retains its statistical significance in the State Department PTS model. Overall, the assessment of the clauses' effect during civil war is rather unimpressive in the general failure to achieve statistical significance: the duration clause achieves statistical significance in only one of six models; the ban against dissolving the legislature fails to achieve statistical significance in any model; and the legislative declaration achieves it in only one of six models. The list of nonderogable rights is significant only in the non-fixed-effects model. Thus under conditions when the state faces the highest level of threat, the state of emergency provisions are relatively weak protections against the more egregious category of repression.

The sporadic and inconsistent performance of the state of emergency provisions under conditions of civil war continues when we move the analysis to repression of civil liberties. When I condition the models on civil war, the emergency clause fails to perform at all in the broad civil liberties model, which was actually the case in the unconditioned analysis except that the list of nonderogable rights had a beneficial effect in the non-fixed-effects model. The clauses perform better in the individual civil liberties models, although the performance is somewhat inconsistent. For example, in the fixed-effects model one or two clauses in each model produces a coefficient that achieves acceptable levels of statistical significance, but no clause is statistically significant in more than one of the models. The duration clause has the beneficial effect the ICJ/ILA would predict in regard to freedom of speech/press. The size of the impact is substantial; a maximum increase would be associated with an .86 decrease in the level of repression on a 3-point scale. Legislative declaration is statistically significant only in the freedom of association/assembly model. In the association/assembly and religious freedom ordered probit models, the list of nonderogable rights produces a harmful effect, but the ban against dissolving the legislature produces a beneficial effect. Thus we end up with the list of nonderogable rights having the most prevalent effect and with its being associated with greater repression of civil liberties but less repression of personal integrity rights during civil war. This result may reflect international standards to some extent in that the ICCPR does not allow states to derogate from articles that protect rights such as the right to life or that ban torture. However, the ICCPR delineation of nonderogable rights also includes the freedom of thought, conscience, and religion, and the constitutional provision for nonderogable rights is associated with more not less repression of religious freedom during times of civil war. Overall judicial independence performs much less consistently in the presence of civil war, producing statistically significant effects in only two of the non-fixed-effects models and in four of the ordered probit models. It is particularly notable that an independent judiciary is not associated with less repression of religious freedom or freedom of speech/press during civil wars in any model.

I next broaden my conceptualization to include either form of violent threats (civil war or violent rebellion). Table 6.6 reports the analysis conditioned upon violent threats. Most significantly, in states under these types of threat, none of the clauses is statistically significant in the fixed-effects personal integrity abuse models, and only two clauses produce statistically significant coefficients in the ordered probit personal integrity model: the duration clauses have a harmful effect in two of three models, and the ban against dissolving the legislature is significant in the Amnesty International-based model. The performance in the civil liberties models is much more sporadic and thin when the threats are broadened to include violent threats beyond just civil war. None of the clauses produces statistically significant coefficients in the broad civil liberties model. The coefficients for the ban against dissolving the legislature are statistically significant in both freedom of association/assembly models, and the duration clauses produce coefficients that are negative and statistically significant in both freedom of speech/press models. The list of nonderogable rights is statistically significant in only one model and is positive—in the fixed-effects religious freedom model. Judicial independence performs more strongly and consistently in these models—it fails to produce statistically significant coefficients only in the non-fixed-effects religious freedom model.

Rather than conceptualizing the conditional divide as violent or nonviolent, Table 6.7 conditions the models on states experiencing midlevel threats, which here are conceptualized as some form of threat short of civil war that

Table 6.6. State of Emergency Coefficients from Conditional Threat Models: Countries Experiencing Violent Threats (Civil War and Violent Rebellion)

	PTS-SD	*PTS-AI*	*CIRI Index*	*FH Civil Liberties*	*Speech/ Press*	*Association/ Assembly*	*Religion*
Fixed-Effects Models							
Legislative Checks on Declaration (–)	–.05 (.07)	–.06 (.07)	.31 (.14)	.01 (.05)	.12 (.05)	–.03 (.05)	–.01 (.04)
Duration Clause (+/–)	.07 (.08)	–.05 (.10)	–.18 (.14)	–.07 (.06)	–.14 (.05)***	–.05 (.05)	–.02 (.03)
Ban against Dissolving Legislature (–)	.13 (.09)	.08 (.11)	.31 (.21)	.02 (.07)	–.06 (.06)	–.11 (.06)*	.08 (.05)
List of Nonderogable Rights (+/–)	– .15(.14)	–.18 (.19)	–.11 (.40)	–.04 (.11)	.14 (.10)	.03 (.11)	.18 (.09)**
De Facto Judicial Independence (–)	–.10 (.06)**	–.07 (.05)*	–.47 (.09)***	–.15 (.04)***	–.09 (.04)***	–.06 (.04)*	–.01 (.03)
Ordered Probit							
Legislative Checks on Declaration (–)	.02 (.04)	–.01 (.04)	.07 (.04)	. 03 (.04)	.05 (.05)	.05 (.05)	.04 (.06)
Duration Clause (+/–)	.15 (.05)***	.10 (.05)	.12 (.04)***	.05 (.05)	–.03 (.05)**	–.01 (.05)	.06 (.07)
Ban against Dissolving Legislature (–)	–.01 (.06)	–.09 (.06)*	.03 (.06)	.06 (.06)	.06 (.06)	–.12 (.06)**	.01 (.08)
List of Nonderogable Rights (+/–)	–.01 (.10)	–.08 (.10)	–.01 (.09)	–.08 (.09)	.11 (.12)	–.02 (.11)	.19 (.15)
De Facto Judicial Independence (–)	–.20 (.06)***	–.10 (.06)**	–.21 (.05)**	–.26 (.06)***	–.30 (.06)***	–.14 (.07)**	–.15 (.08)**

Full standard models estimated. Only constitutional provision and judicial independence coefficients reported. Fixed effects and ordered probit estimation with robust standard errors. Standard errors in parentheses. *Significant at the 10 percent level. **Significant at the 5 percent level. ***Significant at the 1 percent level. All tests one-tailed except where no direction predicted (+) predicted positive direction, (–) negative, and (+/–) no predicted direction.

seeks to make substantial alterations to the political system (organized nonviolent rebellion and organized violent rebellion). Looking first at the models of repression of personal integrity rights, I find no statistically significant coefficients for the various clauses in the fixed-effects models; however, consistent with previous research the duration clauses produce positive coefficients that are statistically significant in all three non-fixed-effects models. The list of nonderogable rights is positive and statistically significant in two of the three non-fixed-effects models. In addition the ban against dissolving the legislature is statistically significant in only the Amnesty International model. Under these conditions, the emergency clauses produce only one statistically significant coefficient in the religious freedom models (legislative checks on declaration in the fixed-effects model). The duration clause has a beneficial effect in both freedom of speech/press models. And the ban against dissolving the legislature produces statistically significant coefficients in both the assembly/association models and the speech fixed-effects model. As in the previous analysis, judicial independence performs more strongly and consistently in these models; it fails to produce statistically significant coefficients only in the non-fixed-effects religious freedom model.

Finally, I condition the models to include just those states experiencing nonviolent threats, and these results are reported in Table 6.8. In previous studies, none of the state of emergency clauses was found to have a statistically significant relationship with repression of personal integrity rights. Here I find this not to be the case. Granted, in the fixed-effects model only two coefficients are statistically significant, but in the Department of State PTS ordered probit model all the coefficients are statistically significant. However, the list of nonderogable rights and the duration clauses have a harmful effect rather than a beneficial one. These two provisions do not produce statistically significant coefficients in the Amnesty International model, although the two beneficial provisions do. One of them (ban against dissolving the legislature) is also statistically significant in the CIRI index model. None of the provisions achieves statistical significance in the broader civil liberties model. The problematic list of nonderogable rights is statistically significant in both freedom of speech/press models and increases repression. The ban against dissolving the legislature produces a coefficient that achieves acceptable levels of statistical significance in both association/assembly models. The duration clause demonstrates a rare beneficial effect in the speech/press model, but the effect is limited to the ordered probit model. Only one

Table 6.7. State of Emergency Coefficients from Conditional Threat Models: Only Countries Experiencing Midlevel Threats (Rebellions Short of War)

	PTS-SD	*PTS-AI*	*CIRI Index*	*FH Civil Liberties*	*Speech/ Press*	*Association/ Assembly*	*Religion*
Fixed-Effects Models							
Legislative Checks on Declaration (–)	–.04 (.07)	.03 (.07)	.24 (.12)	.05 (.06)	.13 (.05)	–.01 (.05)	–.06 (.04)*
Duration Clause (+/–)	–.01 (.08)	–.11 (.10)	–.25 (.15)	–.07 (.06)	–.10 (.05)**	–.06 (.05)	–.02 (.03)
Ban against Dissolving Legislature (–)	.16 (.10)	.11 (.12)	.38 (.19)	.02 (.08)	–.10 (.06)**	–.06 (.06)*	.02 (.07)
List of Nonderogable Rights (+/–)	–.06 (.16)	–.06 (.24)	.04 (.42)	–.01 (.13)	.15 (.12)	–.05 (.12)	.13 (.11)
De Facto Judicial Independence (–)	–.12 (.05)**	–.09 (.06)*	–.41 (.11)***	–.14 (.02)***	–.11 (.04)***	–.06 (.04)*	–.02 (.02)
Ordered Probit							
Legislative Checks on Declaration (–)	–.01 (.04)	–.04 (.04)	.04 (.04)	.06 (.04)	.02 (.04)	.04 (.05)	.02 (.06)
Duration Clause (+/–)	.16 (.05)***	.09 (.05)**	.10 (.04)***	.06 (.04)	–.02 (.05)**	.01 (.05)	.05 (.07)
Ban against Dissolving Legislature (–)	–.01 (.06)	–.09 (.06)*	.01 (.05)	.05 (.06)	.07 (.06)	–.08 (.07)**	.09 (.08)
List of Nonderogable Rights (+/–)	.20 (.10)**	.10 (.10)	–.02 (.09)	–.11 (.10)	.19 (.12)*	.16 (.12)*	.14 (.16)
De Facto Judicial Independence (–)	–.29 (.06)****	–.18 (.06)***	–.21 (.05)**	–.25 (.06)***	–.30 (.06)***	–.17 (.07)***	–.18 (.08)**

Full standard models estimated. Only constitutional provision and judicial independence coefficients reported. Fixed effects and ordered probit estimation with robust standard errors. Standard errors in parentheses. *Significant at the 10 percent level. **Significant at the 5 percent level. ***Significant at the 1 percent level. All tests one-tailed except where no direction predicted (+) predicted positive direction, (–) negative, and (+/–) no predicted direction.

Table 6.8. State of Emergency Coefficients from Conditional Threat Models: Countries Experiencing Nonviolent Threats

	PTS–SD	*PTS–AI*	*CIRI Index*	*FH Civil Liberties*	*Speech/ Press*	*Association/ Assembly*	*Religion*
Fixed-Effects Models							
Legislative Checks on Declaration (–)	–.08 (.06)*	.03 (.06)	–.01 (.11)	.02 (.04)	.05 (.04)	–.04 (.04)	–.07 (.03)***
Duration Clause (+/–)	–.02 (.07)	–.12 (.09)	–.34 (.13)***	–.03 (.05)	–.07 (.05)	–.04 (.05)	.01 (.03)
Ban against Dissolving Legislature (–)	.03 (.08)	.10 (.10)	.13 (.16)	–.03 (.07)	–.08 (.07)	–.08 (.05)*	–.02 (.06)
List of Nonderogable Rights (+/–)	–.01 (.19)	–.21 (.20)	–.25 (.40)	–.01 (.14)	.27 (.12)**	–.06 (.12)	–.06 (.07)
De Facto Judicial Independence (–)	–.12 (.05)**	–.01 (.06)	–.33 (.08)***	–.14 (.03)**	–.09 (.03)***	–.08 (.03)***	–.02 (.02)
Ordered Probit							
Legislative Checks on Declaration (–)	–.06 (.03)*	–.07 (.03)**	–.03 (.03)	.01 (.03)	.02 (.04)	.02 (.04)	.01 (.05)
Duration Clause (+/–)	.11 (.04)***	.02 (.04)	.01 (.04)	.05 (.04)	–.02 (.05)**	.03 (.05)	–.01 (.06)
Ban against Dissolving Legislature (–)	–.13 (.05)***	–.15 (.05)***	–.07 (.05)**	–.01 (.05)	.07 (.06)	–.10 (.05)**	.02 (.07)
List of Nonderogable Rights (+/–)	.24 (.10)**	.14 (.10)	.11 (.08)	–.04 (.09)	.19 (.12)*	.01 (.11)	.04 (.14)
De Facto Judicial Independence (–)	–.29 (.06)*	–.19 (.05)***	–.23 (.05)***	–.30 (.05)***	–.30 (.06)***	–.26 (.06)***	–.16 (.08)**

Full standard models estimated. Only constitutional provision and judicial independence coefficients reported. Fixed effects and ordered probit estimation with robust standard errors. Standard errors in parentheses. *Significant at the 10 percent level. **Significant at the 5 percent level. ***Significant at the 1 percent level. All tests one-tailed except where no direction predicted (+) predicted positive direction, (–) negative, and (+/–) no predicted direction.

provision influences the repression of religious freedom in these states—the legislative declaration clause—but once again it does so in only one model.

Conclusions

The ICJ and ILA have promulgated international standards that are intended to function as constitutional safeguards to protect against human rights abuse during states of emergency. The constitutional safeguards, which carry the weight of paramount law, are assumed to provide to regimes advance knowledge of the extent and limit of their emergency powers, and the constitutional provisions are assumed to provide objective criteria that represent the public consensus, by which the government's conduct during states of emergency may be evaluated by domestic and international publics. These two organizations recommend that state constitutions clearly set out the conditions under which states of emergency may be declared and exercised so that (1) regimes that resort to emergency clauses in good faith will know in advance the extent and limit of their emergency powers; and (2) regimes not disposed to respect the limits of their authority may be judged according to the extent to which they live up to these specific rules. In this chapter I addressed three core questions: Why do states adopt these recommended constitutional provisions for states of emergency regulation? Does the formal commitment to these international standards make a difference in actual state behavior? In other words, to what extent do the promises actually lessen state repression of these promised rights during periods of threat? Under what types or levels of threat do these provisions work best? In regard to the state of emergency clauses, I did not find nearly as strong empirical evidence to support the world society approach's prediction of a convergence with states adopting similar institutions and structures because global models predicated legitimate state status on these documents—the norm is not to have such constitutional clauses. I extended the world society approach to domestic commitment to these clauses, and, as with the analysis in Chapter 5, I found mixed evidence. Although I found evidence of a global norms cascade, I found no evidence that regional norms or the promulgation of the ILA/ICJ standards influences the level of commitment. I did, however, find some evidence that participation in the ICCPR is associated with higher levels of state of emergency provision. As with the bill of rights analysis, the embeddedness hypothesis is supported only to the extent that the presence of INGOs captures the concept; participation in IGOs appears to have no influence on the adoption and maintenance of these human rights norms in constitutions, or on any of the other provisions studied in this book. The INGO association also provides support for the transnational network hypothesis, which overlaps with the world society approach in its prediction. The role of the INGOs in state commitment is consistent, whether in relation to constitutional provision for core human rights or in relation to state of emergency provisions; but they had no demonstrable effect on commitment to judicial independence. As I have previously suggested, it is possible that while the transnational networks may appreciate the potential rights-protective role of an independent judiciary, they may be more motivated to influence the discourse and formal commitment to rights rather than expand limited resources to enhance the power of an institution that in many states has not played a rights-protective role but often has served to legitimate the abuses of an authoritarian regime, especially during periods of threat. My analyses support somewhat the domestic threat hypothesis in that the presence of civil war did decrease the odds of adopting or maintaining state of emergency provisions; but the overall impact was rather small, and other forms of violent opposition had no effect.

As in the previous chapters, I also examined the expectations that regimes facing electoral uncertainty would seek to "lock in" the benefits of formal rights, and I found even more substantial support for these expectations than in the judicial independence commitment models and the bill of rights models. The competitiveness of political participation continues to produce one of the largest effects in any of the commitment models. As in Chapters 4 and 5, I find strong, consistent evidence to support critics' claims that economic liberalization and globalization, at least in the short term, do not encourage commitment to international human rights norms. The consistency of these findings across the entirety of my constitutional provisions gives substantial credence to the malign perspective.

The effects of state of emergency clauses on political repression are far from clear and appear to be conditional on the level and type of threats occurring within the regime. Still, we are able to identify notable patterns and to draw implications from them. When we look at the overall effect of the clauses, without conditioning their effect on threat level and type, we identify several trends in regard to personal integrity abuse. First, the ban against dissolving the legislature has a consistent beneficial effect on this form of repression generally. Second, increasing the role of the legislature in declaring states of emergency has only a weak sporadic effect. Third, and most important, we see strong evidence that duration clauses encourage or facilitate repression of this sort but find only weak evidence that the other problematic clause, the nonderogable rights clause, will have a harmful effect on personal integrity rights. When I conceptualize civil liberties broadly and do not condition my analysis on threat, we see that only one clause makes a difference—the nonderogable rights clause—and it has a beneficial effect rather than a harmful one. When I examine the three types of individual rights restrictions, I find that the constitutional clauses produce only beneficial effects, but the effects vary by freedoms. The duration clause and ban against dissolving the legislature reduce the likelihood of repression of freedom of speech/press and association/assembly. Only the legislative check is associated with reduced political repression. One constant across each of these analyses is the continuing, consistent influence of an independent judiciary on state willingness to resort to repression as a policy tool. These general analyses suggest that the emergency clauses can both constrain and facilitate a regime's willingness and opportunity to engage in coercive force against its citizens. The clauses that increase the legislature's check on states of emergency offer the strongest potential in discouraging both categories of abuse. The two clauses that have been identified previously as problematic continue to demonstrate the potential of facilitating rather curbing state repression, but only in regard to the more egregious category of repression. The clauses produce the expected beneficial effect in limited categories of civil liberties. Thus it is difficult to express confidence in the clauses' general effectiveness in discouraging repression of either sort.

Since the state of emergency clauses I examine here are intended to regulate state behavior during times of threat, I engaged in a series of analyses in which I limited the focus to the level of threat present in the state. I examined states experiencing civil war, states experiencing any form of violent threat, states facing midlevel threats that fell short of violence, and states experiencing nonviolent forms of threat. When I conditioned the analysis of the broad range of civil liberties restrictions, I find that none of the clauses has an effect, regardless of the level or type of threat to the regime. One of two problematic clauses—the duration clause—continued to cause concern about its unintended consequence of facilitating repression. It produced only harmful effects in regard to personal integrity abuse, especially when midlevel threats and violent threats were present, but somewhat even in regard to low-level threats. The beneficial effect of this clause was evident only in regard to freedom of speech and press. Thus, again, caution seems to be merited in the promulgation of these clauses. The other problematic clause—the nonderogable rights clause—produces little redeeming evidence, with one important exception: it reduces the odds of personal integrity abuse during civil war. However, there is some evidence that it facilitates repression of personal integrity rights during midlevel threats and lower-level threats. Its effect on civil liberties is thin and sporadic, but the evidence, with only one exception, suggests that the clauses encourage or facilitate civil liberties restrictions across threat levels. Again, caution seems to be merited in the promulgation of these clauses, and domestic and international publics would be wise to monitor regimes closely for violations of rights that are clearly nonderogable under international norms. While the other clauses are not associated with increased levels of repression of either sort, their performance across threat levels and types of rights is thin and inconsistent at best. Ultimately, judicial independence, which consistently decreases the likelihood that a state will engage in either category of political repression, appears to be more important as a guarantor of rights, with one notable exception, during periods of civil war.

Chapter 7

Protecting Human Rights: Conclusions, Implications, and Where We Go from Here

Numerous scholars and legal commentators have posited that the world society of states has converged upon a set of ideals regarding human rights behavior and the appropriate institutions to promote and protect those ideals. These ideals include a written constitution or the equivalent, an entrenched bill of rights, and democratic processes and institutions, which increasingly include a judicial check on state power to protect an internationally recognized set of human rights. In this book I have presented clear evidence of substantial formal acceptance of the human rights norms in constitutional documents, as well as acceptance of the international norms for judicial independence. The formal commitment to these norms, while strong and growing, does not approach universality in the sense of commitment we have witnessed in regard to the international human rights treaty regime. The trends in constitutionally adopting these norms coincide with the tremendous wave of constitution writing that occurred during the post-Cold War transitions, and the subsequent creation of many newly independent states. The driving question of this work has been whether the remarkable growth in formal adherence to this global script of rights and institutional standards has led to a concomitant decrease in the willingness of states to repress their own citizens' fundamental rights and freedoms. I have sought to answer this question by drawing upon a variety of approaches within the social sciences reflected in a growing body of literature committed to understanding the question of why states repress their citizens.

Why Do States Repress Their Citizens?

In these chapters I have built upon the growing empirical human rights literature, expanding our understanding of state actors' decisions to employ the tools of repression against their citizens, and in particular developing a broader understanding of why states incorporate international standards of human rights and judicial independence into their paramount domestic law, and identifying the factors that affect their subsequent translation into practice. Before examining these commitments and their effects I revisited what has become known as the "standard model" of repression and expanded it forward in time to cover almost three decades and the global set of states. I also adapted the standard model to reflect developments in the literature concerning the conceptualization and measurement of democracy, and I explored measurement issues in regard to civil liberties. I explored more thoroughly the conflicting expectations regarding the effect of military regimes. My finding that military regimes are more likely to employ personal integrity abuse and less likely to employ restrictions on civil liberties supports Davenport's (2007b) overall assessment that military regimes are less likely to repress civil liberties "because they tend to avoid involving themselves with the political processes which are normally responsible for these repressive activities (i.e., legislatures and courts)" but are more likely to "use repressive techniques which are more directly within the realm of their expertise—physical violence" (500), a phenomenon that clearly encompasses repression of personal integrity rights. My study also sheds light on the long-standing controversy over whether the inconsistent findings regarding the influence of leftist regimes on political repression reflect a State Department bias or a legitimate association. While it has been argued that "the tenets of Marxist-Leninist theory about the need for a dictatorship of the proletariat" would suggest that Marxist-Leninist regimes may be more inclined toward repression (Poe and Tate 1994, 858), my results here support Keith's (2002a) further explanation that in these regimes, control of society and of personal freedoms has often been so complete that the regime might be less likely to need to engage in these more severe abuses of personal integrity rights, which is exactly what I find—along with finding that these regimes are more likely to control a broad range of citizen behavior of the sort that might reduce the need to employ more severe forms of repression, such as those measured by personal integrity rights abuse. These results also support Davenport's (2007b) findings.

Subsequently I expanded the standard model to account for state embeddedness in global society, examining the influence of INGOs as well as state membership in IGOs and human rights treaties. I also broadened our attention to liberal economic theory and examined the influence of WTO membership, trade, and foreign direct investment. I find generally that the influence of INGOs and IGOS is quite weak, especially once I control for judicial independence and constitutional provisions. The impact of treaty membership is somewhat mixed, but generally positive, when controlling for reservations and declarations. Indicators of liberal economic theory produce one of the most consistent effects across all models of repression, and the effect always supports critics of the theory, who claim that these conditions encourage rather than discourage repression of personal integrity abuse and restrictions on civil liberties. My primary contribution in this book lies in the substantive examination of the role of judicial independence and constitutional rights protections in reducing state repression. To better understand their association with political repression, and in order to more rigorously model the provisions effects, I first addressed the issue of why states commit formally to the international human rights norms and the international norm of judicial independence.

Why Do States Commit?

I believe that the analyses in this book represent the first systematic cross-national empirical examination of the question of why states commit in constitutional documents to international human rights standards and international standards for judicial independence. To address this question, I have examined the dominant approaches within the social sciences that have primarily sought to explain state commitment to international human rights treaties. I have presented strong empirical evidence to support the world society approach's prediction of a convergence with states adopting similar institutions and structures over time because the global society expects that they should in order to attain legitimate state status—I found convergence in regard to promulgation of constitutions with bills of rights and provisions for judicial independence, but I found less convergence in regard to the more controversial state of emergency clauses. I demonstrated that constitutional promises of judicial independence were not "cheap talk," as realists would posit, meant to merely superficially satisfy the concerns of potential investors or the demands of opposition groups or INGOs; and I found no evidence to suggest a general decoupling effect posited by some scholars applying the world society approach. I do not take this general finding to mean that no countries make empty promises of judicial independence for state legitimacy or material interest, but rather I suggest that generally states do not engage in these empty promises, or, if they do, they may be caught in their own rhetoric and eventually provide some level of judicial independence. This evidence supports the constructivist approaches in that the choice to adopt provisions for judicial independence appears to reflect the diffusion of norms, both globally and regionally, and follows the promulgation of the final sets of standards set forth through the United Nations. While the evidence of diffusion of norms supports the world society approach, I find no evidence that state embeddedness in the international community influences the incorporation of these standards into state constitutions, nor do I find an observable influence of a transnational network at this stage. I remain somewhat cautious about these findings, as the time frame of analysis with IGO and INGO measures ends in 2000 because of the lack of IGO/INGO data; thus a significant portion of the post-Cold War era remains unexamined in these models. In addition, the INGO data do not control for whether the organizations specifically have a human rights mission.

I found much more mixed evidence when I extended this approach to domestic rights commitments. I found no evidence of a global norms cascade, as I did with judicial independence, but I did find consistent evidence of a regional diffusion, at least in regard to the broader bundle of rights, and some evidence of a regional effect on due process rights. I found no evidence that embeddedness in the broader world, as measured by IGO participation, influences formal rights commitment; but, unlike with judicial independence commitments, I did find strong, consistent evidence that the increased presence of INGOs influences formal commitment to rights provisions, a result that also supports the transnational network theory. It is possible that while the transnational networks may appreciate the potential rights-protective role of an independent judiciary, they may be skeptical about committing limited resources to empower an institution that may have a history of legitimizing and even facilitating an authoritarian regime's abuses of human rights. I also found that prior commitment to the ICCPR was consistently associated with higher levels of constitutional commitment across each category of rights under study here.

I extended the world society approach to domestic commitment to state of emergency clauses, and, as with the analysis of commitment to fundamental freedoms and rights, I found rather mixed evidence. While I found evidence of a global norms cascade, I found no evidence that regional norms or the promulgation of the ILA/ICJ standards influenced the level of commitment. I did, however, find some evidence that participation in the ICCPR is associated with higher levels of state of emergency provision. As with the bill of rights analysis, the embeddedness hypothesis is supported only to the extent that the presence of INGOs captures the concept; participation in IGOs appears to have no influence on the adoption and maintenance of these human rights norms in constitutions, or on any the other provisions studied in this book. The INGO association also provides support for the transnational network hypothesis, which overlaps with the world society approach in its prediction. The role of INGOs in state commitment is consistent, whether in relation to constitutional provision for core human rights or in relation to state of emergency provisions. Thus, as a whole the constructivist approach receives fair to moderate support across all three forms of commitment.

I also apply or extend the dominant theories within the comparative courts literature regarding commitment to judicial independence and/or judicial review and find substantial support when applied to the commitment model of judicial independence. Regimes facing electoral uncertainty (because the state is newly democratizing or because of the emergence of strong multiparty competition) appear to adopt or maintain constitutional provisions for judicial independence in order to foster the possibility of having an alternative forum in which they may influence policy should they lose control of the regime through elections or in which their political and civil rights may be protected against the new majority. Subsequent evidence suggests that treating the judiciary as insurance may pay off, at least in regard to the potential severity of political repression of core rights. When I examined the expectations that regimes facing electoral uncertainty would seek to "lock in" the benefits of formal rights, I found strong and consistent evidence that regimes with strongly competitive political participation are more likely to adopt and maintain the constitutional freedoms and found moderate evidence of the same effect in regard to new democracies. I also examined these expectations in regard to the adoption of state of emergency clauses and found even more substantial support for these expectations than in the judicial independence commitment models and the bill of rights models. Judicial independence appears to be perceived as a reliable form of insurance for the future.

The positive perspective of economic liberalization predicted that an interdependent economy and trade would indirectly encourage states to adopt or maintain constitutional provisions for core rights, I found no evidence of this "dividend"; instead I found consistent evidence supporting the malign perspective that economic liberalism is not likely to lead to these dividends but actually decreases the probability of meaningful reform and a regime's commitment to formal judicial independence, bill of rights provisions, or the adoption of state of emergency provisions. All three indicators of economic liberalism and globalization were consistently associated with *less*, not more, formal protections. This evidence parallels the large body of evidence that Abouharb and Cingranelli (2008) produced in regard to the IMF and World Bank structural adjustment programs; their evidence strongly suggested that the ameliorative effects of economic liberalization were not just overstated but rather the effects in reality were contrary to rights provision. I reach the same conclusion.

Overall, though, the results from my commitment models suggested optimism that the formal commitments would be translated into action, given the role of norms, prior treaty commitment to international human rights norms, and the potential ongoing role that INGOs and a competitive party system would continue to play in committed states.

Does Commitment Matter?

My analyses clearly demonstrate that formal commitment to judicial independence is not simply an empty gesture—these constitutional provisions do indeed influence actual levels of achieved judicial independence across the global set of states, even when controlling for selection effects and other factors. Not surprisingly, I also find that achieved levels of judicial independence are influenced by a variety of factors. Economic resources matter: the greater the state's economic wealth, the more likely the state is to foster independence in the judiciary, while the more resource constraints the state faces, the less likely it will be to provide for an independent judiciary. Economic liberalization is not associated with the actual fulfillment of judicial independence, although here, unlike in regard to commitment and repression, I do not find evidence to support the malign perspective that economic liberalism would decrease the likelihood of judicial independence. I do find some evidence that embeddedness in the global society increases *de facto* judicial independence, but only in that a state's participation in IGOs is associated with increased levels of judicial independence. The presence of

INGOs does not make a difference any more than it did in regard to formal commitment.

Threats such as civil war and international war do affect a regime's willingness to allow judicial independence, but the effect largely disappears once I control for legislative constraints on the executive and for party competition. The influence of the formal provisions ultimately depended upon these components of democratization whose positive influence on judicial independence was also dependent upon the formal provisions. Democracy produces the strongest effect, next to military regimes, which are considerably less likely to allow for an independent judiciary generally. I also find evidence to support Ferejohn, Rosenbluth, and Shipan (2004), who argue that courts are more able to act independently when political fragmentation limits the ability of politicians to engage in court-curbing action such as jurisdiction-stripping, court-packing or even constitutional amendment. Some environmental factors, such as colonial legacy and legal system, which are largely invariable across time, fail to influence judicial independence in most models. However, I do find some support that states with prior British colonial experience are more likely to have independent judiciaries and that states with civil law systems are less likely to have independent judiciaries. As a whole I would conclude, not surprisingly, that formal provisions by themselves alone only weakly influence the actual independence of the judiciary, which ultimately is also influenced more by a broader set of electoral conditions, resource capabilities, and constraints, and to some extent by violent threats to the regime.

My primary interest in this book is explaining states' use of tools of repression, and thus I engaged in a series of analysis to examine whether optimists' or skeptics' expectations were supported in the real world of state repression. Optimistic expectations were supported in regard to promises of judicial independence and lists of fundamental freedoms and rights—these promises do reduce state propensity to employ coercive action; however, state of emergency clauses were much less consistent in their effect, and in some circumstances were associated with greater repression rather than less. First, I find that even when controlling for selection effects, the achieved level of judicial independence does in fact reduce the likelihood of both repression of personal integrity rights and restriction of civil liberties. Thus judicial independence seems to have earned its place as an "essential feature of liberal democracy" and an "essential guardian of the rule of law" (Steiner and Alston 1996, 711); although these roles are also shared by democratic institutions, especially a competitive party system. In terms of its impact on repression of personal integrity, judicial independence outweighs that of democratization but is substantially less than the impact of civil war. However, in the case of civil liberties restrictions, while the impact of judicial independence is relatively large, the level of democratization slightly outweighs the influence of judicial independence. On the other hand, its influence surpasses that of civil war in regard to repression of this broader set of liberties that presumably affects a larger segment of the population than does personal integrity abuse. The evidence lends overwhelming support to the domestic institutions argument that an independent judiciary can increase the material and reputational costs to regimes employing coercive force against their citizens to such an extent that regimes would be deterred from employing these tactics as severely or frequently. An independent, rights-supporting judiciary may over time also socialize both the public and the regime toward a rights consciousness that under most circumstances may remove the tools of repression from the menu of appropriate policy options.

Second, I tested the optimistic perspective that formal commitments to fundamental freedoms such as freedom of speech, press, assembly, association, and religion would allow persons to openly criticize and challenge the regime without the threat or application of coercive state action, and that formal due process rights would provide recourse to a legal remedy, and impose material and reputational costs to the regime were it to engage, thus over time discouraging the regime from selecting this costly policy tool. Thus, I argued, from the opportunity and willingness framework, that bills of rights or particular formalized freedoms potentially change the menu of appropriate choices, change the costs of inappropriate choices, and influence the values through which the regime will evaluate the choices. Overall, the evidence suggests that the formal commitments are much more likely to curb repressive state behavior in regard to the broader set of civil liberties than in regard to the more egregious repression of personal integrity rights. While due process rights did lessen the probability of personal integrity abuse, the formal provisions were largely dependent upon the presence of an independent judiciary. Individually, the due process protection appeared to be largely driven by provision for fair trials and public trials. The provision for fair trials operated on repression independently of judicial independence, whereas the public trial provision was dependent upon the level of judicial independence. This relationship clearly merits future study, particularly further delineation of fair trial protection beyond the explicit enumeration of a "right to a fair trial." And in regard to public trial provision it would be fruitful to study the connection between public trials provisions in bills of rights that enumerate a right to a public trial and provisions in judicial sections of constitutions that require the judiciary to hold trials in public.

I also found evidence that the personal freedoms index reduced the likelihood of repression of two sets of individual freedoms (speech and press, assembly and association) but not the third, freedom of religion. Concomitantly, I found that this form of repression was the one form not consistently influenced by judicial independence. This result suggests that the translation of a formal promise of religious freedom into the actual free exercise of religion faces more significant cultural hurdles than the other freedoms, and that the judicial arena may not be immune to those cultural influences in regard to this freedom. I did find one encouraging link in regard to religious freedom: while the presence of INGOs has no effect on repression of the other four freedoms, I did find evidence that a broader INGO presence decreased the likelihood of repression of religious freedom. Thus their effect was evident where it is perhaps most needed, in the area of repression that is only weakly affected by constitutional protections and an independent judiciary.

Third, I examined the effects of state of emergency clauses on political repression, which turned out to be far from clear and to be conditional upon the level and type of threats occurring within the regime. Still, I was able to identify some notable patterns and to draw implications from them. When we look at the overall effect of the clauses, without conditioning their effect on threat level and type, I identify several trends in regard to personal integrity abuse. First, the ban against dissolving has a consistent beneficial effect on this form of repression generally. Second, increasing the role of the legislature in declaring states of emergency has only a weak sporadic effect. Third, and most important, we see strong evidence that the duration clauses will encourage or facilitate repression of this sort; but I find only weak evidence that the other problematic clause, the nonderogable rights clause, will have a harmful effect on personal integrity rights. When I conceptualize civil liberties broadly and do not condition the analysis on threat, I find that only one clause makes a difference—the nonderogable rights clause—and it has a beneficial effect rather than a harmful one. When I examine the three types of individual rights restrictions, I find that the clauses produce only beneficial effects but the effects vary by freedoms. The duration clause and ban against dissolving the legislature reduce the likelihood of repression of freedom of speech/press and association/assembly. Only the legislative check is associated with reduced political repression. One constant across each of these analyses is the continuing, consistent influence of an independent judiciary on state willingness to resort to repression as policy tool. These general analyses suggest that the state of emergency clauses can both constrain and facilitate a regime's willingness and opportunity to engage in coercive force against its citizens. The clauses that increase the legislature's check on states of emergency offer the strongest potential in discouraging both categories of abuse. The two clauses that have been identified previously as problematic continue to demonstrate their potential to facilitate rather than curb state repression—but only in regard to the more egregious category of repression. The clauses produce the expected beneficial effect in limited categories of civil liberties, so it is difficult to express confidence in the clauses' general effectiveness in discouraging repression of either sort.

Since the state of emergency clauses are intended to regulate state behavior during times of threat, I engaged in a series of analyses in which I limited the focus to the level of threat present in the state. I examined states experiencing civil war, states experiencing any form of violent threat, states facing midlevel threats that fell short of violence, and states experiencing nonviolent forms of threat. When I conditioned the analysis of the broad range of civil liberties restrictions, I found that none of the clauses has an effect, regardless of the level or type of threat to the regime. One of two problematic clauses, the duration clause, continued to produce the unintended consequence of facilitating repression. It produced only harmful effects in regard to personal integrity abuse, especially when midlevel threats and violent threats were present. The beneficial effect of this clause was evident only in regard to freedom of speech and press. The other problematic clause—nonderogable rights clause—produces little redeeming evidence, with one important exception: it reduces the odds of personal integrity abuse during civil war. However, there is some evidence that it facilitates repression of personal integrity rights during midlevel threats and lower-level threats. Its effect on civil liberties is thin and sporadic, but the evidence, with only one exception, suggests that the clauses encourage or facilitate civil liberties restrictions, across threat level. While the other clauses are not associated with increased levels of repression of either sort, their performance across threat levels and types of rights is thin and inconsistent, at best. Ultimately, judicial independence, which consistently decreases the likelihood that a state will engage in both categories of political repression, appears to be a more important guarantor of rights during times of threat, with one regrettable exception, during periods of civil war.

The Implications of This Work

The results of these analyses have strong implications for actors and institutions within the international community that support the development of democratic institutions and the reform of judicial or legal systems more specifically. Efforts to entrench an independent judiciary formally in a documentary constitution are not futile; however, they are not sufficient. Ultimately, the impact of the formal provisions is dependent upon core components of pluralistic democratization such as fostering a competitive party system and establishing legislative checks on the executive branch. Judicial independence is unlikely to be fully realized unless the state has sufficient resources to fund the infrastructure and institutional access to the public that allow the judiciary to function effectively, to attain legitimacy in the broad public, and to serve as an ultimate check against abusive power. As a whole my analysis of constitutional provisions for rights suggests that optimists are fairly justified in their expectation that such provisions are indeed more than mere window dressing and are more than mere codes that "govern the allocation of functions, powers and duties" of government officials (Finer 1974, 145–47). Instead they appear, especially in the case of civil liberties, to "articulate the ideals or intentions of the communities they serve" and "provide standards against which the governors can be measured by the governed and by themselves" (Andrews 1964, 21, 24). The evidence suggests that the provisions may indeed extend the reach of the rule of law and provide individual protection from the overextension of governmental power; but it appears that the standards of justice and the level of protection of the individual are thinner in regard to personal integrity rights. Given the egregious nature of even low levels of personal integrity abuse, it is perplexing that the potential "rights consciousness" that arguably develops around a bill of rights would not extend as readily or consistently to the more egregious forms of repression such as torture, killing, and disappearance, which the state is more likely to resort to during times of threat.

Skepticism is most merited in regard to the promulgation of the state of emergency clauses. I would not go so far as to recommend that states not adopt emergency clauses. I would encourage states that adopt such provisions to include strong legislative and judicial checks on each stage of the process, especially in regard to renewing states of emergency. I would urge caution in adopting lists of nonderogable rights without specific language carefully delineating the limited circumstances under which any rights might be derogated. I believe that domestic and international nongovernmental organizations and the broader international human rights community would be wise to monitor closely regimes that declare states of emergency, even when presumably regulated by strong constitutional provisions for such emergencies or by international treaty commitments. Ultimately, each of my analyses brings me back to the conclusion that the most important reform priority is insuring the independence of the judiciary and healthy political participation and competition.

Where We Go from Here

I recognize the limitations of these analyses and am hopeful that they will point the way to future research, my own as well as others'. Further examination of the role of INGOs is imperative. In order to achieve this, we need to develop better measures of INGO presence and state participation and support of these organizations, and we need to extend the coverage across time and space. We need to be able to capture and assess the level of resource capability as well as to delineate the primary objectives of the INGOs, at least identifying those that have a human rights mission. In addition, we need to broaden our examination to other organizations such as bar associations that may play a role in constraining state repression. Several of the constitutional measures also merit further exploration. For example, it would be beneficial to further delineate fair trial protection beyond the explicit enumeration of a "right to a fair trial" and to examine other components of this protection that may be enumerated in constitutions, such as the right to a speedy trial and the right to counsel. It would be fruitful to study the connection between public trials provisions in bills of rights that enumerate a right to a public trial and provisions in judicial sections of constitutions that require the judiciary to hold trials in public. In order to understand fully the role of the judiciary in state repression or provision of rights, scholars need to develop a cross-national measure of core dimensions of the judiciary—its ability to function effectively and afford broad and meaningful access to the public, which is necessary to attain legitimacy in the broad public and to serve as an ultimate check against abusive power (Prillaman 2000). In addition, my measure of judicial review fails to capture many of the variations of constitutional review that may inform our understanding of how judges' use of this power may facilitate or constrain their regime's opportunity and willingness to engage in political repression. I also believe that our attempts to understand the law's effect on repression, especially during periods of threat, must extend beyond an examination of paramount law and international law, to examine statutory law such as national security laws or decrees, which may conflict with these broader promises. Currently, we lack sources to create reliable cross-national measures of statutory laws. Finally, I acknowledge that my focus has ignored a much broader set of state human rights behavior such as equality rights, basic needs and development rights, and cultural and social rights, which clearly are influenced by international and domestic law, and for which the judiciary has a potential role as guarantor. I expect that these relationships are even more complex than the ones I address here. I hope that the work of this book may inform future studies that continue to expand the exploration of the role of law and courts in protecting human rights.

Notes

Chapter 1

1. Five states are signatories but have not ratified the convention: Bhutan, Djibouti, Grenada, Nauru, and SãoTomé and Principe.

2. Eight states are signatories but have not ratified the convention: China, Comoros, Cuba, Guinea-Bissau, Laos, Nauru, Pakistan, and São Tomé and Principe.

3. Six states are signatories but have not ratified the convention: Belize, Comoros, Cuba, São Tomé and Principe, South Africa, and the United States.

4. The United States is a signatory but has not ratified the convention.

5. Ten states are signatories but have not ratified the convention: Bahamas, Comoros, Dominican Republic, Gambia, Guinea-Bissau, India, Nauru, Pakistan, São Tomé and Principe, and Sudan.

6. The United States and Somalia are signatories but have not ratified the convention.

7. First-generation rights are civil liberties and political rights that emerged during the European and U.S. revolutionary eras; second-generation rights are economic, cultural, and social rights that emerged later and were strongly shaped by revolutionary movements in Russia and China (DeLaet 2006, 19).

8. Arguably, there is a *jus cogens* for the prohibition against torture, according to the International Criminal Tribunal for the Former Yugoslavia that binds all states (*Prosecutor v. Furundžija*, 121; *International Law Reports* 213, 2002).

Chapter 2

1. The norm requires state parties consider asylum claims and prevents the state from forcibly returning the applicant to his or her country of origin if they have a well-founded fear that they will be persecuted there because of race, religion, nationality, membership in a social group, or political opinion.

2. He finds similar results in regard to Articles 21 and 22 of the CAT and in regard to the Optional Protocol, although he notes that the beneficial effect of ratification tapers off the more democratic the state becomes.

Chapter 3

1. Examples of level 5 repression were seen in Afghanistan in 1985 and Colombia in 1991. The Philippines in 1990 and Libya in 1987 are examples of level 4 countries. Cuba in 1991 and Ghana in 1982 are examples of level 3 countries. Congo in 1985 and Cameroon in 1987 are examples of level 2 countries. Benin in 1991 and Oman in 1991 are examples of level 1 countries. Full sets of examples and excerpts of country reports for each level of repression are available in Gibney and Dalton (1996).

2. The most notable absence in the Department of State–based measure is the United States.

3. There is some misunderstanding about our previous use of this measure; at no time have we ever combined the political rights index with the civil liberties index (see Neumayer 2005), as we believe that the political rights index more appropriately reflects electoral democracy, and we carefully distinguish among electoral democracy, personal integrity, and liberalism in our models (Poe and Tate 1994; Poe, Tate, and Keith 1999; Keith 2002a; Keith, Tate, and Poe 2009).

4. CIRI notes: "'Some' censorship means the government places some restrictions yet does allow limited rights to freedom of speech and the press. 'No' censorship means the freedom to speak freely and to print opposing opinions without the fear of prosecution. It must be noted that 'None' in no way implies absolute freedom, as there exist restrictions on information and/or communication. Even in democracies there are restrictions placed on freedoms of speech and the press if these rights infringe on the rights of others or in any way endanger the welfare of others. Finally, in practice, if the government owns all of any one aspect of the media, such as all radio stations or all television stations, then that country receives a ZERO."

5. The categories include: (1) low violence/low restriction, (2) low violence/moderate restriction (the number of cases made this category too small for statistical analysis), (3) low violence/high restriction (the number of cases made this category too small for statistical analysis), (4) moderate violence/low restriction, (5) moderate violence/moderate restriction, (6) moderate violence/high restriction, (7) high violence/low restriction, (8) high violence/moderate restrictions, and (9) high violence/high restrictions.

6. It is possible that other points within the scale infer a presence of violence, but it is not clear where. The explicit 4-point scale on political terror that is embedded in the Rule of Law sub-component checklist suggests that political terror (and thus violence) is only captured there.

7. In addition, I found an overall correlation of .81 for the two scales.

8. To illustrate the magnitude of its impact, Poe, Tate, and Keith (1999) demonstrated that an ongoing civil war would have an effect on the repression scale that levels out at around 1.5 on a 5-point scale of repression, with other factors in the model held equal (308).

9. Davenport (2007b) uses Geddes' (1999) somewhat broader definition, which delineates military regimes as those in which "a group of officers decides who rules and influences policy" (Davenport 493; Geddes 4).

10. 1979 and 1981 are lost in the models because of the use of the lagged dependent variable. The data set includes the global set of independent states whose independence is recognized by the United Nations (thus Taiwan and Palestine are excluded). Newly independent states are included in the data set at the point at which they have been independent for more than six months. Finally, following Poe and Tate (1994) and Poe, Tate, and Keith (1999), states must have an annual population of at least 150,000 to be included.

11. These results are available from the author. The magnitude was slightly higher; for example, using the Department of State PTS measure, the coefficient for democracy in the fixed effects model was -.07, which suggests that maximum change in the level of democracy would produce a decrease of close to .5 on the 7-point scale.

Chapter 4

1. Hirschl (2000) notes that "nearly every recently adopted constitution or constitutional revision contains a bill of rights and establishes some form of active judicial review" (92).

2. Becker argues and I agree that impartiality is different from and should not be confused with independence. It may not be possible for a nonindependent judge to be impartial, but it is certainly possible for an independent judge (in the sense used in these definitions) to be partial (say, because he/she is racist or hates business people, etc., etc.). Nevertheless, writers on independence frequently do lump impartiality with independence. The practice seems to do no harm in the context of this research.

3. As with impartiality, I think it best not to conflate legitimacy and independence, but the practice seems to do no harm in this research.

4. In addition to the seven elements that emerge from the United Nations principles I consider two more questionable elements (hierarchical system and judicial review) in the sections that follow.

5. This may be the appropriate place to acknowledge the obvious fact that a formal written constitution is not the only mechanism through which nations structure courts, judicial independence, and rights. Clearly, statutes, legal codes and doctrines, and even customs also structure a nation's "constitution" and the interpretation of its written "Constitution." Our reliance on the latter is primarily a matter of necessity. We must tolerate the irony of a using a data source that leads us to code one of the world's oldest "constitutional" regimes, the United Kingdom, as having "no constitutional provisions" because it has no written constitution and the birthplace of judicial review, the United States, as having no constitutional judicial review because the practice was

established through Supreme Court doctrine. It is simply impossible to implement and code a broader definition of national constitutional practices. The importance still placed on written constitutions and their formal provisions is evident in the large-scale constitution drafting that has gone on during the Third Wave of democratization.

6. Ginsburg and Moustafa (2008) argue that even though the electoral logic does not hold in the context of authoritarian regimes, the underlying condition that leads democratic regimes to empower judiciaries—disaggregation of interests within a governing regime—may intensify an authoritarian regime's willingness to allow for at least limited judiciary autonomy. Widener (2008) argues that a variety of motivations can inspire semidemocratic or authoritarian regimes to recognize the advantage of an independent court, particularly in regard to purposes of internal control. For example, she argues that courts provide authoritarian regimes a cheaper alternative to the constant administrative supervision of bureaucrats under the "police patrol" model and instead allow "aggrieved individuals and firms [to] bring their complaints to courts and sound a 'fire alarm'" (236). Other motivations include the potential (1) "to resolve local disputes that might end up otherwise on the streets"; (2) to signal to the international community "good international citizenship," and (3) "to distinguish itself from its predecessors, who themselves abused the rule of law" (236–37). She cautions however that the willingness of these regimes "to delegate power to an independent court tends to be fairly ephemeral" (237) and that "judicial independence is never won once and for all" but rather "is constantly renegotiated" (247).

7. In many constitutions it was easy to identify the provision for judicial review because the document explicitly stated that courts exercise "constitutional review" or "judicial review." In other cases, I used Ackermann's (1989) definition as the standard for determining whether constitutional or judicial review existed: right and duty conferred on a court or particular courts of a country to interpret authoritatively the constitution of that country, to decide authoritatively the constitutionality of laws, executive and administrative acts, and, in appropriate cases, to declare such laws and acts invalid and unenforceable when they conflict with the country's constitution (60).

8. I ran several preliminary models testing lagged effects; a lag of one year performed best.

9. The U.S. Department of State further notes: "Once individual country reports were completed, the Bureau of Democracy, Human Rights and Labor, in cooperation with other Department of State offices, worked to corroborate, analyze, and edit the reports, drawing on their own sources of information," and "these sources included reports provided by U.S. and other human rights groups, foreign government officials, representatives from the United Nations and other international and regional organizations and institutions, experts from academia, and the media" (U.S. Department of State 2009).

10. The Department of State reports are summative and typically use phrases such "has a fully independent judiciary" or "has a judiciary that is somewhat or partially

independent" or that through the year "there was pressure from the executive" or that "there was a high level of corruption within the judiciary." For examples of the actual language in the reports, see the appendix to this chapter.

11. Rosenn (1987) also notes that the civil law tradition in Latin America, in which judges are traditionally weak and lack the power, prestige, and deference associated with common law judges, has long denied a creative, independent role for judges. He argues that while most Latin American constitutions have added the power of judicial review, asking Latin American judges to perform this function broadly is to "plunge them into a political role for which they are ill-prepared by both temperament and experience" (33).

12. The University of Ottawa Law School website, available at http://www.droitcivil.uottawa.ca/world -legal-systems/eng-monde.php, offers the following definitions:

Civil Law Systems: [T]he countries found in this category have drawn mainly on their Roman legal heritage in addition to other sources, and while giving precedence to written law, have resolutely opted for a systematic codification of their ordinary law. Also found in this category are countries, generally of the mixed law variety, that have not resorted to the technique of codifying law but that have retained to varying degrees enough elements of Roman legal construction, "as a written reason," to be considered affiliated to the civil tradition. On the other hand, we also find countries in this category where Roman influence was weaker but whose law, codified or not, rests on the notion of legislated law which in many ways resembles the systems of countries with a "pure" civil tradition (for example, Scandinavian countries that hold a unique position within the "Romano-Germanic" family).

Common Law Systems: Like that of civil law, the common law system has taken on a variety of cultural forms throughout the world. Notwithstanding the significant nuances that such diversity can sometimes create, and which political circumstances further accentuate, this category includes political entities whose law, for the most part, is technically based on English common law concepts and legal organizational methods which assign a pre-eminent position to case-law, as opposed to legislation, as the ordinary means of expression of general law. Thus this category includes countries or political entities that may not always have close ties with the English tradition and that sometimes possess an abundance of codes, legislation and non-jurisprudential normative instruments, but for which common law jurisprudence retains its character as the fundamental law (e.g., California).

Customary Law System: Hardly any countries or political entities in the world today operate under a legal system which could be said to be typically and wholly customary. Custom can take on many guises, depending on whether it is rooted in wisdom born of concrete daily experience or more intellectually based on great spiritual or philosophical traditions. Be that as it may, customary law (as a system, not merely as an accessory to positive law) still plays a sometimes significant role, namely in matters of personal conduct, in a relatively high number of countries or political entities with mixed legal systems. This obviously applies to a number of African countries but is also the case, albeit under very different circumstances, as regards the law of China or India, for example.

Muslim Law System: The Muslim legal system is an autonomous legal system which is actually religious in nature and predominantly based on the Koran. In a number of countries of Muslim persuasion it tends to be limited to personal status, although personal status can be rather broadly defined.

Mixed Legal Systems: The term "mixed," which we have arbitrarily chosen over other terms such as "hybrid" or "composite," should not be construed restrictively, as certain authors have done. Thus this category includes political entities where two or more systems apply cumulatively or interactively, but also entities where there is a juxtaposition of systems as a result of more or less clearly defined fields of application.

13. See Landman (2005, 43–44 and 171–176) for further details.

References

Abouharb, Rodwan, and David Cingranelli. 2006. "The Human Rights Effects of World Bank Structural Adjustment, 1981–2000." *International Studies Quarterly* 50: 233–62.

———. 2008. *Human Rights and Structural Adjustment.* New York: Cambridge University Press.

Ackerman, Bruce. 1991. *We the People, Vol 1: Foundations.* Cambridge: Harvard University Press.

Ackermann, L.W. H. 1989. "Constitutional Protection of Human Rights: Judicial Review." *Columbia Human Rights Law Review* 21: 59–71.

Alfatooni, Afra, and Michael Patrick Allen. 1991. "Government Sanctions and Collective Protest in Periphery and Semiperiphery States." *Journal of Political and Military Sociology* 19: 29–45.

Amnesty International. 1998. "Zambia: Misrule of Law—Human Rights in a State of Emergency," available at: http://www.amnesty.org/en/library/asset/AFR63/004/1998/en/60e7315c-db00-11dd-903e-e1f5d1f8bceb/afr630041998en.pdf.

Amnesty International. 2009. Country report on Myanmar. Accessed January 12, 2011. http://report2009.amnestry.org/en/regions/asia-pacific/myanmar.

Andrews, William G. 1964. *Constitutions and Constitutionalism.* New York: Van Nostrand.

An-Na'im, Abdullahi Ahmed. 2003. *Human Rights under African Constitutions: Realizing the Promise for Ourselves.* Philadelphia: University of Pennsylvania Press.

———. 2006. *African Constitutionalism and the Role of Islam.* Philadelphia: University of Pennsylvania Press.

Apodaca, Clair. 2001. "Global Economic Patterns and Personal Integrity Rights after the Cold War." *International Studies Quarterly* 45: 587–602.

———. 2004. The Rule of Law and Human Rights." *Judicature* 87: 292–99.

———. 2007. "The Whole World Could Be Watching: Human Rights and the Media." *Journal of Human Rights* 6: 147–64.

Apodaca, Clair, and Michael Stohl. 1999. "United States Human Rights Policy and Foreign Assistance." *International Studies Quarterly* 43:185–98.

Beatty, David. 1994. "Human Rights and the Rules of Law." In *Human Rights and Judicial Review,* ed. David M. Beatty. Dordrecht: Martinus Nijhoff.

Beck, Thorsten, Philip E. Keefer and George R. Clarke. 2010. *Database of Political Institutions.* World Bank. http://econ.worldbank.org/WBSITE/EXTERNAL/EXTDEC/EXTRESEARCH/0,,contentMDK:20649465~pagePK:64214825~piPK:64214943~theSitePK:469382,00.html.

Becker, Theodore. 1970. *Comparative Judicial Politics.* Lanham, Md.: University Press of America.

Beckett, Paul. 1987. "Elections and Democracy in Nigeria." In *Elections in Independent Africa,* ed. Fred Hayward. Boulder, Colorado: Westview Press.

Beer, Lawrence Ward. 1992. "Introduction: Constitutionalism and the United States." In *Constitutional Systems in Late Twentieth Century Asia,* ed. Lawrence W. Beer. Seattle: University of Washington Press..

Bilder, R. B. 1989. "International Third Party Dispute Settlement." *Denver Journal of International Law and Policy* 17: 471–503.

Bissell, Richard, Clara Haignere, John McCamant, and Mark Piklo. 1978. "Varieties of Political Repression." Unpublished manuscript.

Blasi, Gerard J., and David L. Cingranelli. 1996. "Do Constitutions and Institutions Help Protect Human Rights?" In *Human Rights and Developing Countries,* ed. David Cingranelli. Greenwich, Conn.: JAI.

Blaustein, Albert P. 1971–1993. *Constitutions of the World.* Nashville: W. S. Hein.

Boli, John, and Greg M. Thomas. 1997. "World Culture in a World Polity: A Century of Non-Governmental Organization." *American Sociological Review* 62:171–90.

Boli-Bennett, John. 1976. "The Expansion of National States, 1870–1970." Ph.D. diss., Stanford University.

Booth, John, and Mitchell Seligson. 1989. *Elections and Democracy in Central America.* Chapel Hill: University of North Carolina Press.

Buchmann, Claudia. 1996. "The Debt Crisis, Structural Adjustment and Women's Education: Implication for Status and Social Development." *International Journal of Comparative Sociology* 37: 5–30.

Bueno de Mesquita, Bruce, George W. Downs, Alistar Smith, and Feryal Marie Cherif. 2005. "Thinking Inside the Box: A Closer Look at Democracy and Human Rights." *International Studies Quarterly* 49: 439–57.

Buergenthal, Thomas. 1981. "To Respect and to Ensure: State Obligations and Permissible Derogations." In *The International Bill of Rights: The Covenant on Civil and Political Rights,* ed. Louis Henkin. New York: Columbia University Press.

Caine, Burton. 1987–88. "Panel Discussion: The Influence Abroad of the United States Constitution Judicial Review and a Bill of Rights." *Temple International and Comparative Law Journal* 2: 59–78.

Cameron, Charles M. 2002. "Judicial Independence: How Can You Tell It When You See It? And, Who Cares?" In *Judicial Independence at the Crossroads: An Interdisciplinary Approach,* ed. Steven B. Burbank and Barry Friedman. New York: Sage Publications.

Carey, Henry F. 2002. "The Postcolonial State and the Protection of Human Rights." *Comparative Studies of South Asia, Africa and the Middle East* 22: 59–75.

Carey, Sabine, and Steven C. Poe. 2004. "Human Rights Research and the Quest for Human Dignity." In *The Systematic Study of Human Rights*, Sabine Carey and Steven C. Poe, eds. New York: Ashgate Publishing.

Carleton, David, and Michael Stohl. 1987. "The Role of Human Rights in U.S. Foreign Assistance Policy: A Critique and Reappraisal." *American Journal of Political Science* 31: 1002–18.

Cea, Jose Luis. 1987. "Chile's Difficult Return to Constitutional Democracy." *PS: Political Science* 20: 665–73.

Chayes, Abraham, and Antonia Chayes. 1993. "On Compliance." *International Organization* 47: 175–205.

Chowdhury, Subrata Roy. 1989. *Rule of Law in a State of Emergency*. New York: St. Martin's Press.

Cingranelli, David L., and Thomas E. Pasquarello. 1985. "Human Rights Practices and the Distribution of U.S. Foreign Aid to Latin American Countries." *American Journal of Political Science* 29: 539–63.

Cingranelli, David L., and David L. Richards. 2010. The Cingranelli-Richards (CIRI) Human Rights Dataset. URL: http://www.humanrightsdata.org.

Cingranelli, David L., and David L. Richards. 1999a. "Respect for Human Rights after the End of the Cold War." *Journal of Peace Research* 36: 511–34.

———. 1999b. "Measuring the Pattern, Level, and Sequence of Government Respect for Human Rights." *International Studies Quarterly* 43: 407–17.

Clark, David. 1975. "Judicial Protection of the Constitution in Latin America." *Hastings Constitutional Law Quarterly* 2: 405–42.

Cole, Wade M. 2005. "Sovereignty Relinquished? Explaining Commitment to the International Human Rights Covenants, 1966–1999." *American Sociological Review* 70: 472–95.

Constitutional Design Group. 2008. "Judicial Independence." Accessed January 12, 2011. http://constitutionmaking.org/ files/judicial_independence.pdf.

Cross, Frank. 1999. "The Relevance of Law in Human Rights Protection." *International Review of Law and Economics* 87–98.

Cumaraswamy, Dato' Param. 1995. Report of the Special Rapporteur on the independence of judges and lawyers. Pursuant to Commission on Human Rights resolution 1995/36.

Daes, Erica Irena. 1983. "The Individual's Duties to the Community and the Limitations on Human Rights and Freedoms under Article 29 of the Universal Declaration of Human Rights." UN Doc. E/CN.4/Sub.2/432/Rev.2 (1983).

Dahl, Robert. A. 1971. *Polyarchy: Participation and Opposition*. New Haven, Conn.: Yale University Press.

Davenport, Christian. 1995a. "Assessing the Military's Influence on Political Repression." *Journal of Political and Military Sociology* 39: 683–713.

———. 1995b. "The Weight of the Past: Exploring Lagged Determinants of Political Repression." *Political Research Quarterly* 49: 377–403.

———. 1995c. "Multi-Dimensional Threat Perception and State Repression: An Inquiry into Why States Apply Negative Sanctions." *American Journal of Political Science* 39: 683–713.

———. 1996. "'Constitutional Promises' and Repressive Reality: A Cross-National Time-Series Investigation of Why Political and Civil Liberties Are Suppressed." *Journal of Politics* 58: 627–54.

———. 1999. "Human Rights and the Democratic Proposition." *Journal of Conflict Resolution* 43: 92–116.

———. 2007a. *State Repression and the Domestic Democratic Peace.* New York: Cambridge University Press.

———. 2007b. "State Repression and the Tyrannical Peace." *Journal of Peace Research* 44: 485–504.

———. 2007c. "State Repression and Political Order." *Annual Review of Political Science* 10: 1–23.

Davenport, Christian, and David A. Armstrong. 2004. "Democracy and the Violation of Human Rights: A Statistical Analysis from 1976 to 1996." *American Journal of Political Science* 48: 538–54.

Davis, David R., and Michael D. Ward. 1990. "Deaths and the Disappeared in Contemporary Chile." *Journal of Conflict Resolution* 34: 449–75.

DeLaet, Debra. 2006. *The Global Struggle for Human Rights.* New York: Thomson-Wadsworth.

de Tocqueville, Alexis. 1966. *Democracy in America,* ed. J. P. Mayer. New York: Harper and Row.

Di John, Jonathan. 2005. "Economic Liberalization, Political Instability, State Capacity in Venezuela." *International Political Science Review* 26: 107–24.

Dixon, William J. 1994. "Democracy and the Peaceful Settlement of International Conflict." *American Political Science Review* 88: 14–32.

Donnelly, Jack. 1998. *International Human Rights.* Boulder, Colo.: Westview Press.

Duvall, Raymond D., and Michael Stohl. 1983. "Governance by Terror." In *The Politics of Terrorism,* ed. Michael Stohl. New York: Marcel Dekker, 179–219.

Elkins, Zachary, Tom Ginsburg, and James Melton. 2009. *The Endurance of National Constitutions.* New York: Cambridge University Press.

Elster, Jon, 1993. "Introduction." In *Constitutionalism and Democracy,* ed. Jon Elster and Rune Slagstad. New York: Cambridge University Press, 1–18.

Epp, Charles R. 1998. *The Rights Revolution: Lawyers, Activists, and Supreme Courts in Comparative Perspective.* Chicago: University of Chicago Press.

Europa. 1979–2005. *World Year Book.* London: Europa Publications Limited.

Fein, Helen. 1995. "More Murder in the Middle: Life-Integrity Violations and Democracy in the World, 1987." *Human Rights Quarterly* 17: 170–91.

Ferejohn, John. 1999. "Independent Judges, Dependent Judiciary: Explaining Judicial Independence." *Southern California Law Review* 72: 353–84.

Ferejohn, John, Frances Rosenbluth, and Charles Shipan. 2004. "Comparative Judicial Politics." Accessed January 11, 2011. http://www.yale.edu/leitner/comparative judicial politics.pdf..

Fields, A. Belden. 2003. *Rethinking Human Rights for the Millennium*. New York: Palgrave Macmillan.

Finer, S. E. 1974. *Comparative Government*. Middlesex, Eng.: Penguin Books.

Finer, S. E., Vernon Bogdanor, and Bernard Rudden. 1995. *Comparing Constitutions*. Oxford: Oxford University Press.

Finkel, Steven E., Aníbal Pérez-Liñán, Mitchell A. Seligson, and Dinorah Azpuru. 2006. "Effects of U.S. Foreign Assistance on Democracy Building: Results of a Cross-National Quantitative Study." Vanderbilt University.

Finkel, Steven E., Aníbal Pérez-Liñán, Mitchell A. Seligson, and C. Neal Tate. 2008. "Deepening Our Understanding of the Effects of U.S. Foreign Assistance on Democracy Building: Final Report." Vanderbilt University.

Finn, John E. 1991. *Constitutions in Crisis: Political Violence and the Rule of Law*. Oxford: Oxford University Press.

Finnemore, Martha, and Kathryn Sikkink. 1998. "International Norm Dynamics and Political Change." *International Organization* 52: 887–917.

Fiss, Owen. 1993. "The Limits of Judicial Independence." *University of Miami Inter-American Law Review* 25: 58–76.

Fitzpatrick, Joan. 1994a. "Protection against Abuse of the Concept of 'Emergency.'" In *Human Rights: An Agenda for the Next Century*, ed. Louis Henkin and John Lawrence Hargrove. Washington, D.C.: American Society of International Law.

———. 1994b. *Human Rights in Crisis: The International System for Protecting Rights during States of Emergency*. Philadelphia: University of Pennsylvania Press.

Flanz, Gisbert H. 1997–2009. *Constitutions of Countries of the World*. New York: Oceana Publications. Updated annually.

Franklin, James. 1997. "IMF Conditionality, Threat Perception, and Political Repression: A Cross-National Analysis." *Comparative Political Studies* 30: 576–606.

Freedom House. 2010. *Freedom In The World 2010: Erosion Of Freedom Intensifies*. http://www.freedomhouse.org/uploads/fiw10/FIW_2010_Checklist_Questions.pdf.

Friedman, Gil, and Harvey Starr. 1997. *Agency, Structure, and International Politics*. London: Routledge.

Frühling, Hugo E. 1993. "Human Rights in Constitutional Order and in Political Practice in Latin America." In *Constitutionalism and Democracy: Transition in the Contemporary World*, ed. Douglas Greenberg et al. New York: Oxford University Press.

Garro, Alejandro Miguel. 1993. "Nine Years of Transition to Democracy in Argentina: Partial Failure or Qualified Success?" *Columbia Journal of Transnational Law* 31: 1–101.

Gartner, Scott Sigmund, and Patrick M. Regan. 1996. "Threat and Repression: The Non-Linear Relationship between Government and Opposition Violence." *Journal of Peace Research* 33: 273–87.

Gastil, Raymond. 1980. *Freedom in the World: Political Rights and Civil Liberties, 1980.* New Brunswick, N.J.: Transaction Books. Geddes, Barbara. 1999. *Authoritarian Breakdown: An Empirical Test of a Game-Theoretic Argument.* Los Angeles: University of California Press.

Gibney, Mark. 2011. The Political Terror Scale. http://www.politicalterrorscale.org/.

Gibney, Mark, and Matthew Dalton. 1996. "The Political Terror Scale." *Policy Studies and Developing Nations* 4: 73–84.

Gibney, Mark, and Michael Stohl. 1988. "Human Rights and U.S. Refugee Policy." In *Open Border? Closed Societies? The Ethical and Political Issues,* ed. Mark Gibney. Westport, Conn.: Greenwood Press.

Gilpin, Robert. 1987. *The Political Economy of International Relations.* Princeton: Princeton University Press.

Ginsburg, Thomas. 2003. *Judicial Review in New Democracies: Constitutional Courts in Asian Cases.* New York: Cambridge University Press.

Ginsburg, Thomas, and Tamir Moustafa, eds. 2008. *Rule by Law: The Politics of Courts in Authoritarian Regimes.* New York: Cambridge University Press.

Gleditsch, Kristian S., and Michael D. Ward. 1997. "Double Take: A Reexamination of Democracy and Autocracy in Modern Polities." *Journal of Conflict Resolution* 41: 361–83.

Go, Julian. 2003. "A Globalizing Constitutionalism? Views from the Postcolony, 1945–2000." *International Sociology* 18 (1): 71–95.

Goldstein, R. J. 1978. *Political Repression in Modern America: From 1870 to the Present.* Cambridge, Mass.: Schenkman.

Goodliffe, Jay, and Darren G. Hawkins. 2006. "Explaining Commitment: States and the Convention Against Torture." *Journal of Politics* 68: 358–71.

Goodman, Ryan, and Derek Jinks. 2003. "Measuring the Effects of Human Rights Treaties." *European Journal of International Law* 14: 171–83.

Grossman, Claudio. 1990. "States of Emergency: Latin America and the United States." In *Constitutionalism and Rights: The Influence of the United States Constitution Abroad,* ed. Louis Henkin and Albert J. Rosenthal. New York: Columbia University Press.

Guarnieri, Carlo, and Patrizia Pederzoli. 2002. *The Power of Judges: A Comparative Study of Courts and Democracy.* Oxford: Oxford University Press.

Gurr, Ted Robert. 1970. *Why Men Rebel.* Princeton: Princeton University Press.

———. 1986. "The Political Origins of State Violence and Terror: A Theoretical Analysis." In *Government Violence and Repression: An Agenda for Research,* ed. Michael Stohl and George A. Lopez. Westport, Conn.: Greenwood Press.

Hafner-Burton, Emilie M., and Kiyoteru Tsutsui. 2005. "Human Rights in a Globalizing World: The Paradox of Empty Promises." *American Journal of Sociology* 110: 1373–1411.

Haile, Minasse. 1996. "The New Ethiopian Constitution: Its Impact upon Unity, Human Rights, and Development." *Suffolk Transnational Law Review* 20: 1–84.

Harrelson-Stephens and Rhonda Callaway. 2003. "Does Trade Openness Promote Security Rights in Developing Countries? Examining the Liberal Perspective." *International Organizations* 29: 143–58.

Harrigan, Jane, and Paul Mosley. 1991. "Assessing the Impact of World Bank Structural Development Lending 1980–1987." *Journal of Development Studies* 27: 63–94.

Hartman, Joan F. 1981. "Derogation from Human Rights Treaties in Public Emergencies." *Harvard International Law Journal* 22: 1–52.

Hathaway, Oona A. 2002. "Do Human Rights Treaties Make a Difference?" *Yale Law Journal* 111: 1935–2042.

———. 2005. "Between Power and Principle: An Integrated Theory of International Law." *University of Chicago Law Review* 72: 469–536.

———. 2007. "Why Do Countries Commit to Human Rights Treaties?" *Journal of Conflict Resolution* 8: 588–621.

Hayward, Fred, and Jimmy Kandeh. 1987. "Perspectives on Twenty-Five Years of Elections in Sierra Leone." In *Elections in Independent Africa,* ed. Fred Hayward. Boulder, Colo.: Westview Press.

Henderson, Conway. 1991. "Conditions Affecting the Use of Political Repression." *Journal of Conflict Resolution* 35: 120–42.

Henderson, Conway. 1993. "Population Pressures and Political Repression." *Social Science Quarterly* 74:322-33.

Henkin, Louis. 1979. *How Nations Behave: Law and Foreign Policy.* New York: Council on Foreign Relations.

Henkin, Louis, and John Lawrence Hargrove. 1994. In *Human Rights: An Agenda for the Next Century,* ed. Louis Henkin and John Lawrence Hargrove. Washington, D.C.: American Society of International Law.

Herman, Edward, and Frank Brodhead. 1984. *Demonstration Elections: U.S.-Staged Elections in the Dominican Republic, Vietnam, and El Salvador.* Boston: South End Press.

Hibbs, Douglas A., Jr. 1973. *Mass Political Violence: A Cross- National Causal Analysis.* New York: Wiley.

Higgins, Rosalyn. 1976–77. "Derogations under Human Rights Treaties." *British Yearbook of International Law,* 48: 282–320.

Hilbink, Lisa. 2007. *Judges beyond Politics in Democracy and Dictatorship.* New York: Cambridge University Press.

Hirschl, Ran. 2000. "The Political Origin of Judicial Empowerment through Constitutionalization: Lessons from Four Constitutional Revolutions." *Law and Social Inquiry* 25: 91–149.

Hirschl, Ran. 2004. *Towards Juristocracy: The Origins and Consequences of the New Constitutionalism*. Harvard University Press

Hoffmann, Stanley. 1956. "The Role of International Organizations: Limits and Possibilities." *International Organization* 10: 357–72.

Holmes, Stephen. 1988. "Precommitment and the Paradox of Democracy." In *Constitutionalism and Democracy*, ed. Jon Ulster and Rune Slagstad. New York: Cambridge University Press.

Howard, A.E. Dick. 1991. "The Essence of Constitutionalism." *In Constitutionalism and Human Rights: America, Poland, and France*, Kenneth W. Thompson and Rett T. Ludwikowski, eds. New York: Lanham.

Howard, Robert M., and Henry F. Carey. 2004. "Is an Independent Judiciary Necessary for Democracy?" *Judicature* 87: 284–90.

Humana, Charles. 1992. *Humana World Human Rights Guide*. New York: Oxford University Press.

Human Rights Watch. 2005. *Human Rights Watch World Report 2005* - Azerbaijan , 1 January 2005, available at: http://www.unhcr.org/refworld/docid/421da30d2.html.

Human Rights Watch. 2005. "Nepal: State of Emergency Deepens Human Rights Crisis," available at http://www.hrw.org/en/news/2005/01/31/nepal-state-emergency-deepens-human-rights-crisis.

Human Rights Watch. 2010. "Egypt: Government Renews State of Emergency, available at:http://www.hrw.org/en/news/2010/05/11/egypt-government-renews-state-emergency.htm.

Huntington, Samuel P. 1957. *The Soldier and the State: The Theory of and Politics of Civil-Military Relations*. Cambridge, Mass.: Belknap Press of Harvard University Press.

International Commission of Jurists (ICJ). 1983. *States of Emergency: Their Impact on Human Rights*. Geneva: International Commission of Jurists.

Jarquin, Edmundo, and Fernando Carrillo. 1998. *Justice Delayed: Judicial Reform in Latin America*. Washington, D.C.: Inter-American Development Bank.

Johnson, Kenneth. 1976. "Scholarly Images of Latin American Political Democracy in 1975." *Latin America Research Review* 11: 129–40.

Joireman, Sandra Fullerton. 2004. "Colonization and the Rule of Law: Comparing the Effectiveness of Common Law and Civil Law Countries." *Constitutional Political Economy* 15: 315–38.

Katzenstein, Peter J. 1996a. *The Culture of National Security: Norms and Identity in World Politics*. New York: Columbia University Press.

———. 1996b. *Cultural Norms and National Security: Police and Military in Postwar Japan*. Ithaca, N.Y.: Cornell University Press.

Keck, Margaret, and Kathryn Sikkink. 1998. *Activists beyond Borders: Transnational Advocacy Networks in International Politics*. Ithaca, N.Y.: Cornell University Press.

Keck, Thomas. 2002. "Activism and Restraint on the Rehnquist Court: Timing, Sequence, and Conjuncture in Constitutional Development." *Polity* 35: 121–52.

Keen, David. 2005. "Liberalization and Conflict." *International Political Science Review* 26: 73–89.

Keith, Linda Camp. 1999. "The United Nations International Covenant on Civil and Political Rights: Does It Make a Difference in Human Rights Behavior?" *Journal of Peace Research* 36: 95–118.

———. 2002a. "Constitutional Provisions for Individual Human Rights (1976–1996): Are They More than Mere 'Window Dressing?'" *Political Research Quarterly* 55: 111–43.

———. 2002b. "International Principles for Formal Judicial Independence: Trends in National Constitutions and Their Impact (1976 to 1996)." *Judicature* 85: 194–200.

———. 2004. "National Constitutions and Human Rights Protection: Regional Differences and Colonial Influences." In *The Systematic Study of Human Rights*, ed. Sabine Carey and Steven C. Poe. Burlington, Vt.: Ashgate Publishing.

Keith, Linda Camp, and Jennifer S. Holmes. 2009. "Determinants of Asylum Grants: A Rare Examination of Factors Typically Unobservable in U.S. Asylum Decisions." *Journal of Refugee Studies* 22: 224–41.

Keith, Linda Camp, and Ayo Ogundele. 2007. "Legal Systems and Constitutionalism in Sub-Saharan Africa: An Empirical Examination of Colonial Influences on Human Rights." *Human Rights Quarterly* 29: 1065–97.

Keith, Linda Camp, and Steven C. Poe. 2000. "The U.S., the I.M.F., and Human Rights." In *The United States and Human Rights: Looking Inward and Outward*, ed. David P. Forsythe. Lincoln: University of Nebraska Press.

———. 2004. "Are Constitutional State of Emergency Clauses Effective? An Empirical Exploration." *Human Rights Quarterly* 26: 1071–97.

Keith, Linda Camp, C. Neal Tate, and Steven C. Poe. 2009. "Is the Law a Mere Parchment Barrier to Human Rights Abuse?" *Journal of Politics* 71: 644–60.

Kelley, Judith. 2007. "Who Keeps International Commitments and Why? The International Criminal Court and Bilateral Non-Surrender Agreements." *American Political Science Review* 101: 573–89.

Keohane, Robert. 1984. *After Hegemony: Cooperation and Discord in the World Political Economy.* Princeton: Princeton University Press.

King, Justice L.J. 1982. "Minimum Standards of Judicial Independence." *Australian Law School* 58: 340–45.

Knack, Stephen. 2004. "Does Foreign Aid Promote Democracy?" *International Studies Quarterly* 48: 251–66.

Koh, Harold H. 1996. "The 1994 Roscoe Pound Lecture: Transnational Legal Process." *Nebraska Law Review* 75: 181–98.

Kornhauser, Lewis. 2002. "Is Judicial Independence a Useful Concept?" In *Judicial Independence at the Crossroads: An Interdisciplinary Approach*, ed. Stephen B. Burbank and Barry Friedman. Thousand Oaks, Calif.: Sage Publications.

Krasner, S. D. 1993. "Sovereignty, Regimes, and Human Rights." In *Regime Theory and International Relations*, ed. V. Rittberger and P. Mayer. Oxford: Oxford University Press.

Krueger, Eric, and Steven C. Poe. 1998. "Testing Models of United States Foreign Policy: Foreign Aid During and After the Cold War." *Journal of Politics* 60: 63–85.

Landes, William, and Richard Posner. 1975. "The Independent Judiciary in an Interest-Group Perspective." *Journal of Law and Economics* 18: 875–901.

Landman, Todd. 2005. *Protecting Human Rights: A Comparative Study*. Washington, D.C.: Georgetown University Press.

La Porta, Rafael, Florencio López-de-Silanes, Cristian Pop-Eleches, and Andrei Shleifer. 2004. "Judicial Checks and Balances." *Journal of Political Economy* 112: 445–70.

Larkins, Christopher M. 1996. "Judicial Independence and Democratization: A Theoretical and Conceptual Analysis." *American Journal of Comparative Law* 44: 605–26.

Lasswell, Harold. 1950. *Politics: Who Gets What, When, and How*. New York: P. Smith.

Leeds, Brett Ashley. 1999. "Domestic Political Institutions, Credible Commitments, and International Cooperation." *American Journal of Political Science* 43: 979–1002.

Lillich, Richard B. 1985. "Current Development: The Paris Minimum Standards of Human Rights Norms in a State of Emergency." *American Journal of International Law* 79: 1072–81.

Linz, Juan. 2000. *Totalitarian and Authoritarian Regimes*. Boulder, Colo.: Lynne Rienner.

Lipset, Seymour Martin. 1959. "Some Social Requisites of Democracy: Economic Development and Political Legitimacy." *American Political Science Review* 53: 69–105.

Lopez, George, and Michael Stohl. 1992. "Problems of Concept and Measurement in the Study of Human Rights." In *Human Rights and Statistics: Getting the Record Straight*, ed. Thomas B. Jabine and Richard P Claude. Philadelphia: University of Pennsylvania Press, 216–34.

Ludwikowski, Rett R. 1996. *Constitution-making in the Region of Former Soviet Dominance*. Durham, N.C.: Duke University Press.

MacGuigan, Mark. 1965. "The Development of Civil Liberties in Canada." *Queen's Quarterly* 27: 273.

Madani, Hamed. 1992. "Socioeconomic Development and Military Policy Consequences of Third World Military and Civilian Regimes, 1965–1985." Ph.D. diss., University of North Texas.

Madison, James. 1788. Letter from James Madison to Thomas Jefferson (Oct. 17, 1788), in 5 The Writings of James Madison, 1787-1790, at 269.

Maduna, Penuell M. 1989. "Judicial Review and Protection of Human Rights under a New Constitutional Order in South Africa." *Columbian Human Rights Law Review* 21: 73–83.

Magaloni, Beatriz. 2008. "Enforcing the Autocratic Political Order and the Role of Courts: The Case of Mexico." In *Rule by Law: The Politics of Courts in Authoritarian Regimes,* ed. Tom Ginsburg and Tamir Moustafa. New York: Cambridge University Press.

Marshall, Monty G., and Keith Jaggers. 2011. "Polity IV Project: Political Regime Characteristics and Transitions, 1800–1999." University of Maryland. Accessed April 24, 2011. http://www.systemicpeace.org/polity/polity4.htm.

Martin, David. 1991. "Roundtable Discussion." In *Constitutionalism and Human Rights: America, Poland, and France,* ed. Kenneth W. Thompson and Rett T. Ludwikowski. New York: Lanham.

McColm, R. Bruce (survey coordinator). 1990. *Freedom in the World: Political Rights and Civil Liberties, 1989–1990.* Lanham, Md.: University of America Press.

McCormick, James M., and Neil Mitchell. 1997. "Human Rights Violations, Umbrella Concepts, and Empirical Analysis." *World Politics* 49: 510–25.

McKinlay, R. D., and A. S. Cohan. 1975. "A Comparative Analysis of the Political and Economic Performance of Military and Civilian Regimes." *Comparative Politics* 8: 1–30.

McKinlay, R. D., and A. S. Cohan. 1976. "Performance and Instability in Military and Nonmilitary Regimes." *American Political Science Review* 70:850-64.

McNollgast. 2006. "Positive Political Theory and the Law: Conditions of Judicial Independence." *Journal of Contemporary Legal Issues* 15: 105–27.

Mearsheimer, John J. 1994. "The False Promise of International Institutions." *International Security* 19: 5–26.

Meernik, James, Eric L. Krueger, and Steven C. Poe. "Testing Models of U.S. Foreign Policy: Foreign Aid during and after the Cold War." *The Journal of Politics* 60:-63-85.

Meyer, John W., John Boli, Greg M. Thomas, and Francisco O. Ramirez. 1997. "World Society and the Nation-State." *American Journal of Sociology* 103: 144–81.

Meyer, William H. 1996. *Human Rights and International Political Economy in Third World Nations.* Westport, Conn.: Praeger.

Milgrom, Paul R., Douglass C. North, and Barry R. Weingast. 1990. "The Role of Institutions in the Revival of Trade: The Medieval Law Merchant, Private Judges, and the Champagne Fairs." *Economics and Politics* 1: 1–23.

Mitchell, Christopher, Michael Stohl, David Carleton, and George A. Lopez. 1986. "State Terrorism: Issues of Concept and Measurement." In *Government Violence and Repression: An Agenda for Research,* ed. Michael Stohl and George A. Lopez. Westport, Conn.: Greenwood Press.

Mitchell, Neil J., and James M. McCormick. 1988. "Economic and Political Explanations of Human Rights Violations." *World Politics* 40: 476–98.

Moderne, Frank. 1990. "Human Rights and Postcolonial Constitutions in Sub-Saharan Africa." In *Constitutionalism and Rights: The Influence of the United States Constitution Abroad*, ed. Louis Henkin and A. J. Rosenthal. New York: Columbia University Press.

Mondlane, Luis. 2003. "Mozambique: Nurturing Justice from Liberation Zones to a Stable Democratic State." In *Human Rights under African Constitutions: Realizing the Promise for Ourselves*, ed. Abdullahi Ahmed An-Na'im. Philadelphia: University of Pennsylvania Press.

Moran, Theodore H. 1998. *Foreign Direct Investment and Development.* Washington, DC: Institute for International Economics.

Moravcsik, Andrew. 2000. "The Origins of Human Rights Regimes: Democratic Delegations in Postwar Europe." *International Organization* 54: 217–52.

Morgenthau, Hans J. 1948. *Politics among Nations.* New York: Knopf.

Most, Benjamin A., and Harvey Starr. 1989. *Inquiry, Logic, and International Politics.* Columbia, S.C.: University of South Carolina Press.

Moustafa, Tamir. 2007. *The Struggle for Constitutional Power: Law, Politics, and Economic Reform in Egypt.* New York: Cambridge University Press.

Moustafa, Tamir . 2009. "Law and Resistance in Authoritarian States: The Judicialization of Egypt." In *Rule by Law: The Politics of Courts in Authoritarian Regimes,* ed. Thomas Ginsburg and Tamir Moustafa. New York: Cambridge University Press.

Murphy, Walter F. 1993. "Constitutions, Constitutionalism, and Democracy." In *Constitutionalism and Democracy: Transition in the Contemporary World,* ed. Douglas Greenberg et al. New York: Oxford University Press.

Mutua, M. 2001. "Justice Under Siege: The Rule of Law and Judicial Subservience in Kenya." *Human Rights Quarterly* 23: 96–118.

Neumayer, Eric. 2003a. *The Pattern of Aid Giving—The Impact of Good Governance on Development Finance.* London: Routledge.

———. 2003b. "Is Respect for Human Rights Rewarded? An Analysis of Total Bilateral and Multilateral Aid Flows." *Human Rights Quarterly* 25: 510–27.

———. 2003c. "Do Human Rights Matter in Bilateral Aid Allocation? A Quantitative Analysis of 21 Donor Countries." *Social Science Quarterly* 84: 650–66.

———. 2005. "Do International Human Rights Treaties Improve Respect for Human Rights?" *Journal of Conflict Resolution* 49: 925–53.

Olson, Mancur. 1993. "Dictatorship, Democracy, and Development." *American Political Science Review* 87: 567–76.

Pahl, Michael R. 1993. "Concealing Justices or Concealing Injustices? Colombia's Secret Courts." *Denver Journal of International Law and Policy* 21: 431-40.

Park, Han S. 1987. "Correlates of Human Rights: Global Tendencies." *Human Rights Quarterly* 9: 405–13.

Perlmutter, Amos, and Valerie Plave Bennett. 1980. *The Political Influence of the Military: A Comparative Reader.* New Haven, Conn.: Yale University Press.

Pion-Berlin, David. 1984. "The Political Economy of State Repression in Argentina." In *The State as Terrorist,* ed. Michael Stohl and George Lopez. Westport, Conn.: Greenwood Press.

Poe, Steven C. 1992. "Human Rights and Economic Aid Allocation under Ronald Reagan and Jimmy Carter." *American Journal of Political Science* 36: 147–67.

———. 2004. "The Decision to Repress: An Integrative Theoretical Approach to the Research on Human Rights and Repression." In *The Systematic Study of Human Rights,* ed. Sabine Carey and Steven C. Poe. Burlington, Vt.: Ashgate Publishing.

Poe, Steven C., Sabine C. Carey, and Tanya C. Vazquez. 2001. "How Are These Pictures Different? A Quantitative Comparison of the U.S. State Department and Amnesty International Human Rights Reports, 1976-1995." *Human Rights Quarterly* 23: 650-77.

Poe, Steven C., Suzanne Pilatovsky, Brian Miller, and Ayo Ogundele. 1994. "Human Rights and U.S. Foreign Aid Revisited: The Latin American Region." *Human Rights Quarterly* 16: 539–58.

Poe, Steven C., and Rangsima Sirirangsi. 1994. "Human Rights and U.S. Economic Aid during the Reagan Years." *Social Science Quarterly* 75: 494–509.

Poe, Steven C., and C. Neal Tate. 1994. "Repression of Human Rights to Personal Integrity in the 1980s: A Global Analysis." *American Political Science Review* 88: 853–72.

Poe, Steven C., C. Neal Tate, and Linda Camp Keith. 1999. "Repression of Human Rights to Personal Integrity Revisited: A Global Cross-National Study Covering the Years 1976–1993." *International Studies Quarterly* 43: 291–313.

Poe, Steven C., C. Neal Tate, Linda Camp Keith, and Drew Noble Lanier. 2000. "The Continuity of Suffering: Domestic Threat and Human Rights Abuse across Time." In *Paths to State Repression: Human Rights and Contentious Politics in Comparative Perspective,* ed. Christian Davenport. Boulder, Colo.: Rowan Littlefield.

Political Handbook of the World. 1979-2005. New York: Published for the Center for Comparative Political Research of the State University of New York at Binghamton and for the Council on Foreign Relations by McGraw-Hill Book Co.

Powell, Emilia Justyna, and Sara McLaughlin Mitchell. 2007. "The International Court of Justice and the World's Three Legal Systems." *Journal of Politics* 69: 397–415.

Powell, Emilia Justyna, and Jeffrey K. Staton. 2009. "Domestic Judicial Institutions and Human Rights Treaty Violation." *International Studies Quarterly* 53: 149–74.

Prempeh, H. Kwasi. 1999. "A New Jurisprudence for Africa." *Journal of Democracy* 10 (3): 135–49.

Prezworski, Adam, Michael E. Alvarez, Jose Antonio Cheibub, and Fernando Limongi. 2000. *Democracy and Development: Political Institutions and Well Being in the World, 1950–1990.* New York: Cambridge University Press.

Prezworski, Adam, and James Raymond Vreeland. 2000. "The Effects of IMF Programs on Economic Growth." *Journal of Development Economics* 62: 385-421.

Prillaman, William. 2000. *The Judiciary and Democratic in Latin America.* Westport, Conn.: Praeger.

Pritchard, Kathleen. 1986. "Comparative Human Rights: An Integrative Explanation." *Policy Studies Journal* 15: 110–28.

Questiaux, Nicole. 1982. "Study of the Implications for Human Rights of Recent Developments Concerning Situations Known as States of Siege or Emergency." UN Doc. E/CN.4/Sub.2/1982/15.

Ramseyer, J. Mark. 1994. "The Puzzling (In)Dependence of Courts: A Comparative Approach." *Journal of Legal Studies* 23: 721–53.

Ramseyer, J. Mark, and Eric B. Rasmussen. 2003. *Measuring Judicial Independence: The Political Economy of Judging in Japan.* Chicago: University of Chicago Press.

Rapley, John. 1996. *Understanding Development: Theory and Practice in the Third World.* Boulder, Colo.: Lynne Rienner.

Rasler, Karen. 1986. "War, Accommodation, and Violence in the United States, 1890-1970." *American Political Science Review* 80:921-45.

Regan, Patrick M. 1995. "U.S. Economic Aid and Political Repression: An Empirical Evaluation of U.S. Foreign Policy." *Political Research Quarterly* 48: 613–28.

Regan, Patrick, and Errol A. Henderson. 2002. "Democracy, Threats, and Political Repression in Developing Countries: Are Democracies Internally Less Violent?" *Third World Quarterly* 23: 119–36.

Reisman, W. Michael. 1990. "Sovereignty and Human Rights in Contemporary International Law." *The American Journal of International Law* 84: 866-877.

Richards, David L. 1999. "Perilous Proxy: Human Rights and the Presence of National Elections." *Social Science Quarterly* 80: 648–65.

Richards, David L., Ronald Gelleny, and David Sacko. 2001. "Money with a Mean Streak? Foreign Economic Penetration and Government Respect for Human Rights in Developing Countries." *International Studies Quarterly* 45: 219–39.

Risse, Thomas, Stephen C. Ropp, and Kathryn Sikkink. 1999. *The Power of Human Rights: International Norms and Domestic Change.* Cambridge: Cambridge University Press..

Risse, Thomas, and Kathryn Sikkink. 1999. "The Socialization of International Human Rights Norms into Domestic Practices: Introduction." In *The Power of Human Rights: International Norms and Domestic Change*, ed. Thomas Risse et al. New York: Cambridge University Press.

Rosenblum, Marc R., and Idean Salehyan. 2004. "Norms and Interests in U.S. Asylum Enforcement." *Journal of Peace Research* 41: 677–97.

Rosenn, Keith S. 1987. "The Protection of Judicial Independence in Latin America." *University of Miami Inter-American Law Review* 19: 3–35.

Rosenthal, Albert J. 1990. "Afterword." In *Constitutionalism and Rights: the Influence of the United States Constitution Abroad*, ed. Louis Henkin and Albert J. Rosenthal. New York: Columbia University Press.

Rottman, Andy J., Christopher J. Fariss, and Steven C. Poe. 2009. "The Path to Asylum in the U.S. and the Determinants for Who Gets In and Why." *International Migration Review* 43: 3–34.

Russell, Peter. 2001. "Towards a General Theory of Judicial Independence." In *Judicial Independence in the Age Of Democracy: Critical Perspectives From around the World*, ed. Peter H. Russell and David M. O'Brien. Charlottesville: University Press of Virginia.

Sadasivam, B. 1997. "The Impact of Structural Adjustment on Women: A Governance and Human Rights Agenda." *Human Rights Quarterly* 19: 630–55.

Salehyan, Idean, and Marc R. Rosenblum. 2008. "International Relations, Domestic Politics, and Asylum Admissions in the United States." *Journal of Politics* 61: 104–21.

Sartori, Giovanni. 1997. *Comparative Constitutional Engineering: An Inquiry into Structures, Incentives, and Outcomes.* New York: New York University Press.

Schmitter, Philippe C., and Terry Lynn Karl. 1991. "What Democracy Is . . . and Is Not." *Journal of Democracy* 2: 75–88.

Schoultz, Lars. 1981. *Human Rights and United States Policy toward Latin America.* Princeton: Princeton University Press.

Schwartz, Bernard.1993. *A History of the Supreme Court.* New York: Oxford University Press.

Seiderman, Ian D. 2002. *Attacks on Justice: A Global Report of the Independence of Judges and Lawyers.* 11th ed. Geneva: Centre for the Independence of Judges and Lawyers of the International Commission of Jurists.

Shapiro, Martin. 1981. *Courts: Comparative and Political Analysis.* Chicago: University of Chicago Press.

———. 2008. "Courts in Authoritarian Regimes." In *Rule by Law: The Politics of Courts in Authoritarian Regimes*, ed. Thomas Ginsburg and Tamir Moustafa. New York: Cambridge University Press.

Sherif Adel Omar, and Nathan J. Brown. 2002. *Judicial Independence in the Arab World.* United Nations Development Program.

Sidell, Scott R. 1988. *The IMF and Third World Instability: Is There a Connection?* New York: St. Martin's Press.

Siegan, Bernard H. 1994. *Drafting a Constitution for a Nation or Republic Emerging into Freedom.* Fairfax, Va.: Locke Institute.

Sieghart, Paul, 1983. *The International Law of Human Rights.* Oxford: Clarendon Press.

Simmons, Beth A. 2009. *Mobilizing for Human Rights.* Cambridge: Cambridge University Press.

Simmons, Beth A. 2000. "International Law and State Behavior: Commitment and Compliance in International Monetary Affairs." *American Political Science Review* 94: 819–36.

Small, Melvin, and J. David Singer. 1982. *Resort to Arms: International and Civil Wars, 1816–1980*. Beverly Hills, Calif.: Sage Publications.

Sprout, Harold, and Margaret Sprout. 1956. *Man-Milieu Relationship Hypothesis in the Context of International Politics*. Princeton: Center for International Studies, Princeton University.

———. 1965. *An Ecological Perspective on Human Affairs*. Princeton: Princeton University Press.

———. 1968. *An Ecological Paradigm for the Study of International Politics*. Princeton: Center for International Studies, Princeton University.

———. 1969. "Environmental Factors in the Study of International Politics." In *International Politics and Foreign Policy*, ed. James N. Rosenau. New York: Free Press.

Steiner, Henry J., and Philip Alston. 1996. *International Human Rights in Context: Law, Politics, Morals*. Oxford: Clarendon Press.

Stohl, Michael. 1975. "War and Domestic Violence: The Case of the United States, 1890-1970." *Journal of Conflict Resolution* 19:379-416.

Stohl, Michael. 1976. *War and Domestic Political Violence: The American Capacity for Repression and Reaction*. Beverly Hills: Sage. Stohl, Michael .

Stohl, Michael, and David Carleton. 1985. "The Foreign Policy of Human Rights: Rhetoric and Reality from Jimmy Carter to Ronald Reagan." *Human Rights Quarterly* 7: 205–29.

Stohl, Michael, and George Lopez. 1984. *The State as Terrorist*. Westport, Conn.: Greenwood Press.

Stotzky, Irwin P. 1993. "The Tradition of Constitutional Adjudication." In *Transitions to Democracy in Latin America: The Role of the Judiciary*, ed. Irwin P. Stotzky. Boulder, Colo.: Westview Press.

Tate, C. Neal, and Torbjorn Vallinder. 1995. *The Global Expansion of Judicial Power*. New York: New York University Press.

Taylor, Charles, and David Jodice. 1983. *World Handbook of Political and Social Indicators*. New Haven: Yale University Press.

Tiede, Lydia Brashear. 2006. "Positive Theory and the Law: Judicial Independence: Often Cited, Rarely Understood." *Journal of Contemporary Legal Issues* 15: 129–61.

UN Treaty Collection, accessed December 2009.

United Nations. 1985. United Nations High Commissioner for Human Rights. *Basic Principles on the Independence of the Judiciary.*, adopted by the Seventh United Nations Congress on the Prevention of Crime and the Treatment of Offenders held at Milan from 26 August to 6 September 1985 and endorsed by General Assembly resolutions 40/32 of 29 November 1985 and 40/146 of 13 December 1985.

———. 1987. *Human Rights: Status of International Instruments*. Geneva: Centre for Human Rights.

———. 1993. World Conference on Human Rights. Vienna 14-25 June 1993. *Vienna Declaration and Programme of Action*, adopted on 25 June 1993 (A/CONF.157/23).

———. 1995. *The Report of the Special Rapporteur on the independence of judges and lawyers, Dato' Param Cumaraswamy,* submitted pursuant to Commission on Human Rights resolution 1995/36.

———. 1996.United Nations Background Note. "The Independence of the Judiciary: a Human Rights Priority." http://www.un.org/rights/dpi1837e.htm.

USAID. 2000. Guidance for *Promoting Judicial Independence and Impartiality.* Rev. ed. Washington, D.C.: Office of Democracy and Governance, Bureau for Democracy, Conflict, and Humanitarian Assistance, U.S. Agency for International Development. Accessed January 11, 2011. http://www.usaid.gov/our_work/democracy_and_governance /publications/pdfs/xpnacm007.pdf.

U.S. Department of State. 1999 through 2007. *Country Reports on Human Rights Practices.* Washington, D.C. http://www.state.gov/g/drl/rls/hrrpt/index.htm.

van de Walle, Nicholas. 2001. *African Economies and the Politics of Permanent Crisis, 1979–1999.* New York: Cambridge University Press.

Vreeland, James Raymond. 2008. "Political Institutions and Human Rights: Why Dictatorships Enter into the United Nations Convention against Torture." *International Organization* 62: 65–101.

Vreeland, James Raymond. 2003. *The IMF and Economic Development.* Cambridge: Cambridge University Press.

Walker, Scott, and Steven C. Poe. 2002. "Does Cultural Diversity Affect Countries' Respect for Human Rights?" *Human Rights Quarterly* 24: 237–63.

Waltz, Kenneth. 1979. *Theory of International Politics.* Reading, Mass.: Addison-Wesley.

Weingast, Barry R. 1995. "The Economic Role of Political Institutions: Market-Preserving Federalism and Economic Development." *Journal of Law, Economics, and Organization* 11: 1–31.

———. 1997. "The Political Foundations of Democracy and the Rule of Law." *American Political Science Review* 91: 245–63.

Wiener, Myron, and Ergun Ozbudun. 1987. *Competitive Elections in Developing Countries.* Durham, N.C.: Duke University Press.

Wilkinson, Paul. 1976. *Terrorism versus Liberal Democracy: The Problems of Response.* London: Routledge.

Wotipka, Christine Min, and Francisco O. Ramirez. 2007. "World Society and Human Rights: An Event History Analysis of the Convention on the Elimination of All Forms of Discrimination against Women." In *The Global Diffusion of Markets and Democracy,* ed. Beth A. Simmons, Geoffrey Garrett, and Frank Dobbin. New York: Cambridge University Press.

Zack-Williams, Alfred B. 2000. "Social Consequences of Structural Adjustment." In *Structural Adjustment: Theory, Practice and Impacts,* ed. Giles Mohan, Ed Brown, Bob Wilward, and Alfred B. Zack-Williams. London: Routledge.

Zanger, Sabine C. 2000. "A Global Analysis of the Effect of Political Regime Changes on Life Integrity Violations, 1977–93." *Journal of Peace Research* 37: 213–33.

Ziegenhagen, Eduard A. 1986. *The Regulation of Political Conflict.* New York: Praeger.

Index

Acknowledgments

As many in the human rights community will know, this work is in some ways incomplete. Neal Tate and I planned to write this book together at a time when we were already missing our partnership with Steve Poe. We were in the data gathering process when Neal was struck by the illness that eventually took his life. I contemplated simply abandoning the project, which was already overdue, but with the encouragement of Bert Lockwood and Peter Agree, I belatedly began the book solo. While I missed Steve and Neal tremendously in writing this book, I felt their presence and support continually. I missed very much chatting and arguing with them over the shape of ideas and their expression, the depth of Neal's fascination and experience studying the judiciary, and the inspiration of Steve's unflagging commitment to work that might make a difference in the real world. I dedicate this book to them in great appreciation for the role they have played in my life—first as mentors, then as colleagues and dear friends.

The data collection for this book was supported through funding either directly or indirectly by the Political Science Department at the University of Iowa, the Political Science Department at Vanderbilt University, and Finkel, Pérez-Liñán, Seligson, and Tate's USAID grant funding the New Foreign Assistance, Democracy and Human Rights project. Research assistance from Naeda Elliott and Lance Mogard at the University of Iowa helped me to develop the de facto measure of judicial independence. Vanderbilt University provided the funding for Naeda Elliott to continue the coding as a law student at the University of Iowa. I thank both universities for their support, and Naeda for her dedication to the study of law and judicial independence. Her assistance was invaluable. The extension of the constitutional measures was funded through Finkel et al.'s USAID grant. I express thanks especially to Marina for her assistance on this project. I also express appreciation for the direct support I received from the grant.

I would like to express special thanks to my editors, Peter Agree and Bert Lockwood, who enthusiastically supported this project from the time that I first approached them, and especially for their continued support as the project was put on hold indefinitely, and then for their confidence and encouragement as I decided to take on the project alone. I am thankful not only for the support of my work but also for their dedication to human rights scholarship. I also want to thank the anonymous reviewer for helpful suggestions and guidance in shaping the project, as well as for his encouragement.

Finally, I have important personal acknowledgments to make. First, to my son, Adam, and his partner, Summer Lopez, both of whom work in the *real* world of human rights and constantly inspire me and provide me with a much broader perspective and insight than I can claim on my own. And always, to my twin sister, Brenda, who listens patiently to my excited yammering and whining complaints about my research, when she would rather be chatting about food, cooking, and dancing with me, but always is there with friendship and wise counsel. And to Mom and Dad, who step in without hesitation to offer relief with an invitation to dinner or with a not-too-subtle reminder that I work too much and should play more often. And to Joe the Artist—special thanks. And finally to Maggie the Corgi, who constantly reminds me that there is nothing in life more engaging than chasing a squirrel up a tree or as sweet as finding a stray M&M on the floor.

www.ingramcontent.com/pod-product-compliance
Ingram Content Group UK Ltd.
Pitfield, Milton Keynes, MK11 3LW, UK
UKHW041853031026
15587UKWH00006B/1210/J

9 780812 243819